Calculating Property Relations

GEOGRAPHIES OF JUSTICE AND SOCIAL TRANSFORMATION

SERIES EDITORS

Deborah Cowen, University of Toronto
Nik Heynen, University of Georgia
Melissa W. Wright, Pennsylvania State University

ADVISORY BOARD

Mathew Coleman, Ohio State University
Sapana Doshi, University of Arizona
Zeynep Gambetti, Boğaziçi University
Geoff Mann, Simon Fraser University
James McCarthy, Clark University
Beverly Mullings, Queen's University
Harvey Neo, National University of Singapore
Geraldine Pratt, University of British Columbia
Ananya Roy, University of California, Berkeley
Michael Watts, University of California, Berkeley
Ruth Wilson Gilmore, CUNY Graduate Center
Jamie Winders, Syracuse University
Brenda S. A. Yeoh, National University of Singapore

Calculating Property Relations

CHICAGO'S WARTIME INDUSTRIAL
MOBILIZATION, 1940–1950

ROBERT LEWIS

THE UNIVERSITY OF GEORGIA PRESS
Athens

© 2016 by the University of Georgia Press
Athens, Georgia 30602
www.ugapress.org
All rights reserved
Set in 10/12.5 Minion Pro by Graphic Composition, Inc., Bogart, Georgia

Most University of Georgia Press titles are
available from popular e-book vendors.

Printed digitally

Library of Congress Cataloging-in-Publication Data

Names: Lewis, Robert D., 1954– author.
Title: Calculating property relations : Chicago's wartime industrial mobilization, 1940–1950 / Robert Lewis.
Description: Athens, GA : University of Georgia Press, 2016. | Series: Geographies of justice and social transformation ; 29 | Includes bibliographical references and index.
Identifiers: LCCN 2016014715 | ISBN 9780820350127 (hard bound : alk. paper) | ISBN 9780820350134 (paperback : alk. paper)
Subjects: LCSH: Industrial mobilization—United States—History—20th century. | Industrial policy—United States—History—20th century. | Military-industrial complex—United States—History—20th century. | World War, 1939–1945—Illinois—Chicago—History.
Classification: LCC HC110.D4 .L49 2016 | DDC 940.53/1—dc23 LC record available at https://lccn.loc.gov/2016014715

CONTENTS

List of Illustrations   vii
Acknowledgments   ix
List of Abbreviations   xi

Introduction   1
CHAPTER 1 Calculation and Industrial Property   11
CHAPTER 2 Industrial Sites and Wartime Mobilization   32
CHAPTER 3 Mobilizing Chicago's Wartime Industrial Property   56
CHAPTER 4 Chicago's Wartime Industrial Sites   76
CHAPTER 5 War Factories and Industrial Engineering   106
CHAPTER 6 The Disposal Regime: Factories and National Security   129
CHAPTER 7 Disposing of Chicago's War Factories   152
CHAPTER 8 The Site Politics of Defense Factory Disposal   177
CHAPTER 9 Property, Calculation, and Industrial Space   198
APPENDIX Wartime Factory Expansion   215

Notes   219
Manuscript Sources   257
Index   259

ILLUSTRATIONS

FIGURES

2.1 How subcontracting accelerates defense production, 1942   37
3.1 Acme Steel, Riverdale, 1940   64
4.1 Regional geography of procurement, 1940   78
4.2 New defense factories, Chicago, 1940–1945   82
4.3 Douglas Aircraft assembly plant, 1944   83
4.4 Aircraft production networks   85
4.5 Factory additions for war purposes, Chicago, 1940–1945   87
4.6 Total investment in defense factories, Chicago, 1940–1945   95
6.1 Advertising War Department industrial facilities, 1947   137
6.2 Steel plant advertisement, 1946   138
6.3 *Plant Finder*, 1948   139
7.1 Selling the Studebaker plancor to National Tea, 1949   161
7.2 Floor plan of Howard Foundry   170
8.1 Kropp forging building (plancor 1293)   179
8.2 "Republic Builds for D.P.C."   184

TABLES

2.1 State and private expenditures on defense factories, 1940–1945   35
2.2 Corporate concentration of construction and supply awards, 1940–1945   39
4.1 Wartime factory investment by type and source, Chicago, 1940–1945   79
4.2 Suburban share of industrial fixed-capital investment in eighteen metropolitan areas   91

4.3 Wartime investment by zone in Chicago, 1940–1945   94
4.4 Wartime investment in selected areas of the Calumet, 1940–1945   100
4.5 Largest construction awards in the Calumet, 1940–1945   101
5.1 Sanderson and Porter's building contracts, 1940–1941   117

ACKNOWLEDGMENTS

Over the last few years, I have been lucky enough to have enjoyed considerable backing from the department's two chairs. Joe Desloges and Virginia Maclaren are models of how to provide support for academic research and writing. Similarly, department staff members—most notably Mariange Beaudry, Mary-Marta Briones-Bird, Candace Duong, Nina Duras, Jessica Finlayson, Kathy Giesbrecht, Yvonne Kenny, Marika Maslej, and Dean Robson—have provided various forms of help over the years. I appreciate their work and patience. I would like to thank Bryon Moldofsky for the maps. A large number of colleagues and friends in Toronto and elsewhere have helped me in one way as I have worked on this book. In particular, I would like to give a special thank-you to Christian Abizaid, Bob Beauregard, Alana Boland, Deb Cowen, Rick DiFrancesco, Mike Ekers, Matt Farish, Gunter Gad, Emily Gilbert, Paul Hess, Richard Harris, Debby Leslie, Ted Muller, Scott Prudham, Katharine Rankin, André Sorensen, Matti Siemiatycki, and Dick Walker.

I have been fortunate to have received a four-year operating grant from the Canadian Social Science and Humanities Research Council to undertake the research for this study. Despite the major changes that have taken place to the Council over the years, many of which emerged from having to fight the Harper government's insidious attempts to turn social science work into a technocratic and profit-making business, Canadian scholars can still count on receiving funding for research on a range of intellectual matters. Thanks to all the people—academics and administrators alike—for fighting to preserve the integrity of a state-funded grant system.

I am heavily indebted to an excellent group of research assistants. Charlie Strazzeri and Jason Cooke provided able help in the early stages of the research. More recently, Nick Lombardo has provided exceptional assistance, helping me collect and interpret a range of materials in Chicago and Toronto. Patrick Vitale is the only person to have read an entire draft of the manuscript. I owe him a great many thanks for his intellectual insights, numerous grammatical corrections, and thoughtful (and rigorous) comments. The book is much better because of Patrick's and Nick's work.

A book of this sort depends on the skills, kindness, and good graces of archivists and librarians. I would like to make a special thank-you to the staff at the National Archives and Records Administration in College Park and Chicago, the Chicago Public Library, the Chicago Historical Museum, and Special Collections at the University of Illinois at Chicago. As always, I have benefited greatly from the able support of people working in the interlibrary loans and the acquisition sections of the University of Toronto library.

Similarly, I would like to thank the staff at the University of Georgia Press for all their work. The publication of the book has benefited from the efforts of Mick Gusinde-Duff and Jon Davies, both of whom shepherded the manuscript through all of the various stages of review, revision, and production. Several anonymous reviewers have made copious comments, all of which added immeasurably to the book's clarity and focus. Jane Curran has been a terrific copyeditor, helping me delete numerous infelicities and redundancies. It is greatly appreciated. I would like to thank Deb Cowen, Nik Heynen, and Melissa Wright for making it possible for me to publish my book in their series.

My Toronto family and friends have provided much support, laughs, and love over the years. Thank you. Finally, I dedicate this book to the young writers of my Toronto family, Yonah, Lev, and Calvin. Although their writing has a different purpose than mine, they too know the joys and agonies of putting words on the page.

ABBREVIATIONS

ANMB — Army and Navy Munitions Board
CAC — Chicago Association of Commerce (and Industry)
CPA — Civilian Production Administration
CPL, MR — Chicago Public Library, Municipal Reference
CPL, SC — Chicago Public Library, Special Collections
DPC — Defense Plant Corporation
GSA — General Services Administration
IMA — Illinois Manufacturers' Association
ICD — Illinois Council of Defense
IWC — Illinois War Council (World War II) records, Illinois State Archives
MHC — Metropolitan Housing Council
NDAC — National Defense Advisory Commission
OCO — Office of the Chief of Ordnance
OCWS — Office of Community War Services
OPA — Office of Price Administration
OPM — Office of Production Management
RFC — Reconstruction Finance Corporation
RPDC — Real Property Disposal Case Files, War Assets Administration
SPB — Surplus Property Board
SWPA — Surplus War Property Administration
WAA — War Assets Administration
WPB — War Production Board

Calculating Property Relations

INTRODUCTION

The mobilization of the metropolitan Chicago economy had already begun on May 26, 1940, when President Franklin Roosevelt informed the American people about his administration's program of rearmament. The more observant of Chicago's residents would not have needed Roosevelt's pronouncements to know that something was afoot. It was hard not to notice that Chicago industrialists from all corners of the metropolis were opening closed factories and reactivating machinery to meet British war orders and the promise of even more orders from the U.S. military. It was difficult to miss that workers across the city and the suburbs were filling openings at the South Chicago steel mills, the district's numerous machine shops, and the Loop's business offices. Eager to find a way to shape the new world of armament production, union leaders were reassessing the political and economic realities of the war's workplace. Similarly, Chicago's corporate executives were jockeying with military and federal mobilization agency officials for supply contracts and construction awards and were rushing to meetings to plan how they and their companies could be part of Roosevelt's new mobilization plans. Likewise, city, suburban, and state politicians were building campaigns to bring new industry, new laboratories, and new infrastructures to their locality. Most Chicagoans wanted to take advantage of the opportunities afforded by the promise of war. Little did they know in the spring of 1940 just how much the war would contribute to the expansion of the metropolitan economy over the following five years.

At the center of this expansion was the industrial site, a fixed space consisting of, among other things, factory buildings, railroad sidings, and infrastructures linked to the outside world through a complicated set of political, economic, and social relationships. Industrial sites are places of concern for agents invested in a site's origins, character, operations, and eventual demise. The interests of developers, factory engineers, corporate executives, politicians, unions, and the working class are intimately bound up with industrial space. The fact that agents have different and competing social, economic, and political interests in the functioning of factories, mills, and workshops ensures that industrial sites are places of conflict and deliberation. In pursuing their interests, agents make sociopolitical and numeric calculations about how to proceed given available resources and existing socioeconomic conditions.

Between 1940 and 1950 the calculations shaping the industrial site were reframed as the government and military decisively intervened in the matters of the private firm. Before 1940, federal involvement in industrial property was minimal at best. Legislation drawn up during the Progressive and New Deal periods regulated some activities taking place on privately owned industrial property, most notably legislation regarding monopolies and working conditions. For the most part, however, the government did not seriously contest manufacturers' control of the physical form or social relations of industrial property. Similarly, the direct intervention of the military in the affairs of private industrial property was, with a few exceptions, virtually nonexistent before war broke out in 1939.

Wartime mobilization, however, changed the relationship of the federal government and the military to the industrial site. While industrial executives would remain rulers in their industrial kingdoms, they did have to learn how to accommodate greater intervention in their affairs from government and military leaders. One of the many effects of this was to resituate industrial property in the sociopolitical calculus of government-business relations. Three elements were key to the new calculus of industrial property: the government's financing of wartime mobilization; the acquisition of land and the building of factories by the government and military; and the coordination of the wartime industrial economy by the government, military, and private sector. The new property relationships created after 1945 by the three central institutions of the military-industrial complex did not end with the war. The existence of an unprecedented stock of state-owned industrial property at the time of the surrender of Germany and Japan forced the state to answer questions about the place of federal industrial property in the early postwar economy. This study of the calculative refashioning of Chicago's industrial property between 1940 and 1950 explores the questions raised about the government's ownership of industrial sites and the impact this had on the military-industrial complex.

The broad-sweeping changes made to the social relations of industrial property were signaled by Roosevelt in May 1940 when he told the American people that "the Government of the United States stands ready to advance the necessary money to help provide for the enlargement of factories, the establishment of new factories, the employment of thousands of necessary workers, the development of new sources of supply for the hundreds of raw materials required, the development of quick mass transportation of supplies." Roosevelt was true to his word. Between 1940 and 1945 the U.S. government directly invested more than $17.2 billion in new factory units, indirectly supported factory construction valued at more than $6 billion, poured $196 billion into supply contracts, and produced millions of new manufacturing, construction, and service jobs. In just over five years the U.S. government financed the building of the largest war economy the world had ever known.[1]

The May fireside talk indicated Roosevelt's desire to bring the free enterprise system into the heart of the U.S. war effort while ensuring that the federal government worked with corporate America to achieve his program of industrial mobilization. To this end, the president promised that his administration would provide funds for private industry to produce war commodities. While federal agencies would underwrite the war economy, industrial corporations would produce the required jeeps, bombers, and ships. As he told his audience, "Private industry will have the responsibility of providing the best, speediest and most efficient mass production of which it is capable." In return for turning the peacetime industrial economy into a wartime one under the aegis of the federal government, private industry would be handed significant control over the direction and coordination of the wartime economy. As Roosevelt noted, "The functions of the businessmen whose assistance we are calling upon will be to coordinate this program—to see to it that all of the plants continue to operate at maximum speed and efficiency."[2] The production of war materials was to be a public-private partnership.

This partnership oversaw the construction of an unprecedented expansion of industrial facilities and relied on private operation of government-financed factories built on government-owned property. Private and public land across the nation, from the suburbs of Chicago, Los Angeles, and Houston to rural land in Georgia, Kansas, and Michigan, was converted into industrial property. In the process, the federal government, military, and industry created a partnership centered on the state's coordination of industrial policy and investment; the military's demand for war products and a greater role in industrial affairs; and the deployment of businesses' industrial experts. Roosevelt's program of mobilization required executives from America's largest corporations to operate America's war machine, the government to underwrite industrial expansion and factory construction, and the military to generate demand for war products.

Three issues mentioned in Roosevelt's fireside chat are central to this study of Chicago's government-financed industrial sites. One is that Washington bureaucrats and industrialists drew up plans for the creation of a wartime economy. Even before Roosevelt went on the air, corporate leaders in New York, Chicago, Los Angeles, and elsewhere were working out private industry's role in the new political economy of wartime production. While a few were opposed to state-led industrial mobilization, others, driven by a heady brew of patriotism and profits, were already in Washington helping the bureaucrats of the new mobilization agencies draw up the war economy blueprint. A regime developed consisting of federal financing of factory space, private production of war products, and military demand for commodities. The creation of new industrial sites and the conversion of existing ones to wartime uses were on the radar of industrial executives from an early date. Industrial leaders were already working with government and military officials in Washington to build a mobilization program that produced war commodities in government- and military-financed factories on government- and military-owned industrial property. This initial planning established the basis for the public-private partnership that developed around the country's war factories.[3]

The second issue is that the military became directly involved in industrial property and industrial production, although this was not obvious in May 1940. It would have been difficult to assess so early on just how powerful a player the military would become in channeling funds to industrial sites, in providing supply contracts, and in allocating scarce resources. The military's flexing of its muscles since the mid-1930s, however, did point to its search for more funding, a larger fighting force, and greater authority over production. Even if Roosevelt's administration in 1940 did have an inkling of the military's growing influence over industrial facilities, they did not know the specific trajectories this would take. The making of the war economy was contingent on creating and assembling knowledge about industrial property, much of which was controlled by the military. The implementation of information about production demands, the allocation of scarce resources, and the location of production units, however, was not straightforward. The government's ability to build war factories emerged out of the reworking of the calculative actions of the members of this public-private partnership—government policy makers, Army and Navy Munitions Board officers, and corporate executives. Two outcomes of this were a realignment of industrial politics and the recalculation of the rights associated with industrial property.[4]

Finally, Roosevelt argued that what happened in the factories, streets, and homes of America's industrial centers was vital to the success of the industrial construction program and mobilization.[5] Roosevelt emphasized the role of defense factories to the nation in his speech. A nationally planned, state-financed, privately run industrial war economy, however, had to be mobilized at the local level. The plans of federal bureaucrats, corporate executives, and military planners had to be rooted in decisions and actions taken where production was to take place.[6] The local level, however, was not an unmediated reflection of political decisions made at the national level. The everyday of the local shaped national decision making. Munition officials and government officials operating out of Chicago, Seattle, and Buffalo were linked to manufacturers in other industrial centers and to military and civil mobilization officials in Washington. The local and the national were mutually constitutive. Place was not separate or subordinate to national, international, or global concerns. The articulation of local dealings with circuits of relations crisscrossing the nation and the world resulted in the making of industrial sites in Chicago that were produced out of the flows of capital, ideas, and people across space.[7] Place's place in national networks was central to the building of America's war economy.

Working through these issues, I make three interrelated arguments about the building and disposal of state-owned industrial property between 1940 and 1950. In the first place, I argue that the military-industrial complex relationship was refashioned by the calculative actions associated with the role of industrial property in the federal government's industrial mobilization program.[8] Wartime mobilization did not create the military-industrial complex. Its origins in the nineteenth century have been well documented. Nevertheless, the scope, scale, and character of the state-industry-military nexus were altered by changes made to industrial property relations after 1940 and the subsequent building and disposal of thousands of state-financed industrial sites between 1940 and 1950. The American state was militarized in an unprecedented manner during the war, and industry was inexorably drawn into the administrative structures of the federal government and the military. The powerful military-industry alliance that emerged during the war became permanent after 1945.[9] A detailed examination of the more than six hundred industrial sites in metropolitan Chicago that received direct and indirect federal funding allows me to probe state-directed changes to industrial property and outline the ways in which these changes were part of the changing dynamics of the military-industrial complex during the war and the immediate postwar years.

The military-industrial complex is a contentious notion. Much of the criticism, quite correctly, revolves around the idea that it cannot carry the weight of all of its different parts.[10] Organizationally, the military-industrial complex is fragmented and contingent. The complex's different agents function in a contested world where there is no simple, overarching rationale for their interactions. Nevertheless, the concept can be productively used to explore the question of state-financed industrial facilities. Conceptually, it revolves around the provision of munitions and supplies to the military by industrial firms. This, by definition, requires a complex set of interrelationships centered on industrial production and industrial property. Heuristically, it allows us to make an analysis of the key calculative agents responsible for developing wartime industrial sites and for disposing of these facilities before the Korean War, and to work through the social relations of state-industry-military interaction. Using the idea of the military-industrial complex does not mean downplaying historical processes or discarding the nuances of historical contingency. Rather, focusing on how individuals, groups, and institutions operate within wartime and early postwar networks allows us to analyze their worlds. This provides a flexible framework for understanding how the discrete events of the militarization of industrial property constitute the broader political economy of industrial mobilization.

The second point I make here is that state investment in wartime industrial property had a specific metropolitan geography. A study of eighteen industrial metropolitan areas shows that a disproportionate share of investment went to suburban areas. A detailed case study of Chicago indicates that wartime investment in factories led to the development of a metropolitan fringe dominated by new sprawling government-funded defense factories and a privately funded city center populated by small additions to existing factories.[11] This was not planned; the bipolar geography of industrial investment was unintended. The decentralization of industrial capital during World War II was not a new phenomenon. As several writers have made clear, the depositing of large lumps of investment on the metropolitan fringe had been taking place for a hundred years or more.[12] Industrial suburbanization in Chicago and elsewhere after World War II accelerated greatly. To some extent, this was directly related to wartime investments. In Chicago, some of the large defense factories built by the federal government in places such as Melrose Park and North Chicago or the very edge of the central city were taken over by large corporations seeking suburban locations. Federal and military investment in industrial property between 1940 and 1950 changed the balance of metropolitan industrial geographies in Chicago and elsewhere.

The final argument is that the building and decommissioning of defense facilities was necessarily a local process. The success of national policies of mobilization and disposal depended on how the relations of the military-industrial complex were played out locally. The building of federally financed war factories could only be realized by the operations of economic and political relationships at the local level. While civil, military, and corporate leaders mobilized the war economy, purchased industrial property, financed factory construction, determined production requirements, and formulated surplus plant disposal policy, it was only by being placed in a material world of local business and political life that these could be successfully accomplished. Most studies of wartime industrial plants have focused on industries operating at a national scale. We know a great deal about the overall effect of disposal on, among others, the aluminum and the steel industries.[13] Little attention, however, has been given to the impact of plant disposal on the industrial economy of a specific place.[14]

Roosevelt wasn't concerned with the disposal of defense factories in May 1940 when the overriding issue faced by the military-industrial complex was building a profitable industrial economy that could quickly produce a sufficient amount of war materials for America to win the war. The president's immediate concern was to kick-start mobilization and to coordinate the bumpy relations that came with converting a peacetime economy to a wartime one. The question of how to dispose of surplus industrial land, buildings, and machinery once victory was ensured was of little interest. By 1944, with victory in sight, the government turned its attention to the question of what to do with the thousands of industrial facilities that it owned. The government's response to dealing with this property and how to proceed in its relationship with private industrial property raised important questions about the state's role in manufacturing and the postwar relationship between the civil state, the military, and industry.[15] Answers to the questions raised about the building and disposal of industrial factories would have enormous repercussions on the militarization of American life, the place of corporations and industrial sites in the emergence of the national security state, and the character and strength of the military-industrial complex.

My focus on the importance of local political and economic dynamics contrasts with the work by historians, sociologists, and political scientists who typically view wartime mobilization and the military-industrial complex through the lens of the national. By using federal industrial sites created in Chicago during the war and redeployed after 1945 as the focus of the book, I show that the military-industrial complex was produced at a variety of scales, from the factory to the national.[16] This view provides a richer understanding of the dynamics of wartime mobilization, the calculative actions of political and business leaders, the social relations of property, state-industry relations, and the making of industrial space.

Chicago's war machine and the industrial sites in which it was embodied had to operate in situ. This point has been made by Roger Lotchin, who notes that national policy makers, industrial executives, and military officials could only instantiate industrial production by working with alliances mobilized at the local level.[17] Government, military, and industrial managers operating in Washington, many of whom had deep local attachments, channeled public investments into federally financed factory additions, new government-owned factories, supply contracts, and research labs. Working with government and military officials who operated out of the offices of national mobilization agencies located in Chicago, local industrial managers and politicians managed how these investments were translated into the material sites and infrastructure that produced the American war machine. Local boosters in Chicago and elsewhere worked with agents operating at the national and regional levels to channel billions of dollars into industrial facilities that would underpin America's mobilization program.

The most effective way to study the multiscalar processes of the military-industrial complex between 1940 and 1950 is through an examination of one place. As Michael Bernstein and Mark Wilson have noted, case studies show the workings of the military-industrial complex by mobilizing "the insights and techniques of 'microhistory' in an effort to refine and strengthen the abstractions and conceptions framed by more general theories of social and historical change."[18] The case study paints a rich and detailed picture of the political, economic, and social dynamics of one place while making direct connections to a set of issues that link that place to other scales: from a munitions factory to a Washington, D.C., agency office to the European battlefield. The story of defense plants in American localities between 1940 and 1950 has the potential to inform us about the character of capitalist industrial relations, the changing role of the state, property relations, and the influence of the military in the private industrial realm.

The focus of this book is metropolitan Chicago.[19] There are several reasons why metropolitan Chicago is an excellent choice for a study of federal investment in manufacturing facilities and the development of wartime industrial spaces. First, the metropolitan region was the country's largest recipient of state and private capital investment in wartime manufacturing plants. With more than $1.3 billion poured into new productive capacity between 1940 and 1945, Chicago easily outpaced the other leading recipients of industrial funding: New York City, Detroit, Philadelphia, and Los Angeles. Second, federal funding was invested in a variety of firms: suburban corporate steel mills experienced substantial expansion; new massive airplane engine factories were built on city and suburban greenfield sites; and specialized, precision instrument makers across the city had small additions made to their workshops. The breadth of Chicago's industrial spectrum allows me to explore the impact of the emerging public-private partnership on the development of capitalist industrial relations around defense plants. Third, Chicago's political and business leaders were actively involved in industrial mobilization and at the national and regional scale. Many Chicago industrial executives worked for mobilization agencies in Washington. As the regional center of the Midwest, Chicago was home to a wide range of agencies and departments, such as the Chicago Ordnance District, that coordinated local mobilization with national planning directives and policy coming out of Washington.

The final reason is the availability of excellent archival sources. A range of materials on the building and disposal of Chicago's defense plants is held at the National Archives (such as those of the War Assets Administration and Office of the Chief of Ordnance) and local depositories such as the Chicago Public Library, Chicago History Museum, and University of Chicago. The digitization of local newspapers, most notably the *Chicago Tribune*, has made the search for material on local mobilization and disposal much easier. While newspapers have their weaknesses, their emphasis on local events complements archival holdings that typically focus on the national level. Unfortunately, the range of local municipal records in the Chicago region is abysmal. Very little of interest for this study is available.

The single most important source for this study of Chicago's government-financed industrial sites is the real property case files held in the National Archives at College Park, Maryland, and Chicago. These files consist of materials that trace the history of the building and disposal of all state-financed industrial sites.[20] The material was created by federal officials as part of their effort to sell the facilities. In most cases, the files are very large, running into several hundreds and, in some cases, thousands of pages. The more substantial files contain materials from various sources. Some are from units internal to government agencies (such as the Engineering Division of the Defense Plant Corporation, and the Real Estate Review Board of the War Assets Administration). In other cases, the material consists of letters from firms seeking to buy or lease plancors at the end of the war; appraisers, credit-rating companies, auctioneers, and industrial engineers working on contract for agencies; and local and state politicians looking to increase their constituency's industrial base.[21] The real property case files and other archival documents allow me to trace a detailed historical geography of metropolitan Chicago's wartime industrial sites between 1940 and 1950.

In chapter 1 I sketch out the broad conceptual and historiographical ideas that animate the study. In doing so, I argue that the defense factory, both during and immediately after the war, was a calculative object subject to the machinations of a small group of officials, officers, and businesspeople firmly ensconced in the thickening networks of the military-industrial complex. Chapter 2 considers the processes shaping industrial mobilization in the United States. It focuses on the ways in which military officials, federal policy makers, and corporate executives operating at the national scale worked with local officials and businesspeople to build industrial sites in places such as metropolitan Chicago.

The remaining chapters explore the building and disposal of federally owned industrial sites in Chicago and its surrounding suburbs, industrial cities, and rural districts. Metropolitan Chicago was home to the country's largest agglomeration of state-funded wartime fixed-capital investment. The story of the making and disposing of the metropolitan area's state-owned industrial sites is laid out in six chapters. Chapter 3 examines the processes driving the mobilization and assembly of Chicago's wartime industrial spaces, with especial attention given to the particularities of the local political and industrial world. Chapter 4 presents the key elements of the industrial landscape created by the state's fixed-capital investment. The chapter starts with a discussion of the various types of industrial spaces and the uneven metropolitan geographies that were created by this investment. This is followed by a case study of the Calumet district that illustrates the central features of the wartime manufacturing landscape. Chapter 5 explores the role of industrial engineering companies in the making of three new, large, and important industrial war sites in metropolitan Chicago: the Elwood ordnance plant, the Seneca shipyards, and the Buick aircraft engine factory at Melrose Park.

The final three chapters focus on the disposal of metropolitan Chicago's state-owned industrial facilities. Chapter 6 examines the assembling, measuring, and disposal of Chicago's wartime facilities, emphasizing the ways in which industrial plants became incorporated into the idea of the national security state. Chapter 7 considers the creation of new forms of knowledge about government factories by agents of the military-industry complex. The final chapter explores the relationship between defense factory disposal and place making through four case studies: the relationship between postwar defense contracts and the sale of a wartime factory to Kropp Forging; the entangled character of the disposal of two steelmaking sites; the place politics of the Bendix Aviation plancor; and a court case between the federal government and Ahlberg Bearing over state-owned industrial property.

This brings to a close a history of the building of new wartime factories with state funds and the disposal of these plants to private interests. In metropolitan Chicago, and this is the case for most other areas of the United States, the federal government and military's massive involvement in the provision of productive wartime fixed capital would have a long-standing impact not only on urban centers but also on military-state-industry relations.

CHAPTER 1

Calculation and Industrial Property

An industrial site is a calculative good. The very character of the capitalist factory and its associated appurtenances is embedded in a calculative understanding of the world. This was the point made by Karl Marx and Friedrich Engels in 1848 when they noted that the triumph of industrial capitalism was fixed "in the icy waters of egotistical calculation."[1] For them and others, capitalism and political governance are inherently calculative. Marx's factory owners seek ways to extract surplus value and intensify the labor process. Michel Foucault's prison wardens and Christian thinkers make calculations about the workings of the human body. David Harvey's financiers produce reckonings about the profits to be made from investing excess capital in urban places. James Scott's state officials use calculating techniques to make the world more legible.[2] In all cases, public and private institutional agents are located in a world of calculative deliberation or reckoning. While these calculations are not always rational, they are always concerned with measuring the world. Calculative action is the search for a way to interpret, bound, and rationalize the world. The representation of the world as calculative makes a complex world more understandable by creating boundaries that distinguish objects from one another and by allowing actors to interpret and rationalize objects and actions. Calculation is typically understood to have numeric outcomes. The agents involved with the factory, for example, are concerned with devising numerical calculations to questions about its operation. How much does that land cost? How many workers will be needed on the production line? How profitable is the factory? How much should be invested in new machinery? Should workers be paid by the piece or by the hour? In such cases, the answers are always numeric.

Calculation, however, does not begin or end with the number. The "icy waters of egotistical calculation" may well be concerned with numerical answers to sociopolitical questions, but it is also concerned with the ways that industrial entrepreneurs, military leaders, and politicians interpret the world outside the number. Without this, the number could not exist. Calculation requires interpretative positions that precede and follow the quantitative response. The numeric answer, whether it is how many workers are required or the cost of land, is rooted in the social relations of industrial property. A simple question about how many workers are needed requires information about, for example, the labor market, government legislation, and industrial competition. The cost of industrial property is embedded in, among other things, questions of local economic policy, land-use zoning, and transport facilities. All of these concerns entail a qualitative understanding of the factory world, labor markets, and industrial property markets. Without an interpretative understanding of the world, calculative agents would be unable to render the world as knowable through the number. In other words, calculative action is both quantitative and qualitative.[3]

Working through the literature on calculation, property relations, militarization, and wartime metropolitan history, this chapter argues that the construction and dismantling of the state-owned defense factory during World War II was predicated on these two mutually constitutive sides of calculation. The industrial site was a calculable good that was fixed as part of America's industrial mobilization program and the postwar defense program.

Calculation and the Industrial Site

As Marx and Engels's comments on the rise of "icy calculation" in bourgeois society suggest, the idea of calculating agents has been key to the understanding of the development of capitalist society. Writers such as Karl Polanyi, Sidney Pollard, and Max Weber have pointed to the rise of the intertwined processes of capitalist commodity markets and the need for the state to intervene in the regulation and management of these markets.[4] As one part of this, property markets became inscribed into a new order of capitalist market calculation and rationalization that developed simultaneously with the growth of bourgeois power over everyday life. Land had to be valued, measured, and used in such a way to minimize the contradictions of the private market and the disorder that came with the incompatibility of politics and the economy. This order consisted of building a structure to safeguard property rights while allocating land to appropriate use in the marketplace. As Harvey notes, "Capitalism cannot do without land price and land markets as basic coordinating devices in the allocation of land to uses."[5] The land market, however, is more than a coordinating device of land allocation and use; it is also a relation in which calculative agents work to give order to capitalist property rights.

The study of calculation today centers on two main approaches: Foucauldian and political sociology. Although there are obvious overlaps, especially in the prominence given to state practices and rationality, there are important differences between the two approaches. Foucauldians build on Weberian ideas of measurement, rationalization, and bureaucratic control to determine how the politics of the number underpins the modern world. Numbers make an object representable, something that can be calculated and worked on by government. As Rueben Rose-Redwood has recently noted, this literature draws on governmentality "to examine how a governmental power is exercised through the deployment of political technologies of calculation."[6] From this perspective, objects as different as markets, shellfish, and slum housing are rendered calculable through devices that function to serve government purposes.[7] This position has obvious strengths, most notably the close attention given to calculative technologies, the emphasis on rationality as a key component of political practice, and the importance of calculation for political and moral purposes.

A second strand rooted in the political sociology of objects takes a more expansive view of calculation. From this perspective, the Foucauldian position "makes politics too much of a technical and instrumental matter and places too much emphasis on rational state control."[8] In contrast, political sociology seeks to unpack the tension-filled, contingent relationships that characterize calculation. Rather than Foucault's polished sheen of human action and the determinative direction of governmentality, Michel Callon and others focus on a range of calculative agents who operate across the blurred boundaries between objects and behavior. Rather than working through the imperatives of governmentality, political sociology emphasizes the specific apparatus of the calculative act.[9] Most importantly, as Callon emphasizes, the qualitative side of calculation is based on framing the objects as distinct from one another. It is only when a thing is disentangled from other objects that it can be successfully calculated. As Callon and Fabian Muniesa note, "Calculation starts by establishing distinctions between things or states of the world, and by imagining and estimating courses of actions associated with those things or with those states as well as their consequences."[10] Objects are not unconnected or isolated; they can only be understood in relation to other objects.

The political sociology position extends the political economy view of the state, markets, and class by bringing calculative politics to an analysis of industrial property. An object such as industrial land or a factory becomes calculable only when it is framed as different from other objects by individuals who have the authority to demarcate boundaries between entities. With the rise of industrial capitalism, the state and business established the boundaries of industrial property that clearly separated it from other forms of property, allowed for the building of an allocative system of value and use, and ensured that it functioned in a way that was both rational and calculable. In developing and defending boundaries between objects, individuals drew on preexisting networks while creating new networks of individuals, groups, and institutions, as was evident as manufacture moved from proto-industrialization to proprietary and corporate capitalism. In the case of industrial property, this required an ongoing assessment of the principal players in the property market. By the twentieth century, the key actors were the federal government, the courts, the military, the real estate industry, financial institutions, and industrial companies. Finally, numeric calculation is inextricably interwoven with the nonnumeric. The number is qualitative. The pricing of property, for example, is relational and can only occur once the value of land is calculated in regard to the social, political, and economic relations in which it exists.

The mutually constitutive character of calculation can be demonstrated in the case of wartime industrial property. The advent of war in Europe in 1939 forced the American state, the military, and business to rethink the place of private industrial property in industrial mobilization. Preexisting notions of what constituted industrial property were no longer viable. Private interests could not effectively incorporate the demands of full-scale industrial mobilization into their production operations. The state had to intervene. As property is a malleable "system of laws, practices and relations," it can be reworked to accommodate new social, political, and economic conditions.[11] While there is a degree of fixity to property relations in any society, they are open to change in times of stress and crisis, as was the case during World War II when unprecedented demands were placed on industrial production and, by extension, industrial property. As this study shows, the result was the emergence of a new calculative object: the government-owned defense factory.[12] During World War II the government-funded industrial site and factory became framed as different and separate from other industrial property. A network of calculating actors from government, the military, and industry created a production space centered on a new form of property relations.

The government defense factories built between 1940 and 1945 were primarily distinguished from private production spaces by the source of financing and ownership. Defense factories were created by mobilizing and realigning preexisting networks. To be framed as a defense factory, and as different from other factories, it had to be made a legitimate object and delimited from other property. As such, the government factory was part of a network of relationships that included specific groups and excluded others. The key agents that underpinned the factory as a calculable object during World War II and the immediate postwar period were federal policy makers, military officials, and business executives. The agents of the military-industrial complex delimited the factory as a calculable object and by so doing opened it up to monetary, legal, political, and other forms of calculative actions.

This suggests that the social relations that underpin the framing of an object have to be stabilized for effective calculation to take place. As Dan Slater explains, calculation relies on the creation of "a stable and reliable context in which objects and obligations are clearly mapped and can be intersubjectively recognized."[13] The framing of an industrial site as an object financed for the most part by the state and not by private interests during World War II depended on the building of reliable encounters and the development of appropriate behavior between those operating in the emerging network. One example of this would be the signing of legally sanctioned and non-arbitrary contracts between mobilization agencies and industrial engineering firms to build defense plants. Another would be the contested but nevertheless directed meetings between different interests to determine resource allocation among the competing arms of the military. In all cases, calculative relations had to be fixed, demarcated, and workable.

The search for stability among a set of competing interests puts immense pressure on all those involved in calculating property markets. The hierarchical character of capitalist relations ensures that the choices are controlled by a group of political and business leaders who typically work together in some form of alliance. Almost without exception, those making calculations about industrial property were middle- and upper-class white men. There were few if any women or people of color in government or industry who played a significant role in the mobilization or disposal of industrial space. While women and visible minorities populated the production line and the administrative offices of the mobilization and disposal agencies, they did not play a direct role in calculation. It was a world dictated by white men who already had powerful positions within government, the military, and industry. These calculative agents sought to use state-industry relations to their own ends and to create a stable object—state-owned industrial property—that could be worked on by members of the military-industrial complex.

Regardless of the character and strength of any alliance, the decisions to be made about any particular event or object have to be ranked in order of importance. The ranking of these self-interested agents involves making quantitative and qualitative judgments simultaneously. After a list of possible options has been created and ranked, agents must identify and describe the actions that turn these options into material effects. The options available to an English nineteenth-century capitalist for extracting more profit could be to sweat more work out of the laborer or to install new machinery. In the case of the twentieth-century financier, the options may be to invest capital in Los Angeles office property or the New Delhi subway. In all cases, the agent has to list and then prioritize options. Once the options are ranked, the factory owner or financier can attempt to operationalize the decisions. A successful calculation involves framing the object in such a way that a clear way forward to its implementation can be discerned. These decisions, all of which involve a numerical effect, require qualitative deliberation. Played out on material landscapes, these deliberations create spaces of calculation. In the same sense, industrial sites are calculative spaces; they are a focus of specific class-based social relations that determine who controls and oversees the creation and use of this particular type of industrial space.

Industrial spaces of calculation are defined by four elements.[14] In the first place, they are material and tangible objects—land, buildings, machinery, roads—operated on by calculative agents such as real estate agents, planners, bankers, company managers, and union leaders. The imperatives of war, government policy, and business opposition to industrial mobilization forced the state to consider alternatives to privately funded defense plants. Calculating that America had to get involved in war production, the Roosevelt administration, after consulting with military and business leaders, had worked out the basic lineaments of industrial mobilization by the summer of 1940. Central to this calculation was the decision to move ahead with the construction of government-financed defense factories. Working with a range of private sector actors, including industrial executives, real estate agents, and industrial engineers, the state directly invested more than $17 billion in industrial facilities and indirectly underwrote another $6 billion. By the end of war, the state had built an assemblage of factories, roads, utility lines, and machinery geared to constructing the largest war machine the world had ever known.

A second element of these industrial spaces is that they are defined and ordered by legal structures and practices. These establish the basis for actions by agents on industrial sites, from providing the legal basis for the character and extent of property rights and labor relations to the power that government agencies have over what takes place in industrial sites. In the case of the construction of World War II factories, legislation introduced after 1940 gave the federal government and the military the right to create publicly financed and operated industrial space.[15] This legislation, which covered a range of issues such as prices, labor, raw material, and housing, gave the state broad authority over most areas impinging on industrial mobilization and the building of defense factories. Similarly, the surplus property and industrial reserve acts passed between 1944 and 1948 laid the basis for the disposal of federally owned industrial buildings and the incorporation of private property into the national security system. As calculative action, government legislation established the parameters and legitimacy of what could be done in specific contexts and by whom.

A third feature is that calculative agents must follow the procedures that determine which objects are to be worked on and outline the way things are to be done. The creation and operation of industrial sites, for example, involve rules and practices about the purchase of property, the construction of factories, the allocation of scarce resources, and the working of the production process. Along with passing various pieces of legislation, the federal government and the military implemented a range of powerful agencies that oversaw the locations for defense factories, determined which corporations would operate government-owned factories, coordinated the construction of industrial facilities across the country, and channeled resources from one area to another. Federal agencies such as the National Defense Advisory Commission and the Defense Plant Corporation and military ones such as the Army and Navy Munitions Board established the procedures and practices that mobilized the political calculations about industrial mobilization.

Finally, calculative spaces are shaped by monetary issues. Agents involved with industrial sites assess the cost of their interactions, from the price of land to the cost of producing a good. All of these decisions intersect with one another and are shaped and reshaped by other elements. The first major financial decision that shaped the building of state-owned industrial facilities was the Roosevelt administration's calculation in early 1940 to move ahead with industrial mobilization. This was followed over the ensuing years by the channeling of vast resources to the federal and military mobilization and disposal agencies. Business decisions to convert from civilian to defense production and to build new facilities for manufacturing munitions involved switching financial resources from one place to another. Together, these four elements establish the framework for calculative action.

The process of producing effective calculations about industrial mobilization and industrial sites, however, is neither straightforward nor seamless. Calculative agents are unable to make fully informed decisions and judgments despite their frequent claims to the contrary. For a variety of reasons, they function in a milieu in which they have incomplete information. This could be because agents—military officials, government bureaucrats, and corporate executives, for example—keep information from each other or because they are unable to assimilate the vast amount of information that surfaces in any complex situation. Agents also operate in a world of truncated interactions. Institutional and geographic boundaries restrict movement of information, while interpersonal relations are frequently curtailed by actions outside of the agent's control: telephone calls are not returned, forms are not filled in, people leave positions. Geographic relations are made more problematic by the difficulty of communicating across physical distance. These restrictions on the flow of information only make local actions and decisions more important to the building of an industrial regime and the success of national policy making.

Calculative action is predicated on discontinuous and truncated information. Agents often find themselves in situations that are beyond their control. Calculative action is their attempt to order this state of disorder. For example, labor leaders are greatly constrained in planning wartime industrial plants by their inability to undermine the power of military officials and corporate executives. Decisions about how to proceed are also structured by past decisions. The tendency for the social arrangements of political and economic institutions to be self-reproducing over time produces systems that are routinized and hard to change. It can be very difficult for those new to a system or outside of existing networks to break down well-worn practices. Social and geographic distance only accentuates these problems. At any one time, the options open to agents such as industrial engineers, federal and labor officials, or local politicians to shape an industrial site rests on and is conditioned by the past and the state of the present.[16]

Calculation, then, is the way in which agents work to produce bounded and rational order out of disorder. In order to do this, calculative agents frame objects as singular and distinct from other objects. Once framed, an object is subject to actions that have consequences. A material object such as a factory is framed by legislation that legitimizes it and makes it legible; it is worked on by practices and procedures that are typically framed by the legislation; and it becomes the focus of financial resources that allow agents to implement the calculation. Roosevelt's calculation that the state had to become centrally involved in the construction of industrial factories and the production of commodities was dependent on a particular network of class-based decision makers from government, the military, and business. The implementation of industrial mobilization in turn created new networks that drove and shaped the course of actions. These networks involved drawing in people from all scales, which linked the national with the local, the political with the economic, and the civil with the military. In all cases, the attempt to create calculated order was both numeric and qualitative.

The Industrial Site, the Militarized State, and World War II

These reflections help us understand industrial sites as spaces of calculative militarization and the economic, social, and political processes that are mobilized to organize society around military action and violence. One of the ways that historians have chronicled the militarization of American life is through the military-industrial complex. The central themes of this work on the history of the complex have been a critique of corporate capitalism and the relationship of the state to big business, the charting of the political-economic changes associated with the rise of the defense industry, and outlining the relationship between key industries and the armed forces.[17] More recently, work has focused on the cultural geographies of military affairs, both on and off the battlefield and outside the military-industrial complex.[18] In all cases, the focus has been on how military power is "dependent on the legitimation of spaces" that constitute the processes and form of militarization.[19] This concern with the authority invested in and the legitimization of the geographies of militarization has led to studies of, among other things, landscape formation, the creation of military knowledge, the normalization of military effects, and the geographical formation of military ideologies and power.[20] Research on the military-industrial complex and the geographies of militarism has clearly established the creation of a militarized state as part of everyday social relations.

Building on this work, I explore the calculative relations of factory building during World War II and the immediate postwar period and show how these relations shaped the social relations of property and the industrial site.[21] Even though the state had actively intervened in industrial affairs since the end of the nineteenth century, industrial sites before 1940 were framed as private spaces, not government or militarized spaces. Industrial mobilization changed this by forcing military-industrial complex leaders to recalculate the meaning, role, and relations of industrial property in American life between 1940 and 1950. This involved reconfiguring the social relations of property to meet the demands made by the federal government and the military around industrial mobilization and demobilization. These changes involved building new boundaries around how industrial property was financed, owned, and controlled. Even though these changes were resisted by many sectors of the business world in the early years of the war, the imperatives of national industrial mobilization and international geopolitical realities forced all calculative players to agree to rethink the relations of industrial property.[22] Although the state would withdraw from involvement in many areas of industrial activity after the war, it remained committed to maintaining the relationships that bound it to the military and business. The close relationships that developed in the postwar period between the members of the military-industrial complex around research and development, national security, and military procurement were new elements of a militarized state that differentiated it from the prewar version.

The reframing of industrial property after 1940 by the militarized state had three elements.[23] In the first place, it involved building an elaborate professional structure made up of competing agencies to coordinate and implement state policy. These agencies, boards, and committees worked, among other things, to build new technological innovations, to ascertain the amount and allocation of resources necessary for the building of new factory space, to define the scale and type of the munitions required by the armed forces, and to determine the location and type of new production facilities. Second, the federal government created legislation that permitted militarized control over industrial space and allowed the state and the military to have a greater role over industrial management. Finally, the Roosevelt and Truman administrations worked to ensure that substantial funds flowed to mobilization and disposal programs. The result was the creation of a militarized state that had important repercussions for industrial property both during and after the war.

The militarized state as it emerged after 1940 had a long history. Its origins lay in the growing ties between the federal government, military, and business after the Civil War. By the end of World War I, "centralized control over a planned economy [had been] . . . established and carried out by representatives of the government, the business community, and the military. In so doing, institutional lines were obliterated."[24] These relations became more elaborate in the interwar period with the military's increasing interest in industrial sites as part of the broader calculations about its place in American life, although very little was actually implemented before 1940. The National Defense Act of 1920 had several effects, including building a knowledgeable military staff and gearing wartime military plans to the economy. The 1930 Industrial Mobilization Plan became the blueprint for future wartime plans. A place for industrial sites was written into the plan, but with very few concrete outcomes. The publication of the Special Senate Committee to Investigate the Munitions Industry (Nye Committee) findings in 1936 changed little. While Nye and his committee members pointed to a number of issues, such as wartime profits and the corporate role in World War I, they did not adequately address the question of industrial sites and military production. The scale and scope of militarized industrial production and military control over manufacturing space continued to be limited and episodic as late as 1939.[25]

The military's inability to effectively frame industrial sites as part of its mobilization plans ensured that the country was ill prepared for an emergency such as war. Attempts to identify factories that could be part of a national munitions program before 1940 floundered on small budgets, inadequate legislation, and wrangling between the military-industrial complex partners. While their activities allowed the army and navy to assemble material on companies that could provide munitions under emergency conditions, the armed forces were unable to effectively mobilize industrial sites as a component of the modern military. The military-industry relationship was still ad hoc and fragmented. The fact that the New Deal captured an inordinate amount of the federal government's attention during the 1930s only accentuated the problems. Together with the strength of isolationism, the Nye Committee findings, and business opposition to government intervention, these factors worked to ensure that economic mobilization was neglected and that the military made little progress in identifying and mobilizing private industrial space. Accordingly, the United States had few military facilities when war broke out in September 1939. The few that had been active during World War I had been dismantled or converted to peacetime production. At the end of 1939, the United States stood sixteenth in terms of size of the military, "sandwiched between Spain and Bulgaria."[26] The armament industry was correspondingly very small. Industrial sites remained outside of military influence.

German aggression and the advent of war in the fall of 1939 forced the state to undertake a rapid reappraisal of the place of industrial property in military matters. The geopolitics of war created alliances that established different ways of understanding the factory, most notably the recalculation of the industrial site in America's mobilization program. Roosevelt's speeches of May 1940 clearly signaled that the industrial site could no longer be the sole prerogative of private industry. Building on the tentative beginnings established over the previous twenty years, the federal government brought the factory more closely under its control. The result was that industrial investment, information, labor, and materials were recalculated during the war. The framing of the industrial site as an object of concern led to creation by wartime mobilization agencies of a substantial body of quantitative and qualitative material on issues such as the value of industrial property, the availability of construction materials, and the composition of the labor force. This understanding of the factory and property relations created networks that linked Washington committee rooms with corporate boardrooms, military bases, city halls, and subcontractor offices. The post-1939 calculations about the state's place in production and property matters worked to recalibrate how industrial sites were understood and worked on.

This calculative politics of industrial property during the war and in the immediate postwar period had two effects on the militarized state. The first was to force military-industrial complex leaders to rethink the importance of industrial sites in national policy. As early as 1939 it was no longer assumed that the federal government's role in commodity production would continue to be a simple regulatory one. As the war in Europe intensified and the pressure to enter the war grew, it became increasingly obvious to government and military leaders that the state would have to be more than a provider of government contracts for defense commodities produced by private corporations on their own property. The state's role of facilitating social consensus and promoting capitalist relations had to be balanced by a more direct intervention into industrial matters, both during and after the war. Massive investment in factory space for the production of wartime materials was a central feature of this intervention. The question of what to do with state-owned industrial sites at the end of hostilities became a key concern after 1944. These questions were part of broader changes to state capacity and industrial policy making, including legislation that oversaw the building of a wartime and postwar economy; agencies that managed and controlled industrial mobilization between 1940 and the Korean War; and the recruitment of scientific, military, and corporate experts into federal policy making.[27]

The second effect was the reorganization of state, military, and corporate relations in light of the policy of investing in industrial property and wartime factories. Government and military officers were deployed in a policy-making role at the heart of the mobilization and disposal agencies. This administrative body was strengthened by corporate executives who came to wield great control over the industrial economy. The three calculative institutions of the military-industrial complex worked, often acrimoniously, to direct the war economy. This involved refashioning industrial, military, and political relations. It also required rethinking the industrial site, which was no longer to be the sole domain of the industrialist. Mobilization and regulatory agencies became key centers through which calculative agents reworked the social relations of property and channeled investment into industrial spaces. The creation of mobilization agencies, such as the War Production Board, allowed state industrial and military leaders to work together to build new industrial spaces and to convert the industrial economy to war production. Similarly, new agencies were established to dispose of the industrial site in the postwar period.

The post-1940 reformulation of industrial policy, investment, and property emerged out of policies introduced during the New Deal. As Gregory Hooks has argued, "Administrative advances and strategic policy tools forged by the New Deal were absorbed and adapted to the nascent national security state during and after World War II."[28] Despite a series of obstacles, the federal government was able to shift a share of its administrative capacity gained during the 1930s to the wartime agencies running industrial mobilization. In part this was because of the ability of the Roosevelt administration to transfer practices and personnel from the New Deal to wartime agencies. It was also due to the increasing pressure to find administrative solutions to the imperatives of mobilization. The government had little choice but to forge ahead with building capacity devoted to production once the Roosevelt administration had framed factory construction as central to the war effort, had decided to move ahead with large-scale state investment in factory sites, and had committed substantial funds to constructing a war machine. Building on New Deal precedents, the wartime state developed an industrial policy consisting of instrumental norms, routinized methods of work and decision making, a codified system of law, and a bureaucratic social hierarchy. The basic outline of a militarized state centered on unprecedented government investment in industrial production was built on earlier state intervention in infrastructures and welfare.[29]

The erection of this state-directed, militarized industrial regime during the war was characterized by competition between competing visions over industrial matters and the prerogatives of property. The liberal tradition that was so influential during the 1930s eventually succumbed to the onslaught of a conservative and more business-friendly tradition during the war.[30] The vision entailed moving away from ideas of state regulation and collective action to one emphasizing national security issues and the withdrawal of the state from regulation of the economy and corporate behavior. Similarly, the ability of the state to use real property to advance collective ends increasingly became under attack. The effect was to strengthen policies promoting industrial expansion by reducing regulation of industrial and financial corporations and to facilitate state investment in industrial sites.[31]

The conclusion of the early debates about the state's wartime role was to subject the industrial site to recalculation. The industrial site was no longer simply a private object, one that the state had little right to intervene in and control.

Rather, the federal government heavily committed to investment in new industrial facilities and to dictating industrial output. Wartime deliberations forced the state into industrial matters on a scale and in a way that had never been seen before. The state would become the primary investor in industrial facilities and the owner of industrial property. These decisions, however, set into motion a set of policy-level calculations. How was the state going to channel investment into buildings, machinery, and equipment at new industrial sites? How much capital was to be invested and in what industries? Where was this investment to be located? What sort of legislation and new agencies had to be created? Who was going to be included in the decision-making process? These and many other questions became central to the calculations of the wartime civil state and its partners, the military and industry.

Disposing of Defense Factories, the Militarized State, and National Security

The winding down of wartime production and the search for postwar "normalcy" required rethinking the status of state-owned wartime industrial property. The factory had to be reframed for a peacetime world. The politics of factory building had to be recalculated for the new socioeconomic conditions of postwar America. Even though it was agreed that the federal government would dispose of state-owned property at the end of the war, the state did not immediately relinquish control over its wartime plants. The process was drawn out over several years as factories became part of the calculus of the national security state and postwar industrial policy. This is in contrast to what happened at the end of World War I, where the few government-owned properties that did exist were disposed of with little fanfare.[32] The situation was quite different in 1945, both in terms of what to do about state-owned industrial factories and the military's desire to maintain control over what they considered to be key defense facilities. The problem facing military-industrial complex leaders was what to do with the more than 1,600 state-owned manufacturing sites valued at more than $17 billion.[33]

Deliberations about how to proceed started as early 1943, with two main interest groups vying to control the destiny of government manufacturing facilities. Left-leaning state officials and academics believed that industrial property should remain in public hands to be used for state-directed economic reconstruction. Military officers, industrial officials, and conservative politicians argued that the defense factories should be sold as quickly as possible to private interests. Not surprisingly, the latter won the battle, and a disposal program designed to sell wartime plants to private industry was established, although this did not happen in a straightforward way.

Government officials moved ahead with the disposal of state-owned industrial property. This required calculating the property relations of the industrial sites after 1945 in a different way from how they were understood during the war. Wartime mobilization agencies were dismantled and replaced by new ones with a mandate to oversee and coordinate the selling off of the large number of industry facilities. A large bureaucracy developed to assemble information about manufacturing sites deemed surplus to government needs and to rationalize the procedures and practices by which factories were sold or leased to private interests. Legislation such as the 1944 Surplus Property Act established the legal basis for plant disposal and created an administrative apparatus to dispose of surplus industrial facilities. Disposal of industrial facilities to private interests and the creation of a new set of calculative actions could only take place once the wartime industrial site had been framed as surplus to government and military requirements.

Disposal of wartime factories was slow at first, only picking up by the second half of 1946. An extensive advertising campaign and the relatively low costs of the facilities ensured that many of the more enticing industrial plants were quickly purchased by firms, oftentimes those that had operated them during the war.[34] By the end of 1948, the War Assets Administration (WAA), the agency charged with disposal, had sold many of the most viable properties. Despite the agency's best efforts, however, some industrial facilities were impossible to sell. Nevertheless, by the time of the Korean War, the government had successfully washed its hands of a significant share of its wartime manufacturing facilities.[35]

At the same time that industrial property was being sold to private interests, the federal government was also looking to bring industrial facilities into the national security state. The factory was no longer viewed by the state simply as a private profit-making object that had to be regulated to minimize political and economic disruptions internal to America. Industrial assets became a calculative element of the postwar national security system. This movement to link production sites with postwar state policy emerged out of America's new place in the global order and was linked to the government's need to intervene in industrial matters to protect U.S. political and economic interests overseas. Business, military, and congressional leaders vigorously argued for the need to defend national borders, contain Soviet expansionism, and promote economic and political expansionism abroad. They were successful. At home, a national security regime framed by the 1947 National Security Act sought, among other things, to unify the armed forces and increase the military budget, to build new institutions such as the National Security Council and the Central Intelligence Agency, and to reorganize Congress to better implement the changing demands of national security.[36] As noted by several writers, the building of a national security state, with its emphasis on both national and economic security, worked to strengthen the partnership between the state, the military, and business.[37]

Despite the work by Melyvn Leffler and others on the changing place of industrial matters in national life, little has been said about the place of industrial property in the immediate postwar national security state.[38] The administrative structure used to oversee wartime mobilization established the basis for ongoing state intervention in postwar industrial matters. The contested, but yet successful, wartime alliance continued into the postwar period, although operating in a different way. The growing power of the military along with increasingly powerful conservative factions in Congress gave impetus to government interest in the production of war materials. The National Industrial Reserve Acts of 1947 and 1948 allowed the federal government to control privately owned industrial property in the name of national security. Unlike during the war, where the focus was on production of wartime products, the emphasis after 1945 was to keep a set of industrial plants ready for use in an emergency. Even though the state formally disposed of a great deal of its industrial property to private companies in the postwar period, decommissioning defense factories and creating a national industrial reserve forged a new set of relations around industrial property in the early postwar period.

It is critical to understand that the state's presence in manufacturing before and after World War II differed in significant ways. In prewar years, outside of fiscal and antitrust policy, patent law, and New Deal regulation, the American state did not directly intervene in industrial affairs. It spent little on the defense industry. In 1939 its military production units consisted of six ordnance factories, which supplied less than 5 percent of the army's wartime requirements.[39] Even though the state had become more involved in labor issues and production regulation in the 1930s, its role was minimal and centered on legislation that established the state as a mediator between capital and labor. The most intrusive state practice was antimonopoly legislation. The 1890 Sherman Act and its amendments over the following years reflected the state's need to assuage the bruising power of the corporation. But even this, despite a handful of spectacular results, had little effect on corporate control over the American economy. While the state had been essential to the rise and reproduction of capitalist relations, it rarely intruded in the actual operations of manufacturing. The war changed this, and the state did not relinquish its reins on many aspects of industrial production with the end of hostilities in 1945.

The postwar militarized state continued to actively regulate manufacturing assets. This was evident in many arenas: large-scale funding of science and technology; the maintenance of a large number of ordnance factories; the formation of a factory national reserve that was to be activated for the production of munitions in a time of emergency; the leasing of wartime state-owned factories to private firms; the provision of large defense contracts; and the creation of studies and reports about industry. These elements did not congeal to form a well-thought-out and coherent industrial policy. It is a long list. Most of what became industrial policy, however, was ad hoc, contested, and disorganized.

Nevertheless, a postwar national security policy emerged out of the development of the wartime emergency, the growing power of the federal government, the decision to demonize the Soviet Union, and the need to construct a bureaucracy that would both defend and extend America's imperial power. In the process, industrial plants became part of the calculations that built the national security state in the early postwar period.

Metropolitan Geographies and Industrial Calculation

Metropolitan regions are centers of industrial calculation that work to bring "disparate production activities into advantageous relation with one another."[40] They provide industrialists with access to a large labor pool, a range of tradable intermediate goods, and technological spillovers. The agglomeration economies that underpin metropolitan economies allow firms to gain benefits from locating close to one another. Propinquity minimizes costs while maximizing access. Locational fixity offers a built environment consisting of assets, information, and resources. Industrial and social boundaries frame the possibilities of interaction by defining movement and social interaction. The benefits of the metropolitan concentration of economic activity for industrial producers are to reduce costs of transportation, communication, and labor, to facilitate the flow of information and capital, and to integrate activities within a broader industrial and political organizational form. The success of metropolitan complexes such as Chicago is predicated on a closed system that functions through place-based systems of vertical and horizontal integration.[41]

The capitalist metropolis is also created through calculations about industrial relationships that occur outside the industrial complex. Territories are relational in that they are constituted through active interaction within the complex and are articulated outside the complex. They are places in which industrial relations are "stretched out." These multiscalar, stretched-out relationships can be locationally close as in the relations of propinquity that facilitate access and pool resources in a metropolis. Scale is used to organize and, in the process, is deployed to control the world. In order to do this, leaders of the military-industrial complex have to create, shape, and implement knowledge, transportation, and production relationships stretching across regional, national, and international scales. In this way, metropolitan territories do not exist as finished, self-contained entities. Rather, they are, as Ray Hudson notes, "complex and unbounded lattices of articulations constructed through and around internal relations of power and inequality."[42] The industrial success of a metropolitan district such as Chicago is centered on the ability of producers to be linked to a world outside the metropolis.[43]

In all cases, manufacturing takes place at specific sites and with local inputs.

Production takes a material form. Accordingly, industrialists build place-based relationships around issues such as the installation of new public infrastructures, the building of local networks of financiers, industrialists, and state officials, or the creation of pools of labor. All of this requires ranking options about place-based investment strategies linked to decisions that are stretched out at multiple scales. In the case of industrial fixed-capital investment in metropolitan districts between 1940 and 1945, the options open to federal authorities to install an effective mobilization system were framed and limited by the war's socioeconomic and political conditions. As this book demonstrates, the militarization of American industrial relations was played out in material industrial sites. The ability of industrial and military officials to capture control of the levers of federally generated wartime mobilization ensured that America's metropolitan districts were shaped according to a militarized logic. Chicago became an important militarized metropolis as a result of its role in the country's factory construction and its place as a regional center of mobilization agencies.

One area of wartime calculation that occupied the attention of the leaders of the military-industrial complex was the scale and location of industrial sites.[44] The politics of fixed-capital investment was played out in the corporate boardrooms of a few cities, in the corridors and offices of Washington, and in the places where new industrial facilities were constructed. Capitalist social, political, and economic relations are grounded in the ways in which places are constructed, understood, and fought over. Moreover, once in place, the scale and lumpiness of fixed capital ensures that it cannot be easily moved or dismantled. It has a long life that provides places with economic relations that are hard to change in the short to medium run. In the process, fixed-capital investment restricts the choices that capitalists can make and ensures that the options available for change in any place are limited.[45] As such, an industrial locale, whether it is a large vacant property site, an industrial district within a region such as the Calumet district, or a sprawling metropolis such as Chicago, is a calculative issue.

Most studies of industrial mobilization, the militarized state, and the military-industrial complex have focused on questions at the national scale while neglecting how they were actualized at the metropolitan scale. Studies of wartime mobilization have explored shifts in federal policy, the conversion from peacetime to wartime production lines, population migration, and the growth of industries such as synthetic rubber. Research on the military-industrial complex has emphasized Washington's politics and how negotiations between the executive, legislature, and military contributed to the formation of corporate-state relations and the development of a new administrative regime. What is missing is an understanding of the way that the material practices of the relations between the military, industry, and civil government were played out and formed by the capitalist social relations of place. As a result, questions about the role of territorial complexes such as Chicago in the process remain unanswered. What this book shows is that calculations about industrial property and factories at the local scale were central to industrial mobilization.

While some writers have contributed to an understanding of wartime social and economic change, few have actually explored the history of wartime industrial sites.[46] There are some exceptions. Perry Duis and Scott La France have studied Chicago's changing industrial character and geography of war production.[47] Sarah Jo Peterson has explored how the relationship between the Ford Motor Company and the federal government created a large bomber plant and new residential area in Willow Run outside of Detroit.[48] Willow Run is an exemplary case of the interaction between the federal government and the corporation in the planning of new militarized spaces, the development of state-financed wartime mobilization, and the building of the military-industrial complex. Likewise, Gary Weir has looked at the interplay between local industrial practices and national policy in the building of American wartime submarine shipyards. As he notes, "The demands of war brought together the three vital components required to create a naval-industrial complex for submarines: naval commitment, a capable industrial base, and scientific support."[49] These processes were brought together in place. All of these studies demonstrate the political economy of wartime mobilization stretched across space, linking specific places into a larger network of economic and knowledge relations that were centered on industrial sites such as shipyards and bomber plants.

As these writers suggest, the national policies and institutional relations associated with state industrial investment are rooted in the multiscalar relations of place. As Lotchin notes, it is necessary to undertake studies "from the bottom up" if one wants to better understand the dynamics of wartime mobilization and the military-industrial complex.[50] This is true of the investment in and ownership of new industrial space beginning in 1940 and the disposal of these industrial assets to the private sector at the war's end. The calculations of the military-industrial leadership about where to locate state investment were embedded in the politics of place. The localization of federal construction and supply contracts was central to the growth of industrial capacity, increasing production output, the building of new industry-state relations, and greater corporate control over the industrial landscape. While federal policy and interagency hostilities in Washington shaped the character and scale of mobilization, the material effects of national policy occurred in place. Decisions made at the local level about production levels, resource allocation, financial arrangements, and subcontracting relationships determined the political economy of wartime industrial sites. These sites were rooted in a specific location and dependent on local political and economic pressures.

To calculate industrial property is to be place dependent in three ways. First, the circulation of capital through space has to be balanced by the fixing of capital in place.⁵¹ Investment in property is only possible if it is economically and geographically bounded; capital circulation has to be matched by institutional boundaries that make circulation possible and by spatial boundaries that facilitate investment. During World War II, federal agencies devised new financial instruments to facilitate the flow of investment into defense factories and supply contracts, implemented a range of labor supply and capital-labor relations to manage production, and allocated scarce resources from other projects to build wartime industrial sites in particular places. Manufacturers realized surplus value by selling output from these material sites to the military, or, if subcontracting to other defense firms, through a set of supply contracts made between the state, the military, and industry.

Second, places are lived-in spaces that are linked to other places. On the one hand, they have a name, boundaries, and distinctive identities. Chicago is not Houston, which is not Kansas City. They differ in all manners of ways. Places are heterogeneous entities comprising, among other things, different populations, labor pools, political institutions, and industries. Class, race, and gender politics differ from place to place and structure local labor markets. The different forms taken by growth alliances shape the way places develop. On the other hand, places are nonbounded entities linked to relations that stretch outside place. Decisions made in Washington by the mobilization agencies affect the scale of investment in factories in Omaha and Detroit. Calculations by large airplane corporations such as Douglas or Boeing about whether to close a factory or reduce employment are felt in districts outside of Los Angeles or Seattle. In this way, places are, as Ray Hudson notes, "open, discontinuous, relational and internally diverse."⁵² The simultaneously bounded and unbounded character of place shaped the ability of the state, military, and industry to put in place its massive war machine.

Finally, the relationship between place and industrial property is shaped by the character of local alliances or urban regimes. The ability of local coalitions to create niches of attraction within a locale such as cultural amenities or infrastructures and to channel external private capital and public funding to them is well known.⁵³ The same was true during the war. In this case, the ability of territorial growth machines to capture federal supply, engineering, and construction contracts strongly shaped the local wartime economy. A small and select group of powerful agents engaged in a set of ongoing calculations that sought to bring national resources to their locality and to turn those captured assets to their profit. The mobilization of old as well as new social networks was vital to their success. These networks allowed members to share political knowledge, to create new economic opportunities, and to fashion a standardized set of administrative technologies that facilitated external linkages. Local alliances promoted the investment and circulation of capital within specific places by establishing the boundaries of what was local and what was not, by defining who was in the network, and by capturing external assets and deploying internal assets, industrial and otherwise. They created fixed nodes of accumulation and administrative capacity that was linked to the national and international worlds.

Conclusion

Wartime mobilization revolved around militarized calculations forged in metropolitan and rural districts. Building on existing industrial practices and networks, the military and the federal government worked with industrialists and local leaders to refashion the social relations of industrial property and to assemble a collection of state-financed industrial sites in metropolitan areas such as Chicago. Private and public investment in new industrial spaces and equipment increased industrial capacity, initiated new state-private relations, and changed America's metropolitan areas. Existing industrial sites were enlarged; new ones were created. An integrated industrial complex of buildings, roads, railroad tracks, docks, and pipelines was built. Existing industrial sites were modernized and expanded, while new industrial spaces in greenfield sites were built. Industrial sites were formed out of the calculative relations of the wartime version of the military-industrial complex. These relations were actualized in place through the capitalist calculations of local alliances that captured capital investments and supply contracts for their own ends. A series of private and private-public calculations operating at different scales refashioned the territorial complex. The preexisting networks and practices of manufacturers in America's industrial districts were reframed in such as a way to deliver the necessary commodities to the military. Delivery could be realized only when prewar practices and networks were joined with the calculations involved in the making of a wartime economy and the investment by federal agencies of vast funds into industrial sites.

This book examines the impact of the calculative actions of the military, civil government, and industry on the industrial sites of one metropolitan landscape. Chicago's story, while distinctive, captures many of the elements common to place making in other wartime metropolitan areas. Between 1940 and 1945 the American government directly invested in manufacturing facilities on an unprecedented scale. Investing billions in entirely new factories and new factory additions had repercussions that not only changed the character of American society during the war but also lingered long after the war had ended. It made the federal government the country's largest owner of manufacturing plants. The resulting involvement in the funding, coordination, and operation of industrial sites forced the state to get involved in industrial matters in a way and on a scale that had never before been experienced. The political, economic, and social relationships of war refashioned and strengthened the relations that had existed between the government, the military, and corporate America before the war. The fate of many of the state's wartime defense factories was tied to the development of a national security state. Finally, places, from nonindustrial areas in the South to the country's largest industrial metropolises hugging the Great Lakes, were shaped by and in turn shaped the production of America's wartime industrial sites. The calculative decisions of federal officials, military officers, and industrialist executives relating to industrial property and industrial expansion were felt in most parts of the country. Perhaps no other place in the United States was a more important wartime industrial center than Chicago. The rest of the book explores the impact of the calculative decisions of the military-industrial complex on the Windy City's industrial property.

CHAPTER 2

Industrial Sites and Wartime Mobilization

According to a 1947 Civilian Production Administration (CPA) report, wartime industrial mobilization was "an achievement without precedent in magnitude, complexity, and duration." As the report's author notes, this achievement was built around three elements, the first of which was "unprecedented production." America's factories produced ships, planes, and ordnance materials on a scale never before realized. The second involved "sweeping transformations in the entire economic structure." New industrial sectors (synthetic rubber) were created; relatively new ones (aircraft and aluminum) were expanded; and a few older industries received a major boost (machine tools and iron and steel). The final element involved "fundamental changes in the Government itself."[1] Wartime mobilization required rebuilding the apparatus of the federal state, developing war-related agencies, and creating a different set of relationships between the civil government, the military, and industry. One key effect of the recasting of industry-state networks during World War II was to bring the industrial site directly into the purview of the federal government and the military.

Writers have shown how the calculative actions of government, military, and economic institutions realigned the relationship between a militarized state and industrial space.[2] Framed as public-private partnerships, industrial sites became objects of intense concern for a variety of business, political, and military interests. Seeking to profit from the opportunities afforded by the wartime emergency, business leaders looked to create new productive space and equipment, convert production lines from peacetime to wartime use, establish new supply chains, material sources, and labor markets, and work with new institutional forms. Government officials, on the other hand, scrambled to put into place a new set of policies that would effectively frame wartime mobilization and a new set of agencies that would assemble the necessary expertise and information and build the administrative machinery to administer the allocation of raw materials and channel federal investment into industrial buildings, machinery, and equipment. Looking to take advantage of the unprecedented funds available for military goods, personnel, and facilities, military leaders sought to control the allocation of these federal funds and forge strong relations with industry leaders. In doing so, they furthered their position as key players in the institutional framework of the American state. The result was that the federal government became the major investor in wartime factories and as such reworked the legal, ideological, and material elements of the industrial site, both during and in the immediate aftermath of the war. In the process, wartime mobilization agencies, industrial corporations, and the military reassembled industrial networks and reshaped the industrial geographies of the war.[3]

Building on this work, this chapter argues that the achievements of America's wartime mobilization were made possible by the successful framing of the industrial site as a calculative object by the agents of the military-industrial complex. This calculative relationship formed around the creation of an organizational apparatus, legal mechanisms, and monetary allocative systems by the government, industry, and military geared to the building of government-financed factory space. The agents of the military-industrial complex framed the social and economic boundaries of the industrial site. The scale and character of the government and the military's involvement in the financing, locating, and operation of the industrial site were unprecedented. The industrial site became an entity subject to the machinations of coalitions of social, political, and business actors who looked to create new boundaries around the industrial world. The single most important element of these new industrial relations was the questioning of the prerogative of the capitalist to unilaterally determine the production world. Calculating that full-scale mobilization under emergency conditions required intensive involvement in the working of the production system, military and civil leaders rationalized their attempts to direct the mobilization of America's industrial base and to have control over factory sites. The chapter starts with an outline of the making of the American industrial war machine. This is followed by a discussion of the rationale of the new industrial order, the framing of military-industry-state networks, and the assembling of knowledge about metropolitan industrial sites.

America's War Machine

Wartime mobilization was made possible by redefining the social relations of industrial property and the federal role in industrial space. For the first time in American history, the government significantly intervened in the ownership and construction of industrial sites. In some cases, ownership consisted of financing, designing, and building new production plants; in others, it involved building additions to thousands of existing privately owned factories and converting production lines of many more. The state also intervened by providing indirect support through accelerated depreciation rates and production controls. In all cases, the industrial production site—industrial land, buildings, and machinery—was understood in a new way. In order to meet their mobilization needs, the federal government and the military framed industrial property as an object of direct interest. The defense factory was placed within a new organizational structure, operated under new legal strictures, and received unprecedented state investment. No longer was industrial space the sole prerogative of private capital.

State intervention in the expansion of the country's productive capacity cannot be taken for granted. In May 1940 when Roosevelt called for industrial expansion, the United States was ill prepared for industrial mobilization. This was not helped by the reluctance of private capital to invest in new productive capacity. Many Americans, both inside and outside of government, wanted a slow defense buildup. For some businesspeople, the conditions of 1940 did not warrant extensive mobilization of productive capacity and the changes this would have for the everyday running of their businesses. Others continued to believe that the state had no role in industrial matters, which should be left to private interests. Infighting among federal-military factions and the inability to create effective mobilization agencies did not help matters. Administratively, the development of effective machinery was hampered by the failure to build the appropriate agencies to oversee mobilization, while the development of cumbersome procurement regulations hindered the state's mobilization plans. Framing the industrial site as an object to be worked on by government was not straightforward. It was only with the attack on Pearl Harbor that full-scale industrial mobilization was successfully undertaken.[4]

The federal government, however, had framed the necessity of intervening in the provision of new factory space even before Pearl Harbor. Roosevelt's call for full-scale expansion of government-financed plants in 1940 was the first significant statement about the industrial site as a federal object. Over the next year, the government became fully committed to investing in industrial property. The state's investment in industrial sites was huge. Between June 1940 and June 1945, $23.1 billion of federal and private capital was invested in thousands of factories. Of this, almost three-quarters ($17.2 billion) was authorized by the government. The private sector's contribution to the building of new industrial space, which only totaled $5.9 billion, was overshadowed by that of the state, with the result that a substantial share of the nation's manufacturing assets became the property of the federal government. In one estimate, federal industrial expenditure accounted for more than half of the value of all the industrial facilities that existed in 1939. In another, the figure was much lower. Regardless, for the first time in its history, the U.S. government had become heavily involved in building and financing manufacturing plants. By the end of the war, it controlled a substantial share of the country's industrial facilities.[5] As Dwight

TABLE 2.1 State and private expenditures on defense factories, 1940–1945

Industrial sectors	Cost ($millions)	State funded ($ millions)	State funded (%)	Structures ($ millions)	Structures (%)
Aircraft	3,894	3,474	89.2	1,556	40.0
Chemicals	3,525	1,973	56.0	1,014	28.8
Explosives	2,857	2,831	99.1	2,002	70.1
Guns	2,747	2,399	87.3	912	33.2
Ships	2,605	2,381	91.4	1,552	59.6
Iron and steel	2,265	1,303	57.5	715	31.7
Nonferrous metals	1,531	1,160	75.8	658	43.0
Machinery	1,032	482	46.7	101	9.8
TOTAL	23,066	17,166	74.4	9,444	40.9

SOURCE: Civilian Production Administration, War-Time Manufacturing Plant Expansion Privately Financed, 1940–1945 (Washington, D.C.: CPA, 1946), p. 5.

Green, the governor of Illinois, noted, "Government has become the country's biggest business."[6]

Public and private investment in industrial property took three forms and occurred in a small number of industries. New factories, most of them authorized by the military and heavily financed by federal agencies, accounted for a significant share of wartime fixed-capital investment. More than two-thirds of the investment ($15.8 billion) went to new plants—entirely new facilities separate from existing factories. The remainder was accounted for by "expansions" to existing manufacturing sites ($4.8 billion) and "conversions" of existing facilities to a new function ($2.5 billion).[7] Five industrial groups accounted for three quarters of "new" facilities (Table 2.1). Accounting for $14.4 billion of the total, the leading groups by value were aircraft, explosives, and guns. The 3,827 federally financed projects were ten times larger on average ($4.1 million against $400,000) than the 14,746 ones financed by the private sector. Of the total wartime investment, $9.5 billion went to structures and land, and $13.6 billion was spent on equipment. Federal investment had a powerful effect on the scale and character of industrial capital formation. During the war years it amounted to approximately $2.4 billion a year on average. This stands in sharp contrast to prewar figures: in the 1920s capital formation averaged about $600 million a year, and in the 1930s it averaged $300 million a year. In sum, the massive government investment in new industrial facilities created "the greatest increment to manufacturing capital recorded in modern industrial history."[8]

Federal investment in defense factories pushed manufacturing employment to new heights. In 1939 there were 10.9 million industrial workers in the United States. In November 1943, 17.7 million workers were employed in America's factories. The CPA estimated that three sources were responsible for the 6.8 million new manufacturing jobs: 2.1 million resulted from increased production in prewar factories and private expansion not directly related to war production; another 1.0 million came from employment in war-created privately financed plants; and 3.7 million workers found work in war-created federally financed plants. In other words, state-owned factories were the largest contributor to wartime employment growth. This expansion of state-based employment was accompanied by equally dramatic changes to the workplace.[9] Many new workers had little experience in manufacturing, while those that did tended to be categorized as low skilled. One result of the disjuncture between the absence of a skilled labor force and the demand of rapid mobilization was the reorganization of the workplace. As Marilynn Johnson shows in her study of wartime Oakland, California, local shipyard managers "reorganized work itself, breaking down traditional craft divisions and diluting skills accordingly." This was the case throughout the country.[10]

Industrial mobilization relied on effective supply chains, procurement practices, and effective subcontracting systems. As a poster put out by the Public Information Program of the National Association of Manufacturers in 1942 noted, subcontracting was critical to defense production (Figure 2.1). As the caption reads, hundreds of firms across the country were tied into an extensive subcontracting system that contributed to the ability of a small number of corporations to build tanks. In order to produce tanks, aircraft, ships, and other defense products, the federal government authorized $196 billion in supply contracts during the war. In 1941 in response to the demands of wartime production, a new procurement program replaced the prewar system of competitive bidding with negotiated contracts, allowing for stable profit rates for defense contractors, more easily navigated negotiations between the procurement agencies and industrial firms, and faster production turnover times.[11] The new production relationship was voiced in 1945 by Robert A. Lovett, the assistant secretary of war for air, when he told the Senate hearings on the disposal of aircraft war plants that the aircraft industry is "one link in a chain." In the view of government officials such as Lovett, government's financing and ownership of industrial sites was "a matter of national security" and was essential to the ability to maintain supply chains.[12]

If anyone understood the importance of the industrial site for the mobilization of the industrial economy it was Lovett. Working under Henry Stimson, the secretary of war, Lovett oversaw the expansion of America's aircraft fleet, the reorganization of the workplace, the creation of new supply chains, and the development of vast aircraft factories. He did this by working hand-in-hand with the military and private firms to create new organizational apparatus, channel federal funds to defense factories and supply contracts, and translate federal legislation into workable practices. But Lovett was more than a successful state technocrat who helped shift aircraft production into the broader framing of

FIGURE 2.1. How subcontracting accelerates defense production, 1942. The federal government poured billions of dollars into supply contracts during the war.
Source: Public Information Program, National Association of Manufacturers.

wartime mobilization. Both before the war and after his stints in government, he was a partner in one of the most prominent New York private banks, Brown Brothers Harriman and Company. From his rarified position in America's leading financial circles he had the inside scoop on the dynamics of the nation's business worlds. He was a man who knew his way around the corridors of power and used his knowledge and contacts to shape the intertwined histories of the militarized state and business. Deploying these attributes, he became a builder of the wartime industrial order.[13]

Large-scale federal funding of industrial manufacturing sites and the development of a procurement system by Lovett and others reinforced the economic power wielded by corporate America. On the eve of the war a few large corporations controlled an overwhelming share of the economy. In 1940 just 5 percent of firms employed 70 percent of the country's workers. Concerted action, uniform policy, and collusive cooperation created economic concentration and powerful political alliances in sectors such as steel and petroleum. Eight financial groups, including those of the Morgan, Mellon, and Rockefeller families, controlled 29 percent of the total nonfinancial and banking assets of the 250 largest corporations. The eight groups had close ties with each other and with the nation's most powerful trade associations, the United States Chamber of Commerce and the National Association of Manufacturers. The country's main financial powers also had access to the boardrooms of political power in Washington and elsewhere through their links to businesspeople turned politicians such as Lovett and the hundreds of executives who came to run the mobilization agencies for a nominal annual income (dollar-a-year men).[14]

The war increased the control of big business over the economy. The share of employment in industries most heavily involved in defense, such as electrical machinery, transport equipment, and petroleum, grew in firms with more than 500 employees from 48 percent in 1939 to 62 percent in 1944. As a 1946 Smaller War Plants Corporation (SWPC) report noted, "It is quite clear that it was the industrial giants, the biggest of the big firms, which made the greatest gains during the war."[15] Full-scale industrial mobilization changed the political climate around the place of the corporation in American economic life. Industrial expansion after 1939 quickly soaked up the unemployed and stimulated economic growth across all sectors. The antitrust movement, which had occupied a central place in the politics of the 1930s, was undercut by the political cadre's growing acceptance of the centrality of the large corporation to the mobilization of the American economy. The government's concern about the ill effects of corporate power on the national economy was increasingly replaced by the concern to have corporations gear up for war.[16]

The growing acceptance of the codependence of corporations and the military ensured that most of the nation's industrial investment flowed to large firms. Even though support for small business could be found in Roosevelt's administration and Congress, the military and big business were able to argue that only large vertically and horizontally integrated corporations could successively oversee the massive and complex industrial expansion needed to win the war. From their viewpoint, significant and rapid mobilization could only be achieved by corporations with the appropriate organizational and productive resources. Accordingly, there was no clear plan to convert small business to military production. The federal response to the pressure applied by the SWPC tended to be ad hoc at best. As a result, "the giants expanded greatly, while all other firms, especially small business, suffered a substantial decline."[17]

A handful of large corporations dominated government construction awards and supply contracts. As Table 2.2 shows, other than Curtiss-Wright Aircraft, the ten firms with the largest construction awards were prewar American corporate giants. The same is true for defense contracts. Between June 1940 and September 1944, supply contracts valued at $175 billion were awarded to 18,539 corporations. Of this, two-thirds of the value of the prime contracts ($117 billion) went to the top 100 corporations; 55 percent to the largest 33 corporations; and 30 percent to the largest 10 corporations. Contracting policies favored large corporations with factories in the country's metropolitan areas. As Gregory Hooks makes clear, the rationale of industrial and military leaders for state

TABLE 2.2 Corporate concentration of construction and supply awards, 1940–1945 (thousands of dollars)

Operator	Construction awards	Operator	Supply awards
Du Pont	1,148,773	General Motors	13,260,961
General Motors	1,030,722	Curtiss-Wright Aircraft	6,447,833
U.S. Steel	888,694	Ford Motor	4,820,403
Alcoa	796,760	Bethlehem Steel	3,750,515
Hercules Powder	521,221	Douglas Aircraft	3,703,266
Curtiss-Wright Aircraft	489,249	United Aircraft	3,650,253
Bethlehem Steel	449,914	General Electric	3,361,751
Ford Motor	415,853	Consolidated Vultee Aircraft	3,284,057
Chrysler	371,545	Western Electric	2,920,954
General Electric	353,344	Lockheed	2,610,572

SOURCE: Compiled from Civilian Production Administration, War Industrial Facilities Authorized, July 1940–August 1945 (Washington, D.C.: CPA, 1946); Civilian Production Administration, Alphabetical Listing of Major War Supply Contracts: Cumulative June 1940 through September 1945 (Washington, D.C.: CPA, 1946).

support of industrial concentration was that "large firms offered the greatest reliability." In other words, as the SWPC noted, the "Enormous centralization of prime contracts in corporations engaged in such a variety of industries clearly meant an increase in the concentration of the American economy."[18] Wartime mobilization reinforced big business control over industrial production.

The industrial site became framed as a calculated object and part of a broader struggle over who controlled industrial production during the war. The demarcating of the war factory as the responsibility of the federal government, with the support of the military and industry, set into motion a set of decisions that changed who owned and controlled industrial property and how the state intervened in the production process. Working with industrial and military officials, government bureaucrats calculated the scale, character, and location of new industrial plants using forms of measurement, administration, and interest that were dedicated to the task. The resulting new administrative and manufacturing boundaries reformulated relationships within the military-industrial complex. In order to create and maintain thousands of industrial sites and hundreds of thousands of contracts, federal and military officials had to work with big corporations. This was clear to Jesse Jones, the secretary of commerce, when he noted that "the vast capabilities of our largest industrial corporations were necessary to win the recent war and will be necessary to win the next one."[19] While Jones assumed the importance of the government's need to work with corporations, the implementation of its new interest in industrial sites was not straightforward. A campaign to convince skeptics was necessary.

Rationalizing a New Industrial Order

Neither industrial mobilization nor the building of state-owned industrial sites was uncontested. Corporate leaders were hostile to federal intervention in their affairs, and many in Roosevelt's administration were reluctant to invest billions of federal dollars into industrial property. In 1940, most federal officials with any degree of executive power supported private enterprise, although to varying degrees. Outside of regulating workplace conditions, wages, and the right to unionize, few supported the state actively entering the industrial realm.[20] In the minds of those state officials, at least in principle, there was a clear boundary between industry's role as producer and the state's as regulator. Principle, however, was reduced to pragmatic calculation by the exigencies of crisis in general and the demands of war more specifically. By the late 1930s, Americans, exhausted by years of depression, looked to a government willing to introduce pragmatic solutions to problems rather than those guided by reform principles.[21]

One element of this pragmatic shift from the late 1930s involved greater federal intervention in industrial matters and the framing of industrial sites as state property. In order to orchestrate the massive expansion of industrial facilities, the state had to take on responsibility as the primary coordinator of industrial mobilization and to become the major financial investor in industrial facilities. It was clear, however, that this would not be possible without the active collaboration of the military and industry. This could not be taken for granted. The successful creation of industrial sites as the joint responsibility of the federal government, the military, and industry depended on bringing all of the key players into the frame. This required appealing to the interests of the participants who would be responsible for building new factory space.

The rationale for government intervention in the industrial realm was explained in a paper given at the annual meeting of the American Economic Association in 1942. In his presentation, Hans Klagsbrunn set out the ways in which the government had framed the peacetime factory as a defense plant. A government lawyer and an architect of the federal financing of wartime industrial plants, he told his audience that a good deal of thought had been given in government and military boardrooms "to the ways and means of making this country what has since often been called 'the arsenal of democracy.' A workable solution had to be found for the many difficult technical, military, financial, managerial, and manpower problems."[22] It turned out that the solution depended on building state-financed manufacturing sites. Klagsbrunn told the American economists at the conference that the government was compelled to get involved in the mobilization of industrial space because it had to reduce present-day economic dislocation, to ensure rapid construction of the appropriate industrial sites, and to secure postwar stability. The government would plan, coordinate, and fund the construction of necessary industrial facilities.

Klagsbrunn's speech laid out the agents (government, industry, and military) who would determine what the solution was (the defense site) and the elements (factories and machinery) that comprised the solution. Behind the state's decision to play a key role in the creation of new industrial space was the unwillingness of private industry to immediately convert to making war products. According to Klagsbrunn, corporate reluctance to invest in new industrial plants jeopardized mobilization. Many companies were unenthusiastic about constructing new manufacturing facilities because financing was expensive and difficult to obtain. For many, federal tax laws and industrial regulations were a burden. Even if they were willing to work within the constraints imposed by government regulation, industrialists feared that their firm would become overcapitalized and indebted. Many remembered the difficulties encountered at the end of World War I as well as the problems of overcapacity and low demand in the 1930s. There was no desire to repeat the mistakes of the past.[23]

Klagsbrunn drew on his experience working with New Deal agencies to create a modern, effective mobilization plan. His academic and government background provided him with the connections and tools to undertake changes to the relationship between the state, the military, and industry. A lawyer who attended Yale, Harvard, and the University of Chicago, he joined the Reconstruction Finance Corporation (RFC) in 1933, where he worked on issues that would later shape the organizational structure of state-owned industrial plants. Established by President Herbert Hoover in January 1932 with a mandate to stimulate the economy, the RFC was one of the chief funding agencies for wartime industrial facilities. Seven years later in the fall of 1940, Klagsbrunn was one of the architects of the Defense Plant Corporation (DPC). The DPC, a subsidiary of the RFC and the single most important investor in wartime industrial plants, provided loans of $7 billion to build or make additions to more than 2,300 defense production facilities during the war.[24]

As Klagsbrunn's role illustrates, the social and administrative capacities created by New Deal policies and programs underpinned mobilization and the building of industrial facilities. The institutional and ideological framework embodied in the New Deal shaped federal intervention in industrial matters during the 1930s in several ways. The federal government's right to intervene in a range of social and economic matters and its budding partnership with industry was legitimized. It became widely recognized that the state would act as mediator between competing interests and that it was the only institution able to bring stability and order to the industrial economy. Building on the social reform movement before the Great Depression, New Deal policy makers made it clear that many of the issues plaguing the United States were structural and not individual, and that government intervention was necessary if order was to be maintained.[25] The ideas, programs, and state capacity created during the 1930s were refashioned and incorporated into the industrial mobilization program.

The institutional and ideological continuities between the policies of the New Deal and wartime America, however, were not seamless. The building of the country's defense plants was not the result of a simple transfer of New Deal ideas into a wartime context. The working of the wartime state differed in some important ways from the earlier period, despite the continuities. By the late 1930s, government leaders were much more willing to work with rather than to challenge corporate capitalism. As a result, industrial mobilization was heavily influenced by those willing to work with private industry. By 1940, Roosevelt had sided with and brought into the upper echelons of the mobilization program men such as the head of the Tennessee Valley Authority, David Lilienthal, and the progressive senator from Nebraska, George Norris. The old-styled liberals left in place had a difficult time finding leadership roles in the administration. The changing position of liberals was paralleled by the ascendancy of Republicans in Congress, the linking of liberalism with communism, and the increasing importance of national security issues for many in and outside the Roosevelt administration. All of these issues posed problems for the transfer of New Deal ideas to a wartime setting.[26]

Nevertheless, the Roosevelt administration's decision to invest political and economic capital in full-scale mobilization was grounded in the experience it gained promoting social and economic programs during the 1930s. Indeed, in the face of reluctant private interests, federal policy makers believed they had little choice but to invest in manufacturing facilities in order to ensure an adequate supply of war materials. Roosevelt made this clear in his 1940 talks. In mid-May he told Congress that his government's "immediate problem" was to provide "a greatly increased additional production capacity" to build planes. Among other things, this required appropriations from Congress totaling almost $1.1 billion "to increase production facilities for everything needed for the Army and Navy for national defense." This, he argued, could not wait, as "we require the ability to turn out quickly infinitely greater supplies."[27] In his opinion, immediate state-directed industrial mobilization was necessary if this was to be successful.

Ten days later, he told his listeners that the government had to proceed with industrial investment though "there are many among us who closed their eyes" to the war in Europe. Roosevelt knew that he had to gain the support of corporate leaders if the plan was to succeed. Accordingly, he started by throwing a sop to executives: "I know that private business cannot be expected to make all of the capital investment required for expansions of plants and factories and personnel which this program calls for at once. It would be unfair to expect industrial corporations or their investors to do this."[28] Nevertheless, he knew that it was necessary to increase the number of facilities that could be used to manufacture war materials. Turning his attention to how this could be achieved,

Roosevelt opined that the state had to invest in the expansion of existing manufacturing facilities and the construction of new plants. In order to win the war, according to the Roosevelt administration's calculus, the federal government had to become an owner of industrial property.

This rationale for state intervention in industry and the financing of defense plants did not go uncontested. Opposition from business interests ensured that the implementation of a defense plan in 1940 was a rocky affair. Until the bombing of Pearl Harbor, there was widespread support for isolationists who voiced their dislike of America's foreign entanglements. Similarly, dragging up arguments used against the New Deal regulation of the economy, many businesspeople argued that the state had no right to finance or own industrial facilities. For many, it was incumbent on the state to ensure that public funding did not turn into "state socialism" and for business leaders to maintain control over the use of public funds. The Roosevelt administration's foray into state intervention in business affairs through legislation such as the 1933 National Industrial Recovery Act terrified many on the right as it signaled an unacceptable crossing of the private-public boundary. Similarly, some New Deal liberals were opposed to the opportunities for profiteering and the use of government funds to pay for privately operated industrial plants and equipment. New Dealers feared that giving too much control to private interests within the state apparatus would undermine the social and economic reforms of the 1930s.[29]

By late 1941, however, the voices of dissent were becoming overwhelmed by the voices of internationalism and patriotism. Despite fierce opposition from some business quarters, the arguments for state investment in industrial plants became increasingly louder. The conflicting forces operating within the state, corporate, and military boardrooms came to a consensus. Among other things, this involved framing industrial property as an object to be underwritten by federal funds and fashioned by members of the military-industrial complex. This was made possible by reworking existing state capacity, shifting from the old framework of "direct managed adjustment" to one centered on the use of budgetary tools in order to thwart industrial and social dislocation, to induce prosperity, and to build up the economy.[30]

In many cases, state capacity embedded in older New Deal agencies was passed directly onto wartime agencies. One important case of this was the merging of the Work Projects Administration and Public Works Administration into the Federal Works Agency (FWA). The FWA was instrumental in building bases, airports, bridges, and roads used by the military during the war years. In terms of defense factories, the most notable example of the shift of state capacity to mobilization was the DPC, which was created in August 1940 to purchase and lease land, structures, and equipment for the manufacture of war goods by private firms. In all cases, the administrative and policy-making apparatus of the state was retooled for war as liberals with their long experience working with New Deal programs "seized World War II as an opportunity to promote government-funded construction for preparedness efforts."[31]

In building an industrial mobilization program, the wartime coalition adopted many of the tenets and practices built up during the New Deal. These were used to frame the calculative actions that underpinned federal intervention in industrial production and the construction of industrial sites. This reworking did not fundamentally alter a political economy centered on state-assisted free enterprise or the prerogative of corporate control over production. But, by building on the precedent of New Deal programs, the Roosevelt administration created the capacity that enabled the military-industrial complex to coordinate the industrial economy in a manner and on a scale that it had never done before. It allowed key calculative actors to directly intervene in the making of productive facilities and the production of goods for the emergency period. It also allowed the military to become actively engaged in promoting factory building and to become the dominant player in the state's investment process.[32] The building of state-funded industrial sites reflected the emergence of an industrial order centered on a new set of government, industry, and military calculative relationships.

Building Defense Factories

At the time of the German invasion of Poland in September 1939 the United States did not have the apparatus in place to build defense plants and implement industrial mobilization. The best that could be said about the military's interwar preparedness program was that it was ineffective. As two historians note, "Although the Army's industrial mobilization plan was never put into effect, it does not follow that the years of planning were entirely fruitless."[33] Nevertheless, the program's outdated procurement policies, confusion about where to locate defense factories, and ineffectual administrative structures presented serious problems for rapid and successful industrial mobilization. Undertaking an effective mobilization program, however, was necessary if the United States was to wage war in Europe and the Pacific. The corollary to this political calculation was the need to construct an operational set of practices that both mobilized industry and allowed the state to invest in a battery of plants geared to war production.

To this end, the building of government-financed factories was a central element of the Roosevelt administration's industrial mobilization plan. By early 1941 the government had created the basic form and mechanisms that would shape mobilization. As we have seen, this was due in large part to the incorporation of state capacity created during the 1930s into wartime agencies. Along with the practices and procedures acquired from New Deal agencies, the activities of the 1930s "strengthened the federal bureaucracy, allowed the federal government to gain unprecedented influence in capital markets, and helped introduce a new era in labor relations."[34] It was also due to the ability of the three agents of the military-industrial complex to cobble together a set of institutions to build defense plants. Working together, but often at loggerheads, the War and Navy Departments and four civil agencies—the War Resources Board (August–November 1939), the National Defense Advisory Commission (NDAC) (May 1940 to January 1941), the Office of Production Management (OPM) (January 1941 to January 1942), and the War Production Board (WPB) (January 1942 to October 1945)—directed wartime industrial preparations, private investment, and state investment.[35] Although mobilization practices were constantly changing, the structure that framed how the state would invest in wartime industrial sites had been created by NDAC by January 1941.

The framework put in place to build state-owned industrial sites consisted of two main elements. The first was the development of policies, procedures, and strategies that established state-directed mobilization. Policies related to, among other things, factory location, production controls, and labor management, were implemented in conjunction with military and industrial officials. A large civil and military bureaucracy was established to devise and implement the rules, procedures, and practices required for the building of industrial sites. The second element was the passing of control over the building of industrial sites to business and military leaders. The administrative capacity put into place after August 1939 allowed military and industrial leaders to become the ultimate arbiters of wartime industrial space. Together, these elements framed state-finance industrial sites as key elements of wartime mobilization.

The NDAC created the basic structure of the federal apparatus to build and operate defense factories. This consisted of establishing offices to assess and monitor mobilization (the Bureau of Research and Statistics), labor supply and relations (Labor Division), and production output and expenditures (Industrial Production, Industrial Management, and Industrial Materials). The OPM and WPB built on the NDAC's early attempt to create a viable structure and created more effective methods of operation and mobilization.[36] All of the mobilization agencies included a powerful corporate presence. Industrial executives gained direct access to policy making in their role as dollar-a-year men and as members of wartime planning agencies. As such, "economic elites were well-placed to bring their opinions to bear in important World War II policies" and to influence the character and direction of the mobilization agencies.[37]

The industrial and financial executives who dominated these agencies "used their authority to protect prewar competitive patterns and to support wartime military demands."[38] The position of industrial executives in the mobilization agencies allowed them to tap into the vast flow of federal resources and to increase their firms' employment, revenues, and profits. More important than the profit margins of individual firms, perhaps, the combined forces of big business and centralized government authority worked to intervene in several areas. Building on lessons taken from the New Deal, the government introduced national and sectoral industrial planning into its sphere of activity, established wide-reaching and long-lasting networks to facilitate corporate control over resource allocation, and helped form industrial cartels that shaped economic policy both during and after the war.

The military was also a considerable force in industrial planning and the building of wartime industrial plants. One area in which the military exercised significant authority was the provision of ordnance. The scale and character of the military's wartime procurement program heavily determined the scale and character of defense factory construction. When the United States entered the war in December 1941, already in place was an elaborate legal and administrative mechanism for procuring munitions that was controlled by big business leaders who used their entrenched positions to defend their firms' interests. A powerful coalition formed that consisted of these executives and their allies who occupied strategic positions in the procurement departments of the military and federal mobilization agencies. As a result, the procurement system established by the end of 1941 became the basis for the rest of the war and for the Cold War as well.[39]

Military leaders controlled defense factory building. The army and navy's mobilization agencies invested heavily into the country's new defense factories. The armed services invested $8.7 billion in manufacturing facilities across the country. Military procurement bureaus received money from Congress, which allowed them free rein over how this was spent. An important element of this expenditure was the authority to organize the construction of industrial plants built and operated by private-sector wartime contractors. From 1940 the military established extensive construction and industrial networks with large industrial corporations such as DuPont and Hercules and industrial engineering firms such as Sanderson and Porter, and Day and Zimmerman. Together, this military-private partnership built and operated the military's wartime industrial facilities. Furthermore, military managers had key decision-making positions inside the civil mobilization agencies. The fact that the military was a relatively autonomous unit ensured that many of its calculations about industrial mobilization and the building of new factory space were effectively insulated from permanent federal agencies and the emergency wartime agencies.[40]

The financing of new industrial sites was central to wartime mobilization. In the beginning, the NDAC committee on plant financing hoped to channel private investments into commercial-type defense facilities operated by private corporations. However, it quickly became apparent that neither the private sector nor Congress was willing to generate the conditions to supply sufficient funding to meet the demand for wartime goods. This left the NDAC mobilization officers in a difficult position. On the one hand, it was necessary for the government to ensure rapid construction of defense plants while maintaining economic stability and protecting private enterprise. On the other hand, private funding was not forthcoming. Even the industrialists who were willing to invest in new capacity found it difficult to obtain financing from private financial sources.[41]

More successful than the earlier attempts at underwriting defense factory construction was the five-year amortization program. First enacted into law in October 1940, it allowed wartime contractors to write off the capital costs of facilities created or acquired for national defense at 20 percent annually for five years. The NDAC saw tax amortization as a means to induce private investment. As the historian of the army's mobilization program explains: "It is clear that the amortization law for World War II was abundantly successful in providing badly needed capacity for war production. It succeeded not only because it offered protection against losses but because it also made a frank appeal to the profit motive."[42] Accelerated depreciation required a certificate of necessity signed by an authorized mobilization agency, such as the military's Army and Navy Munition Board. Certificates were granted only if new construction was deemed essential to the production of more defense goods. Tax amortization was used to cover nearly $6.5 billion in new plants and equipment, which accounted for more than a third of wartime industrial investment.[43]

Even though amortization was successful, it was inadequate to the scale and nature of the problem. Another way of financing the construction of wartime factories was needed, one that gave the government greater control over the character, scale, and location of production facilities. The solution was the government-owned, privately operated factory. It had several advantages over the certificate of necessity. First, the government's acceptance of the entire risk of financing factory construction reduced the levels of negotiation that were part of the depreciation model and ensured that building could be completed quickly. Second, government control of financial policy ensured that government-owned plants could be located in strategic rather than economic locations. It was less beholden to private decisions about where war factories should be constructed. Third, the new model gave Roosevelt's administration greater oversight of what sort of industrial facilities were to be constructed. Finally, it was possible to directly allocate state-funded funds to firms that had received war orders but did not have the necessary production facilities.[44] Because of these advantages, the government-owned, privately operated model became the most important method used to build wartime factories.

The DPC was the main agency to finance state-owned industrial property. Although there was talk of such an agency in the winter of 1939/1940, it was not until the summer and fall of 1940 that it was created. The White House approved the program for financing expanded war production, and the rationale was laid out in Roosevelt's address of May 26. This in turn led the RFC to ask Congress for powers to give defense loans for factory construction. Less than a month later, on June 25, 1940, legislation was passed that gave the New Deal agency extensive mobilization powers. The government-financed defense plants had been successfully framed and were made manifest in the legislation. The act consisted of three parts: the government was to provide the bulk of money for industrial plant facilities; the government should own the plants; and the plants should be operated by private industry. Out of this measure, in August 1940 the RFC created four major defense subsidiaries, one of which was the DPC. Construction of DPC-financed war factories began in September 1940. By April 1941 the DPC had authorized $4 billion of defense expenditures. By the end of the war it had authorized 2,300 investments in manufacturing plants and equipment valued at almost $7 billion. Most of its investments were in steel, aviation, synthetic rubber, chemicals, ordnance, shipbuilding, and machine tools facilities.[45]

The framing of the wartime industrial facility as a government-financed object to be run by private corporations allowed the DPC and the other government and military agencies to pour an unprecedented amount of capital into industrial property. By the end of 1940, despite resistance to state intervention in industrial affairs, industrial property had been framed as central to mobilization. The framing allowed the government and its military and industry partners to create the apparatus and mechanisms of a war economy, which included creating the means to establish new manufacturing facilities. Legislation was put into place that mobilized calculations about industrial space. The state channeled funds through major agencies, most notably the civil mobilization agencies, the Treasury, the DPC, and the War and Navy Departments. Private firms designed, built, and operated the facilities, while firm profits came from supply contracts that were filled through factory operation.[46] The result was a government- and military-financed and directed war economy carried out by big business.

Calculative Spaces: Assembling Knowledge

The ability of military-industrial complex officials to build wartime industrial plants relied on the creation of information about factories that could be used to calculate wartime needs. Knowledge had to be produced and assembled by government, military, and industrial officials on a large number of issues, such as the location and cost of land, the amount of available materials, and the scale, character, and location of the labor force. Creating knowledge about industry was not new in 1940. Both business and the state had collected numeric and qualitative information about production sites for a hundred years or more. There were listings of industrial firms that went back to the nineteenth century.

Manufacturing details had been systematically collected by the Census Bureau since 1810. By 1940, a great deal of information on capital, labor, and many other variables by region, state, and municipality was available in the manufacturing census. The Sanborn insurance liability maps provided detailed information at the site level from the 1860s.[47] Some private organizations had compiled listings of firms' capital, employment, products, and addresses for a hundred years. Inventories set out in the Thomas Register of American Manufacturers, for example, provided a national listing of firms and their subsidiaries. Perhaps most importantly of all, credit-rating firms such as Dun and Bradstreet and its predecessors furnished information about individual companies.[48] In other words, calculative knowledge about investment, product lines, and factory location was circulating through industrial, financial, and government channels as early as the nineteenth century.

The demands of building industrial sites for wartime mobilization, however, necessitated a more elaborate and extensive regime of calculative knowledge. The need to obtain more information about the country's factories combined with federal investment in defense plants forced the state to become more interested in the factory. The government's prewar inventory of firm-level details gathered by the census office and the military was replaced by a search for more detailed knowledge of industrial sites. Federal agencies and the armed forces assembled information in order to calculate the ways in which industrial sites could be used and to make a systematic analysis of the facilities needed to ensure the production of adequate levels of military materials. The need for more detailed knowledge of firms' internal workings became an imperative once the state moved from the prewar regulation of firms' revenues and behavior through such devices as tax and antimonopoly legislation to wartime financing and owning industrial facilities. While the federal government's interest in industrial matters was not entirely new, there was little precedent for the way it would develop after 1940.

One precedent for government intervention in industrial matters was during World War I. In this case, however, mobilization and knowledge creation "was largely a story of hasty improvisation to meet unforeseen crises and to fill the void left by inadequate planning and preparation."[49] Unprepared, the federal government used the General Munitions Board and the War Industries Board to create mobilization policies, to acquire basic industrial information, and to establish the procedures necessary to facilitate wartime production. The little planning that did occur was geared to mobilizing private industrial interests. The War Industries Board was "no more than an extension and elaboration of the regulatory mechanism the state had built up to monitor the large corporations since the late nineteenth century." Little systematic knowledge was created. While partially successful, the state was loath to intervene in the private realm. Accordingly, by the end of the war, the federal government had little knowledge of the nation's industrial capacity beyond a basic inventory of factories and their location.⁵⁰

The problems of industrial planning during the Great War forced the military and the federal government to reassess their options for the future. The National Defense Act of 1920 authorized the War Department to plan the economic mobilization of both the armed services and the entire wartime economy. The Industrial Mobilization Plan of 1930 became the blueprint for future wartime plans. The Special Senate Committee to Investigate the Munitions Industry in the mid-1930s outlined ways of organizing industrial mobilization. The creation of the Army and Navy Munitions Board and the Army Industrial College recognized the need for collaborative planning of war production requirements. This expansion of industrial planning during the interwar years had an impact on defense planning during World War II. The most important decisions involved producing knowledgeable military staff, linking wartime military plans to the economy, and making a survey of the nation's industrial plants. By the time the state turned to war, the military had assembled information, among other things, about the nation's production lines, firm locations, employment levels, and fixed capital. More importantly, the ongoing collaboration between the military and business allowed for the development of credible intergroup relations by 1940 that "provided the glue of the successful military-corporate alliance."⁵¹

While meager, these interwar preparations allowed military authorities to build an apparatus capable of making more measured calculations about the country's industrial issues. By the advent of the war, the state and military had amassed information that assessed the urban, regional, and national stock of investment, employment, and credit. Government and military planners by 1940 had created a body of information about industrial sites that linked firms to political alliances between military-industrial complex officials and producer networks to form a broad defense regime. In order to determine a firm's suitability for access to federal prime contracts and factory investment awards the state had to compile information that was more than a simple listing. It had to penetrate the private shell of the firm to ascertain its ability to perform as part of a large network of war firms. The interwar plan devised by the military-industry collaboration did not produce a substantial information base that could be used for the Second World War's mobilization. It did, however, pave the way for ongoing collaboration during the war.⁵² The information gathered by the state was formatted in ways that facilitated the calculated investment of federal finance into manufacturing spaces and industrial production under the control of a military-corporate alliance.

The functioning of this new analytical approach to industrial sites is outlined in a 1941 Calvin Hoover paper on "the requirements of a war economy." A professor of economics at Duke and former adviser to various New Deal agencies, Hoover was well positioned to discuss the shift of a largely private industrial economy into a joint public-private war economy. In his paper, he laid out the elements necessary for an analysis of the mobilization of the war economy. In order for effective calculations to be made about industrial sites, this analysis required the government to acquire detailed knowledge about industry, including the development of methods to increase munitions output, the balancing of defense and consumer goods production, and the mobilization of defense labor. Calculative agents working in the mobilization agencies also had to work out the impact of the expansion of wartime industrial production on issues such as consumer spending and housing. In order to do this, the government had to devise ways to introduce price controls, to control credit spending, and to build wartime housing. Finally, the government had to establish priorities if scarce resources, from labor to structural steel, were to flow to the appropriate war industries. According to Hoover, the conversion from a peacetime to a wartime economy and the success of industrial mobilization rested on a careful and effective calculation of the options and their impact.[53]

A similar analytical approach to situating wartime industrial sites was made by Morris Copeland. A statistician at the WPB, Copeland had worked as a professor of economics at Cornell and the University of Michigan, the executive secretary of the U.S. Central Statistical Board, and the director of research at the U.S. Bureau of the Budget before the war. An adept administrator, economist, and statistician, he was eminently qualified to outline the main elements of production planning in a 1942 paper. In the process of discussing the increases necessary to industrial production and coordination, he outlined three elements required for successful mobilization: a procurement bidding system, production facilities, and government entry into manufacturing. To ensure that industrial sites could be effectively managed required the government, among other things, to create procedures for advanced planning, to gain effective control over the flow of the factors of production, and to ensure that supplies were delivered on time to production sites. This involved creating unprecedented types of information on firms, industries, and locations and the extensive analysis of this growing body of industrial materials.[54]

Over the course of the war, the government and military's mobilization agencies and their assorted divisions, committees, and bureaus assembled a massive amount of statistical data and prepared informed qualitative analysis for military, business, and civil leaders. Industrial property was subject to calculative knowledge. There were two main parts to this. The first was the creation of an up-to-date industrial inventory. Civil and military officials compiled listings that included information about plant size, equipment, transportation, labor, and raw materials. These inventories made it possible for mobilization officials to determine the type, scale, and location of industrial plants that could be called on to produce war commodities. It also allowed mobilization officials to determine what sorts of new facilities had to be built. The second part of the massive wartime information gathering effort was to analytically link this growing inventory of information about industrial firms to mobilization policy. The aim here, although it was never fully realized, was to calculate how information about industrial firms and related issues, such as labor and transportation, could be connected with an integrated national world of production that would further industrial mobilization.

Despite good intentions, it was extremely difficult for the government to link the growing body of knowledge about industrial sites to industrial policy. While the military gathered significant amounts of data about industrial firms, the utilization of the data remained limited as the tensions endemic to interagency rivalry undermined effective use of material. Information from different agencies that might have been useful to answer questions about how to fulfill the demands for war facilities, equipment, and products remained isolated as long as the relations among the key players were uncoordinated, contradictory, and overlapping.[55] This was reinforced by poorly constructed administrative structures and the lack of university-trained economists, statisticians, and engineers.

Creating effective information about industrial sites was difficult. For example, from May 1942, the WPB's Construction Bureau oversaw the administration of L-41, the license to build wartime structures. It faced several problems, most notably a lack of authority over construction, the inheritance of an inadequate administrative structure, and ongoing hostility from the armed forces. On top of this, the bureau was unable to acquire sufficient information to undertake a well-considered construction program. Even when the appropriate information was available, the military and industry worked against the planned implementation of balanced war production.[56] While increased knowledge about what was needed grew exponentially, the ability to satisfy those needs often remained limited. The state's power to utilize the vast body of industrial site and production capacity data was severely circumscribed.

Nevertheless, mobilization agencies did devise a workable system of utilizing industrial knowledge. As with most mobilization issues it was the NDAC that set out the key features for how to assemble and utilize knowledge about industrial property. The commission established the methods of measuring, monitoring, and mobilizing information about industrial sites. The OPM and the WPB added administrative weight to the process of information assembly and data analysis. As previously discussed, the power of the mobilization agencies centered on the incorporation of business and military leaders who had substantial power over policy. Corporate leaders worked with state officials to establish policies and programs that measured (e.g., the Bureau of Research and Statistics), monitored (e.g., defense labor policy guidelines and certification procedure for military contracts), and mobilized (e.g., procurement and tax amortization) industrial sites within a corporate framework.[57]

Corporate leaders worked with mobilization officials and academics to build up knowledge about industry. The primary function of the NDAC's Production Division was to assemble materials for the manufacture of war materials. Headed by William Knudsen, the president of General Motors, the board worked hand-in-hand with industry and the military to model the mobilization process on corporate practices. This required, among other things, "gathering and estimating military requirements, establishing the productive capacity of the economy for specific goods, and determining whether new industrial plant and equipment was necessary." The OPM's Bureau of Research and Statistics and Production Planning Board provided material for mobilization. The former, which was headed by Stacy May, a Rockefeller Foundation social scientist, was composed of academics, economists, and statisticians. They created data that were used to calculate the military's industrial requirements. The Production Planning Board also worked closely with the armed services. Similarly, the WPB's Statistics Division and the Committee on Industrial Facilities and Construction oversaw the collection, analysis, and administration of war mobilization materials.[58]

Corporate leaders were able to use new forms of knowledge to increase their firms' power. The case of the WPB's concentration of the production program is a case in point. A mechanism created in July 1942 to calibrate industrial efficiency and expand production, the program aimed to concentrate all wartime production of an industry into a few factories. This involved maximizing total production while curtailing nonessential civilian production and converting civilian industries to war production. One result of this knowledge was the creation of two types of tools to manage resource restrictions: M orders adjusted supply to demand by imposing material restrictions; and L orders balanced demand with supply by limiting output. In order to concentrate war manufacture into the most efficient defense factories, the WPB had to acquire knowledge of the industry's plant capacity, production processes, managerial assets, labor availability, and factory location. This required an extensive data-gathering exercise and a statistical analysis of an industry as a whole and of its individual firms.[59]

Other government bodies sought information about production facilities. A vast body of knowledge about the demands for factory space was constructed by the statistical and planning boards mandated to guide mobilization. Stacy May's Bureau of Research and Statistics generated material on all sorts of questions, many of which touched directly on production facilities, including material shortages, labor supply, and production output. The Army and Navy Munitions Board employed a large workforce gathering and analyzing data on a variety of issues including construction material availability, allocating scarce resources, and assisting in procuring materials necessary to building factories. The DPC operated a large workforce in several divisions including real estate, financial, engineering, and machine tool, all of which undertook studies, assessments, and evaluations of both potential and existing agency projects.[60]

An astonishing array of materials was gathered by mobilization agencies. This gave government, military, and corporate leaders access to extensive bodies of information and modes of analysis that allowed them to calculate how to proceed with industrial mobilization. Central to this was rethinking the social relations of property. Previously, most knowledge of the factory was internal to the corporation. Executives had a broad sense of capital needs, employment levels, market situations, and so forth. The war changed this, as it was necessary for the federal government and the military to gain access to industrial information about industrial property and production. During the war, the state assembled firm information that previously had not been needed, widened the frame of material considered to be in its interests, and used this material to make critical calculations about wartime industrial property.

Conclusion

In February 1945, Robert Patterson, the undersecretary of war, wrote to Henry Stimson, the secretary of war, outlining the reasons why the federal government had worked with private entrepreneurs to build the wartime industrial regime. In Patterson's opinion, it was necessary "not only because it was the system in which we believed, but because it was the system we had, and any attempt to change it suddenly would have brought dangerous confusion and delay."[61] What Patterson pointed to was the centrality of capitalist production to the federal system of mobilization and the necessity of incorporating industrial executives into the making of Washington's industrial property policy. The construction of defense factories depended on the direct incorporation of private and financial interests into a federally directed coalition. Men such as Patterson, Stimson, and those with whom they worked in the federal state, such as Robert Lovett, the assistant secretary of war for air, and John McCloy, the assistant secretary of war, cooperated with industrial corporate executives.[62] Not only had they come from that world and were fully conversant with the ideological and material practices of capitalist business, but they also brought their knowledge of the material imperatives of business to government.

The building of new industrial sites required erecting a state apparatus that allocated the necessary resources to meet desired ends—making war goods, creating war profits, and protecting corporate markets. It was impossible to build new industrial spaces within the preexisting structures of the state and the social relations of property. New ones had to be created. Through the experience it gained during the 1930s, the federal government was able to construct new agencies, policies, and regulations to oversee the allocation of investment, the rethinking of property rights, the purchase of industrial land, and the deployment of labor. New relations and functional links were forged between the civilian state, the military, and business. A new set of military-industrial complex relations was built. The mobilization of industrial America and the investment of billions of dollars into new industrial plants would have been impossible without the reframing of federal, industrial, and military relations.

State investment in manufacturing facilities had far-reaching implications for war mobilization, business-state relations, and the character of industrial sites. Together, the triad of the state, the military, and industry framed industrial space in a different way and, in the process, incorporated industrial sites within a new set of calculated relationships. The emergence of a reformulated military-industrial complex during the war was not unexpected. It had taken place during World War I, although on a smaller scale. For the most part, production remained separate from government action. This was not the case after 1940. The framing of the industrial site as a federal responsibility ensured that there would be a different relationship between the state and business. Military, government, and corporate cooperation after 1940 was a rational response given the logic of the prevailing political-economic system. Large corporations had advantages that could not be found elsewhere. Their control of the national economy meant that they had the required plant capacity, technical expertise, and established suppliers to respond to the high-volume demands of the military. Moreover, they had the quality-control systems and research staff needed to meet the exacting standards for complex weapons production.

Given the ideological position of the vast majority of those working in the mobilization program, there was little reason to believe that state and military officials would not work with corporate executives to build up the basic industrial infrastructures of wartime industrial sites. Nevertheless, the ease with which corporate executives gained control over the levers of industrial property and resources allocation speaks to a world that was neither rational nor judicious. The unprecedented power that wartime mobilization gave to America's corporations resulted in their control over the wartime economy and ensured that they built a much tighter relationship with the federal government, especially the military and conservative factions.

CHAPTER 3

Mobilizing Chicago's Wartime Industrial Property

In December 1941, *Commerce*, Chicago's leading business magazine, declared the city "the world's greatest and most diversified industrial workshop." In the magazine's opinion, mobilizing Chicago's industrial sector was vital to the country's war effort. The city's "vast unused capacity" could be "converted to defense needs at a rapidly accelerating rate" and would strengthen the national economy by creating much-needed industrial expansion, reducing unemployment and producing war products. The war could also boost the local economy. After more than ten years of dismal industrial growth, the war offered Chicago managers the opportunity to kick-start the world's greatest industrial workshop and to refurbish, expand, and build new industrial sites.[1]

In fact, industrial executives were already involved in expanding the metropolitan area's industrial capacity by the time the United States entered the war. Between June 1940 and November 15, 1941, the federal government placed more than 5,000 supply and construction contracts valued at more than $1.2 billion with 1,190 Chicago concerns. Furthermore, according to a Chicago Association of Commerce (CAC) estimate, other local firms received another $1 billion over this period for subcontracting work, industrial expansion, and supply contracts. The result was that by the time of Pearl Harbor, Chicago's firms were already "rearming the nation."[2] Over the next four years all indicators showed dramatic industrial growth. By the time the war ended, Chicago industrialists, civil state agencies, and the military had invested close to $1.4 billion in new factory space; the U.S. Army and Navy had invested almost $10 billion in supply contracts; and manufacturing jobs had grown from 616,000 in 1939 to more than one million.[3] World War II reinvigorated metropolitan Chicago's industrial economy.

Public and private investment in new wartime industrial spaces made Chicago the nation's leading wartime metropolis. The ability of local and national agents to channel more than a billion dollars of construction work into Chicago relied on the restructuring of property relations and the framing of Chicago's factory space as a joint private-public object. No longer subject solely to private initiatives, the building and operation of the wartime factory involved resetting both local and nonlocal industrial and property relationships. Industrial relations were recast as government military and business officials calculated the new world of industrial production. Property relations were changed to accommodate government and military intervention in factory construction. This chapter explores this calculative action through the emergence of a wartime industrial economy, the flow of federal investment into new industrial fixed plant, and the growing closeness between the agents of the military-industrial complex. As the focus of a new type of public-private partnership and a new set of calculative relations, the wartime industrial site demonstrates some of the key economic and political changes taking place to America's wartime industrial economy.

Boosting Chicago

Metropolitan Chicago was an industrial powerhouse when the United States entered the war in December 1941. The city's 350,000 wage earners worked in more than 8,400 factories, mills, and workshops. The city was surrounded by a range of industrial towns and suburbs, from steel-producing Gary to metal-working Cicero, and further out, an assortment of farming areas. Metropolitan Chicago was a leading producer of steel, meat, furniture, machinery, and radios.[4] The Windy City consolidated its position as the nation's second largest industrial metropolis during the war by capturing a significant share of private and public investment in industrial property. While there were few factories producing munitions in 1940, the metropolitan area's wide range of steel, machine tools, and related industries provided an excellent base for the conversion to war production. The shift from a peacetime economy to a wartime one was made possible by constructing and equipping defense factories. With more than $1.3 billion of the nation's wartime capital investment, metropolitan Chicago had the largest arsenal of defense plants in the country by the end of the war.

The switch from a dormant peacetime economy to a buzzing wartime one was not an easy task, not so much due to the metropolitan area's industrial mix as due to the reluctance of many industrial executives to convert their operations to war production and the lack of investment in new industrial facilities for many years. By 1939, ten years of low rates of capital investment in factory space had weakened Chicago's industrial base. According to the real estate analysis company F. W. Dodge, Chicago's manufacturing firms had invested less than $340 million in fixed capital during the 1930s. Not surprisingly, the early 1930s, when compared to the last five years of the 1920s, which saw total investment in industrial sites of over half a billion dollars, were dismal years for industrial growth. And the situation was not much better in the late 1930s. The reported investment of $33 million spent on new factory space in 1939 was well below the amounts spent for 1936 and 1937, which totaled $40 million and $70 million, respectively.[5] One consequence of this long-term lack of investment in new facilities was that when America began gearing up for war, Chicago was home to a large number of old, obsolete, and dilapidated industrial sites.

The need to invest in the metropolitan area's factory sites was clear to the local coalition. Although attempts had been made during the 1930s to entice industrial growth, the election of a new leader for the CAC in 1939 accelerated the drive to boost industrial investment. In October 1939, not long after becoming the association's chief executive, Leverett Lyon announced the inauguration of the Greater Chicago Plan. Before coming to the CAC, Lyon had completed a very successful career at the University of Chicago, Washington University, and the Brookings Graduate School, where he specialized in marketing strategy and industrial policy. He brought this expertise to the problem of Chicago's industry. To help him, he hired E. P. Querl, a former industrial commissioner for the Los Angeles Chamber of Commerce, to head the association's industrial division. Querl's mandate was to have corporations invest in new industrial concerns and to open up new industrial property.[6] According to Oscar Mayer, the CAC's president, the city had a great deal of "idle industrial property and dozens of sizable vacant factory buildings and warehouses awaiting development." To be successful, Lyon and Querl had to recalibrate the demand for and supply of factory space by matching idle industrial properties with new concerns.[7] Only with investment in new industrial sites and the building of factories could Chicago's industrial economy be rejuvenated.

Despite its grandiose title, the Greater Chicago Plan had little to recommend it, centered as it was on the tired strategy of advertising the region's locational advantages. The strategy consisted of two parts. To start with, the region's elites had to band together to build a program to expand the city's industrial base. Once this was done, they had to advertise Chicago's assets to national business leaders. The resulting private investment, the argument went, would have multiplier effects through the community and make Chicago even more desirable to industry. To mobilize these ideas, the CAC would make a survey of the district and organize "a selling force of experts equipped to carry Chicago's industrial story to every industrial executive in the country."[8] In a new twist to the old strategy, the dismal years of the 1930s could, in the minds of Lyon and Querl, help make Chicago even more attractive. Building on Mayer's point, a booklet distributed to 5,800 executives, engineers, underwriters, and banks in 1940 argued, "Chicago has dozens of sizeable vacant factory buildings and warehouses begging for wage paying tenants. It has more than 100 square miles of well located, but idle, industrial property." The new plan would allow the city to reap the fruits of industrial underinvestment during the Depression.[9]

The city's growth coalition wanted to use the Greater Chicago Plan to link

Chicago to the nation's mobilization program. Two obstacles stood in the way: First, although many Chicago firms could easily convert to war production, for others it would take a great deal of work, dedication, and money. Second, many local manufacturers were hostile to government intervention in production matters and worked actively against the development of a national defense economy. Nevertheless, industrial leaders were coming to terms with the reality of national war conditions. Slowly they began to work with the federal government to increase industrial investment and convert the city's industrial potential into wartime production.[10] By the second half of the 1940, a large number of the region's manufacturers were committed to mobilization and were actively engaged in the creation of a militarized economy.

This commitment required a business-government alliance at the state and federal levels dedicated to building a local war economy and defense factories. Believing that war production offered high profits, industrialists began to drum up war contracts in Washington. In the early stages, however, Chicago lagged behind its competitors in attracting supply contracts and construction investment. This was partly due to the reluctance of Chicago's industrialists to seriously consider wartime production as a viable option. More importantly, at least in the minds of those sitting in Chicago's corporate and political boardrooms, the problem lay in Washington. Basking in the CAC's booster programs, Chicago's media, political, and business officers frequently complained about the intransigence and inefficiency of Washington-based agencies.

They also complained that mobilization agencies were ignoring Roosevelt's plan to locate defense plants in the interior.[11] Foreshadowing the postwar concern with industrial dispersal as a strategy to escape Soviet bombing, the *Chicago Tribune* pointed out that "the major part of the nation's [aircraft] industry is still concentrated on the seaboards—areas most vulnerable to attack in case of war." A map shaded to show this concentration only strengthened the case. A month later, an editorial opined that the Roosevelt administration was paying only "lip service" to the interior policy, and that most army work remained concentrated in the Pittsburgh-Boston-Wilmington industrial triangle. The correspondent argued that even though wartime plant expansion in this triangle may have created scale and scope efficiencies, these gains were of "less importance at the moment than security against bombing or invasion offered by inland sites" such as Chicago.[12]

These complaints continued to surface. In September 1940, Lyon told the press that Chicago was not receiving its "proportionate share of the country's defense orders."[13] This grumbling continued despite the trickle of contracts. It came to a head in the fall of 1941 when city boosters claimed that Chicago, despite its excellent industrial sites, labor skills, and managerial talents, had "not received its share of the war contracts." The state governor, Dwight Green, complained that "Illinois, the third state in population and in industrial capacity, ranks fourteenth in the volume of arms contracts it has received." W. Homer Hartz, the Chicago regional director of the Office of Production Management (OPM), declared that the metropolitan area was being neglected, charging "Washington officials" with failing "to give him a satisfactory explanation for this." He was so incensed that he resigned from the OPM and resumed his duties as the president of the railway equipment manufacturer Morden Frog and Crossing. In early 1942, Illinois senator Scott Lucas and congressman Raymond McKeough complained that the building of war plants on the coasts was being done at Illinois's expense.[14]

While the disproportionate share of government contracts may have resulted from a bias against Illinois as Hartz argued, it probably had more to do with the difficulties of building a workable mobilization policy. The ability of federal officials to build an operational process of production expansion and factory building was restricted by Roosevelt's policy of undermining agency leaders, while the "confusion over targets, lack of enforcement, and poor internal coordination" hindered effective mobilization.[15] Despite the country's growing patriotism, the interest in fighting a common enemy, and the huge amount of economic and political resources allocated to mobilization, agency officials found it difficult to implement an effective system of industrial production. Despite the administrative and personnel continuities they had with New Deal agencies, mobilization officials faced numerous teething problems and tense relationships with other interests involved in gearing up for and the operation of wartime production.

Although located "between mountains," Chicago was considered a problem area by military officials. One reason was the absence of war industries. Despite the scale and breadth of its industrial economy, Chicago had few aircraft firms and a small petroleum-refining base. Labor supply quickly became an issue as the unemployed surplus of the 1930s was quickly absorbed as the war economy heated up and men went off to fight in Europe and the Pacific. Chicago along with the other older industrial centers along the coasts and the Great Lakes faced increasing difficulty finding workers to work in war industries.[16] Colonel Donald Armstrong, the executive officer of the Chicago Ordnance District, made this clear when he stated in November 1940, "it is clearly desirable to prevent the concentration of new industries for national defense in areas such as Chicago, where the load of rearmament will already be a serious burden as time goes on." Accordingly, when policy makers did look to the interior between "the Alleghenies and the Rockies," their gaze took them to the areas of large labor surpluses found in the cities and countryside of Missouri, Kansas, and Nebraska.[17]

The problems of locating war work were not unknown to the officials creating mobilization policy. Effective management remained elusive as competition between super-agencies, tensions between government policy makers, military officials, and corporate experts, and the problems of converting a gigantic peacetime private economy to war production conspired to undermine what was believed to be a rational mobilization program. For leaders of the mobilization agencies, such as Donald Nelson at the OPM and those at the War Production Board (WPB), these pressures made it difficult to find satisfactory answers to the questions about factory location and plant expansion. This was reinforced by a split between policy makers in the agencies responsible for factory expansion. Political infighting between those who advocated greater corporate control (such as Jesse Jones and William Knudsen) and those who sought greater federal control over the mobilization (Clifford Durr and Emil Schram) ensured that a cohesive program of factory construction was impossible to achieve.

The wartime factory became a contested space, and its location became open to competing pressures. On the one hand, entrenched corporate interests centered in major industrial centers such as Chicago, New York, and Los Angeles sought to attract federal contracts and construction awards to existing sites, the majority of which were along the coasts and the Great Lakes. On the other, especially in the earliest stage of mobilization, much of the corporate world strongly opposed government investment in manufacturing sites. As the military's prime concern was to reduce production time, it was willing to invest in plants wherever maximum speed could be attained. Local governments and business groups throughout the country, meanwhile, were demanding a greater share of defense money.[18]

These competing groups placed those in charge of factory investment in a quandary. Robert Patterson, the undersecretary of war, tried to minimize tensions when he told an April 1941 senate hearing that investment was finding its way to all corners of the country despite the problems. In terms of defense contracts, he continued, "there has been no geographical favor in any phase of the procurement program." Taking the corporate line, he argued that war products such as ships and planes had to be built where production facilities already existed. Despite this, defense contracts were being spread out, and areas such as Indiana and Kansas had received substantial government investment. He told the committee that "efforts have been made to place the [war] plants in the interior and to disperse them to the greatest extent possible," but "plants must be located where there is adequate labor supply, transportation, power, and other essentials for production."[19] In his view, the realities of production forced federal policy makers to continue to invest heavily in older industrial districts.

Despite this shaky start, Chicago became one of the nation's largest war producers and home to America's largest body of government-financed industrial property. Building on the region's prewar industrial potential and their promotional campaign, Illinois and Chicago politicians and business executives induced recalcitrant industrialists and Washington mobilization leaders to invest in factory expansion. They made a convincing case that diverting federal construction funds to Chicago would benefit both national mobilization targets and individual firm profits.

Central to the success of the booster efforts was the growth coalition led by local politicians and the CAC. Chicago's mayor, Edward Kelly, was a key player. He used his influence with Roosevelt and his control over one of the country's largest industrial centers to push Chicago's case.[20] Among other things, he made several trips with CAC leaders and local firm executives to the nation's capital in 1940 and 1941 to lobby for a larger share of war spending. In May 1940, for example, Mayer, Lyon, and Querl went to drum up war contracts and to inform War Department officials of the "advantages offered by Chicago for the manufacture of war materials."[21] Similarly, several state politicians made their way to Washington to argue Illinois's case. Perhaps the most important trip was taken in late 1941. Governor Green and Murray Baker, vice-chair of the Illinois Council of Defense (ICD), traveled to Washington to plead for more contracts and larger industrial investment in defense factories. Along with the state's Democrat and Republican congressional representatives, Green and Murray met to discuss Illinois's share of war prime and construction contracts with key federal OPM officials.[22]

A lunch hosted by Green and Murray on November 25 was attended by fifteen congressmen, members of the ICD, and, most importantly, two OPM officials, Donald Nelson, director of the supplies, priorities, and allocation board, and Floyd Odlum, director of the division of contract distribution. Green started the proceedings with a description of the state's locational advantages. This was followed by a deluge of statistics from Baker and Carter Jenkins, the ICD coordinator, and biting comments from several congressmen, all of whom demanded more investment in Illinois. Impressed by the sales pitch, the federal officials agreed. Odlum told the lunch crowd that "Illinois has not received its portion" of war work, while he promised that "within the next three months you're going to see a great many more jobs placed in Illinois." As well as these promises elicited from Nelson and Odlum, the Illinois governor was also able to gain support from Secretary of Commerce Jesse Jones, Secretary of the Interior Harold Ickes, and several military leaders. As he rode the train back to Chicago, Green exclaimed, with evident pleasure, "I believe we've done some good."[23]

Meanwhile, back in Chicago, the CAC, worried about ongoing neglect from Washington, heavily advertised the city's industrial advantages to outside interests. The desire to overturn the Depression's economic problems and to capture more of the defense largesse triggered a concerted attempt by the city's political and industrial communities to work together to reap the rewards of wartime mobilization. While the budding partnership between all levels of government and business around industrial mobilization rested on the building of new industrial space, the onus for enticing new firms to a locale such as Chicago continued to rest with local boosters. Reports, such as the two volumes of *The Report of the Chicago Land Use Survey*, directed by the Chicago Plan Commission and conducted by the Works Projects Administration, documented opportunities and problems facing local industry as it geared up for war. In other reports, Chicago's leaders assembled what they considered to be the appropriate information needed in order to sell the city to the federal agencies responsible for allocating war construction funding and war material supply contracts. These reports and surveys tabulated the metropolitan area's diversity of industries, varied labor force, available land, abundant utilities, and first-rate transportation and research facilities.[24]

The region's boosters pushed two main points in their reports. The first was to convince federal mobilization leaders that Chicago had the "requirements of *invulnerability*."[25] They cited, for example, that the Calumet district was "located far from the coasts[,] and industries may operate without dependence on ocean routes exposed to attack, and with relative immunity from bombing raids."[26] They had made this point earlier in a report of the city's industrial assets. In an attempt to counter the draw of interior states, they stressed that Chicago's industrial sites were "inland and protected from the exposed Mexican border and well removed from the eastern and western seacoasts." Here the writer built on national decentralization discourse and took aim at the city's competitors on the Atlantic and Pacific seaboards. With their susceptibility to air attack from Europe and Asia, it was argued that factories in New York, Philadelphia, and Los Angeles were not as secure as those in Chicago. The report also established Chicago's other advantages. Despite the growing squeeze on labor supply, local boosters proclaimed that Chicago's workers had the "skills and experience in the operations and processes used in the manufacture of aircraft and airplane engines, and nearly every other industrial skill."[27]

The second point focused on the strength of the area's agglomeration of industrial assets. Survey after survey proclaimed Chicago's industrial prowess and the city's availability for war production. Unrivaled in its human and technical resources, Chicago could be quickly transformed into a militarized metropolis. According to its boosters, the region's metal industries, skilled workers, efficient transportation systems, and first-rate research facilities ensured rapid conversion to war production. With appropriate funding and polices in place, industrial sites such as the extensive Acme Steel plant in the Riverdale section of Chicago could be quickly converted to war production (Figure 3.1). Boosters argued that by utilizing Chicago's large number of industrial sites, Chicago could become the nation's center of heavy war materials: "Heavy and light ordnance, tanks, trucks, and tractors may be produced by Chicago transportation equipment and allied 'hard metal' fabrication plants with less time lost in retooling, redesigning, and rebuilding than in other locations because the United States' heaviest manufacturing and milling plants are established and operating in the

FIGURE 3.1. Acme Steel, Riverdale, 1940. Chicago was home to a large number of metalworking factories, such as Acme Steel, that could be quickly converted to war production.
Source: Pullman State Historic Site.

Chicago Area."[28] Local boosters were eager to expand existing industrial capacity and to capture a share of growth industries. As one report averred, "New aviation plants, located in Chicago, will be removed from the present focal points of the aviation industry, thus providing the much needed decentralization in this industry. Chicago's basic manufacturing facilities are ready and able *now* to provide materials and workers for this purpose."[29]

Chicago's boosters wrote these reports to convince federal and military officers that the region could be a prime defense manufacturing center. The boosters reckoned that promoting the region's strengths would entice capital investment to the metropolis. Using the timeworn strategy of enticing corporations by emphasizing the city's locational assets, the CAC and other local organizations looked to sell the city's industrial charms to a new customer, the federal government. For the previous seventy or so years, Chicago's business and political leaders had aimed their booster rhetoric almost exclusively at private industry, seeking to attract new manufacturing firms to the city. The war changed this strategy. While they still maintained their interest in luring private capital to Chicago, local leaders were also busy trying to tempt federal and military officials to invest in new factory space and to provide defense contracts.

The boosters' calculations were successful. After a slow start, Chicago became a leading war industrial center. By November 1943 more than $980 million had been invested in new factory space in the Chicago manufacturing district. This investment made Chicago the principal wartime recipient of wartime funding. It was followed by New York ($880 million), Detroit ($577 million), San Francisco ($478 million), and Philadelphia ($477 million). Similarly, contracts (exclusive of subcontracts) from June 1940 through December 1943 totaling more than $7.7 billion made Chicago a leading beneficiary of orders for war products.[30] This trajectory continued over the next two years. By the end of the war, the more than $1.3 billion invested in wartime factory buildings, equipment, and machinery made the Chicago metropolitan area the country's largest recipient of wartime facility funding. Almost $10 billion of wartime supply contracts placed the region as one of the nation's leading defense contractors.

Chicago was home to the country's largest set of defense plants and some of its most important industries, such as aircraft. Mobilization and industry leaders found Chicago's locational assets to be extremely useful for the building of entirely new assembly plants and the expansion of existing component supplier factories. As one writer noted in 1944: "Chicago, which was long a source for such components in aviation production such as precision machine parts, steel castings and forgings, electrical wiring and equipment and products in the radio and electronics field, now has several primary aircraft manufacturers, three makers of aircraft engines and a large producer of aircraft engine parts, aircraft carburetors, Norden bomb sights and airplane propellers."[31] The aircraft industry was to play a significant role in Chicago's wartime development. This was due to the desire of Chicago's growth alliance to increase its market share and profits by undertaking place-based calculations about the making of a militarized economy. The numeric and qualitative calculations involved in building a wartime economy and the rethinking of the social relations of property resulted in the construction of a militarized metropolitan economy and a war-based public-private partnership.

Assembling Industry for War

Chicago's political and business leaders controlled the local organizations that national leaders used to build the region's industrial sites. In the process, a new institutional framework was created as different interests worked to push forward their respective agendas. Taking lessons from New Deal programs, city boosters moved quickly to coordinate different and sometimes conflicting knowledge that local business and political leaders had of industrial sites.

Information taken from reports and surveys published in the early 1940s allowed local elites to assemble a body of information on metropolitan industry that pushed the idea that the Chicago economy was a militarized space. They assembled a variety of calculating national, state, and local institutions that primed Chicago's industrial sites for war.

Chicago's growth alliance worked with federal and military mobilization agencies to turn the city's peacetime economy into a massive war machine. This began as early as the German invasion of Poland. In September 1939, the Illinois Manufacturers' Association (IMA) established a Committee on National Defense. Its purpose was to work with the Chicago Ordnance District to cement "present and future relationships growing out of the European war."[32] This was easier said than done. The IMA, which was established in 1893 to fight unions and labor legislation, was deeply conservative and extremely hostile to mobilization. Suspicious of all New Deal programs, the association was isolationist and fought all forms of regulation, except for those deemed essential to its own interests. This position was not representative of all IMA members though, and from 1939, some worked to convince the association to back America's entry into the war. After Pearl Harbor, even the most recalcitrant isolationist could no longer deny the cause of war, and the IMA threw its support behind rearmament.

As would be expected given its isolationist and conservative position, the IMA was not particularly effective in mobilizing Chicago's economy. Its Committee on National Defense, established in 1939, had little effect on government-directed industrial expansion and the creation of government-financed industrial sites. Chaired by Brigadier General Thomas Hammond, former president of the Whiting Corporation, and Major F. Preston, chief of the Chicago Ordnance District, the committee boasted a board of executives from some of the state's largest industrial corporations. Despite its professed intentions and weighty membership, and the military's desire for increased munition production, the committee did little to push mobilization forward. At best it railed against the "shackles" placed on industries, authorized resolutions to pressure Washington, and made lists of firms receiving war contracts—worthy stuff for a conservative business institution, but not useful for mobilizing the Chicago economy.[33]

Similarly, in March 1941 the IMA surveyed local industry with the aim of making an inventory of the region's productive capacity. One aim was to strengthen the links between local and nonlocal agents by keeping "national defense planning officers informed" of Chicago's industrial assets. Another was to facilitate the flow of local information by "suggesting to primary contractors where they may sublet some part of the job."[34] Once again, despite the professed aims of building up the local economy by linking up with outside interests, there was little to show for the association's efforts. Despite the absence of any obvious successes however, the IMA's mobilization agenda must have established a climate for cooperation between different elements of the city's economic and political elites in the following years. This, in turn, must have helped in the creation of Chicago's industrial sites and the making of the local war economy.

In comparison to the ineffectual IMA, the CAC had greater impact on militarizing the local industrial economy. Using its extensive industrial expertise and networks, the association turned Chicago into a massive munitions-producing economy and built an impressive body of defense plants in the region. Established in 1904, the CAC, along with the Board of Trade, was the most important business organization in the city. The CAC's membership was "composed of corporations and individuals from every industry and from every type of commercial, professional and financial interest." In its view, the association's objectives were framed to "prove beneficial to the community as a whole, to industry as whole, and to commerce as whole."[35] Despite the obvious and self-serving rhetoric, its claim to represent Chicago's capitalist class in a broad sense was accurate. Unlike the IMA, which drew its support from the more conservative elements of Illinois's business class, the CAC was willing to work with nonbusiness groups, and its membership was drawn from a wider spectrum of political beliefs. This broad support base and a conciliatory politics of business informed the CAC's industrial and political calculations about how to transform the local economy into a war machine and to channel investment into the region's industrial sites.

In this spirit, five days after Roosevelt's May 26, 1940, fireside chat, the CAC organized a Committee on the National Defense Program. The committee's aim was to examine "the means by which the resources and personnel of Chicago could be adjusted to the country's needs." In other words, the CAC was looking to frame local industrialists and their factories within the new world of war. In order to do this, the CAC started by asking all Chicago manufacturers to survey their plants "with a view to their adaptability to the production of war surpluses." The CAC also established committees to cultivate relations with the federal government and the U.S. Army and Navy.[36] The CAC organized its industrial department to build a multiscalar public-private partnership consisting of strong links between local industry and federal and military agencies. To this end, the committee had set up a machinery inventory service for the army, a clearinghouse for defense planning and purchasing, a list of primary contractors in the region, and lines of liaison with military procurement officers by the end of 1940. They had established a new set of industrial relations that would transform the local economy for war.[37]

The CAC also worked with the state and the city's defense committees. The Chicago Commission on National Defense was created on March 6, 1941. It was chaired by Mayor Kelly and had seventy-one members taken from the area's business, industrial, and civic institutions, including the CAC. Similarly, Governor John Stelle created the Illinois Emergency Defense Council in December 1940. The new governor, Dwight Green, signed into existence the Illinois Council of Defense, a revamped version of Stelle's committee, in April 17, 1941.[38]

The purpose of both organizations was to build the Chicago war economy and to attract construction investment. By early 1941, then, the region's primary business and political institutions had framed the local economy as part of the federal war program and were working on strategies to capture a significant share of the country's prime contracts and factory construction awards. Over the next three years, these committees linked Chicago manufacturers with civil and military mobilization agencies. They liaised with various civil and military officials, undertook surveys of industries to establish war production potential, and gave workshops to local business owners on how to obtain war contracts. As Republican congressman Evan Howell said in the winter of 1942, the committees must be credited with "securing millions of dollars of added arms business for the state's industries."[39]

The CAC remained the city's key organization responsible for coordinating and promoting war production. By the end of 1940, local industrialists were using the association's connections to find new ways of moving to war production and promoting investment in new factory space. In May 1940 and January 1941, the CAC surveyed its membership about available production facilities. This material was used by federal and military officials to plan contracts and to identify industrial property that could be turned into wartime factories. A barrage of booster articles and listings of firms receiving prime and construction contracts in the monthly *Commerce* worked to keep metropolitan manufacturers abreast of the growing volume of war work coming into the district. The association worked with educational institutions to mount a campaign in order to strengthen the defense program. Several conferences, on topics ranging from labor relations to retailing, were organized "for the purpose of analyzing mutual problems."[40] The association's activities were critical to assembling material about the scale, location, and viability of the city's industry. This information was passed onto civil and military agencies and became part of the calculus for the building of the region's wartime industrial base.

Illustrative of the CAC's calculative role in shaping Chicago's industrial sites was the Defense Problem Service, established in 1940, whose mandate was to provide services to manufacturers seeking war work. The CAC was aware that the new committee was a necessity if local industrialists were to take advantage of the billions of dollars of construction and supply awards flowing from Washington. Most factory managers were unfamiliar with the intricacies of state bureaucracy, despite the availability of business loans by the Reconstruction Finance Corporation (RFC) after 1934. The Defense Problem Service was established to remedy this situation by helping local managers and executives sort through the different government systems and to provide assistance with interpreting federal industrial construction and supply purchasing methods.[41] It assisted firms in both their political and numerical calculations about how to convert their workplace to war production by pooling information that local firms could share about how to obtain federal supply contracts and building awards. The service linked local firms with military procurement officers and offered industrialists information about government and military services located in Chicago. In this way, the CAC was able to help managers sort through the various agency bureaucracies to target the appropriate people and agencies in the Chicago and Washington offices.

The Defense Problem Service also undertook an advertising campaign to showcase the role of Chicago manufacturers in the war effort. A December 1941 list of more than a thousand prime contractors promoted the extent of Chicago's industrial capacity to the rest of the world, identified the region's industrial base and industrial facilities, and demonstrated that Chicago had the human and physical resources to get things done. The service also established a War Problems School, which brought in experts to discuss issues ranging from how to deal with federal priorities and price controls to how to get access to war construction contracts and construction awards. The thirty-four sessions that took place in 1944, for example, involved 69 Washington officials and 230 Chicago-based federal executives, as well as several businesspeople.[42]

Another association event illustrates the importance of the assembling of calculative actors to coordinate the national and local worlds of the military-industrial complex. The Defense Production Clinic, a three-day workshop held at the Stevens Hotel in October 1941, was organized by the OPM contract distribution division and the CAC. It brought together in one place key mobilization agencies, including the navy, army, Chicago Commission on National Defense, Illinois Chamber of Commerce, IMA, Illinois State Council for Defense, and business groups from Illinois, Indiana, Wisconsin, Iowa, and Michigan. The purpose of the clinic, according to Hartz, was "to promote the farming out of armament jobs to smaller plants."[43]

It was a well-attended and successful workshop. According to one observer, it was the "largest industrial market place ever arranged in this country to encourage the diffusion of armament work."[44] More than 150 large companies had booths where they laid out their requirements and materials: blueprints, machine specifications, and machine tool needs. Other booths were occupied by procurement agencies and various military branches, including ordnance, chemical warfare, quartermasters, signal corps, and air corps. More than 2,200 smaller firms from Chicago and the Midwest attended, looking for subcontracts. The idea of the clinic was not to finalize deals. According to Thomas McEwan, an OPM district manager, only a few contracts were expected to be signed on the spot. Rather, "most of them will be negotiated in more exhaustive dealings later. The preliminary work is being done here."[45] In other words, the workshop provided a calculable space for agents, including the federal government and the CAC, to come together to decide how to proceed with making war work and war spaces. The workshop established an expansive network of manufacturers stretching from Chicago and the Midwest to the rest of country to mobilize the war economy.

Other key calculative agents were the financial institutions that worked with industrialists, the military, and federal agencies to channel investment into industrial property. Investment banks took on a bigger role supplying capital for factory construction during the war.[46] In total, private institutions funded 14,746 wartime plant projects totaling $5.9 billion. As early as the fall of 1940, it was reported that commercial banks had $3 billion available for financing factory construction and that "idle reserve funds" could be used to underwrite factory expansion. The first significant loan occurred in November 1940 when New York and Chicago banks provided a ten-year loan of $12 million at 2.5 percent interest to Douglas Aircraft to finance a multiplant expansion program. The government indirectly underwrote the financing of defense factory construction as security for loans from military supply contracts. By coordinating the flow of capital between different calculative agents and into defense factories, financial institutions were key elements of the military-industrial complex during the war.[47]

Several Chicago financial institutions worked with other institutions across the country to underwrite wartime factory expansions. Of the 605 Chicago firms that built factory space between 1940 and 1945, only 48 did not receive any private investment. In 427 of these cases, private financial institutions were the only ones to invest in a manufacturing plant. In a few of these cases, the investment was more than a million dollars, while in two—Pan American Refining (Whiting) and Carnegie Steel (South Chicago)—it was more than $47 million and $21 million, respectively. In contrast to federal financing, the majority of private loans were for sums of less than $200,000. Another 128 firms received capital for expansion and machinery from both private and federal institutions.[48] Davidson Manufacturing, the pump and office equipment maker, illustrates this point. In December 1941 the company received a $300,000 loan from the Harris Trust and Savings Bank and the RFC to expand its facilities to make aircraft cannons. Similarly, nine months later, several banks floated a $200 million loan to Bendix Aviation to expand production space at its Chicago factory.[49] Private investment institutions were involved in financing the expansion of a large number of Chicago war firms.

Despite this, financial institutions played a minor role in terms of the value of new defense facilities. Loans tended to be small in value, accounting for 24 percent of the total spent. Much more important was the federal government. One of the key ways that the state underwrote the building of new industrial facilities and shaped private investment practices was the certificate of necessity, a financial instrument that allowed the federal government to directly underwrite the entire value of new facilities through tax deductions. The Revenue Act of 1940 created a "method of fixing, in advance of the war or emergency period, the amount of depreciation a taxpayer might deduct on a facility constructed or acquired after a certain date for emergency purposes." In doing so, it granted the holder the right to amortize the facility over a five-year period rather than the typical twenty years and gave "a proper depreciation allowance" during the "extraordinary conditions prevalent in times of national emergency." Over the course of the war, 43,000 certificates of necessity were issued with an estimated cost of $7.3 billion. Of these, 39,000 were issued by the army and navy, and 4,000 by the WPB.[50]

The federal government directly financed a significant share of the construction expenditure. Few financial institutions were willing to underwrite war expansion without state protection, and few manufacturers were prepared to risk overcapitalizing their facilities. Federal intervention in capital markets was motivated by the need to balance several issues, including the desire to maintain economic stability, to ensure rapid construction, and to secure postwar stability.[51] For these reasons, state managers calculated that the government had to become directly involved in industrial investment.

The Federal Reserve played a pivotal role in the public-private partnership by linking private investment sources, federal agencies, and war producers. This was a new role for the Reserve banking system. Before the war, Reserve banks had played a minor part in industrial financing. This would change during World War II. After November 1940, new regional offices, both in Chicago and elsewhere in the country, provided manufacturers with information about government war needs and the credit available to finance war production and construction. The intent was to facilitate credit expansion and to ensure that as much as possible of this found its way to war industries. There was little direct investment by the Federal Reserve; more important was the building up of reserves so that investors and commercial banks could purchase government securities. The Federal Reserve banks also authorized private banks to provide credit under several programs to firms with war contracts.[52]

The Federal Reserve Bank of Chicago connected local investment and commercial banks, mobilization agencies, and city war firms. The Chicago bank used an agreement between the National Defense Advisory Commission and Federal Reserve governors to encourage the city's private banks to extend loans for working capital purposes under the V, VT, and T loan programs.[53] Local manufacturers such as Armour and Borg-Warner received tens of millions of dollars in V-loans from a variety of bank syndicates, underwritten by the local Federal Reserve. The Federal Reserve also connected local manufacturers to the broader corporate war economy. In the fall of 1940 it hired an officer "to handle all problems relating to the field and technical activities of smaller business enterprises."[54] Throughout the war it continued to link local manufactures with national corporations.

The Chicago Reserve framed the defense factory as a state object by linking the calculative actors involved in wartime industrial production and construction. In March 1941, for example, it established a defense coordinator with a mandate to find new defense goods producers, to assist firms in bidding on contracts, to aid firms in purchasing materials, and to help companies construct new production facilities. This flow of information between the government and local institutions (the Reserve, banks, and firms) was vital to the local and national war effort.[55] As Daniel Nelson, the government's small business director, explained in November 1940, the Reserve banks must ensure "that there will be no interruption in the flow of materials due to inadequate financial resources or lack of credit and capital facilities."[56]

Chicago also became a center for coordinating war activities. In October 1939, most federal agencies with regional offices in Chicago represented long-standing, executive branch agencies (Internal Revenue and Immigration and Naturalization) and more recent New Deal agencies (Home Owners' Loan Corporation). War mobilization, however, changed this. After 1940, most New Deal offices in Chicago disappeared or were reduced in size, while several war agencies opened offices. In August 1944, forty-nine federal agencies had Chicago offices compared to only thirty-two in October 1939. Of these, twelve were directly related to war. The employment levels of several others had grown in response to the war effort. Agencies such as the National War Labor Board, the War Manpower Commission, and the Office of Price Administration opened regional offices in the early years of the war.[57]

The number of Washington agencies with Chicago offices expanded enormously after Pearl Harbor. In December 1941, two Chicago realtors went to Washington to assist the transfer of 10,000 workers in twelve federal wartime agencies to other cities, including Chicago. At the same time, five of the thirteen government agencies with more than 3,000 workers were shifted to Chicago.[58] The growing responsibilities of the Chicago Federal Reserve made it necessary to find more working space. In April 1942, the bank took over an additional 6,000 square feet of office space at its La Salle Street building.[59] Five months later, the RFC's Chicago office moved into quarters with 30,000 square feet of floor space. In January 1943, the Office of Decentralization Services employed 3,500 workers in its war accounting bureau on West Adams Street.[60] Chicago had become an important and growing calculative center of wartime administration. As one observer noted, "Chicago is particularly fortunate because all branches of the armed services save one have purchasing and planning offices in the city."[61] Together, the Chicago offices of federal and military agencies linked policies established in Washington with local political and business interests.

The Roosevelt administration's policy of decentralizing office functions helped incorporate Chicago's industrial sites into the national war economy. It quickly became apparent that the awarding of supply and construction contracts could be more effective if it was undertaken at the local rather than the national level. Agencies such as the OPM faced several obstacles to mobilization, such as opposition from industrialists and the military, the need for rapid conversion, industrial bottlenecks, and unclear lines of authority.[62] To overcome these problems and to facilitate the flow of information and resources, the OPM established regional offices in June 1941. Despite some teething problems, the agency and its successor, the WPB, created a new regional organizational structure that stayed in place until the end of the war. Key to the success of this decentralization was the intermingling of personnel from all levels of the state and business. Chicago's office was directed by officials from the OPM, WPB, and "commercial and industrial community of Chicago." This convergence of state and industrial actors at the local level helped integrate Chicago's political and industrial leaders interested in industrial sites into the federal and military bureaucracies.[63]

Other military and federal government procurement agencies established regional offices in Chicago to help coordinate the mobilization of the region's industrial sites. The army, navy, and signal corps, among others, were part of the growing administrative apparatus that coordinated the building and operation of Chicago's factory sites. The Army Air Corps, for example, opened its first fully staffed office outside of Washington in Chicago in March 1942. More than 150 "experts, technicians, engineers, metallurgists, chemists, inspectors, and stenographers were moved to Chicago to perform the huge task" of farming out prime contracts for aircraft parts to local manufacturers. In the words of a *Chicago Tribune* writer, "hundreds of factory owners crowded" the North Wacker offices to provide information about their ability to meet the production needs of the air corps. The IMA and the CAC praised the opening of a local branch by saying that Chicago manufacturers could now meet the demand of government work. Chicago was the central coordinating node of military and civil agencies for the regional economy. Information, capital, and ideas flowed from the city's federal, military, and financial offices to rest of the metropolis and the surrounding region.[64]

The building of Chicago's industrial sites and the supply of production contracts were a direct product of this regional coordinating function. The importance of the procurement agencies for the building of local industrial sites can be illustrated by the Chicago Ordnance District, one of the largest purchasers of war material. Ordnance districts were created by the 1920 National Defense Act with the purpose of building an inventory of possible war manufacturers. Despite the best intentions, the office was unable to create an effective and up-to-date inventory of potential munitions manufacturers in the interwar years. One reason for this was the small size of the office; in 1938 it consisted of an army officer, a civilian, and two stenographers. War changed everything. Two years later the staff exceeded more than 1,400. At the height of the war its administrative numbers totaled close to 5,000. Accordingly, the Chicago Ordnance District was better able to meet the needs of mobilization and to shape the direction and scale of the provision of the region's defense factories.[65]

The Ordnance District oversaw the construction of large specialized plants, the conversion of existing factories, and military solicitation of ordnance material contracts. Ordnance staff were central to the local mobilization process. They incorporated commercial and Federal Reserve bankers, municipal employees, industrialists, military and civil officials, factory engineers, and architects into the effort to build new manufacturing plants and to expand the local war economy. Ordnance worked with local and nonlocal agents to build several factories and to make additions to existing factory space. It was responsible, among other things, for the construction of the massive shell-loading Elwood plant, the building of M-8 and M-20 transportation units with special antimine floors at the local Ford factory, and the production of more than $14 million of ordnance material in an expanded factory at Rheem Manufacturing.[66]

The Chicago Ordnance District consolidated interfirm relations as shown by two cases. Ordnance officers placed a manufacturer of recoil mechanisms, Hannifin Manufacturing, into a sphere of supplier and client relations linked to the war economy. On the one hand, ordnance officers found a firm that had the engineering resources to help Hannifin manufacture a 155-mm gun carriage. On the other, they directed Hannifin to two lucrative markets. The company made pilot mechanisms for the International Harvester's Milwaukee plant and produced recoil mechanisms for howitzers designed and tested by the army at the Rock Island arsenal.[67] The Ordnance office played a similar role for Burgess-Norton, the country's largest wartime maker of tank track bodies, by helping establish the "Burgess-Norton pool." The company "furnished production material and engineering 'knowhow'" for seven other area firms. "In fact about 85% of all American-built tanks were equipped with tank truck bodies built by the Burgess-Norton Pool." It is probably not unconnected that Burgess-Norton's control of the pool and the nation's output of tank track bodies were linked to the fact that the company's president, C. M. Burgess, chaired the Ordnance District's Industry Integration Committee for Tank Tracks. This committee controlled production of components for all tracks produced in the United States.[68]

Chicago's educational institutions were also involved in the building of the wartime industrial economy. The University of Chicago established a defense council under the leadership of its vice-president, Emery T. Filbey, with the intent of acting as a clearinghouse for university defense research. It also established an Institute of Meteorology to provide the military with climatic information and an Institute of Military Studies to offer military officer studies. On the manufacturing front, it worked with other universities (MIT and Purdue), Chicago firms (Galvin Manufacturing, later Motorola), and military units (signal corps) to create and mass-produce radio quartz crystal units. Chicago's vocational schools also joined the war effort by tapping federal appropriations to train workers in defense industrial work. Within fifteen months the city's ten vocational schools had taught twenty-nine thousand workers skills including machine shop practice, aviation manufacture and maintenance techniques, welding, and drafting.[69]

Conclusion

A new set of calculative industrial spaces was assembled in Chicago over the course of the war. A wide range of industrial, political, federal, and military interests worked together to underwrite the militarization of the metropolitan and regional economies and to produce a new set of industrial sites for producing war materials. While this was not without its problems and tensions, local business and political elites did work hand-in-hand with government, industrial, and military leaders in Washington and Springfield to make and implement a series of decisions that resulted in the assembly of an elaborate complex of metropolitan industrial sites. These calculating agents brought the fruits of industrial mobilization to the metropolis and in turn brought Chicago into the war effort. Agents, ranging from ordnance officers, CAC officials, corporate executives, and bankers, coordinated defense activities in Chicago and across the nation, forged industrial networks, and assembled information, contracts, and funding that allowed Chicago to contribute to the war effort.

These calculations reinforced the dominant position of the military-industrial complex in the mobilization of Chicago's militarized industrial space. National, regional, state, and metropolitan interests reframed existing institutions and created new ones during the war. This was not incidental to the practice of war in the metropolis. The institutions that industrialists, financiers, politicians, federal officials, and military officers formed, and the resulting practices and techniques, were not simple by-products of war mobilization. Rather, they were central to war mobilization. Industrial sites were affected accordingly. In the process of mobilizing the institutions, agents from a range of institutions worked on industrial property with several important effects. First, Chicago's industrial base was greatly expanded. Second, new intersecting economic, social, and political relationships were formed that realigned the economic and political networks of Chicago manufacturers at the regional and national scales. Third, the geographic spread of these networks was reworked at various scales as the federal, state, and local actors sorted through the imperatives of war production. Finally, industrial property became an object worked on and shaped by calculating agents in Washington, Chicago, and elsewhere.

CHAPTER 4

Chicago's Wartime Industrial Sites

An array of agents, including federal officials, military officers, industrialists, engineers, lawyers, and politicians, worked to mobilize Chicago's industrial property during the war. These agents did not have equal command over the building of Chicago's industrial space. Calculative power is constituted along class lines. A handful of officials working for the military, government, and corporations across the country controlled the character and delivery of the knowledge, investment, and legislation that shaped the building of Chicago's defense factories. Despite the centralized control of wartime planning, the region's socioeconomic relations were not actions simply "read off" from national and structural forces. The local is not an unarticulated expression of corporate or government calculations administrated from outside. The social relations of place are created by agents working through international, national, regional, and local circumstances. In the case of wartime Chicago, a class-based military-industrial alliance made up of local, regional, and national agents worked to restructure the social relations of property, to build defense plants, and to mobilize Chicago's industry for war.

A coalition consisting of local and national political, industrial, and military leaders used private and public procedural matters, legal forms, and investments to assemble Chicago's war plants. Mobilization agencies established lines of command reaching from Washington to regional offices in Chicago to direct the search for industrial land that would become home to new production facilities and to devise methods to identify factories that could be converted to war production. Government and military officials worked with local businesses to determine which plants had the capacity to accommodate defense contracts. The search for industrial sites and the building and coordination of factory space were framed by legal directives that set out who was involved, what could be done, and where it could be built. These actions established the boundaries of the calculable good—the defense factory, which was subject to specific monetary, procedural, and legal practices. In the process, these formed the limits of a network of calculative actors who constructed a massive body of state-funded manufacturing plants in Chicago.

This chapter examines how investment in defense factories by the leaders of the military-industrial complex refashioned metropolitan Chicago's industrial landscape. Three aspects of the region's wartime industrial property are covered: the private-public relations of defense factory construction; the locational dynamics of wartime investment; and the place-based effects of investment on the Calumet district. A focus on the calculative actions responsible for the construction of Chicago's wartime industrial facilities shows how these factories were embedded in a network of place-based, capitalist relationships. Corporate executives, local politicians and boosters, federal officials, and military officials worked to establish new industrial investment in the metropolitan area. In the process, this spatially structured alliance realigned the industrial geography of metropolitan Chicago between 1940 and 1945 by creating a new set of industrial plants and intensifying the long-term shift of industrial investment away from the city center to the city fringe and surrounding suburbs.

Corporation and Factory Investment

The framing of industrial sites as calculative objects by people employed in the military-industrial complex resulted in the creation of an extensive body of Chicago defense factories between 1940 and 1945. Mobilization agencies channeled more than a $1.5 billion of government funds and certificates of necessity into hundreds of production facilities in Illinois, making it one of the largest recipients of the country's financing of defense plants (Figure 4.1). The billion dollars invested in metropolitan Chicago factories accounted for more than two-thirds of the Illinois amount. More than 1,400 firms received supply contracts valued at $9.8 billion from the military procurement authorities, while other firms subcontracted with nonlocal companies to produce a wide range of wartime products.[1] This construction and supply investment made the Chicago region one of America's major war production hubs. Much of this investment was directly controlled by corporate officials.

A total of $1.38 billion of fixed-capital investment was channeled into 605 Chicago firms during the war. The federal government supplied a substantial share of this investment in new factories and factory additions (Table 4.1). As an indirect government subsidy, 427 plants received private investment through certificates of necessity totaling $195 million, accounting for 14 percent of Chicago's total expenditure. Private investment in Chicago's defense factories was dwarfed by direct federal and military investment in new industrial space. The lion's share came from the Defense Plant Corporation (DPC), the army, and the navy. Forty-nine plants valued at $619 million accounted for 45 percent of the

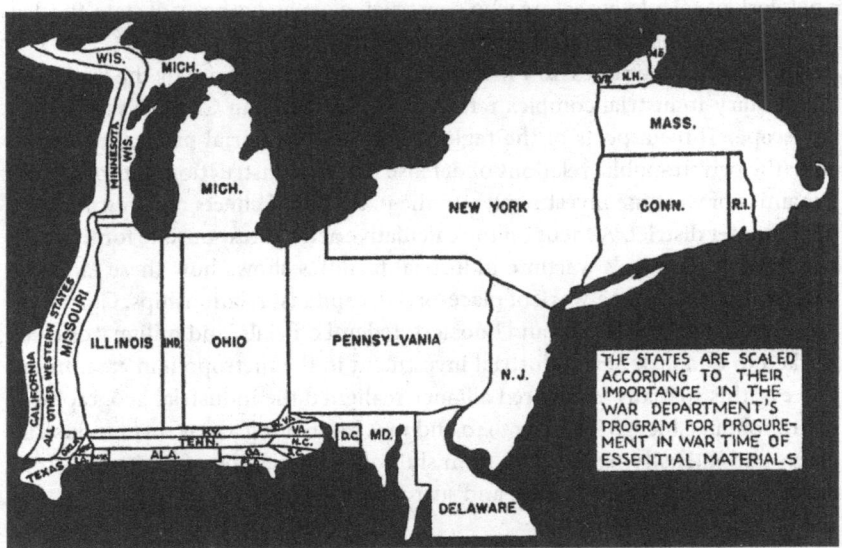

FIGURE 4.1. Regional geography of procurement, 1940. From the very beginning of mobilization the northern industrial states were the nation's major centers for wartime procurement.
Source: Illinois Manufacturers' Association, *Industrial Review* 7 (July 1940): 8.

total received investment from only federal sources. This was almost three times the private-only investment. Another 129 factories received a mix of state and private funding. These industrial facilities accounted for $564 million (or 41 percent) of total investment. Of this mixed funding, two-thirds ($397 million) came from federal agencies, while less than a third ($168 million) came from federally subsidized private sources. Even though state-funded defense plants were outnumbered by factories receiving private investment, nearly three-quarters of the investment (more than $1 billion) in Chicago's manufacturing wartime plants came from direct investment by federal or military agencies.

Federal investment in defense plants was heavily concentrated in a small number of very large factories operated by some of America's leading industrial corporations. The largest forty projects built in Chicago accounted for more than a billion dollars of fixed-capital investment and accounted for 80 percent of Chicago's total capital spending. The largest wartime project was the Dodge-Chrysler airplane engine factory, which cost $182 million. The other thirty-nine investments went to leading corporations in metalworking, transportation, chemicals, electrical equipment, and machine goods. Chicago's new wartime industrial sites were largely operated by blue-chip industrial firms.

Corporate executives as key calculative agents driving mobilization heavily

TABLE 4.1 Wartime factory investment by type and source, Chicago, 1940–1945

	Private only		Public only		Public and private		Total	
Type of investment	No.	$ (000)	No.	$ (000)	No.	$ (000)	No.	$ (000)
Additions to factories	332	174,943	14	30,167	110	535,852	456	740,962
New factory	21	8,994	15	572,381	6	10,570	42	591,945
Equipment only	74	11,073	18	15,530	13	18,534	105	45,137
TOTAL	427	195,010	49	619,023	129	564,956	605	1,378,989

SOURCE: Compiled from War Production Board, *War Manufacturing Facilities Authorized through December 1944 by State and County* (Washington, D.C.: Government Printing Office, 1945). Civilian Production Administration, Industrial Statistics Division, *War Industrial Facilities Authorized, July 1940–August 1945: Listed Alphabetically by Companies and Plant Location* (Washington, D.C.: Government Printing Office, 1946).
NOTE: The totals do not tally, as the type of investment undertaken at two public projects valued at $945,000 cannot be determined.

influenced which firms would receive government investment. Working with mobilization agencies such as the DPC and the Army and Navy Munitions Board (ANMB), corporate executives scanned the locational options across the country and made decisions about where to locate new investment. Chicago business and political leaders worked to attract the interest of corporate executives in a local location. For corporations already located in the region, such as Western Electric and the steel companies, the decision was whether or not to operate an entirely new factory or to build an addition to an existing facility. Corporations with no factories in the metropolitan area, such as Douglas Aircraft, faced a similar situation: Where would they operate a manufacturing plant in Chicago, or did other locations have better industrial sites?

Once they had determined that they would operate a government-funded industrial facility in Chicago, corporate executives worked with local government to scan the region's locational options. Local support was forthcoming, especially for national corporations seeking new sites. The two airplane engine makers, Dodge and Studebaker, for example, lauded the "complete cooperation and assistance from public officials, leaders in education, who are being asked to help in employe [*sic*] training programs, representatives of labor, other key elements in the community, and for the Chicago Association of Commerce, which worked actively to have the plants located here, were also favorably commented upon in connection with the announcements."[2] Similarly, local governments assisted with the building of defense factory infrastructures. The visible hand of the government and military cooperated with the less visible hand of private capital to build Chicago's wartime industrial landscape.

Corporate executives worked with local, military, and federal agencies to build new industrial sites. These agencies maintained downtown offices where, among other things, they signed off on supply and construction awards, undertook surveys of plant capacity and labor availability, and sought industrial sites for new wartime facilities. In the winter of 1940, the procurement branches of the ordnance, quartermaster, signal, and medical corps undertook a survey of the productive capacity of Chicago firms. From this they determined assignment of specific items by firm. The survey also worked out the need for new productive capacity, and this became the basis for the region's construction of defense plants.[3] From Chicago's Loop, civil and military bureaucracies reached out across the metropolis, monitoring industrial activity, assessing industrial sites, letting out contracts, and advising industrial executives.[4]

Military officials were heavily involved in local mobilization. They worked hand-in-hand with Chicago's two leading business organizations, the Illinois Manufacturers' Association (IMA) and the Chicago Association of Commerce (CAC) to promote industrial expansion and the building of new factories. The chief of the Chicago Ordnance District cochaired the state-run Committee of National Defense, which oversaw mobilization programs. The military participated in workshops, lectures, and other programs. These industry-military relations remained the main forum through which industry, the civil state, and the military scanned the metropolis and determined how to mobilize Chicago's industrial sites for the war effort. Along with its participation in the planning, surveying, and evaluation of Chicago's production landscape, the military had a daily presence in the metropolitan area's factories. The navy alone had at least 213 high-ranking personnel working directly and indirectly with industry. Most of these were located in offices in the city's business district offices, but at least 60 worked in industrial plants scattered across the metropolitan area. Naval officers also worked alongside researchers at educational institutions, including the University of Chicago, Northwestern, and Loyola.[5]

The unprecedented scale and scope of the navy's presence in the metropolitan area was part of the broader intervention of the military and the civil state into numerous aspects of everyday life, including industrial administration, university research, and municipal governance. The economic regime centered on the interaction of the civil government, the military, and business required ongoing control and monitoring of capitalist industrial spaces. Wartime mobilization forced local business and political leaders to rethink the management of the local economy and company business plans. Gearing up for war required calculating the place of the industrial property in industrial matters.

New Factories and New Additions

Forty-two entirely new factories costing almost $600 million were built in metropolitan Chicago during the war. In some cases, these were small annexes for existing firms to build dedicated wartime products, such as the Chicago gauge factory operated by R. Krassberg or CP Hall's para-flux factory in the industrial district of Clearing. In other cases, they were among the largest factory complexes in the United States, many of which were located outside the central city (Figure 4.2). Most of the funds for these mainly corporate-operated factories came from the federal government and the military and were spent on sprawling sites on the edge of the city or in the suburbs, such as the $48 million Douglas Aircraft assembly plant in suburban Park Ridge financed by the War Department (Figure 4.3).

The calculative politics behind the construction of the large, federally funded, corporate-operated factory specifically built for defense needs can be illustrated by the Dodge-Chrysler plant, which built B-29 Superfortress bomber engines. By mid-1941 the military decision to quickly expand bomber production required three main calculations. First, who would assemble the plane? After a great deal of consultation a joint-manufacturing team led by Boeing, the designer of the B-29, was chosen.[6] A second calculation was to determine the best engine for the bomber and who would manufacture it. After looking at several options, the government selected the Wright R-3350 engine. It quickly became clear to Wright and its military advisers that successful production of the engine required teaming up with another company. Searching through the corporate alternatives, Wright and military procurement officials gave the contract to Chrysler to build the engines in an entirely new factory. The military procurement agencies favored large firms and the construction of new factories over small firms and the conversion of old industrial facilities. Although there were many reasons why this was the case, the main ones were that it was much easier to work with established firms that had technical expertise, financial and managerial skills, trained workers, and established links with existing firms. New manufacturing plants could be constructed much more quickly and with less trouble on greenfield sites and were easier to furnish with machinery and equipment than existing plants, which were geared to other products and production processes.[7]

The final calculation had to do with where Chrysler would build the engines. Based on an assessment of potential bomber sites, the final choices reflected existing industrial networks and government locational directives.[8] Although some bomber engines were already being built at Woodbridge, it became necessary to find another location, given the New Jersey plant's inability to meet demand. The army scanned the continent for suitable locations, especially in the interior away from the vulnerable coastline and close to the assembly plants (Omaha; Wichita; Marietta, Georgia; and Renton, Washington). After crossing off various options, the choice was finally narrowed down to two cities close to the center of Chrysler's empire, Milwaukee and Chicago.

The two cities entered a bidding war. In a letter to Robert Lovett, the assistant secretary of war for air, Mayor Edward Kelly laid out the argument why Chicago

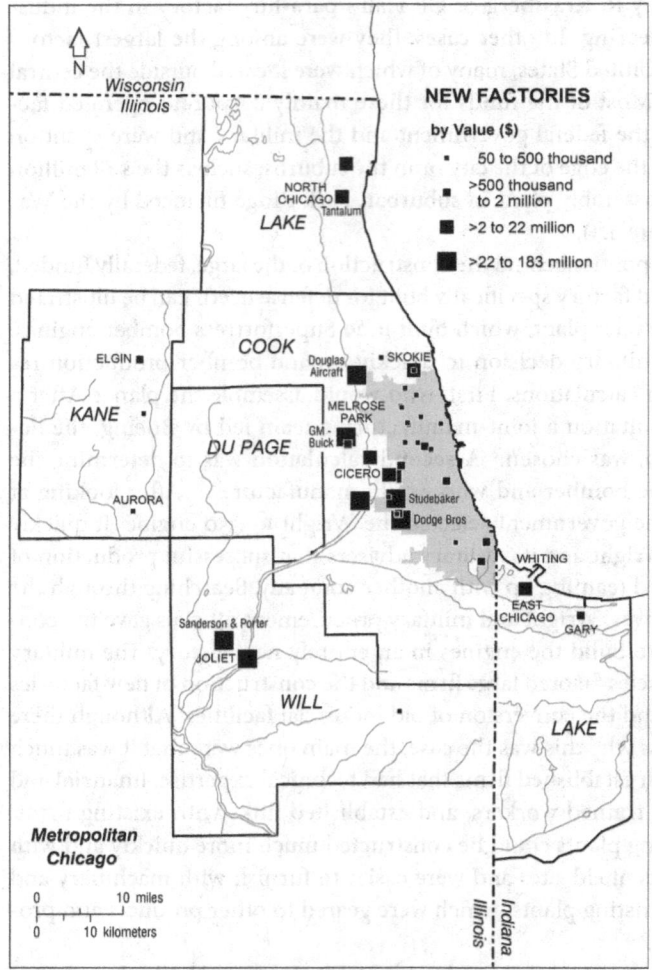

FIGURE 4.2. New defense factories, Chicago, 1940–1945. Most of metropolitan Chicago's forty-two new defense factories were built on the city fringe and in the suburbs.
Source: Material compiled by the author. Map drawn by Bryon Moldofsky.

FIGURE 4.3. Douglas Aircraft assembly plant, 1944. The Douglas assembly plant and airfield was just one of several large government and military production sites built on the metropolitan fringe during the war.
Source: O'Hare Collection, Bensenville Community Public Library.

was the best place for the new factory. The region was both an efficient and safe production center. Far from the vulnerable coastline, the B-29 engines could be built in a city with a range of locational assets without fear of attack. Kelly also provided Lovett with information about four potential sites for the new plant. All of them were in the suburbs or on the city's fringe. Kelly sent a letter, maps of the four sites, a map of industrial areas, and a reference volume about Chicago to Donald Nelson, chair of the War Production Board (WPB). The combination of Chicago's pool of technical abilities, locational assets, and labor supply and Kelly's booster campaign convinced procurement officials that the Windy City was the best choice.[9]

The Dodge plant was enormous. The finished facilities consisted of more than 6.4 million square feet of floor space, nineteen building complexes, and approximately ten thousand machine tools. The factory employed 28,500 workers in late 1944. Construction started in June 1942 and was completed fifteen months later. The cost of the land, buildings, equipment, and machinery came to more than $180 million, making it Chicago's largest new wartime factory.[10]

Indeed, it was so large that the main machining and assembly shop, which covered almost four million square feet of floor space, was broken into seven distinct divisions "each with its own manager, master mechanic, chief inspector and so on down the line, as if each were a separate plant."[11] When it shipped its last engine in August 1945, the factory had delivered 18,413 engines to the four bomber plants.

The selection of Chicago as the place to manufacture the B-29 bomber engines set in train a number of decisions by the aircraft, engine, and automobile companies, the air force, mobilization agencies, and local government that transformed a corner of the city's southwest fringe into a massive industrial site and resulted in the building of one of the world's largest industrial complexes. The building of such an enormous industrial facility required decisions about site, design, product, production process, labor supply, and subcontracting by assorted civil, military, and industrial actors in Washington; Detroit; Paterson, New Jersey; and elsewhere. For it to be successful, however, the theoretical, policy, and military calculations undertaken by nonlocal agents had to be filtered and translated by local agents.

The preparation of the site involved negotiations between local and national officials. Among other things, they approved a contract between the city, the DPC, and Chrysler for the construction of a three-mile, thirty-six-inch water pipe at a cost $562,000, of which $450,000 was covered by the DPC, with the city paying the remainder. The city also passed an ordinance closing off ten miles of streets in order to create an industrial "superblock" site, made engineering tests to determine the site's geological weaknesses, changed the city's zoning regulations to allow manufacturing, and provided bus service for the workers.[12] At the same time, choices had to be made about the architect and builder. With the army's approval, Chrysler turned to Albert Kahn, who had built many of the iconic interwar modernist corporate factories. As one city observer noted, the success of the factory's construction was "largely attributable to the teamwork that has existed between the company officials and the Army Air Force Materiel Command."[13]

Dodge production engineers and managers developed close relations with their counterparts from Wright, the military, federal mobilization agencies, and corporations across the country (Figure 4.4). Dodge and Wright engineers brought their technological knowledge to large-volume engine and airplane engine production, respectively. Military engineers consulted with the engineering personnel of the George A. Fuller Company, which had the contract to build the factory. Many of the parts that went into the engines were supplied by subcontractors. Federal and industrial factory designers calculated what materials to use and which contractors to employ. Technological relationships were forged: company lawyers, engineers, and executives, for example, negotiated with the New York–based Sperry Gyroscope to license the manufacture of

FIGURE 4.4. Aircraft production networks. Dodge was part of an extensive production network system that stretched across industries and spanned the country.
Source: Public Information Program, National Association of Manufacturers.

gyro-compasses at the Chicago plant. At the same time, "thousands of major and minor subcontractors" supplied the Dodge plant with raw materials, tens of thousands of finished and semifinished parts, and subassemblies.[14] Together, this elaborate calculative network transformed a wetland on the city's edge into a modern industrial site built and operated by large corporations.

The calculations that government, military, and industrial officials made about war demand, plant capacity, producer networks and so forth shaped what sort of factory spaces should be built. As just described, the state channeled a huge amount of investment to a small number of very large new defense factories. In older industries with established capacity, the investment in industrial space generally took a different form—the addition to an existing factory. There were three types. A privately financed addition to a factory authorized by a certificate of necessity allowed the company to invest private capital in an addition and to depreciate the construction costs over five years. In a second type of investment, the state or private sources funded an addition built adjacent to a company's property that functioned as an adjunct to an existing production complex. In both cases, the state's role was important, but the scale of its investment was relatively minimal. This was especially the case with certificates of necessity, as they required very little state-industry interaction once the military or federal agency granted authorization. Both of these are in contrast to the final type: the publicly financed addition on the property of a private industrial company (a scrambled plant). In all cases, unlike new factories, additions were heavily concentrated in the central city (Figure 4.5).

Certificates of necessity allowed firms to make private additions to their factories. By the middle of 1940, the federal government was seeking ways to compel private firms to invest in war production while trying to balance the demand for scarce resources. The 1940 Revenue Act allowed firms receiving army and navy war contracts to amortize new construction over a five-year period rather than the typical twenty years. To take advantage of this, firms had to obtain a certificate of necessity from the government agency funding the war contract.[15] The certificates allowed the government to operate from a distance, permitting firms to function as they had always done, investing their own capital to build up capacity. This was a two-pronged calculative decision, with firms having to decide to convert to war production and to expand capacity, and the military and civil state bureaucracies having to identify suitable firms for both the war contracts and the construction certificates. In both cases, judgment and evaluation were necessary components of the calculative action.

Chicago manufacturers looking to expand their factories used certificates of necessity to drum up private capital.[16] During this time, 306 Chicago firms used certificates valued at $42.6 million to increase their manufacturing capacity. Most invested small amounts. The Standard Railway Equipment Company in the industrial suburb of Hammond built a $35,000 addition to help manufacture landing craft. W. C. Ritchie added a $51,000 shell casing manufacturing addition to its South Side factory. A few firms used certificates to invest heavily in new facilities. Carnegie Steel added new capacity valued at almost $7 million to its Chicago and Joliet mills in order to produce steel ingots and rods. Diamond T Motor spent $1.2 million to produce vehicles at its Chicago West Side plant.

Certificates of necessity were an indirect means to entice firms such as Ritchie and Carnegie Steel to undertake war work and to finance new production facilities; they were not a financial instrument by which the federal government was directly involved in financially underwriting new industrial plants. This required ongoing interaction between industrial executives, military officers, and federal officials. As local manufacturers had little experience working with the public sector, the CAC officiated between government technocrats and private businesspeople. Association committees such as the War Problem School and the War Problem Service allowed government officials to provide advice and to answer "highly technical questions in a very specific way." As such, industrialists learned how to take advantage of state largess by obtaining access to munition contracts and construction awards.[17]

Standard Railway's decision to build its small addition, for example, rested on decisions by mobilization agencies and the ANMB about the number of landing craft to be built, the prospective producers, the ability of the Hammond firm to build the craft, and the allocation of scarce construction materials to the

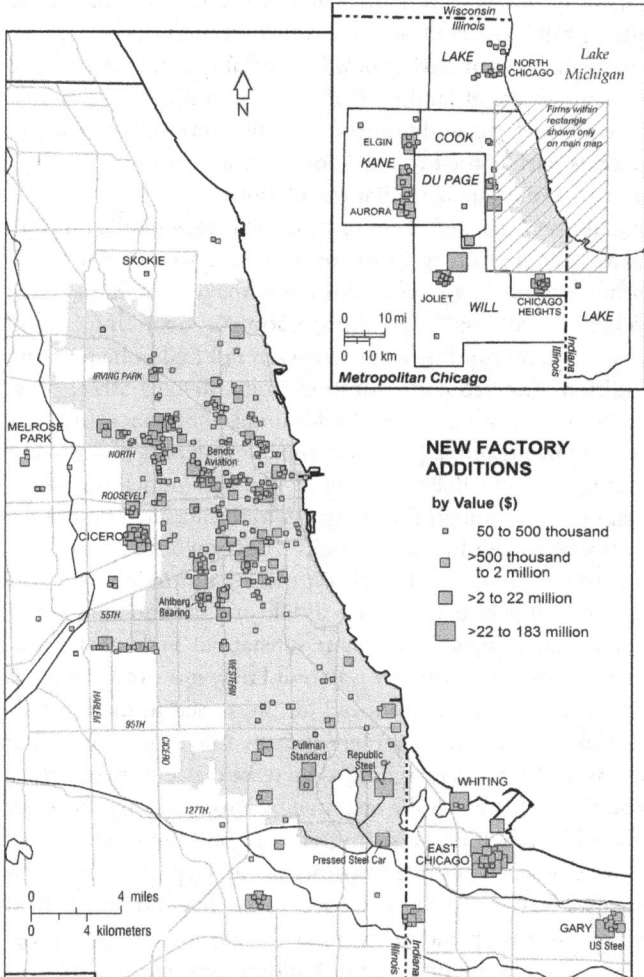

FIGURE 4.5. Factory additions for war purposes, Chicago, 1940–1945. Even though additions to existing industrial space for wartime production were scattered across the metropolitan region, most factory additions were concentrated in the city of Chicago. Source: Material compiled by the author. Maps drawn by Bryon Moldofsky.

addition. Standard Railway, on the other hand, had to consider questions about their technical ability to fulfill the contract, the availability of skilled workers, and the long-term consequences of having new industrial space. In the case of Standard Railway's manufacture of landing craft, federal, military, and industrial agents made procedural, legal, and monetary calculations that operated to frame industrial space as part of the broader mobilization process. It was not alone. Hundreds of firms had to make similar calculations.

A second type of addition consisted of committing private or public funds to building adjacent to an existing factory. Most cost less than $500,000 to build. Borg-Warner, for example, built a $400,000 addition to make 1.5 million clutch units for military vehicles, 2 million fuses, and 150,000 gun operating cranks. The company also used federal funding to produce aircraft hydraulic pressure pumps in a new addition. The $266,000 addition to its Menard Street plant provided the firm with 43,000 square feet of additional floor space and new machinery to make aircraft piston rings. The company was part of a pool of assembly firms—Boeing Airplane, Bellanca Aircraft, and McDonnell Aircraft—building the AT-15 plane. Even though the contracts were cancelled before the factory went into production, the addition was built. The company also received a $3.8 million contract for clutches, while subcontracting out to War Department ordnance plants as well private firms such as Oldsmobile and Dodge.[18]

A small number of the adjacent additions were substantial. Federal and military mobilization agencies worked with firms to build new industrial capacity. After 1940, for example, Kropp Forge produced forgings used in planes, ordnance, tanks, ships, and vehicles for customers such as Cleveland Pneumatic and Eastern Aircraft. As the firm was unwilling to increase capacity, the military decided to fund an addition that would be operated by Kropp during the war.[19] The result was a $2.5 million factory consisting of eight buildings with 78,758 square feet of floor space on 8.7 acres of government land. Capacity expansion increased the company's wartime drop forging capacity fivefold and helped double sales.[20] In the case of Kropp and many other Chicago firms, the government and the military were heavily involved in building new nonprivate production space that was operated by private companies. Kropp faced the same calculative situation as that of Standard Railway and the mobilization agencies, but with the added complication of the federal government's direct intervention in the functioning of a private company and ownership of industrial property.

The final type of additions—scrambled plants—involved the building of federally owned manufacturing facilities and machinery on the property of private firms. Scrambled projects were an extension of the government's relationship with private industry. The War Assets Administration (WAA) defined a scrambled facility as "government-owned personal property located on or used as an integral part for the operation of a private plant." As a production unit embedded within the property lines of an existing firm, the scrambled addition could not be "operated independently on an economic basis."²¹ To be successful, the government-owned factory had to be functionally integrated with the private facilities. The government built scrambled buildings for several reasons. Along with speed of construction, it was "motivated by such considerations as conservation of critical materials, manpower and advantages incidental to the utilization of experienced management and labor."²² The need for rapid mobilization and material conservation forced the state to assume responsibilities it would not have taken in other circumstances. There was no established policy for taking such a course of action. Events of the day forced the various funding agencies—most notably the army, navy, and the DPC—to interweave state-owned facilities with private ones.

It is impossible to determine how much war-related work was undertaken in scrambled facilities, as the records do not provide precise information about where an addition or new factory was constructed. Many federal projects in Chicago took the form of new plants or additions adjacent to existing factories on federally owned land. In these cases, property rights were clearly distinct. That is, they were unscrambled. In others, however, the line between state-owned property and privately owned property was not so clear. Some of the federally funded additions were constructed on land owned by a private company, while other buildings were tightly integrated into industrial plants. In all of its different forms, the scrambled site became an item of intense scrutiny, definition, and analysis. As such, it opened up a different set of possibilities for the everyday relations between the federal government, the military, and industry. Scrambled plants blurred the clear state-private divide and forced the federal government to incorporate itself even more deeply into the working of private enterprise.

Most Chicago scrambled sites were small. Gaertner Scientific, for example, built a second-story addition to its scientific equipment facility, filling it with company-owned machinery as well as with machinery bought from DPC funds totaling $43,000.²³ In the case of Stauffer Chemical, the DPC funded manufacturing facilities valued at three-quarters of a million dollars on an acre of land owned by the company at its Hammond plant. The addition was authorized to augment the company's capacity of sulfuric acid for the manufacture of TNT. As it was a scrambled plant, acid making at the state-owned additions was dependent on the company's sulfuric pit, power facilities, and storage.²⁴

Federal intervention into industrial production took several forms, ranging from state-financed independent factories to the building of small additions with funds taken from certificates of necessity. In some cases, expenditures were minimal, while in others they were huge. Small additions tacked onto existing facilities coexisted alongside some of the world's largest industrial complexes. Large-scale federal investment in Chicago's factory sites refashioned the region's industrial relations of space. Federal involvement in building defense factories was only one possible response to wartime conditions. Indeed, the history of mobilization during World War I and the interwar years suggested that federal involvement would be minimal at best; this turned out not to be the case for World War II. Rather, Roosevelt's administration calculated that it had to directly intervene in industrial mobilization, and in a significant manner. One form this calculated intervention took was indirect and direct financing of manufacturing plants. The production of wartime munitions required massive government investment in new industrial facilities. The result was that urban centers across the country became the home to a mixed form of property and fixed-capital ownership.

Locating Manufacturing Space

The construction of wartime factory space both reproduced and changed the existing distribution of the region's factories. The work on the industrial geography of metropolitan districts has been inconclusive. Some writers argue that it changed very little and that most wartime employment continued to be found in the central city. The clearest statement of this comes from Coleman Woodbury and Frank Cliffe: "The net effect of the war years in the distribution of production workers in manufacturing was very slight." In their opinion, the expansion of wartime production resulted from utilization of existing capacity and by additions to existing factories. Federal officials, military officers, and factory managers were compelled by the exigencies of wartime conditions to build most industrial facilities in established industrial districts. In this view, the metropolitan geography of wartime production "was determined by the prewar pattern of industrial location" because of the effects of industrial agglomeration.[25]

Other writers take an opposite position. Philip Funigiello states that firms left "old manufacturing sites within the central business district for undeveloped, less heavily taxed suburban locations." Similarly, Arnold Silverman argues that investment spurred suburban industrial growth. Perry Duis believes that large-scale industrial decentralization in Chicago resulted from the opening of large wartime production facilities on the metropolitan fringe.[26] Even though these authors provide different reasons for why this happened, the common theme is that the concentration of federal investment in suburban manufacturing facilities was the key feature of metropolitan industrial geography. The suburbanization of production was the defining geographic impact of wartime investment. This section shows that the city fringe and metropolitan suburbs received a vast amount of federal investment in wartime plants, while the older manufacturing districts of the city center received very little new investment.

Evidence from eighteen metropolitan areas on the impact of investment in defense factories supports both sides (Table 4.2).[27] A sizeable share of the nation's fixed-capital investment in manufacturing plants went to central-city

TABLE 4.2 Suburban share of industrial fixed-capital investment in eighteen metropolitan areas

Metropolitan Area	Wartime fixed capital (thousands of dollars)	Suburban share of fixed capital (percentage)	Suburban share of 1939 wage earners (percentage)	Suburban index (capital ÷ wage earners)
Pittsburgh	556,509	86.6	77.3	1.12
San Francisco	437,500	84.3	58.6	1.43
Los Angeles	732,732	77.9	37.2	2.09
Cincinnati	283,397	74.8	39.5	1.89
Buffalo	411,780	64.1	49.8	1.29
New York	1,088,970	64.0	41.4	1.54
Philadelphia	797,841	57.6	39.0	1.48
Chicago	1,378,989	56.9	28.1	2.02
Youngstown	140,745	54.3	62.9	0.91
St. Louis	535,594	53.0	30.1	1.76
Akron	169,494	52.4	23.8	2.20
Detroit	980,406	47.7	42.3	1.13
Houston	507,586	41.2	39.7	1.03
Cleveland	481,836	38.4	22.5	1.71
Dallas–Fort Worth	124,657	34.0	15.3	2.22
Rochester	66,505	1.1	6.7	0.16
Indianapolis	216,863	0.1	8.1	0.01
Toledo	103,895	0	9.1	0

SOURCE: Compiled from War Production Board, War Manufacturing Facilities Authorized through December 1944 by State and County (Washington, D.C.: Government Printing Office, 1945); Civilian Production Administration, Industrial Statistics Division, War Industrial Facilities Authorized, July 1940–August 1945: Listed Alphabetically by Companies and Plant Location (Washington, D.C.: Government Printing Office, 1946).

sites—$3.8 billion of the total of $9 billion (42 percent). In a few cities a significant amount of the metropolitan total went to central factories. In Rochester, most construction awards went to Eastman-Kodak and a few specialized instrument firms. These firms received federal monies to expand their downtown factories to make photographic materials (film, chemicals, and paper) and airplane parts (instruments and lenses). Similarly, a significant share of Cleveland's expenditures went to machinery, metalworking, and electrical appliance factories in the central city, while fifty downtown Toledo firms made, among other things, tank transmissions, plane parts, and chemicals for the DPC, the War Department, the navy, and the Ordnance Department in state-financed additions.

In most cases, however, central cities received a lower share of the metropolitan investment during the war than would be expected given their prewar prominence. This is shown by an index comparing the city/suburb distribution of fixed capital with the 1939 distribution of wage earners.[28] A score of more than 1.0 indicates that the share of suburban fixed capital during the war was greater than what would be expected given the 1939 distribution of wage earners. Only four places (Youngstown, Rochester, Indianapolis, and Toledo) had an index of less than 1, which signified high levels of central-city investment between 1940 and 1945 compared to 1939. Investment in downtown factories was important in only a handful of metropolitan areas.

The evidence for the eighteen districts shows that industrial suburbs were the major recipients of wartime factory investment. The more than $5 billion invested in the suburbs accounted for 58 percent of the total. The creation of new factory complexes, the additions made to existing manufacturing plants, and the installation of new machinery and equipment underwrote the development of the metropolitan fringe as the wartime's main production center. Adjacent suburbs and satellite cities had much higher rates of investment than would be expected given the 1939 industrial employment structure. In some cases, most notably Pittsburgh, San Francisco, Los Angeles, and Cincinnati, at least three quarters of factory investment was located outside of the central city. In all four cases, this was much higher than would have been expected given the prewar distribution of wage earners.

Los Angeles illustrates this point. Two-thirds of its manufacturing employment was found in the city in 1939 despite its reputation as a place dominated by suburbs. During the war, however, military and industrial officials channeled more than three-quarters of all metropolitan fixed-capital investment into suburban factories. The result was that wartime suburban investment occurred at more than two times what would be expected given 1939 production employment. Large aircraft plants such as Lockheed (Burbank), Consolidated Vultee (Downey), and North American Aviation (Inglewood) were particularly likely to be opened up or greatly expanded in the suburbs. Some companies had more than one factory in the suburbs. Of the six Los Angeles aircraft plants operated by Douglas during the war, five were located in the suburban districts of El Segundo, Long Beach, South Gate, Pasadena, and Santa Monica.

Los Angeles was not unusual. In Cincinnati, new facilities and additions to existing factories manufactured aircraft engines, airplanes, machinery, ordnance, ingots, and castings in suburban Lockland, Norwood, Hamilton, Middletown, Mariemont, Newport, and Cheviot. Outside of Pittsburgh, a mix of private and federal money went into factories that made an array of steel products, from pig iron (Jones and Laughlin at Aliquippa) to copper steel wire (Copperweld at Glassport), steel sheets (Carnegie at McKeesport), and tank armor (Continental Foundry at Coraopolis). Other factories were new. The Aluminum Company of America manufactured forgings at the new $27 million plant it operated in Canonsburg, while Koppers United operated a new $60 million butadiene plant in Monaca. Metropolitan Pittsburgh's suburbs and surrounding towns produced a disproportionate range and quantity of products in federally funded wartime factories. The same is true for most major metropolitan areas.

The dominance of the suburbs is not the end of the story though. Some writers argue that neither the city core nor the suburbs were the most important recipients of wartime manufacturing plants. Rather, according to John Kain, most manufacturing expenditure was to be found "within" the central city's "legal boundaries." In his view, the city fringe was the primary recipient of wartime fixed-capital investment.[29] Kain's argument that the city fringe played a significant role in the expansion of wartime plants has purchase. While it is beyond the scope of this study to look at the detailed geography of defense factories in the eighteen metropolitan districts, an examination of 562 Chicago firms provides a more precise locational analysis of wartime industrial expansion.

The evidence for three geographic zones—suburbs, city center, and city fringe—supports all three perspectives. Rather than a simple expansion of the central city or the suburbs, Chicago's geography of wartime manufacturing plants was complex (Table 4.3). The evidence reinforces the earlier point about the importance of the metropolitan suburbs and the satellite towns as the key area for new factory space: $785 million of the $1.37 million (58 percent) of defense investment went to industrial sites outside central-city boundaries. The remaining $580 million (42 percent of the metropolitan total) went to the city's industrial sites. A different picture emerges if we divide the city of Chicago into two zones: the city center and the city fringe. The central zone accounted for only 7 percent of the investment in new facilities, while the city fringe zone accounted for 36 percent. Although smaller than the suburbs, investment on the city fringe was significant. The main investment areas for new factories and additions were Chicago's suburbs and city fringe. The older districts of the central city received an insignificant share of federal spending on wartime industrial facilities.

Capital investment was unevenly distribution through the metropolis (Figure 4.6). All of the region's zones received additions. Even though there was variation, firms in existing industrial districts used federal funding to make additions to, remodel, and renovate old factory space. Additions were uniformly dispersed across the metropolis in terms of the number of projects, but the suburbs and fringe accounted for a larger share of the amount of investment than did the city center—most new plant investment was found in the suburbs.[30] Some of the country's largest new war plants, such as the Dodge and Studebaker engine factories, were located on the city's fringe. New suburban manufacturing plants tended to be located in greenfield sites. Of the twenty-one new suburban facilities, only two were in the older industrial areas of the Calumet (Gary and East Chicago). Most were found in satellite cities with a long but not dominant industrial legacy (Elgin, Joliet, Aurora, St. Charles, and Bellwood) and in entirely new areas (Lincolnwood, North Chicago, Morton Grove, Skokie, and Park Ridge).

One new suburban factory was the Tantalum plant in North Chicago. Fac-

TABLE 4.3 Wartime investment by zone in Chicago, 1940–1945

Investment by type	Metropolitan area No.	Metropolitan area Millions of dollars	City center No.	City center Millions of dollars	City fringe No.	City fringe Millions of dollars	Suburb No.	Suburb Millions of dollars
Equipment only	86	41.6	33	10.0	27	14.1	26	17.5
Additions	434	732.1	151	82.8	144	258.2	139	391.0
New factories	42	591.9	7	1.7	15	214.0	20	376.3
TOTAL	562	1,365.6	191	94.5	186	486.3	185	784.8

SOURCE: Compiled from War Production Board, War Manufacturing Facilities Authorized through December 1944 by State and County (Washington, D.C.: Government Printing Office, 1945); Civilian Production Administration, War Industrial Facilities Authorized, July 1940–August 1945: Listed Alphabetically by Companies and Plant Location (Washington, D.C.: Government Printing Office, 1946).
NOTE: An address could not be found for 43 projects valued at $12.4 million.

tory construction was mobilized by wartime needs centering on a product (tantalum) and a new industry (electronics). It was operated by Fansteel Metallurgical, which had a plant in North Chicago making ignition coils for the infant auto industry. In order to eliminate costly platinum vibrator points, the company experimented with tungsten, which eventually led to working on tantalum, a rare metal highly resistant to corrosion and an efficient heat conductor. Wartime production of tantalum took on a new importance after 1940 because of its use in electronic equipment. The DPC sponsored the building of a specialized factory to produce the commodity. The costs of the North Chicago plant, America's only tantalum plant, came to more than $5.3 million.[31]

The government and military reliance on existing firms and corporate practices had a twofold impact. First, there was little change to the existing geography of metropolitan manufacturing. Few new firms were established, and capital was invested in existing central-city and suburban factory districts. However, and this is the second point, wartime investment deepened uneven patterns of industrial growth within the region. This resulted from the uneven distribution of wartime capital investment: the city fringe and suburbs received the lion's share of investment, while the expansion of central-area production occurred mainly through small amounts of investment authorized by certificates of necessity. The exigencies of war and rapid federal investment accelerated large investment flows into the suburbs and urban fringe. Economic restructuring during the war relied on a level of state intervention never experienced previously, and this resulted in different metropolitan geographies. New factories, which were almost entirely state funded (sometimes in cooperation with corporate interests), were almost entirely to be found in the city fringe or in the suburbs.

The development of the state-funded city fringe and suburbs and a privately

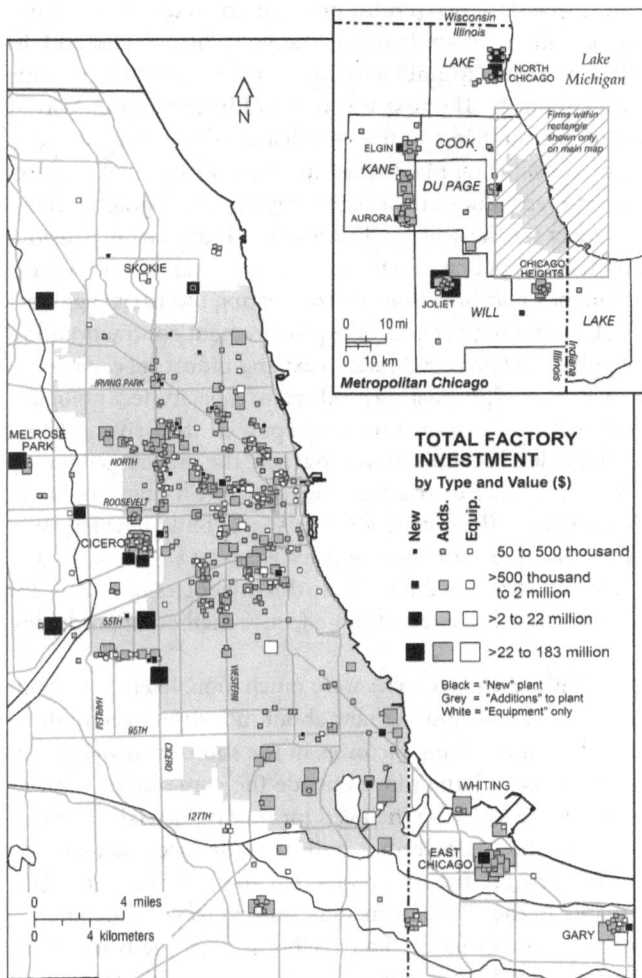

FIGURE 4.6. Total investment in defense factories, Chicago, 1940–1945. A large number of new and old factories in Chicago and the adjacent suburbs produced a wide assortment of war goods.
Source: Material compiled by the author. Maps drawn by Bryon Moldofsky.

funded center was an inadvertent geography, one constructed out of the necessity of wartime mobilization. The military state sought the quickest and, in their terms, most effective means to militarize metropolitan production. This consisted of two main strategies. The first was to build in existing industrial districts. By authorizing private firms to use certificates of necessity to make additions to existing manufacturing plants they funneled investment into existing factory districts and reproduced the existing industrial geography. There was no centralized strategy for the scale and location of industrial expansion, and the translation of national policy into the local setting was ad hoc and inadvertent. The government's plan was to mobilize existing industrial agglomerative dynamics to entice existing firms to take procurement contracts and to use a combination of public and private capital to expand industrial capacity. A firm's ability to take advantage of preexisting production capacity, technological expertise, supplier networks, and labor force underpinned the drive to bring private industry into the federal mobilization program. The prewar geography of industry ensured that the central districts of cities such as Chicago would become a focus of such a strategy. The second strategy was to build new federally financed factories. This was necessary because private capital was unwilling to risk scarce funds in new industrial facilities, while the exigencies of war meant that building plants was the most cost- and time-effective method of producing armaments.

In either case, new additions and factories were much more likely to be built outside of the city core. There was nothing new about industrial decentralization. Manufacturers had been installing factories in the suburbs in significant numbers for one hundred years.[32] The move outside the core during the war continued a long-term trend. Driven by the need for new industrial space and quick turnaround, military-industrial leaders built state-financed factories on vacant land on the urban fringe. The result was that "the locational tendencies of the new war plants in the Chicago area are serving to weld together as well as greatly augment the arc of industrial development on the rim of Chicago."[33] Even though most capital investment was outside of the region's central districts, much of the expenditure on defense factories took place in existing industrial districts on the city fringe and in the suburbs. In the process, they shaped the nature of specific industrial districts, as the next section shows.

The Calumet District: Assembling an Industrial District

The Calumet district provides a glimpse into the dynamics that produced the inadvertent industrial geography of wartime America. By 1940 the Calumet was one of the country's premier manufacturing areas. It contained some of Chicago's largest factories as well as many smaller firms. It was one of the country's major steel districts and was home to U.S. Steel, Republic Steel, Youngstown Sheet and Tube, and Inland Steel. The Calumet's extensive interfirm linkages connected it to firms and institutions elsewhere in the region and the United States. It encompassed a substantial portion of the southern section of the city and a number of independent adjacent municipalities, including Gary, East Chicago, Hammond, and Harvey.[34] It experienced dramatic wartime growth. By 1945 more than a hundred firms were operating industrial sites that received close to half a billion dollars of wartime fixed-capital investment, a third of metropolitan Chicago's total. The Calumet was a wartime industrial powerhouse.

The district's wartime prominence rested on situating the Calumet as a place of public investment by military and industrial officials. District elites sought to take advantage of the government's framing of the industrial site as an investment object for the government and the military. Accordingly, the district became of interest to those working in mobilization agencies and to those involved in local industrial and political issues. A 1942 study by Charles Blessing and Harold Mayer provides a window into the local opinions about how to link federal funds with Calumet industrial property.[35] Blessing had planning degrees from Colorado and MIT. Mayer's dissertation from the University of Chicago was on the city's railway pattern, and he had published on Chicago's zoning, business centers, and residential areas. The aim of their report was twofold: to make sense of the rapid expansion of industry after 1940 and to ensure that the Calumet received a substantial share of the resources flowing from the mobilization agencies.[36] After consulting with district elites, Blessing and Mayer made a survey of the region and laid out the "groundwork ... for a scientific, comprehensive, workable development plan."[37]

To deal with the issue of industrial sites, Blessing and Mayer followed Lyon and Querl's strategy of placing locational factors at the center of the district's wartime development. Nearly two-thirds of the report set out the Calumet's locational assets and how these would allow the district to attract manufacturing investment and supply contracts.[38] The list mentioned many of the assets that Chicago's boosters had long trumpeted: raw materials, transportation, labor, housing, and zoned industrial land. But there was more. The authors also spoke of the district's special advantages for war work. Three were deemed critical. In the first place, the region's inland location protected factories and transportation routes from enemy bombing. Second, they pointed out that war workers would get access to new Chicago Housing Authority units. This would help solve one of mobilization's biggest problems, the housing of industrial workers. Finally, Blessing and Mayer noted that the Calumet's relation to raw material deposits allowed for quick access to materials, most notably coal and iron ore.

As the 1942 report illustrates, the Calumet became an object of intense concern for federal, military, and business officials once full-scale defense production became a reality. Local elites and mobilization agents in Chicago and

Washington made all manner of calculations about the locational assets of the metropolis, the city, and the district. Was Chicago too close to the Canadian border? Could large ordnance plants be placed within built-up urban spaces? How did the Calumet's supply of labor and transportation facilities affect where a defense factory might be located? These and numerous other questions about the selection of industrial property in the district had to be assessed in comparison with competing industrial sites elsewhere.

These sorts of calculations were on the mind of Colonel H. Rutherford in August 1940 when he considered Chicago's eligibility for federal industrial investment. Rutherford was in charge of the selection of new industrial sites for the ANMB. This was perhaps the most important position in the United States to determine the geography of wartime fixed-capital investment. Under Rutherford's command, the armed forces made a preliminary choice of a site. The proposed location was reviewed by the WPB and then given final approval by a mobilization agency. It was extremely rare for these agencies to reject an ANMB proposal. The need to quickly kick-start production compelled the agencies to streamline the approval process and quickly resolve conflict. William Knudsen, the National Defense Advisory Commission's production coordinator and former president of General Motors, made it very clear that the military had to accelerate production as rapidly as possible. He told Congress that the military would determine the location of industrial sites. Rutherford's calculations of what should be built, how much funding should be invested in the new plant, and where the new facilities should be located heavily influenced the development of the Calumet's defense landscape.[39]

When Rutherford told Chicago-area politicians, property developers, financiers, and industrialists that being close to the Canadian border was not an issue and that ordnance plants would not be located in densely populated areas on the eastern seaboard, his words had special meaning, a meaning that reverberated across the metropolitan landscape. They suggested that Chicago, with its impressive range of industrial assets, would be seriously considered as a site for federal investment in industrial facilities. These and other calculations would be based on information garnered from his research staff in Washington, Chicago, and elsewhere about potential manufacturing sites across the country. The decisions made by Rutherford and his staff ultimately shaped the future of economic activity and industrial sites in metropolitan Chicago and the Calumet.[40]

Local elites became very attentive when the air force started looking for suitable sites to build bomber plants in September 1941.[41] In their search to entice new firms and capital to Chicago, local political and industrial elites were eager to take the opportunity to bring a large and prestigious facility to the Windy City. Accordingly, in November 1941, Dwight Green, Illinois governor and chair of the Illinois Council of Defense (ICD), pushed Chicago's case to the army leadership while visiting Washington. Receiving a positive response, the ICD surveyed the metropolitan area for sites, consulted with local real estate agents, politicians, and the Chicago Association of Commerce, and prepared recommendations that laid out potential sites in the region.

The ICD ended up recommending a Calumet site: the Ford-Lansing airport on the Illinois-Indiana state line. In the council's opinion the site had the requisite advantages needed for a bomber assembly plant. With more than 1,400 acres, the site was well connected to three railroads and the Lincoln highway. It was located in the middle of a large labor market. Once built, the factory would have links to numerous suppliers, from large aircraft engine, aluminum, and steel manufacturers to hundreds of smaller instrument, pump, and machine part makers. Finally, of course, Green played up Chicago's inland location and its freedom from enemy attack.[42] The ICD's work, however, was to no avail. Their recommendations did not mesh with the calculations being made by Washington military and federal mobilization officials. In their opinion, issues such as spreading war investments across the country, especially in areas of labor surplus, trumped Chicago's superior industrial assets. The factory construction contracts went to Renton, Marietta, Omaha, and Wichita. The Calumet did not get a bomber assembly plant.

Even when new construction was authorized, the building of new factories was not unproblematic. As the bomber case illustrates, the district faced serious competition from other locales for scarce resources. One uncompleted ordnance plant illustrates this problem. In August 1942, after long negotiations between mobilization officials, the Continental Ordnance Corporation was authorized by the army to build a $45 million mill to manufacture heavy steel castings in East Chicago. Less than four months after receiving authorization, however, the WPB ordered an immediate halt to construction. At this time, the government had spent a million dollars and built a one-story, steel frame building, an uncompleted one-story concrete building, and a two-story administrative building. The project was stopped because the government could not justify the expenditure on the mill's construction materials and machinery, given the time it would take to build the plant. Calculating Continental's needs against what were considered the more pressing demands of rubber, gasoline, and aluminum producers, the WPB felt it had no choice but to stop construction. The Calumet mill had got caught in a wider calculus of resource priorities, industrial hierarchies, and place-based politics. It remained unfinished, and Continental never made any castings.[43]

Despite these setbacks, the Calumet did become one of the country's prime investment destinations. More than $465 million went into 104 industrial sites (Table 4.4). The Calumet received more money for defense factories than many metropolitan areas, including San Francisco and Buffalo. It secured more than Akron, Youngstown, Toledo, and Rochester combined. Close to two-thirds of the investment ($286 million) came from the government, with the remain-

TABLE 4.4 Wartime investment in selected areas of the Calumet, 1940–1945 (thousands of dollars)

Area of the Calumet district	Total investment		Separate private and public awards		Joint government and private awards		Government share of total investment (percentage)
	No.	$	Private $	State $	Private $	State $	
South Chicago	35	168,280	28,033	10,256	8,467	121,524	78.3
East Chicago	16	113,949	7,615	9,973	20,51	75,849	75.3
Gary	13	80,658	2,177	2,070	46,449	29,962	39.7
Whiting	3	47,524	47,524	0	0	0	0
Harvey	8	19,795	1,046	930	4,304	13,515	73.0
Hammond	9	19,709	623	9,596	1,425	8,065	89.6
Indiana Harbor	2	9,164	0	139	5,629	3,396	38.6
Chicago Heights	10	3,628	1,453	0	1,173	1,002	27.7
TOTAL	104	465,524	89,991	32,929	89,291	253,313	61.5

SOURCE: Compiled from Civilian Production Administration, War Industrial Facilities Authorized, July 1940–August 1945: Listed Alphabetically by Companies and Plant Location (Washington, D.C.: Government Printing Office, 1946).

der coming from military-sponsored certificates of necessity and other authorized federal funding. It was heavily concentrated in existing factory clusters in South Chicago, East Chicago, Gary, and Whiting. Few new greenfield sites were opened up. Rather, the military and local firms preferred to build additions to existing factories and to locate entirely new plants close to existing facilities. Agglomeration effects of propinquity, labor, and technological spillovers accumulated over sixty years anchored new concentrations of industrial investment.

Corporate America ruled the Calumet. A large share of the funding was concentrated in a small number of corporations (Table 4.5). Close to 90 percent of the construction awards in the district went to the fifteen largest projects, all of which were operated by America's leading corporations. Large steel, petroleum, and transportation corporations, including U.S. Steel, Standard Oil (Indiana), and Pullman deployed a mix of state and private capital to create new industrial sites and increase production capacity in the Calumet. Unused capacity was taken up, and new capacity was created. Some corporations continued old production lines, such as steel ingots and tubing, while others retooled to manufacture new product lines geared directly to the war, such as armor plate and Freon. Mobilization officials worked with local and corporate leaders to evaluate the pros and cons of the district's industrial sites, to determine economically and politically feasible locales for new capital investment, and to monitor production output and labor conditions. The navy, for example, deployed material inspectors, cost inspectors, vehicle maintenance school managers, ordnance inspectors, and industrial managers at several district factories, including Buda, International Harvester, and Pullman-Standard.[44]

TABLE 4.5 Largest construction awards in the Calumet, 1940–1945

	Construction awards				
Firm	Amount (thousands of dollars)	Government percentage	Supply awards (thousands of dollars)	Location	Product
Republic Steel	94,020	99	1,987	South Chicago	steel alloy
Carnegie (U.S. Steel)	73,068	27	58,065	Gary	tin plate
Inland Steel	50,348	71	49,010	East Chicago	steel ingots
Standard Oil	47,276	0	84,275	Whiting	aviation gasoline
American Steel Foundries	30,758	94	551	East Chicago	armor plate
Carnegie (U.S. Steel)	20,798	0	28,713	South Chicago	steel ingots
Wyman-Gordon	13,799	89	1,490	Harvey	aircraft steel
National Tube (U.S. Steel)	12,669	100	10,524	Gary	steel tubing
Pullman-Standard	12,045	99	44,747	Pullman	aircraft wings
Pullman-Standard	10,522	91	296,310	Hammond	tanks
Pressed Steel	10,255	89	544,898	South Chicago	tanks
Continental Foundry	9,973	85	9,653	East Chicago	steel castings
Phelps Dodge	9,561	100	0	Hammond	copper alloy
Ford	9,272	100	126,258	South Chicago	armored cars
Youngstown Sheet	9,109	38	11,151	Indiana Harbor	steel ingots

SOURCE: Compiled from Civilian Production Administration, *War Industrial Facilities Authorized, July 1940–August 1945: Listed Alphabetically by Companies and Plant Location* (Washington, D.C.: Government Printing Office, 1946); War Production Board, *Listing of Major War Supply Contacts by State and County* (Washington, D.C.: WPB, 1944), vol. 1.

Federal investment underpinned the development of new product and production process technologies in the district. The electrical wire firm Diamond Wire and Cable of Chicago Heights is illustrative. During the war it introduced an innovation for making flexible cord that would be used by firms to produce radios, radar equipment, and naval rockets. The firm cooperated with others to meet the "enormous demand caused by our growing Air Force, Navy and Armored Force." Mobilized by military demands and operating under punishing schedules, company technicians worked with engineers from Western Electric, the Fort Monmouth Signal Laboratory, the Wright Field Aircraft Radio laboratory, and the Navy Bureau of Ships to develop a more cost-effective method for making better-quality cord.[45]

Federal and military funding for factory expansion reformulated the Calumet's industrial property. The Pullman-Standard Car plant at Cottage Grove South and 110th Street was one of the largest industrial complexes in the Calumet. The corporation received supply contracts valued at $296 million from the army to build tanks, artillery shells, and other armaments at both the main factory in the community of Pullman and a rehabilitated one at Hammond, Indiana. Pullman received construction awards totaling more than $8 million to build new manufacturing space and to retool. The company also received navy contracts valued at $45 million to build patrol vessels, which took place in a navy-funded facility at the factory adjacent to Lake Calumet. The award for this addition totaled more than $10.5 million, of which $6.3 million went to building factory space while the remaining $4.2 million went to machinery and equipment.[46] Pullman developed new production technologies for building patrol vessels at this wartime site. Rather than building around a laid keel—the traditional method of ship construction—the company assembled fourteen preassembled sections simultaneously. Once joined, the assembled sections were transferred to the company's buildings on the shore of Lake Calumet for final assembly and launching.[47]

Federal funds also built up the Calumet's industrial complex by rehabilitating disused factories. The restoration of the Pressed Steel factory for tank manufacture illustrates the crucial role that the Chicago Ordnance District had for converting the Calumet to wartime production. In early 1940, the site contained "a ghost plant without roof, floors, or suitable machinery" and employed a skeleton workforce of 15 (Figure 4.5).[48] A few months later, with the guidance of the Ordnance Department, the company signed a contract with British Purchasing Commission to make five hundred M-3, twenty-eight-ton tanks for the British. The first one rolled off the assembly line in July 1941. Contracts from the U.S. Army soon followed, and by the end of the war the company had received supply contracts valued at more than $544 million. The company received more than $10 million to completely refurbish the factory and to equip the factory with machinery and equipment. As a result, the plant's number of employees grew from 293 in January 1941 to more than 4,100 four years later. Over these four years, Pressed Steel workers made 10,750 armored vehicles, almost all of them for the U.S. Army.[49]

The framing of Pressed Steel industrial property as a site for federal funds was central to the Ordnance Department's renewal of the manufacturing facilities. The agency acted as an intermediary between the company, the British Purchasing Commission, and the U.S. Army and turned "this once ramshackle, rusting hulk of steel and brick" into an example of "what industry can accomplish under the stress of war."[50] The Ordnance Department worked with other local and nonlocal calculative agents to scan the metropolitan world for appropriate industrial sites. Once the Pressed Steel plant had been identified, Ordnance officials worked to bring construction awards and supply contracts to the firm. Guided by military plant engineers, tank designers, and company production officials, the rehabilitated industrial site effectively linked national demand for munitions, the practices of procurement agencies, and the expansion of a local industrial concern. As such, it was responsible for helping generate millions of dollars of prime and construction contracts. The calculative strategies of the Ordnance Department in response to meet the demand for tanks transformed a ghost plant into a working industrial site.[51]

The War Department rehabilitated other dilapidated and unused industrial sites in the district. Another example is Buda Company's old foundry in Harvey, an industrial suburb. The War Department rehabilitated the factory to produce marine diesel engines. Government funds were also used to install the necessary machinery and equipment. The total cost of the new manufacturing facilities and machinery was $3.4 million. Along with this building, Buda expanded its working facilities throughout the war, took over the Harvey warehouse of American Stove to add needed capacity in June 1944, and opened an auxiliary plant in Blue Island to make diesel engine parts in February 1945.[52] This rehabilitated building was just one part of a larger network of wartime industrial production units operated by Buda in the Calumet.

The state also invested in scrambled plants in the Calumet. One of the largest was the Wyman-Gordon drop-forging plant in Harvey. Costing more than $11.7 million, it was built as an addition on property purchased from the company. The military built nineteen buildings on sixteen acres of newly acquired government land surrounded by the company's property and production facilities. Wyman-Gordon used the factory to produce twenty thousand tons monthly of drop forgings for aircraft engine crankshafts and propellers for the air force.[53] Despite the war contracts and the new state-owned industrial facilities that they operated, the company was not enthralled with federal investment within the boundaries of their premises. It felt, however, that it had no other choice. The demands of industrial mobilization enforced a calculus of industrial space that favored speed and existing knowledge. As H. Stoddard, Wyman-Gordon's president, told Hans Klagsbrunn, the DPC's executive vice-president, in September 1944, "In our judgment, it [scrambled facilities] saved nearly a year's time in those early days and also a large amount of money as compared with the cost of limiting expansion to new and isolated plants."[54] The imperatives of war forced private companies to accept government intrusion into their control over industrial property.

As the Calumet's rehabilitated, scrambled, and new factories illustrate, federal and military mobilization agencies worked with industrial leaders to build a regional industrial complex in the Calumet geared to producing wartime ordnance of all kinds. In terms of land, factories, and machinery, the state and the military were legally, materially, and administratively entangled in the interests of private capital and could not easily be separated from them. Linking local, regional, and national interests, the state, military, and industry funneled a huge amount of industrial investment into the Calumet by taking advantage of the district's industrial legacy and strengths. The result was the building of one of the country's largest war-producing districts.

Conclusion

The three pillars of Chicago's industrial war economy were the mobilization of existing productive capacity, the creation of new factory space, and the awarding of defense contracts. Federal investment of $1.3 billion of fixed-capital investment refashioned metropolitan Chicago's industrial geography. The teeming central industrial districts surrounding the Loop, which were home to thousands of small, vertically disintegrated, consumer-based firms working out of multistory industrial buildings, received few construction awards. For those that wanted to expand, the only possible route was to restart existing but unused capacity or to obtain vacant space elsewhere in the city. In the face of corporate control of the procurement process and their inability to get a certificate of necessity or a federal construction award, most central-city firms survived the war by producing for the civilian market or by subcontracting with large corporate prime contractors. Most downtown firms missed out on the direct benefits of the military and the state's investments. Working within the confines of existing productive capacity and beholden to the economic might of America's large corporations, the typical central-city firm in Chicago played a small part in wartime mobilization.

In sharp contrast, the rest of the metropolitan area was awash with new fixed-capital investment, much of which went to large corporations. The suburbs and the city fringe accounted for the vast share of the district's new productive capacity. Corporations in suburban districts such as the Calumet and city fringe areas such as the southwest operated huge steel mills and metalworking, chemical, munitions, and aircraft engine factories that had been built with federal funds. Along with the Calumet, many other industrial districts running along the boundary between the suburbs and the city became home to a massive infusion of capital. Productive capacity grew in the older, more established industrial suburban districts in the western part of the metropolis, such as Cicero and Joliet, and in the city close to the railroads. These districts were joined by new factories in less industrial areas such as St. Charles, McCook, and Melrose Park. The same was true to the north. Here, older city districts and newer ones in the suburbs such as North Chicago and Skokie became the home of capital investment in electronic, metalworking, chemical, and instrument factories.

The industrial geography of the Chicago metropolitan area during the war was shaped by a calculative coalition. This coalition, which consisted of local and national federal, military, and industrial leaders, framed Chicago as a central component of a national industrial program. From the beginnings of industrial mobilization, a range of actors identified, worked on, and transformed the metropolitan area's industrial spaces. Federal legislation authorized civil and military mobilization agencies to channel investment, both directly and indirectly, to the region's existing industrial sites and to vacant spaces on the urban fringe that became new defense factories. Corporate leaders were in positions of power where they could influence the scale, type, and location of investment. Mobilization leaders took advantage of Chicago's industrial base. For military and government officials the internal economies of scale and scope enjoyed by the steel mills and the agglomerative networks created by small central-city firms were too good to pass up. Working with the huge body of numeric and qualitative information generated during the war about a dizzying array of industrial issues, the calculations of military-industrial officials were instrumental in making metropolitan Chicago one of the key industrial regions in the country.

CHAPTER 5

War Factories and Industrial Engineering

The building of new industrial sites is a long and complex procedure. The purchase, subdivision, and marketing of land, as well as the conception, funding, design, and construction of a manufacturing plant involves hundreds of processes and thousands of individual decisions. Land speculators and property developers have to consider the price, quality, and location of potential property. Once land has been purchased, developers have to weigh their options about, among other things, land subdivision, building construction, infrastructure installation, and marketing the finished commodity. All of these options involve a range of private sector actors from surveyors and builders to land auctioneers and bankers. Likewise, an assortment of public officials working in registry, planning, and legal offices shape the value, use, and legal status of land. Buyers have to work through the suitability, cost, and location of the industrial property. Driving all of these actions is the search for profits to be made from land conversion and the ability of the state to oversee and contain accumulation. The buying and selling of industrial property is a mutually constitutive capitalist and calculative affair.

The process of building industrial sites was complicated by war conditions. The competition for scarce building materials reduced construction output, and even the introduction of restrictions to nonwar construction did not solve the problem. The hostility of industrial capital to building new capacity in the early years of the war further weakened the movement to erect new factory space. Elaborate bureaucratic schedules slowed industrial construction. Competing federal policies made it next to impossible to fashion a coherent building program. Miscommunication between national, state, and local governments ensured that the completion of new industrial sites was hard won. Federal and military funding and control of wartime industrial space guaranteed that factory building would be a complicated and tense process.

Nevertheless, an unprecedented amount of new factory space was created between 1940 and 1945. Despite the obstacles, the federal government and the military financed and coordinated a massive factory-building program. A large number of state-financed defense factories were built, most of which were operated by private corporations. This chapter explores a neglected yet important element of defense factory building—the role of the private industrial engineering firm working under contract with federal mobilization, military, and disposal agencies. An examination of three of Chicago's industrial sites illustrates the calculative expertise that private industrial engineering companies brought to the making and dismantling of defense facilities between 1940 and 1948. Military and federal officials integrated the calculative expertise embodied in the industrial engineer into the design, building, operation, and evaluation of wartime production facilities. Industrial engineers undertook much of the planning, building, operating, and disposing of many of the large defense plants. Although private engineers did not fundamentally alter the industrial engineering approach of the military, they did ensure that the military was able to build a sufficient number of ordnance and defense factories.

The place-based outcomes of the calculations made by the construction alliance are illustrated here by three defense factories built or appraised by three industrial engineering firms. The involvement of Sanderson and Porter, a New York City firm, in the building of the Elwood ordnance plant just outside of Joliet, a Chicago satellite town, demonstrates how engineers were calculative experts who worked on the design, construction, and operation of defense factories. The two other cases consider how industrial engineering firms were directly involved in assessing manufacturing and determining industrial value. Lockwood Greene's appraisal of the Buick aircraft engine plant in suburban Melrose Park shows how industrial engineering firms contributed to the building of local industrial knowledge and determined the monetary and functional value of wartime industrial plants. Day and Zimmerman's evaluation of the construction of the Chicago Bridge and Iron Company's shipbuilding yards at Seneca, a small town on the outskirts of the metropolis, illustrates how industrial engineers were implicated in making an inventory of industrial space and shaping community fortunes once the shipyard was no longer needed for wartime purposes. The three case studies show how private industrial engineering firms were engaged by civil and military agencies to use their calculative expertise to build, operate, assess, and dismantle metropolitan Chicago's wartime industrial sites.[1] Before turning to the three cases, I give a brief history of the place of industrial engineers in the working of industrial sites and the way in which they were framed as part of the building of the wartime factory.

Engineering Industrial Sites

A range of agents engineered the wartime industrial site. Private industrial engineering companies worked alongside the Corps of Engineers, the Quartermaster Department, the Defense Plant Corporation (DPC), the War Assets Administration (WAA), and other agencies to create, refashion, and dispose of defense factories. This was not to be expected as the army's small Construction Division had little industrial experience before 1940 and had focused most of its attention on the construction of base facilities. At the outbreak of war, the few industrial engineers working for the military were not up to the task of building the necessary munitions factories. As the historians of the Corps of Engineers have noted, in 1939, "After two decades of mobilization planning the War Department still had no effective blueprint for carrying out a large emergency building program." This point was reiterated in February 1940 by Louis Johnson, the assistant secretary of war, when he told the audience at an Associated General Contractors conference "that we have neglected the construction phases of industrial mobilization."[2] The acceleration of the mobilization program and the framing of the industrial site as a federal object after May 1940, however, forced the military to give greater attention to the building of defense factories and to incorporate industrial engineering expertise into their construction. The calculative expertise of private industrial engineering firms was central to this mobilization program in three ways.

First, the government and military involvement in funding, building, operating, and disposing of industrial facilities forced mobilization agencies to have a comprehensive understanding of their character. Government and military officials had to have precise information about an industrial site's legal status in order to evaluate its potential as a defense factory. It was necessary to know who owned the property, what the boundaries of ownership were, and under what conditions of ownership the site operated. Once these were established, accurate inventories of materials and equipment that were to be part of the industrial property were required. These were then used by mobilization agents to make calculations about the scale and character of industrial sites. This information was used to find answers to pressing questions about the availability of construction materials, the area's labor supply, and the character of regional transportation facilities. Private industrial engineering firms worked with government officials to establish the legal and operating basis of industrial property.

Engineering firms also worked with the federal government and the military to calculate the financial costs that constituted the industrial site as a marketable commodity. As owners, and after 1945 as sellers, of industrial property, mobilization agencies had to determine the value of a site's elements—land, buildings, machinery and equipment, and transportation facilities. Once established, these costs were transposed into a set of legible values that functioned as a comparative mediator of the industrial property market. The government, as the owner of the property that would be put up for sale, had to be concerned with the site's cost in order not to place undue pressure on the private property market and the disposal cost. They also had to create financial values that made accounting and real estate sense. In some cases, military and federal engineers and real estate evaluators oversaw these determinations. In many cases, however, the mobilization and disposal agencies contracted with private industrial engineering companies to make a financial assessment of the manufacturing plant. In this capacity, industrial engineers were a key part of the regime's effort to administer and put a value on every aspect of state-owned industrial space.

Finally, mobilization agencies had to work with federal and private industrial engineers to establish how the site was linked to the world outside. Engineers had to evaluate information about a site's access to infrastructure such as roads, railroad sidings, sewers, and utility connections. Industrial engineers mobilized knowledge about the state of market conditions, labor supply, building conditions, and raw material availability. Once compiled, this information was used to compare specific locations and sites. Similarly, mechanical and chemical engineers incorporated current production process technologies into the factory. All of this had to be cooperatively undertaken by federal, military, industrial, and engineering officials. This involved a calculative comparison; sites were evaluated against one another across space. Actions undertaken by the army or navy at one site were measured against those at other sites, both locally and nationally. It was incumbent on mobilization agencies to implement effective calculations. This involved building relationships between state agencies (such as the Bureau of Internal Revenue and the Department of Justice), military agencies (Corps of Engineers and the Army and Navy Munitions Board), industrial firms (operators, contractors, and subcontractors), utility and transportation companies (local and national), and local governments. The industrial engineering firm played a role in these processes and as such facilitated mobilization and the making of industrial spaces.

The wartime functions of industrial engineering companies emerged out of the expertise they accumulated in the building up of America's industrial base. The origins of this are to be found in the construction of canals, railroads, and mills in nineteenth-century New England and the Mid-Atlantic. The industry moved out of transportation and mill construction and into other fields in the late nineteenth century. The nineteenth-century skilled mechanic and mechanical engineer produced both the machinery and the factories on which American industry was built and underpinned the development of production space on America's moving industrial frontier. Large industrial engineering firms that designed, built, operated, and evaluated factories had emerged by the early twentieth century in response to professionalization, increasing demand, and diversification. These companies added utility systems construction and industrial management to their repertoire of expertise by the 1920s.[3]

Despite diversification, industrial engineers remained focused on plant engineering. The need to appraise factory scale, operations, quality, and value had long been required by firms and their competitors. This grew in importance from the end of the nineteenth century as the merger movement amplified the stakes and created the need for more firm information. Historically, a firm's financial power, patent pool, and market share had been handed down from one owner to another either through family networks or the nontechnical services of bankruptcy experts. The rise of the large corporation at the end of the nineteenth century changed this. The scale and scope of corporations required that industrial assets were transferred by more formal professional businesses that specialized in large, technically sophisticated and legally challenging transactions. Increasingly, industrial engineers were brought in to assess and evaluate industrial plants and, in some cases, to introduce scientific management practices. To be successful, corporations had to fix, build, and evaluate their industrial sites and work relations. Industrial engineering firms helped facilitate this process.[4]

Building on this legacy, industrial engineers remained the leading factory builders before World War I. After the war, industrial engineers, along with a growing number of specialized industrial architects such as Albert Kahn, turned their attention to rethinking the factory. The key changes were replacing the classical functional mill-type box with the modernist, open factory and a greater focus on the sociological and technical aspects of the industrial site. In the interwar period, engineers and architects designed new large corporate factories that sought to balance form with function.[5]

The involvement of industrial engineers in factory building continued after 1939. During World War II, a number of industrial engineering firms plied their trade to mobilization agencies. Contracts were not forthcoming at first. It was only in the second half of 1940 after Roosevelt's call to arms that industrial engineering firms were able to tap into federal construction funds. Even though mobilization agencies had their own engineers who could assess the industrial site and build factories, the government and the military called on private engineering companies in order to keep up with the workload and to bring specialized calculative skills to projects. Moreover, the defense factory expansion program unleashed by Roosevelt in 1940 called for specialists in industrial construction. This was particularly the case with large, complex assemblages such as ordnance plants, airplane- and shipbuilding facilities, and steel and synthetic rubber works. All of this added to the work of industrial engineers.[6] As William Enright noted in September 1940, industrial engineering companies "predicted that their services would be in greater demand for the next year of two than at any other time in their history."[7]

Enright was not mistaken. Lockwood Greene, for example, saw its volume of work increase dramatically after 1940, a significant share of which came from war contracts. In March 1941, it was reported that the company had received $196,539 from contracts with the army and the navy in the previous twelve months. This was small compared to $1.2 million received by Stone and Webster Engineering for building the Kankakee Ordnance plant. Another eleven firms were paid large sums by the War Department, and six engineering firms received money under fixed-fee construction contracts over this period. The volume of government work for industrial engineering firms increased over the next three years. For companies such as Lockwood Greene, and Stone and Webster, war was a boon.[8]

War contracts widened their regional reach. The Cleveland firm of H. K. Ferguson opened a branch plant in Houston in 1941 to tap into the construction boom in the South and Southwest. The new branch became the administrative center for the company's numerous wartime construction contracts in the South, including the huge synthetic rubber plant at Baton Rouge and the Rocky Mountain Arsenal at Denver. The company received DPC contracts in 1942 to build new industrial facilities (New York, Buffalo, Chicago, Birmingham, Dallas, and Los Angeles) and make additions to existing facilities (Carteret, New Jersey, East Chicago, Indiana, Neville Island, Pennsylvania, and Baltimore) as part of a program to increase the country's tin capacity.[9] For industrial engineering firms the war was an antidote to the depressed conditions of the previous ten years.

The calculative expertise created over a hundred years or more by industrial engineers was used to build and evaluate America's stock of defense plants. Industrial engineers along with architects were the main designers and builders of wartime factories. They also contributed in other ways. The H. K. Ferguson Company, among other things, provided government officials with ideas about how to speed up factory construction. George S. Armstrong and Company completed surveys of industrial sectors such as rubber, shipping, and light metal for the government and pointed out expected production and construction needs over the course of the war. These two companies took advantage of other forms of wartime largess to shape the character of industrial sites before, during, and after the construction of the defense factory.[10]

The growing scale and scope of industrial engineering commitments to fashioning industrial space ensured that these firms consolidated their relationship with the military-industrial alliance. Throughout the war, industrial engineers continued to work for their traditional employer, the private corporation, which subcontracted out to federal and military agencies. Working with the government and the military opened up a new field of work for engineering companies: federally financed defense factories. In the process, engineers were ensconced as a junior partner in the military-industrial complex. After 1939, engineering companies undertook two key tasks for the army and navy and government agencies such as the DPC, the National Defense Advisory Commission (NDAC), and the WAA. The first task was to design, build, and operate war plants. The second was to assess and evaluate the engineering, financial, and functional components of industrial sites. Wartime factories became the focus of the joint efforts of industrial engineering companies and military and civil government agencies. This cooperation continued after the end of the war as industrial engineering firms worked with the government and the military to determine the condition and value of the state-owned property that was to be sold off to private interests.

Sanderson and Porter and the Elwood Ordnance Plant

On November 2, 1939, Harrison Smith, a partner in the industrial engineering firm Sanderson and Porter Company, called on Colonel J. Clement of the New York district of the Ordnance Department. Spurred by German victories in Europe, and sensing that the United States would soon join the fray, Smith was curious about the preparations being made by the Ordnance Department for loading high-explosive shells. Unable to provide an answer, Clement advised Smith to get in touch with Major Harris at the Philadelphia Ordnance district in Wilmington, Delaware.[11] With this initial contact, Sanderson and Porter started a drive to obtain government contracts to design, construct, and operate defense factories. They were successful. Ten months later the company signed its first contract with the army: the construction of the Elwood Ordnance plant outside of Joliet, an industrial satellite of Chicago.

The Elwood case illustrates the ways in which private engineering companies brought their calculative expertise to manufacture a militarized industrial landscape and, in the process, to strengthen the relationship between the private and public sectors. With the advent of the war and the concomitant increase in the demand for munitions-manufacturing space, the army's Construction Division found it very difficult to find a sufficient number of qualified industrial engineers within its ranks. Accordingly, they turned to private industrial engineering companies for the prerequisite calculative expertise.[12] The framing of the factory as an object to be worked on by mobilization agencies opened up federal coffers, resulting in the channeling of billions of dollars to privately operated but government-financed defense plants. Seeking contracts and driven by entrepreneurial executives, industrial engineering firms such as Sanderson and Porter tapped into the rich lode of federal and military construction awards after 1940 and deployed their engineering networks and expertise to build defense factories across the country. One such facility was the massive Elwood ordnance plant on the edge of the Chicago metropolitan area.

When Sanderson and Porter was established in 1896, its first job was to build a street railway line in Plattsburgh, New York. Over the next four decades it focused on civil, electrical, and mechanical work, specializing in the evaluation of electric powerhouses and other utility projects. In World War I the company built ships for the Emergency Fleet Corporation and designed, constructed, and operated shell-loading plants. In the interwar period it branched out into the burgeoning fields of oil and gas and hydroelectricity. Along with this, Sanderson and Porter opened an industrial department to make surveys of industrial sites. Using its expertise and drive, the company was able to take advantage of the growing funds available for factory construction to win several wartime federal projects. Along with the Elwood scheme, the company designed, built, and operated a number of other defense plants. One such facility was a bomb-loading ordnance facility in Arkansas. Funded by the Chemical Warfare Service, the Pine Bluff Arsenal cost more than $57 million to build and equip.[13]

Sanderson and Porter's first wartime contract was the construction and operation of the federally funded shell-loading plant at Elwood. Winning the contract was not easy, despite the firm's expertise and its aggressive search for government contracts. Even before it competed with other engineering firms for the contracts, Smith had to convince his own firm that it had the administrative abilities, technical expertise, and business contacts to build such a facility quickly and under emergency conditions. With the coming of war in Europe, Smith saw an opportunity to mobilize his expertise gained by working for the American and Russian governments. To take advantage of lucrative wartime opportunities building defense factories, Smith had to gain agreement from the rest of his partners at Sanderson and Porter. Winning them over, Smith initiated the company's first contact with a government representative in November 1939.

The September 1940 contract to build Elwood was the product of an intensive campaign waged by the firm for government and military funding. During the ten months that elapsed between the meeting with Colonel Clement in November 1939 and the contract signing, the company had a succession of meetings with federal and military agents working in the Washington, New York, and Chicago offices of the Ordnance Department, the Bureau of Yards, and the Quartermaster Department, and with the assistant secretary of war. This solicitation of federal work bore no fruit until August 5, 1940, when Smith was informed that the Ordnance Department had authorized the company to build and operate a shell-loading plant. After a false start at one site, the company visited another site outside Joliet in early September. Company and military officials liked what they saw. Negotiations started a week later. Spurred by the imperatives of wartime mobilization, they quickly came to an agreement, signing the contract on September 19. Construction began in late November 1940.[14] Within six months a rural world was transformed into an industrial site on the metropolitan fringe that was born out of the calculative relations of private industry, the military, and the government.

Deciding on sites such as Elwood was not straightforward. Starting in the late 1930s the chiefs of the Ordnance and Chemical Warfare Departments began working with corporations such as DuPont and Hercules to create guidelines for selecting sites and plans that would see private contractors build factories under the supervision of the branch financing each project. The military, however, was not free to choose locations for military reasons only. Decisions were subject to pressure from diverse interests, including Washington officials who were intent on implementing Roosevelt's interior policy and local political leaders who could be for or against defense plants in their region. Final approval rested with the president, the assistant secretary of war, the civilian mobilization agencies, and the private firms that would operate each factory.

Despite the pressure to decentralize, most defense plants were located close to industrial areas in the eastern region of the country. The primary aim of the military was production at the quickest speed and lowest cost; this could only be achieved by locating new factories in districts such as Chicago, which had an array of linkages with construction and manufacturing firms that were necessary for the building and operation of the defense factory. Building plants in nonmanufacturing areas did not make economic sense. As Brigadier General Charles Harris, chief of the Ordnance Industrial Service, explained: "The general consideration was to locate the plants conforming to the ... pattern of existing industry." It was under these competing conditions that Elwood was chosen as a site for the shell-loading facility.[15]

Finding a location and signing a contract were the first steps in framing the economic and political relations between a private corporation and the military for the building of an industrial facility. The next was to assemble a group of industrial engineers and associated professionals from the private sector to work on the Elwood project who could work with the Real Estate and Construction divisions of the Corps of Engineers.[16] Despite the industrial experience gained during World War I, Sanderson and Porter's focus in the interwar years had been on civil work. By 1940 the firm had little in-house ordnance expertise. After working his business networks, Smith found several experienced men to work on the factory's design and construction. The most important were William Canniff and Thomas Burns, both of whom had worked designing ordnance plants during World War I. Pragmatic men who saw an opportunity to take advantage of wartime mobilization jobs, they were enticed by Smith to join Sanderson and Porter.[17] With the team in place, Sanderson and Porter under Smith's leadership and Canniff's and Burn's technical expertise undertook the making of the ordnance factory and the transformation of a rural district into a defense landscape.

The creation of an industrial site and the building of a massive ordnance facility in the Elwood area were not uncontested. Many local residents were angry that their homes were going to be turned into an explosives factory. Less than a week after Sanderson and Porter received the contract, the *Chicago Tribune* reported on unrest among the district's residents and the attempts by the federal government to appease the agitated community. Concerned that the protests could delay the project, the army looked to defuse the situation. To this end, the army sent Colonel Rigby Valliant, chief of the Construction Division, to pacify a disgruntled crowd of two thousand farmers, cottage owners, and Joliet residents at a community meeting in Wilmington on September 24, 1940. Valliant explained to them the seriousness of the situation and justified the choice of the district as an industrial site by using a discourse of science, fairness, and hardball. Many people remained unconvinced, despite their patriotic feelings.[18]

Sentimental and financial calculation came up against imperatives of patriotism and industrial mobilization. Property relations were at the heart of the issue. Local residents and seasonal visitors were dismayed at losing their land, some of which had been in their families for generations. Permanent residents and cottage owners from Chicago were concerned that they would not receive a fair price for their land. Others, of course, were excited by the changes that federal money and a large workplace would bring to the area. While Valliant used patriotism and jobs to overcome sentimental value, he tried to mollify their financial fears by resorting to the rationale of the market. He told them that the government "intended leaning over backward to assure fair treatment to all land owners." He continued by assuring them that land prices would be "decided by sound scientific methods applied by reliable appraisers," most of whom were local real estate agents.[19]

Just in case there was lingering resentment, Valliant turned up the heat. He informed the residents that the government "will not pay for sentimental value the tracts may have to the owners," and that it "can brook no delay." Turning the knife further, he told the audience that it would be better to accept the government's offer than "risk having the price fixed by a city jury in a condemnation action." Despite this, feelings were still running high a few weeks later. The 450 property owners whose land had been expropriated and the locals who were concerned about the changing social, economic, and political conditions continued to find the situation intolerable.[20] The military, however, was in a rush and, having decided that the new ordnance plant would be built in Elwood regardless of local discontent, quickly went about creating a new industrial site and defense landscape on the metropolitan fringe. The public-private imperatives of war and the market, and not individual property rights, were the key elements in this calculation.

The purchase of the Elwood property was part of a national program of military land acquisition. In June 1940 the War Department owned 2 million acres. This had increased to almost 46 million acres by 1946. Much of this land was obtained from temporary leases and transfers from the federal government. Nevertheless, as in the Elwood case, the Real Estate Branch and the Corps of Engineers made outright purchases from private owners of 5.7 million acres at a cost of $360 million. Due to the small size of the branch—it had only nineteen employees in the spring of 1940—and the paucity of specialized officials, the military's real estate officers worked with local real estate brokers who selected the property, assessed its value, and contracted the sale. Although the military tried to purchase the property through negotiation, it did resort to expropriation when necessary. The latter, however, was difficult, costly, and time consuming. Whenever possible, the preference was to appeal to patriotism and financial gain.[21]

Armed with federal dollars, property, legal powers, and administrative procedures, Sanderson and Porter moved into a rural section of metropolitan Chicago to build an ordnance plant. This action brought with it a new set of calculative relationships for the company and the military, involving, among other things, the laying out of the site, the supply of hard-to-get building materials, and the creation of workforce accommodation. Sanderson and Porter brought in a local company of "reliable appraisers" to traverse the farms and cottages acquired by the army to measure land, assess quality, and determine value. The company's advance force, which arrived in September, made precise measurements of the site. Working on location, the team designed the plant, surveyed the territory, demolished homes, barns, and fences, flattened the land, and assembled hundreds of mixed-land-use lots into a single industrial site. The Sanderson and Porter team along with private appraisers and contractors as well as military advisers simplified the landscape and transformed a rural world into a wartime industrial site.[22]

The factory was gigantic. It was not the largest ordnance plant built in the United States during the war—that privilege belongs to the Rock Island facility 150 miles west of Elwood. Nevertheless, the Joliet ordnance complex sprawled over 14,720 acres, had 400 loading buildings, warehouses, and TNT magazines, and employed 8,000 production and administrative workers, while 9 locomotives and 200 freight cars traversed the facility's 85 miles of railroad lines. The Sanderson and Porter plant was home to, among other things, a dazzling array of machines, equipment, furniture, infrastructures, and chemical supplies that were brought in from other factories across the country. Managers and salespeople from construction supply companies and subcontracting firms turned up with, among other things, tractors and trucks, generators and pumps, work tables and lockers, tripods and cranes. The first production unit of the $30 million ordnance plant opened in July 1941, four months ahead of schedule.[23]

In building the Elwood plant, the industrial engineering company was drawn into a specific set of business networks. Defense landscapes built by industrial engineering companies were fixed in place by a set of networks that operated across space. These networks can be documented by information supplied by Sanderson and Porter to the Truman Committee's inquiry into the conflict of interest charges against one of the company's partners.[24] Among this information are lists of the equipment purchased and leased by the firm, and the subcontractors used in the building of the facility.[25] An analysis of these lists shows

TABLE 5.1 Sanderson and Porter's building contracts, 1940–1941

Contract type	All contracts		Chicago contracts		Chicago share of all contracts	
	No.	$	No.	$	No.	$
Construction Equipment	148	149,674	116	113,053	78.4	75.5
Office equipment	216	68,375	132	43,171	61.1	63.1
Engineering equipment	98	19,570	38	11,515	38.8	58.8
Railroad equipment	4	44,032	2	41,317	50.0	93.8
Permanent equipment	78	123,681	59	28,654	75.6	23.2
Rentals	48	14,984	44	11,206	75.9	73.6
Subcontracts	45	—	38	—	84.4	—
TOTAL	646	420,316	429	248,736	66.4	59.2

SOURCE: U.S. Senate, Hearings before a Special Committee Investigating the National Defense Program, Part 6, 77th Congress, 1st session (Washington, D.C.: Government Printing Office, 1941), 1919–37.

how business actors located across the country were implicated in the building of a military production site and a public-private partnership.

The Truman Committee evidence shows that the engineering company was involved in business networks that covered most areas of the United States but were concentrated in the Chicago region.[26] A third of the company's contracts and 40 percent of its expenses were with companies outside of the immediate vicinity (Table 5.1). While Sanderson and Porter's search for equipment reached as far as the Pacific (Los Angeles, Oakland, and Spokane) and the South (Chattanooga), most supplies were found in the Manufacturing Belt. Illustrative of the company's connections across this region are Alvey Gerguson (Cincinnati), Harnishfeger Corporation (Milwaukee), Louis Frey (Boston), and Hauck Manufacturing (Brooklyn), which, respectively, supplied a conveyor system, engine and bucket welders, specialized design instruments, and heaters. Sanderson and Porter renewed their connections with past suppliers and began new ones. Along with their technological and construction expertise, the company brought products shipped in from elsewhere to shape the area's emerging defense landscape.

Firms in the Chicago metropolitan area, however, were the main suppliers of products and expertise. Some were extremely local. Joliet firms, such as Winston Chevrolet (sedans and pickups) and Barrett Hardware (saws and grinders), provided a range of goods. Most, though, were from Chicago. Western Contractor Supply provided the company with heaters, burners, breakers, jacks, hoists, and other construction equipment. Eugene Dietzgen supplied drawing boards, trestles, tripods, and curves. In other cases, firms such as General Electric used its Chicago office to bring in materials such as locomotives from other locales. It is obvious that Sanderson and Porter preferred local suppliers because Chicago firms could produce and supply most of the materials that the firm required and could deliver them more quickly than outside firms. And, if necessary, local suppliers could visit the construction site and make repairs to their products.

Chicago firms also dominated the contract work. In a few cases, contracts were given out to nonlocal specialized firms. One case was Wisconsin Structural Steel, located in Milwaukee, which received a $500,000 award from Sanderson and Porter to supply the ordnance plant's erecting steel. A handful of other firms in Cincinnati (conveyor system), Toledo (spray painting system), First City, Iowa (sewage treatment plant), New York City (concrete), Milwaukee (iron stairs), and Goshen, Indiana (lighting) received contracts from the engineering company. For the most part, though, Sanderson and Porter contracted with Chicago firms to build and install much of the ordnance plant's equipment. Although the Truman Report did not provide the value of the subcontracts, one of the largest must have been the one given to Midwest Construction, a $1,300,000 contract to build and install a group of igloo-type semi-underground magazines for the storage of explosives.[27] Local expertise mattered.

The building of a new industrial site on the metropolitan area's rural fringe by an industrial engineering company was part of a set of local, regional, and national linkages. Cognizant of the opportunities afforded by wartime mobilization, Sanderson and Porter created business, scientific, and financial networks that capitalized on the lucrative business of building defense factories. By working government and military channels, the engineering firm was able to tap into the pool of federal funds available for defense mobilization. The engineering firm operated long-standing networks that gave them access to key personnel with the industrial and construction expertise to turn a residential and rural landscape into an industrial one. They also worked through several more recent business networks that connected their building on the site with local and regional business interests.

Industrial engineering companies such as Sanderson and Porter were calculative experts that transformed the industrial landscape of the United States during the war. Building on its long tradition of industrial expertise, the company built an ordnance plant that was part of a national program of industrial mobilization. Industrial engineers were part of a grouping of civil and military officials who operated under the purview of legally directed procedures rooted in the government's prerogative to expropriate property and to make defense facilities in the name of the wartime emergency. This national coalition worked with a range of local calculative agents, including municipalities and businesses, to transform a small part of the metropolis into an intensely militarized space. Elwood was not unique. Thousands of ordnance and other defense factories were built across the country between 1940 and 1945. The calculative expertise of private industrial engineering companies was used by the military to design, build, and operate many of these plants.

Lockwood Greene and the Buick Aircraft Engine Factory at Melrose Park

Industrial engineering companies were also brought in by civil and military agencies to assess federally owned industrial facilities. One such firm was Lockwood Greene, a firm with offices in New York City and Boston. Founded in 1882, the company designed and built factories, and evaluated factories and other industrial facilities for insurance and purchasing purposes. During the war, Lockwood Greene was contracted by the WAA to appraise the Buick-operated, government-owned aircraft engine factory in the Chicago suburb of Melrose Park. This section considers the way in which the federally owned industrial site was a calculable space that was subject to intensive measurement and evaluation by public and private agents. In order to ensure that the industrial site had financial and locational value, the federal government was required to work with private industrial engineering companies to assess and evaluate defense factories.

The Melrose Park aircraft engine factory illustrates how the industrial engineering company of Lockwood Greene and a few key government, military, and corporate calculative agents (the DPC, Buick, and Pratt and Whitney) viewed and worked on new industrial spaces. The ground for the new engine plant was broken on March 17, 1941, and within six weeks the first assembly line was being set up. Full-scale operations began in January 1942. Construction was finally finished on plancor 39 by September 1943. The manufacturing site consisted of twenty-four test cells and six main buildings—the central one measured 1,305 by 750 feet and contained one million square feet. The total cost for land, buildings, equipment, and machinery by war's end came to more than $125 million, making it Chicago's second largest defense factory. Only the $182 million Dodge-operated plant a few miles to the south was bigger.

The conception, design, building, operation, and evaluation of the Melrose Park site relied on a set of procedures that bound together various institutions and corporations and utilized legal forms such as the mobilization policies and procurement contracts that facilitated industrial expansion. These procedures and legal forms established the basis on which actions could take place. All of this was made possible by decisions calculated to circulate investment from federal agencies and national and local financial institutions to engineering firms, contractors, and industrial corporations.[28]

Lockwood Greene was brought in by the DPC to provide oversight of the production facilities. As part of its mandate to organize and oversee government property, the DPC undertook a series of evaluations of the Melrose Park facility. In these surveys it laid out the legal, financial, and structural aspects of the site. In some cases, the agency brought in outside companies, such as Lockwood Greene, with a specific expertise in assessing industrial facilities to provide another perspective on the property. This was the case with the sprawling Melrose Park engine manufacturing complex. To understand Lockwood Greene's participation in the assessment of the plant, it is necessary to set out the dynamics behind its construction.

Financed by the DPC, the building of the sprawling Buick facility was predicated on a set of interdepartmental and government-industry calculations. Government officials in Washington and Chicago worked with Michigan-based Buick and local firms to engineer, finance, design, and build the Melrose Park factory. General Motors engineering experts worked with the corporation's favored industrial architect, Albert Kahn, to design the plant. Two firms based in Chicago received building contracts valued at millions of dollars: the general construction contract was given to Thorgersen and Ericksen, and the contract for fabricating and erecting the steel frame went to the Mississippi Valley Structural Steel Company.[29] Local political and business officials were also part of the equation, as Buick officials made clear: "Complete cooperation and assistance from public officials, leaders in education, who are being asked to help in employe training programs, representatives of labor, other key elements in the community, and for the Chicago Association of Commerce, which worked actively to have the plants located here, were also favorably commented upon in connection with the announcements."[30] Buick's industrial links spanned the country. The company depended on engineering, construction, and production expertise from headquarters in Michigan. At the same time, a large number of local firms supplied it with various components and parts.[31]

In many ways, federal ownership of the factory during the war and its subsequent disposal to International Harvester in November 1945 illustrate the manner in which the government worked with the military and corporate America to make calculations about industrial sites during both the war years and in the immediate postwar period. The assembling of knowledge about the Buick plant, the making of new relationships around it, and the measurement of industrial space in the plant were typical not only because they were representative of how industrial engineering companies were central to the building and evaluation of other industrial firms, but also because of the way that industrial engineers were brought in by the state-industrial-military coalition to stoke the fires of wartime production.

On October 23, 1943, the DPC published a prospectus of the Buick site. Just two pages long, the prospectus, a legal document required for all state-owned manufacturing facilities, set out all of the site's key measurements without any fuss, wasted words, or superfluous numbers. It began by listing the war factory's function (the production of aircraft engines and parts under contract with Pratt and Whitney), cost ($107 million authorized, $97 million committed and $83 million disbursed), and the names of the operator (General Motors of Flint, Michigan) and the owner (DPC).[32] In order to provide a picture of what was to be worked on and who had the right to make the decisions, the document clearly laid out the boundaries of function, ownership, and use. Without this transparency, the ability to frame the factory as a calculative object and thus make the appropriate decisions about how to engineer, build, and operate the factory would have been severely compromised. What the prospectus established was who had the right to make calculations about the space. As a formal government document, the prospectus provided an inventory of industrial plants that the state had constructed in 1942. This early description and measurement would be used a few years later by Lockwood in its assessment of the factory's value and future once it had been decommissioned.

In order to keep tabs on the state's property it was necessary for federal agencies to make precise and detailed calculations of the industrial site. The prospectus provided the details of the DPC's investment in land, buildings, equipment, and other facilities. The manufacturing site's 135 acres in the industrial and working-class suburb of Melrose Park had 14.5 miles of streets, 6 principal buildings, and 16 auxiliary and minor structures. In clinical detail, the prospectus laid out the factory's floor space, number of stories, and construction materials and lighting. This was followed by an inventory of the 10,000 pieces of production equipment, 3,500 portable tools, 1,000 office mechanical devices, 5,000 pieces of kitchen equipment, and 80,000 items of office and factory furniture.[33]

Here was a massive industrial enterprise tabulated in the cool language of the administrative number and the utilitarian text. Attached to the prospectus was a one-page semimonthly report written by the DPC's engineering department that laid out in even more precise detail the dollars invested in land, buildings, machinery, and other facilities, as well as time schedules of the commitments of these monies, the operation date of DPC-purchased machinery, and information on current and peak employment levels. In the clear, modern language of the industrial engineer-technocrat, the simple prospectus of plancor 39 sets out the state's investment in the industrial realm.

Industrial engineers, both private and public, brought their technical expertise to bear on wartime industrial facilities. The federal government became a significant industrial calculative agent the moment it became involved in financing production, owning manufacturing facilities, coordinating the flow of materials and commodities, allocating scarce resources among competing interests, and working with private companies such as Lockwood Greene to measure and evaluate its property. For the staff at the DPC's Chicago office, calculating the size, employment levels, and number of office items of state-owned factories such as Buick was an everyday event. Working with and thinking through the day-to-day necessities of industrial production with industrialists and industrial engineers became normal practice.

In order to do this it was necessary to undertake two things. First, professionals such as engineers and surveyors had to clearly demarcate the boundary between public and private property. To ensure that there were no legal, financial, or administrative issues, federal agencies had to establish the boundaries of what belonged to them, from the plot lines that encompassed the industrial site to the factory's machinery. Second, a value had to be placed on government property so that it could be sold in the marketplace. This required laying out the character and size of the workforce, the type of production processes and work practices, and the assembling of information from different sites and sets of expertise. This marshaling of information became commonplace for federal industrial engineers. The prospectus and the semimonthly report were completed for every plancor. Through these government forms the government formulated a body of information on their industrial holdings, providing agencies with information about the investments poured into a massive industrial complex such as the Buick plant or smaller expenditures on machine tools to allow a firm to meet its wartime contracts.

Lockwood Greene contributed to the government's industrial engineering material by collecting information about the factory's everyday affairs. The need to dispose of industrial property at the end of the war required the government to bring in private industrial engineering companies to describe, assess, and value industrial sites. Engineering firms were involved in both the building of state-owned industrial sites operated by firms such as Buick and in the government's disposal of wartime property to the private sector once the war was over. Lockwood was one of the industrial engineering companies that mobilization agencies such as the DPC and disposal agencies such as the WAA brought in to help make sense of the dismantling of federal industrial property.

The origins of Lockwood's work on plancor 39 started with communications between DPC offices in Washington and Chicago and the General Motors headquarters in Detroit. The mobilization agency was eager to sell the factory to private interests as quickly as possible, while General Motors was considering whether the wartime plant would fit into its postwar plans. The government and the auto company sought independent companies that could provide them with expert advice on how to proceed with the large Melrose Park facility once the war had come to an end. The first step was to commission a professional appraisal corporation to determine the facility's value and future use of the plancor 39's building, utilities, and yard facilities. The DPC chose Lockwood Greene.

After visiting the factory in the summer of 1944, Lockwood Greene presented its seventy-two-page report at the end of August. The report provided a detailed appraisal of every building, machine, and piece of equipment and came to the conclusion that the normal replacement cost was just over $15 million. A plot plan at a scale of 250 feet to the inch laid out all of the plants' buildings, parking lots, roads, railroad spurs, and storage areas. An accompanying letter dryly summarized the particulars, while discussing what to do with the manufacturing site at the end of the war. The engineering company's view was that it was difficult to know how to proceed with disposal as "we have no way of judging how these buildings will be used." Calculating scale and value were impossible without knowing use. It did venture to state, however, that the plant's 170,000 square feet of manufacturing floor space could be used by one of GM's subsidiary plants.[34] Through its interaction with government and industry officials, the evaluation of a Chicago area plancor, and the preparation of a long report, Lockwood Greene contributed to evaluating and assessing the federal government's industrial holdings and participated in the calculations necessary to relationally frame the plancor within the broader industrial world. Despite Lockwood Greene's recommendation, the Melrose Park plant did not fit into GM's plans.

As the Buick case shows, assessing federally owned industrial space was a joint process binding public and private institutions together in a negotiated calculation that linked government agencies, industrial engineers, and industrial corporations. While the contract between Lockwood Greene and the DPC ended once the report was delivered, the effects of the report continued to determine what happened to the factory. The report established the property's future as a commodity, situated the property within the larger industrial property market, and shaped how it was understood by America's industrial corporations. Without the expertise of industrial engineering firms such as Lockwood Greene, the federal government would not have been able to determine the value of its property and would not have been able to sell its large number of factories to private interests once the war was over.

Day and Zimmerman and the Seneca Shipyards

By 1940, the industrial engineering firm Day and Zimmerman was one of the nation's major consultants to corporations and governments. As this section demonstrates, Day and Zimmerman played a critical role in the assessment of a new wartime federally owned industrial space for disposal to private interests. It shows how private and public actors created specific industrial-government relationships around industrial property. As with Lockwood Greene's work on Melrose Park, Day and Zimmerman's assessment of the Seneca Shipyards was responsible for helping federal disposal agencies make sense of their inventory of defense factories.

Day and Zimmerman undertook two main tasks during the war. First, it designed, constructed, and managed defense industrial facilities such as the Cressona Ordnance plant and Philadelphia's Marine Corps Depot. Elsewhere, the company received a $34 million contract from the army's Quartermaster Department to design, construct, and operate a shell-loading plant near Burlington, Iowa. Similar to Sanderson and Porter's actions in Elwood, Day and Zimmerman's entry into rural Iowa turned a rural area occupied by a handful of people into an industrial site owned by the federal government, overseen by the military, and operated by a large industrial engineering corporation.[35]

The second task was to evaluate existing factories. In the summer of 1940, for example, Day and Zimmerman received a contract to prepare plans for the rehabilitation of Philadelphia's Cramp Shipyards. As part of the "Two Ocean Navy" program initiated in July 1940, the shipyards were reframed as a desirable production site. As a calculable industrial space, the site was made ready to build cruisers under contract with the navy. Day and Zimmerman's job was to evaluate the shipyards, which were in disrepair after years of neglect since their closing in 1927, and to make recommendations about how to fit them up for production. Working with the navy, the new owners, led by financier William Averell Harriman, implemented Day and Zimmerman's recommendations in the fall of 1940. Over the course of the war the shipyard received more than $21 million in navy funding to repair and expand its facilities. Day and Zimmerman's wartime activity was not limited to Philadelphia. In several other places, the industrial engineering company built, operated, and appraised industrial spaces that became incorporated into the calculative deliberations of the nation's mobilization plans.[36]

As the preparation of the Cramp shipyard for war production with federal funding shows, reports from industrial engineering firms framed the industrial site in terms of its legal status, boundaries, and productive condition. As part of thinking through when and where to build industrial facilities, the government and the military had to choose between competing locations, compile information about land ownership, measure property, and decide on the company to build and operate the plant. By 1944, as state-owned industrial plants were put up for sale to the private sector, it was necessary to revalue, remeasure, and reappraise its property. Over the next five years government and military officials recalculated the financial value of its stock of war plants. Much of this was done internally by wartime agencies such as the Army Services Forces and Corps of Engineers, and the various appraisal divisions of the Reconstruction Finance Corporation (RFC), DPC, WAA, and General Services Administration. In other cases, especially in those plancors where disposal was a complicated matter, appraisals were contracted out to industrial engineering firms.

Day and Zimmerman was one of those companies. The Philadelphia firm made appraisals across the country for federal agencies. One was the 1946 evaluation and analysis of the building of the navy-funded shipyards in Seneca, a small town near Chicago that manufactured 157 Landing Ships, Tanks (LST) between 1942 and 1945. These flat-bottomed, oceangoing vessels were designed to transport tanks and people over long distances and to land them on open beachfront. As with the Elwood plant, the shipyard was built on Chicago's prairie fringe. According to one commentator, "A vast ship yard has sprung up almost as if by magic. Eight months ago the spot was just pasture land. . . . But all is changed now." The government expropriated 192 acres of pastureland in early 1942 for $3.2 million. Construction started in May 1942 and ended by the end of the year. The shipyard cost $7.3 million to build, of which $4.2 million went to buildings and another $2.2 million to machinery and equipment. It was a substantial industrial complex with 15 construction berths, railroad spurs that connected directly to the Rock Island and Pacific Railroad, launching basins, docks and piers, various administrative and miscellaneous buildings, and 115 temporary and semi-permanent buildings.[37]

The shipyard assessed by Day and Zimmerman was built by the Chicago Bridge and Iron Company, whose chief activity before 1940 was the manufacture of heavy steel plate equipment, large-scale water systems, and metal bridges. The specialty steel fabricator had three mills: Birmingham, Alabama, Greenville, Pennsylvania, and the Pullman community in Chicago. In the winter of 1942, the company agreed to the navy's request to build and operate the shipyards, which they did by combining in-house, military, and contracted industrial engineering expertise. Over the next few years it shipped specially engineered steel from its three factories to the new shipyards. Using engineering and technical knowledge gained from years of structural manufacturing and installation, the company built a modern factory, assembled a workforce, and introduced innovative shipbuilding practices. The last LST was launched in June 1945. By that time only three thousand of the more than ten thousand workers remained at the site. By August the shipyard had closed completely. Mothballed for a year, it was declared surplus in June 1946 and put up for sale to private interests.[38]

The calculations around the disposal of the facility required an evaluation of the plancor before it was put on the selling block. The WAA made an internal assessment after the shipyards were closed in the summer of 1945. Receiving permission from the military to sell the plant in June 1946, the WAA's Chicago region zone administrator advertised the factory for sale or lease in seventeen national papers. They received only one bid, a paltry offer of $5,000 for a warehouse valued by the agency at $118,000.[39] In the fall of 1946, questioning their own assessment of the plant, and unsure of how to dispose of the facility, the WAA sought advice. The inability to sell off the facility—a large shipyard with a wide assortment of facilities making an extremely specialized product plunked down in the middle of the prairies a thousand miles from the coast—required the WAA to obtain a professional assessment from an industrial engineering company. A reputable industrial engineering firm such as Day and Zimmerman was an obvious choice given its long history of working with shipyards in Philadelphia and elsewhere.

Day and Zimmerman was asked to bring its engineering expertise to bear on a simple question: How could the federal government dispose of the shipyards? The contract called for a two-volume report: the first to cover the property's fair value and the second its reproduction cost.[40] Day and Zimmerman made several assessments. It gave the WAA a detailed evaluation of the shipyard's finances and facilities. In the company's view, there was a vast difference between what it would cost to reproduce the shipyard's facilities and what they could expect to receive in the market. The $3.4 million reproduction cost contrasted sharply with the fair value of $1.3 million the government could reasonably expect to gain given the problems associated with the facility. The company's estimate of fair value was calculated on the "extent to which [land and building] improvements would be necessary" to make the site workable for general manufacturing and "such intangible items as building location and arrangement." Indeed, given the plant's location and the fact that the newcomers would have to compete with competitive private barge manufacturers, Day and Zimmerman concluded that the "actual shipbuilding facilities have no value other than as salvage." The property could be used for general manufacturing purposes once the ship-making facilities had been removed. This argument was backed up by a written description of the project itself, laying out the advantages for prospective industrial buyers.[41]

The Philadelphia engineering firm also undertook an analysis of the locational calculations behind the choice of Seneca as an inland shipbuilding center. The company argued that the 196-acre industrial site with its fifteen shipbuilding berths and hundreds of buildings with access to railroad switches and U.S. Route 6 had been built because of the absence of a local industrial base. Following federal policy that pushed new industrial facilities to areas of labor surplus, the military looked to rural areas such as Seneca, which, unlike other shipbuilding centers that were working to full capacity during the war, had an array of advantages. Most notably, the location on the outskirts of the Chicago region offered Chicago Bridge "labor markets that were not yet overloaded with work," low labor and property costs, and excellent access to national markets through Chicago. Seneca, according to the company's appraisal, was "in an ideal position to serve the whole country."[42] Day and Zimmerman's report showed how local factors of labor and location in rural areas such as Seneca were brought into the calculations of mobilization agencies, national labor markets, and industrial production.

Interest was also generated about the social conditions of the shipbuilding center. Calculations about property lines and market values were paralleled by those about the impact of industrial mobilization on the town itself. In 1944, the Federal Security Agency's Office of Community War Services (OCWS) released a report on the "prairie shipyard." The report was written by the University of Chicago Committee on Human Development, with input from Chicago Bridge, academics (most notably Robert Havighurst of the University of Chicago), the Federal Works Agency, the Federal Public Housing Authority, the United States Public Health Service, and the National Housing Agency. The purpose of the study was "to analyze social changes that have resulted from war industry in this community." Unlike Day and Zimmerman, the OCWS focused on the human side of mobilization through a compilation of statistics on employment, in-migration, population housing stock, and public works projects, providing a description of the town's key elements.[43]

Both the social and industrial engineering reports sought to determine the social and economic consequences of using federal funds and networks to create a new industrial site. As the OCWS author put it, the wartime industrial facilities "are all contributions to the *new* Seneca." The old "village trading center" had been replaced by a new industrial one directly linked to Chicago, where "some of the primary construction of the ships is done." The author also suggested that the report itself was "a signal for renewed *attention* given to Seneca by Government agencies as the production program enters its new and enlarged phase." While Day and Zimmerman were reluctant to make sociological statements about the new industrial site, it did frame the shipyard with "factors external to the property." Its view was that while the town had certain advantages, the WAA's ability to refashion the industrial property and thereby the town for postwar industrial use was limited.[44]

Both Day and Zimmerman and the OCWS were clear in their understanding that federal funding of manufacturing facilities, the building and selling of new wartime industrial sites, and spending on huge wartime production contracts required ongoing coordination and assessment. They were also clear that wartime investment created new social and political spaces as well as industrial ones. Forced by the need to account for government funds and the social, political, and economic consequences of production decisions, war production districts such as Seneca were subject to fundamental changes that brought a variety of agencies, groups, and individuals together under one administrative umbrella. Private industrial engineering companies such as Day and Zimmerman contributed to this new world by using their technical, managerial, and industrial expertise to make sense of the changes. Industrial engineers, who were key calculative agents, had a decisive impact on the long-term impact of wartime investment, the assessment of industrial property, and the making of wartime industrial sites.

Conclusion

The industrial engineering company was a key institution in the building, operation, and disposing of state-funded production facilities both during and after the war. As Fine and Remington point out, "Military construction was to be largely a civilian endeavor."[45] Although there appears to have been little difference between military and private engineering practices, mobilization agencies nonetheless did seek out industrial engineers. One reason for this was that the military's construction branches were seriously understaffed. The wartime agencies were stretched beyond their capacity. Another was that engineering companies brought with them unparalleled expertise about how to build complex industrial plants. The depth of knowledge that companies such as Sanderson and Porter, Lockwood Greene, and Day and Zimmerman had in designing, building, evaluating, and operating industrial spaces could not be replicated within federal and military agencies. Private companies with their deep reservoir of scientific knowledge, managerial skills, and business networks had to be directly incorporated into the federal and military system of defense factory construction if mobilization was to be successful.

These industrial engineering companies provided the state with an engineering expertise that covered the industrial property itself and also placed the site within its wider regional and national context. The state and the military had to have place-based financial, property, and industrial data if they were going to have an accurate understanding of the industrial facilities. They also needed to be able to compare local economic, labor, and housing conditions against each other. As the wartime agencies became increasingly involved in the workings of production and the ownership of industrial property, the need to situate their projects within the wider region became more of an imperative.

The industrial facility was a calculable object for the federal government during the war years and in the immediate postwar period. Faced by the imperatives of war, the difficulty of constructing defense factories, and the cost of building new industrial space, the state had to do two things: it had to generate a greater awareness of the industrial world in which its investments were embedded; and it had to become involved with a large number of nongovernmental agents such as industrial engineering companies. The public-private relationships that were formed through these actions reformulated the military-industrial complex by bringing in the industrial engineers as a junior partner. The relationships also worked to reframe the industrialization of the communities in which the state had invested in the postwar period.

CHAPTER 6

The Disposal Regime

Factories and National Security

By the end of 1943 the interest of military-industrial complex officials in building state-owned war plants was on the wane, and they were turning their attention to the place of these factories in the American postwar economy. With the continuing success on the battlefields of Europe and Asia, officials began to seriously contemplate what to do about defense factories once the war was over. By April 1945 a solution had been found. Industrial space was no longer to be an object to be financed and owned by the government. Rather, the country's large number of government defense plants were to be sold off to private interests. Reverting back to the prewar patterns, industrial investment was to be left to the private sector. This shift required reframing the place of industrial property in the relationship between the state, the military, and industry. The federal government was to dismantle the apparatus that had been put in place to construct wartime manufacturing facilities and to replace it with one centered on disposing of surplus industrial property. At the same time, some of the defense factories were to be included in an industrial reserve that was part of America's new national security system. The right to control new industrial investment was handed back to the private sector. This postwar industrial disposal regime was rooted in two features of America after 1945: the right of private interests to own and control property, and the emergence of the new system of national security.

This chapter examines the building of this industrial disposal regime between 1943 and 1950. The disposal of industrial plants is important for two reasons. In the first place, it helps us understand the calculations that created the boundary between public and private title. Even though the federal government's mandate after 1945 was to dispose of its industrial property to private interests, it continued to own factories and to liaise with private companies. The line between public and private interests in industrial property was redrawn. In the second place, state-owned industrial facilities continued to have a direct presence in the workings of the military-industrial alliance through their incorporation in the early postwar national security system. Little is known about the role of industrial disposal in this system. At the close of World War II, most Americans were concerned with returning to some form of normalcy and the rebuilding of disrupted lives. The federal government and the military, among other things, were looking to build the administrative and coercive elements of the security state and international policy. Most industrialists were looking to make the transition from a wartime economy and to build up industrial capacity, market, and profits. Nevertheless, the disposal of government-owned property and the creation of an industrial plant reserve did tax the minds of the state, the military, and industry. In the process, as this chapter demonstrates, these key calculative agents created an industrial disposal regime that oversaw the building of a postwar political alliance around state-owned defense factories.

The regime had three key elements. An alliance of military-industrial officials, many of whom had been involved in building defense plants, worked to frame the wartime factory as a problematic object and to devise policy to divest the state of the industrial facilities built between 1940 and 1945. They quickly came to the conclusion as laid out in the 1944 Baruch-Hancock and other reports that the state should "leave the investment process and sell its industrial portfolio to the private sector as soon as possible."[1] The regime also consisted of a set of governmental infrastructures that terminated the life of a factory as a state-operated working object and established the legal and administrative practices that enabled the federal government to dispose of its industrial facilities. The most obvious manifestation of this was the creation of agencies such as the War Assets Administration (WAA) and the passing of legislation such as the 1944 Surplus Property Act and the 1948 Industrial Reserve Act. Finally, military-industrial complex officials were given control over a specific set of federal resources and the administrative apparatus through which industrial disposal and national security policy was implemented. The creation and improvement of this property disposal regime was part of the broader development of the military-industrial complex that emerged during World War II.

Contesting and Framing the Disposal System

In the last two years of the war the federal government created a disposal regime that oversaw the selling of American defense factories to private interests. With the end of the war in sight, the question of the government's right to own industrial property resurfaced. Industrialists, real estate agents, government officials, and others wanted to know what the federal government was going to do with its thousands of industrial properties scattered across the country. In the eyes of many, while the government may have had good reason to finance, build, and own shipyards, ordnance plants, aircraft factories, and foundries, it did not have the right to retain ownership once hostilities were over. The answer was quickly found: sell the state-owned industrial property to private interests and pass legislation allowing for the sale of surplus defense property.

Reframing the defense factory required recalculating the place of the state-owned factory in American economic and political circles. The people engaged in setting out what the disposal legislation would accomplish had to assess the place of state-owned factories in American society, appraise the value of the properties, and evaluate the impact that disposal would have on industries and places. This was not straightforward; the calculations required to pass the appropriate legislation involved a fight over industrial facilities by political, economic, and military interests. The issue of what to do with defense factories engaged the notice of a wide slice of American society, from Roosevelt and Truman down through Congress and its various committees and subcommittees to military officers, civil government agency officials, corporate executives, union officials, local politicians, industry pressure groups, and workers. Despite varied views and participation in this debate, the key players behind the making of the disposal program were, not surprisingly, the federal government, the military, and corporate America.[2]

The question of what to do with war factories appeared on the federal government's radar as soon as America became involved in the war. As early as 1941 some government departments were considering the place of industrial plants in postwar conversion. The Commerce Department's Business Advisory Council established a Committee on Economic Policy. The committee was chaired by Marion Folsom of Kodak and made up of academics, military officers, businesspeople, and bureaucrats; its mandate was to consider problems of postdefense reconversion. Its lengthy 1944 report laid out the types of problems to be encountered in the disposal process and the solutions to overcome these problems.[3] The committee was not alone. Fred Berquist, a Department of Justice economist, for example, reported in 1943 that rapid disposal would have "inequitable impacts" and that it would be impossible to convert all wartime plants to peacetime uses. In his view, "orderly liquidation" was required.[4]

At the same time, studies by academics and federal officials appeared in scholarly journals. Clifton Mack, director of the Department of Justice procurement office, wrote a paper with a Harvard research fellow in 1943 arguing that the growing interest in disposal arose out of the growing shortage of critical materials. In their opinion, selling defense factories would alleviate the demand for steel, copper, and lumber. A year later, John Sumner, an economist working with the Office of Price Administration (OPA), published a paper that explored the impact of public policy on property disposal.[5] The question of what to do about surplus industrial facilities was clearly on the agenda of many working in policy making and academic circles.

Others were concerned about the disposal of state-owned surplus factories. More interested than most were real estate and related industries. In April 1944, for example, the New York Building Commission appointed a committee of real estate, building, and financial executives to look into the issue. Its task, which was to offer suggestions to the federal authorities on how to proceed with disposal, was based on the business class's strongly held conviction that "the construction industry had a 'tremendous stake' in the disposal of war plants."[6] In their view, industrial property had to revert back to private hands. A week later, Herbert Nelson, vice-president of the National Association of Real Estate Boards, warned that the disposal of defense factories would be accompanied by a host of serious problems. Although he refrained from informing the *Chicago Tribune* correspondent what these problems might be, he did state that the association will continue "its campaign for definite disposition procedures that will bring about an orderly liquidation with eventual full return to private ownership."[7]

Groups with strong interests in place and industry, such as chambers of commerce, property associations, and financial institutions, sought to shape the discussion. Those with the greatest capacity to shape federal calculations were industrial executives. Their search for profits and market share in the postwar period forced them to frame surplus plants in relation to markets, capacity, technology, costs, and labor. In their opinion, the ability of private enterprise to control its own destiny would be undermined if industrial property remained in the hands of the state. Accordingly, wartime state-owned industrial facilities had to be placed on the competitive, open market. State intervention in the property market was no longer a necessity now that the war was over. Property relations should return to prewar conditions.

By 1944 the concern with defense factories forced the government to devise a set of principles, create administrative practices, provide funding, and enact legislation to guide their disposal. The most important single intervention was a report written by Bernard Baruch and John Hancock. Released in February 1944, the report called for the creation of a surplus property administrator to coordinate the disposal of all federal and military properties. In their opinion, the government had to follow several principles. The most important was that the postwar state should not operate plants in competition with private industry. Reflecting the interests of most business groups, Baruch and Hancock argued that the state had to withdraw from ownership of industrial plants and had to use the wartime plancors to rebuild the private sector. This point was reinforced a month later by a report from the Truman Committee, which argued for disposing of plants as quickly as possible. Building on growing concerns with postwar security needs, the committee also advocated that some factories be maintained in a standby status in case of future emergencies.[8] The safety of postwar America, the committee stressed, rested in part on the creation of a reserve of industrial plants that would be overseen and coordinated by the government, the military, and industry.

By the end of 1944 a postwar industrial disposal regime was emerging. The key elements of this were summed up by OPA economist John Sumner. In his view, disposal had to fulfill several functions. In the first place, it had to positively affect the private market by containing inflation, controlling the timing and terms of sales, and maintaining the competitive character of the economy by reducing monopoly and helping small business. Second, it had to ensure full employment by selling factories to labor-intensive companies. Finally, it had to support the country's well-being by promoting national security through the permanent maintenance of productive capacities and securing the recovery of public investment by selling at a fair price.[9]

The different parties involved in industrial plants in one capacity or another reached agreement about how to proceed with disposal before the war's end.[10] In February 1944, Roosevelt created the Surplus War Property Administration (SWPA), which was housed in the Office of War Administration. After several organizational changes, the SWPA became the WAA in March 1946.[11] These agencies worked under the legislative ambit of the Surplus Property Act of October 1944. The act had twenty objectives, such as securing the "most effective use" of industrial property, the "reestablishment of a peacetime economy of free independent private enterprise," and the "fair value of surplus property."[12] Although it did not directly address the issue of national security, the act shifted the administrative focus away from plant construction and mobilization and framed defense factories as objects to be sold to private interests. In the process, it established clear boundaries separating surplus plants from other types of factories and the procedures necessary to undertake the reevaluation of wartime industrial sites. Finally, new institutional and legal forms created the financial and administrative resources to be used to sell factories to private interests. With the passing of the October 1944 legislation, the basic calculative structure of the postwar industrial disposal regime was in place.

Selling Wartime Industrial Plants

The implementation of the Surplus Property Act, however, was not a straightforward affair. The agencies entrusted to dispose of the state's industrial sites suffered from internal conflict, poorly defined lines of authority, partisan oversight from Congress, pressure from corporate America, and military intransigence. Disposal proceeded slowly as hard-to-sell factories remained on the books, and the armed forces were reluctant to make their manufacturing plants surplus even after the surrender of the Japanese. Moreover, the many competing objectives in the act worked to undermine an orderly disposal program.

Despite these obstacles, disposal agencies successfully developed practices that framed state-owned industrial properties as commodities that could be sold on the private property market, with the result that billions of dollars of wartime industrial property were sold to American firms. To make this possible, military and government disposal officials had to calculate the place of the defense factory in American society. This involved creating a regime that allowed federal officials to draw lines of authority between the competing sponsors of wartime plants, establish functional disposal procedures, make surveys to determine what was to be sold, build an inventory of surplus properties, and promote and publicize these facilities.

The creation of an effective procedure for selling industrial facilities was not easy. Often at loggerheads, different sponsoring units had competing systems for appraising whether plants should be declared surplus and placed on the market. Will Clayton, the administrator of the SWPA, faced challenges from outside the agency. Clayton, who wanted independence over the disposal regime, fought with Congress, which sought to direct disposal by legislation, and the military, which wanted to maintain control over its industrial properties. Even the clearer lines of responsibility established by the Surplus Property Act did little to promote administrative clarity. Accordingly, the SWPA's first year focused on planning and shaping the disposal process by setting out clearer lines of authority and better working relations between those involved in disposal.[13]

The government, military, and business bodies engaged in disposal did seek to resolve their competing interests. This was made clear in a memorandum written by Colonel Richard Tatlow of the army's real estate and facilities disposal unit.[14] The committee, consisting of representatives from industry, the government, and the military, met in Washington to discuss what to do with the government's defense factories. With the Japanese surrender, the question of how to proceed had become a pressing issue for many agencies, including the Surplus Property Board (SPB), the Reconstruction Finance Corporation (RFC), and the War Department. Questions about the rapid disposal to private interests, the multiplicity of interests in the plants themselves, and the fuzzy boundaries separating the various interests dogged the proceedings. For many, a single disposal agency was essential, as this would lead to "administrative simplicity."[15] This was not lost on the real estate and production sides of the army, the SPB, and the RFC. Tatlow's meeting was an attempt to appeal to these interests by streamlining the disposal process and demarcating clear boundaries of authority and decision making. Following the War Department's suggestion, the committee agreed that the industrial sites "be turned over to a single disposal agency."[16] While slow to materialize, the WAA became that agency. The result was the creation of an institution with calculative powers to determine the future of state-owned industrial property.

The establishment of this institution was paralleled by the increasing cooperation of the military. This spurred disposal. In tune with the Tatlow committee discussion of how to proceed with disposing of wartime industrial property, the military had started to inform the disposal agency of the manufacturing plants they no longer needed as the war wound down. By December 1945, the armed forces had presented the agency with a comprehensive picture of their ship and aircraft needs in the postwar period. Other institutions that owned war plants followed suit. The RFC made significant strides in devising disposal practices for the factories it had funded, including establishing the basis for negotiations between the agency and private companies. On top of this, the WAA had filed most of the required reports on federal industrial plants with Congress, thus allowing the agency to know the full range of plants that were to be sold. More than 430 factories valued at $2.6 billion had been declared surplus by the end of December.[17]

The administrative forms and procedures put in place over the following four years accelerated the disposal of industrial facilities. Nevertheless, the selling of plants proceeded slowly. Worried about this, the WAA created a Price Review Board and gave it the power to speed up disposal. Other important interventions were the reorganization of the Industrial Division, the strengthening of field staffs' ability to facilitate sales, and the introduction of standardized Real Property Disposal Board procedures. Together, these accelerated the disposal process and gave the WAA greater control over factory negotiations. By the end of 1947 almost $6 billion of industrial property had been acquired by the WAA and made ready for sale.[18] Of this, $3.4 billion had been sold or leased, with the remainder still available for disposal. Almost two years later, in the summer of 1949, the total value of industrial real estate available to be sold was $7.8 billion. Of this, $6.4 billion had been disposed of by sale, lease, and other forms of disposal, such as transfer to federal agencies and public organizations. After these impressive few years, the rate of disposal in the following years was trivial.[19]

The disposal agencies undertook a two-part promotional campaign to sell state properties to private interests. The first consisted of informing corporate leaders about the plancors through existing business networks. It was expected that once the availability of industrial plants became known that news would travel through the well-worn corporate communication channels. It is impossible to know how useful these circuits of knowledge were, although given that the world of industrial executives was small and well resourced, the information must have been passed on with some effect.

A much more effective and accountable strategy was a promotional campaign of circulating information about the defense plants. Disposal agencies launched a promotional campaign in 1944 consisting of newspaper advertisements in national and regional newspapers and the publication of annual directories listing the factories available for purchase. The purpose of these drives was to advertise which industrial properties were available and to help manufacturers and other interested people navigate their way through the bureaucratic thickets that had been set up to assess, monitor, and control the flow of state-owned industrial property to the private market. From the very beginning, the WAA reached out to the industrial community through word of mouth and more formal methods.

The WAA alerted the industrial world to the availability of surplus industrial property by advertising in regional and national newspapers. Frequently, several plancors were bundled together in a single advertisement. On September 17, 1945, for example, the RFC ran a full-page advertisement in the *Wall Street Journal* advertising eighteen plants from across the country. As the RFC phrased it, the agency will receive "proposals for purchase or lease of these properties in the interests of continued employment."[20] Eighteen months later, the army advertised thirty-one plants as being available for lease (Figure 6.1). The WAA also advertised one factory at a time. This was often the case with the larger facilities that were proving difficult to sell. A full-page spread in the *New York Times* in June 1946 publicized plancor 422, the Chicago steel mill that had been operated by Republic Steel during the war (Figure 6.2). Along with a detailed description of the war factory, the ad encouraged interested parties to submit a proposal. The WAA informed potential purchasers that the sealed bids received in response to a previous advertisement had been rejected and that the agency was seeking to obtain "a reasonably satisfactory return to the Government."[21] Regardless of the reasons outlined in the sales pitch, the WAA used newspapers to publicize the factories available for sale and to inform industrial executives of the specific terms.

While newspaper ads alerted casual readers to the availability of government-owned defense plants, more serious potential purchasers could seek out government industrial facility listings. The Defence Plant Corporation (DPC) published the first one before the war ended. In March 1944 the RFC dispatched government and private engineers to make an industrial survey of government-owned factories and to publish the results. The directory provided descriptions of 879 factories that were for sale.[22] An August 1945 listing was touted as "an aid to those interested in their utilization for peacetime production." The agency focused on two groups: industrial firms seeking to secure the "additional facilities, required to satisfy widely expanded markets," and government and community groups that would use the facilities to "assure the operation of plants in their communities, thus providing employment and further development of local resources." Arranged by state, the listing gave several pieces of information for each plancor: location, wartime lessee, plant, land, buildings, machinery and equipment, utilities, and transportation. Prospective buyers could receive detailed information—including engineering reports, plot plans, architectural drawings, local amenity information, and illustrated brochures—from the RFC.[23]

These listings turned into an annual publication called *Plant Finder* (Figure 6.3). This inventory of government-owned factories had two main sections:

FIGURE 6.1. Advertising War Department industrial facilities, 1947. Thirty-one government-owned plants are offered for lease.
Source: *Washington Post*, March 2, 1947, M5.

GOVERNMENT-OWNED
STEEL PLANT
FOR SALE or LEASE

The War Assets Administration invites parties interested in the purchase or lease of the South Chicago Steel Plant, owned by the Government, to enter into negotiations with its Iron and Steel Branch at Washington, at the address below, either by letter or conference. This plant is now being operated by lessee under an interim lease arrangement running from month to month and terminable on thirty days notice.

PLANT DESCRIPTION
(Known as Republic Steel Corp. — Plancor 422)

LOCATION: South Chicago, Illinois
LAND: Approx. 160 Acres
BUILDINGS: 27 Major and 28 Minor Buildings
STORAGE YARD: For Iron Ore, Coal and Limestone
COKE PLANT: Capacity—405,000 Net Tons
BY PRODUCT PLANT: Coal Chemical and Benzol Plants
SINTERING PLANT: Capacity—336,000 Net Tons
OPEN HEARTH DEPARTMENT: 4—200 Ton Furnaces
ELECTRIC FURNACE DEPARTMENT: 9—70 Ton Furnaces
BLOOMING MILL: 44"; Capacity—960,000 Net Tons
BAR MILL: 36"—32"; Capacity—480,000 Net Tons
TRANSPORTATION: Rail and Water
WATER SUPPLY: River and City Mains
POWER: Purchased
GAS: Natural Gas—Purchased

The War Assets Administration is seeking to dispose of this plant on a competitive negotiated basis at the earliest possible date. When it appears that negotiations will result in a reasonably satisfactory return to the Government, a cut-off date for any further negotiations and delivery of negotiated bids will be established and all bidders and other interested parties will be given advance notice of such date. Information on this plant can be secured by addressing inquiries to the address below.

A previous advertisement of this plant invited sealed bids for its purchase or lease. Sealed bids received as a result of the previous advertisement have been rejected. This is a re-advertisement for the purchase or lease of the plant and provides for a negotiated purchase or lease instead of sealed bids for purchase or lease.

Address all inquiries and proposals to:

WAR ASSETS ADMINISTRATION
OFFICE OF REAL PROPERTY DISPOSAL
Room 4050, Railroad Retirement Building
Washington 25, D. C.

FIGURE 6.2. Steel plant advertisement, 1946. Like many others, the plancor in South Chicago operated by Republic Steel during the war is put up for sale by the War Assets Administration in 1946.
Source: *New York Times*, June 22, 1946, 10.

FIGURE 6.3. *Plant Finder*, 1948. The *Plant Finder* listed the surplus government-owned industrial plants that were available for sale to private industry. Source: *Plant Finder: A Buyers' Guide* (Washington, D.C.: War Assets Administration, February 1948).

an opening statement and a listing of surplus defense plants by state; and a listing of leased surplus government-owned facilities. The individual factory listing was quite extensive, providing information on the factory's land, buildings, utilities, nearby transportation, and whether it was a national security plant. The one-page opening statement established the *Plant Finder*'s logic. In 1949, for example, this statement, entitled, "So that Private Enterprise May Know," informed prospective buyers that the guide offered them the "facts on available ready-built surplus industrial facilities." It went on to explain the advantages of buying these factories, informing prospective industrialists that the facilities offered a "practical solution" to their plant needs, provided an "economical entrance into new markets," and could be "acquired at material savings as compared with new construction costs." Tantalizingly, firm managers were told that the government would provide credit terms that would "prevent the dissipation of your presently need working capital" and "give you a sound competitive basis over the years to come." Moreover, the WAA offered executives access to "authorized industrial real estate brokers" in order to facilitate the purchasing process. Together, the newspaper advertising campaign and *Plant Finder* assisted the movement of government-owned industrial property to private hands.

The federal campaign for selling its industrial facilities was tied to the calculations manufacturers made about their company's postwar development. With the winding down of wartime production and the reversion to peacetime conditions, industrialists reformulated their plans for the future. Many hoped that the combination of government regulation and private enterprise would kick-start a virtuous cycle of industrial growth. If this was the case, new factory space would be required, and one source of space was government war plants. In this spirit, the WAA worked to incorporate surplus factory space into the calculative thinking of industrial executives. To this end, the agency proclaimed that surplus defense factories would benefit both the state and industry: "Every Government-owned plant put to work by private business means new opportunities for profitable American enterprise and cuts the cost of your Government."[24] Federally owned industrial facilities were reframed as critical elements of industrial growth and private enterprise.

Despite its success disposing of the most saleable properties, the WAA had a much more difficult time selling more specialized factories. By late 1947 the problem had become serious, and the agency needed to find a new strategy. This was made clear when Jess Larson, the WAA administrator, told Congress that "the more marketable surplus real properties have been disposed of, leaving those properties that do not readily attract buyers." The agency was forced to reevaluate its plans for disposing of the remaining plants, which involved reviewing what it knew about surplus factories, reassessing the plancor marketability, and rethinking disposal plans. To this end, a study of "the marketability of plants for their intended or for other uses" allowed the agency to revise the methods of disposal in the light of plant dismantling, scrambled facilities, and the national security clause.[25] The rethinking and reorganization of what to do with difficult-to-sell factories led Larson to introduce new disposal methods.

The most successful was the use of auction companies. Lacking the appropriate expertise, the WAA turned to private enterprise to fill the gap. Desperate to dispose of factories, the agency looked to experienced auctioneers. In much the same way that mobilization agencies sought the expertise of industrial engineering companies to design, build, operate, and evaluate plancors, the WAA looked to the specialized skills of auctioneers to dispose of factories. Private auction houses had, among other things, "extensive facilities for promotion and market contact," qualities that the agency lacked. The auction method was first tested on a Continental Motors plant in Garland, Texas, that had made tank engines. It was successful; the Joseph Day auctioneer company sold the plant to Kraft Foods for $611,000.[26] The system worked so well that Larson increased the number of industrial plants put up for auction. In the fall of 1948, the agency contracted with several auction brokers to sell two dozen war plants. By the end of 1948 the use of auctioneers had become one of the main methods for disposing of surplus industrial space.[27]

The WAA was also concerned with helping executives navigate a course through government bureaucracy. It was clear from wartime experience that industrial managers were concerned about time-consuming procedures and paper work. To help them wade through this morass, the agency printed "self-help" publications, such as *How to Buy or Lease Surplus Real Estate*. The thirteen-page brochure explained how to obtain wartime properties. Prospective buyers were informed that the booklet "sets forth the priorities, pricing, terms, proposed procedures, etc." they would encounter. For each type of property, the brochure discussed how to go about acquiring surplus property. The section on industrial properties described, among other things, how to find the factory (advertisements, *Plant Finder*), the methods used to appraise property ("by well-qualified appraisers or engineers"), how manufacturers could obtain information about facilities (visit regional offices), and the terms of purchase (20 percent cash down, the remainder paid over ten years at 4 percent on unpaid balance).[28] The WAA worked to help private industry have access to industrial properties.

By 1944 the answer to the question about what was going to happen to the thousands of government industrial properties was to sell them to private enterprise. How to actually accomplish this was largely a process of trial and error. The Great War did not provide a precedent for how to proceed; World War I factories were largely financed by private sources. Public funds accounted for only $600 million of a total of $9 billion. Most of this state funding was concentrated in shipbuilding, with little going to other industries.[29] There was little for Woodrow Wilson's government to dispose of. The scale and character of state-owned industrial property during World War II, however, demanded a different response from the Truman administration. The combination of government investment in defense factories and the domestic and international conditions at the end of the war ensured that the disposal of state-owned, military-controlled industrial sites would be framed quite differently from that of the earlier war. As a result, a disposal regime consisting of federal and military agencies created and deployed an infrastructure of policies, legislation, and procedures to oversee the dispersal of billions of dollars of state industrial facilities to private interests. At the same time that the federal government was active in the industrial property marketplace, the military was positioning federal factories as part of the postwar national security system.

Industrial Sites, an Industrial Reserve, and National Security

The government's disposal of surplus property was fashioned by government and military calculations about the place of industrial plants in the country's emerging postwar mobilization program and national security system. Even though the military's ideas of how to deal with factory disposal were slow, unformed, pragmatic, and haphazard, the issue quickly became linked to the building of a national security regime. After the war the United States was a battleground for groups fighting over the political and economic direction of postwar America. Even though there were innumerable fights between civilian and military leaders, different branches of the armed forces, Congress and the White House, Democrats and Republicans, and liberals and conservatives, the struggle fell into two groups. Those in favor of the creation of a security state were pitted against those who supported the continuance of an older political culture. The former were victorious. A national security state developed consisting of a unified armed forces within a new Department of Defense; a larger, permanent military budget; the forging of new institutions, most notably the National Security Council and the Central Intelligence Agency; the creation of a new class of national security managers; and the reorganization of Congress in response to national security demands.[30]

Defense factories became part of the national security system when they were included in the newly created industrial plant reserve. The need for factories that could produce munitions immediately had been on the agenda of military-industrial complex officials from the late 1930s. The military was not slow to note that its inability to quickly mount a fully operating program of industrial production hindered its ability to prepare for war in Europe and Asia. Accordingly, as the war wound down, people from across the ideological spectrum raised the issue of a reserve of standby industrial plants. The thinking behind the reserve was the America military would be a more effective fighting force if a set of industrial plants that could produce the necessary munitions were primed and ready to be quickly mobilized in the event of war. The idea received warm support from influential quarters. In 1944, both the Truman Committee and Robert Patterson, the undersecretary of war, backed the idea of a national industrial reserve.[31] In the same year, a SWPA report estimated that up to $5 billion of military-controlled industrial plants could stay in a standby condition.[32] Several military and congressional subcommittees investigated the issue and found the idea an attractive one.

In other words, federal and military policy makers, not wishing to repeat the problems that plagued industrial mobilization after 1939, looked to implement procedures that would frame a more effective mobilization program and to create a reserve of firms that would produce wartime products on a moment's notice. The key feature of the public-private partnership was that private firms on purchasing a surplus factory had to agree to have one or more of their plants registered by the military as standby facility and, in the event of war, convert their facility to military production. In return, corporations that participated in the reserve program would be among the first to receive wartime military supply contracts. This program blurred the lines between the private and public realms and ensured that relations between industry, government, and the military around industrial facilities would continue in the postwar period.

The success of the government's industrial reserve relied on building knowledge about the location, scale, and character of industries considered essential to national security. A 1944 confidential report by the Army Chief of Engineers on the military's nitric acid facilities illustrates the type of information that was gathered to make calculations about the place of the plants in the industrial reserve. The author recommended that some factories should be sold to private interests, while others deemed essential by the military were to be retained "in a 'stand-by' condition for future operation." Charles Brown, a War Department analyst, noted that the "stock pile" of acid-making plants would provide assurance of "ready, prompt supplies of nitric acid." Otto Sieder, the chair of the Advisory Board on Utilization of Surplus Industrial Facilities, agreed that a few wartime facilities had to be put aside for military purposes.[33]

Similarly, in October 1945, a Senate military affairs subcommittee heard about a plan by the Inter-Governmental Air Coordinating Committee to keep several midwestern engine plants as a peacetime reserve. The committee was assisted in the formulation of these plans by a range of industrial and military agents, including the assistant secretaries of air, war, and navy and members of the Civil Aeronautics Board and the Commerce Department. The idea was to retain six engine plants and ten airframe plants in standby condition. These could then be rented out or operated by the government for the peacetime production of three thousand military planes annually, and, if necessary, they could be quickly converted to producing even more under war conditions.[34]

The idea of an industrial reserve emerged out of both the experience of mobilizing production for World War II and the national security ethos that emerged in the final years of the war. The Munitions Board's rationale for recommending the establishment of a national industrial reserve in 1945 was rooted in the calculations about America's security in the postwar world. The authors of the board's report argued that growing hostilities with the Soviet Union meant that the armed forces had to have rapid access to extensive manufacturing facilities in the event of war. The board repeated the mantra that recent past experience had made it clear that it took time to design, build, and equip industrial plants capable of making large amounts of sophisticated war materials. The logic was that a delay in the mobilization of industrial capacity would endanger national security, and that therefore it was necessary to have a reserve of plants that could be immediately put into operation in case of war. In this scenario, the sale of wartime factories and their conversion to peacetime use without any continuing links to the military would rob the country of vital industrial resources, delay the conversion to a productive war footing, and undermine the nation's security.[35] The imperatives of national security demanded long-term military control over privately owned industrial facilities.

The military was relentless in its desire to create an industrial reserve. Its commitment to maintaining a reserve of industrial facilities is evident in a 1945 Armed Service Forces confidential report on the retention of industrial plants. The purpose of the report was to establish the basic principles for how to select the wartime factories to be retained by the army. Three were highlighted: the number of reserve wartime factories had to able to equip an army of 4.5 million soldiers; the reserve facilities had to be able to be mobilized on a moment's notice; and the reserve production units had to be linked to a research and development program. As the report noted, the military's calculations regarding national security "clearly demonstrate that the Armed Service Forces are placing their faith in the ability of American industry to provide the major portion of the industrial facilities required to produce war material in the event of a future emergency."[36] The report ended by recommending that the army retain sixty-two specialized installations that would form the basis of a military industrial reserve.

The idea of a reserve was not immediately accepted by Congress and business leaders. Afraid of government intervention in industrial matters, some pushed back. Even so, it was never far from the calculations of military planners. The Munitions Board led the charge, conferring with government and business officials about industrial preparedness on several occasions. A June 1946 conference on the subject was attended by military and private interests, including Lamotte Cohu, president of Aircraft Industries; Eugene Wilson, president of the Navy Industrial Association; Frederick Payne, vice-president of the Army Ordnance Association; Major General Edward Powers, assistant chief of Air Staff; Major General Everett Hughes, War Department chief of ordnance; and Vice Admiral

Edward Cochrane, chief of the navy's Bureau of Ships.[37] By the end of 1946, the Munitions Board had clearly decided on a system for keeping industrial plants within the military's embrace and was pushing to have the program in place. It proposed to retain and operate more than 60 war plants and to monitor more than 250 other factories. Anticipating the implementation of a plan, the WAA had already allowed some plants to be sold or leased with the proviso that they be available in the event of war. According to the Munition Board's chair, Cincinnati industrialist Richard Deupree, the military was seeking funds from Congress so that it could have immediate access to aircraft plants, shipyards, and specialized factories making guns, ammunition, and explosives.[38]

As the intervention from business leaders suggests, the military worked with a coalition of allies to mount a campaign to integrate hundreds of the country's manufacturing plants into the emerging national security system. The coalition outlined, publicized, and pushed the need for an industrial reserve. Along with the military, this coalition consisted of conservatives looking to construct a security apparatus, government officials seeking ways to dispose of hard-to-sell industrial facilities, and a public scared by the visions of enemy invasion. The industrial reserve, in this view, would be an important addition to America's arsenal and global influence. By early 1947 the armed services were pushing their case outside of military circles. A spokesman for the Munitions Board informed participants at the Women's Patriotic Conference on National Defense in January that the armed forces had already drafted a plan for industrial preparedness, a plan that included their ongoing control and maintenance of about 150 war factories.[39] At the same time, Kenneth Royall, the undersecretary of war, submitted a report to the secretary of war, Robert Patterson. Royall revealed that the War Department had "plans for continued Government control over 131 war plants" valued at more than $3.5 billion.[40] In March, Donald Nelson, the former chair of the WPB, submitted a report to the president calling for an industrial reserve. By this time, the idea championed by a range of political and economic interests had become an unstoppable force.[41]

The Munitions Board worked hand-in-hand with business organizations such as the Navy Industrial Association to create an industrial reserve. Established in 1919 in response to the country's poor mobilization record during the World War I, the association's mandate was to promote defense-based industries in government and military circles. In March 1947, eighteen industrialists were named to the association's industrial mobilization committee. The list of its members included chief executives from some of America's largest corporations, including General Motors, Bethlehem Steel, Western Electric, Bausch and Lomb, BF Goodrich, Allis-Chalmers, and Fairchild Engine and Airplane. The committee's purpose was to help the Munitions Board prepare an industrial mobilization program. With this in mind, committee members assisted in coordinating industry's contribution to the Munitions Board and the military in general. The committee was to act as liaison between interested groups by supplying information and to help firms get acquainted with the plan of national defense. Central to these functions was the need to create an industrial reserve to underpin their mobilization program.[42]

The efforts of these public and private organizations to build up an industrial reserve required framing wartime defense plants as objects to be worked on and making calculations that linked the available surplus factories with the needs of the military's postwar mobilization program. An industrial reserve was one part of the military's effort to consolidate its control over private industrial production and to build up its industrial resources. Information about and control over a select site of industrial sites was central to this strategy. By 1947, after a couple of years of building business and political relationships, the military was able to push through several pieces of legislation that formally brought some of the country's largest factories under its control. As a 1949 report to Congress noted, "the preservation of Federally-financed World War II manufacturing facilities in an industrial plant reserve became a cornerstone of the industrial mobilization planning efforts within the National Military Establishment."[43] The idea of standby plants in an industrial reserve that had been under discussion since 1940 had become by the late 1940s an accepted component of the postwar national security regime. Working together, leaders from the military-industrial complex produced the reserve by framing the industrial site as a necessary object of national security.

The active commitment of officials from the three branches of the military-industrial complex laid the basis for two pieces of legislation that formally created the industrial plant reserve. The first was a legislated military standby program for wartime industrial facilities. Approved in August 1947, Public Law 364 created a military-controlled reserve of factories. In the process, the law actualized the four elements of calculation by identifying the object (industrial property), procedures (for creating and maintaining a reserve), legal structures (which created the reserve), and resources (allocation of government and military funds). Both the army and the navy were authorized to designate and lease nonsurplus industrial property under their control in order to "promote the national defense" and "the public interest." The act gave the armed forces the right to determine "the continued availability for war-production purposes" of manufacturing facilities and to direct civilian disposal agencies to impose "terms, conditions, restrictions, and reservations" upon the designated property.[44] In other words, the secretaries of war and the navy were authorized to impose national security conditions on selected industrial property. Once the law was passed, the military quickly worked to designate which of the pool of industrial plants were necessary to the "interests of national defense."[45]

The open-ended character of Public Law 364 ensured that it would quickly become politically and administratively problematic even though it had successfully integrated industrial facilities under military control. The main problem was financial. The WAA had the right to certify back to the military those facilities that it could not sell due to the restrictions of the national security clause. The military, however, did not have sufficient funds to purchase or maintain these factories. This left the military at the mercy of the disposal agency's decisions about selling off of potential plants for the reserve.[46] In May 1948, Stuart Cramer, the deputy chair of the Munitions Board, told the hearings before the Committee on Armed Services that the board had lost access to six factories between September and December 1947 and were in danger of losing another fifteen.[47] At the same time, the military's constant pressure to designate industrial facilities as part of the reserve made the WAA's job of disposing of plants more difficult. Neither side was happy. In the opinion of the Munitions Board, a tougher law was required, while disposal officials sought legislation that would make selling surplus defense plants easier.

In April 1948, the government took a step toward resolving this dispute when it imposed a freeze on plancor sales. The White House, after consulting with Defense Secretary James Forrestal, WAA administrator Jess Larson, and the heads of the Munitions Board and National Security Resources Board, stopped all war plant sales for thirty days starting April 8, pending a review by the Munitions Board. According to John Steelman, the assistant to the president, the order's purpose was to "permit the munitions board to review the status and condition of each of the remaining unsold factories with a view to imposing the restrictions of the national security clause on subsequent sales."[48] The survey was part of a "new appraisal of its industrial capacity requirements."[49] The freeze gave the WAA the opportunity to ascertain the state of its stock of surplus plants. More importantly, it allowed the military to determine which manufacturing facilities they wanted as part of what had become their national industrial reserve.

Unsurprisingly, the Munitions Board recommended that 146 government-owned plants should be part of a national industrial reserve, while another 150 to 200 factories should be placed on the security list, thus making them ready for conversion to war production within 120 days. The board's rationale was that plants would be unable to fulfill the purpose for which they were built without a security clause.[50] The survey's recommendations added to the growing pressure from many quarters and paved the way for a bill to create an industrial reserve. Forrestal wrote in support of the bill to the House Armed Services Subcommittee, stating, among other things, that the factories "are important in the larger interest of long-range mobilization planning." In his opinion, the bill before Congress was an improvement on the present system as it provided "a more logical way of retaining plants of this type."[51]

The result of these "logical" calculations was the second major piece of legislation: the National Industrial Reserve Act of 1948. The new legislation provided a more effective system for determining what was to be kept and under what conditions they were to be maintained than its 1947 predecessor. It tightened the military's control over the nation's stock of state-owned industrial facilities by creating clear guidelines about what could be part of the military reserve and by providing funding for the operations and maintenance of plants. A reserve bill was approved by the Senate Armed Services Committee on May 25, 1948.[52] Public Law 883 became law just over six weeks later on July 2. According to Section 2, the act's purpose was to "provide a comprehensive and continuous program for the future safety and for the defense of the United States by providing adequate measures whereby an essential nucleus of Government-owned industrial plants and a national reserve of machine tools and industrial manufacturing equipment may be assured for immediate use to supply the needs of the armed forces in the time of national emergency."[53] The act provided backing for the creation of a pool of industrial plants by the military and allowed the secretary of defense to accept custody of factories that could not be sold.[54] The reserve was to be overseen by a National Industrial Reserve Review Committee consisting of no more than fifteen civilians from "various fields of American industry."[55] The law ensured that those firms with a national security clause that could not be sold or leased in the private market had to be turned over to the Federal Works Agency, which would maintain these industrial plants until they could be sold, leased, or otherwise dealt with. The law was much more effective than its 1947 predecessor and is a testament to the success of the coalition of military and government officials, industrial interest groups, and conservative public opinion in pushing its agenda. State-controlled industrial plants were now firmly embedded within the postwar military-industrial complex.

Even though the number of factories affected by Public Laws 364 and 833 fluctuated over time, a working reserve of industrial facilities was established. By the end of 1948, a total of 201 industrial plants were subject to restrictions.[56] The number increased, reaching 236 plants valued at $3.4 billion by the end of February.[57] Fifteen months later in July 1950, of the 1,595 plants built by the government during the war, 270 were still under the management of the army, navy, and air force; 200 were in reserve either as standby or under stipulation that they be kept in condition to convert to war production within 120 days, while the Munitions Board had completed plans for specific operations on a war footing for 253 of them.[58]

The 1948 Reserve Act directed that unsalable factories be transferred to the General Services Administration (GSA). In many cases the WAA had difficulty selling the plants because of the restrictions placed upon the sale (or lease) by the national security clause. The GSA was responsible for protecting, maintaining, and utilizing the facilities under directives from the secretary of defense. In June 1950 the GSA reserve consisted of sixty factories costing more than $693 million. Most of them were specialized heavy metal facilities unsuited for civilian use. Once transferred to the GSA reserve, facilities were subject to technical surveys to ascertain the degree of deterioration, the scope of the work required to keep them in working shape, and the ensuing cost of maintenance. A report was then sent to the secretary of defense for authorization to place the industrial facilities in a layaway program.[59]

Even though factories had been marked as unsalable, the GSA had to attempt to dispose of them, either by sale or lease. This in turn required another set of calculations. The GSA was directed to make a disposal plan "which provides the basis for determining the classification of the property, the methods and conditions under which the property is to be offered, and the actions that should be taken as prerequisite to offering for disposal."[60] The plan had to include a description of the property; the appropriate numeric, textual, and cartographic information; analyses of the plant's possible and best uses; and other pertinent material. Once the information was compiled, the industrial facility received a classification and a fair value, which was obtained from an appraisal by agency staff or an outside company such as Day and Zimmerman. Finally, the GSA undertook a promotional campaign with help from utility companies, financial institutions, local development commissions, and chambers of commerce. In all cases, the GSA had to work with the defense department and to obtain the approval of the secretary of defense. Being transferred to the GSA was the final stage for many state-owned industrial properties built during World War II. Although only a handful of plants ended up in the GSA's account books, these were large and specialized factories built at government expense that had become postwar "white elephants." Most other wartime facilities were sold to large corporations, largely to the firms that operated them during the war. In a few cases, defense factories were sold to government or other public agencies, but this was unusual.

The creation of the industrial reserve is indicative of the growing interrelationships between government, industry, and the military in the immediate postwar period. The success of calculative agents to frame industrial property as an object to be part of an industrial reserve was built on the attachments formed during wartime mobilization and the search for answers to what to do with wartime factories in the immediate postwar years. For the government this involved shifting their understanding of an industrial site from a place of production to one that had other uses. The industrial reserve helped resolve the problem of what to do with surplus property while providing an administrative response to the country's mobilization program. For the military, it involved framing the factory as a component of the national security system. An industrial reserve would defend America from enemy attack by allowing rapid mobilization of the country's industrial capacity and strengthen the military's domestic position. For industrialists, having a plant that operated in the industrial reserve gave them greater contact with government and military funding agencies. The most notable effect was to give these corporations first priority with defense contracts.

Conclusion

Disposing of the huge body of state-owned wartime industrial facilities after 1945 was "one of the major problems faced by the Government in the transition from a war to a postwar economy."[61] Working with corporate America and the military, the government responded to the problem by creating a disposal regime that gave a small group of actors the calculative tools to oversee the selling of state-owned industrial property to private interests. A coalition of civil, military, and industrial officials worked to reframe defense plants as an object to be sold in the private property market. The central calculation was to convert public property to private property and to boost the expansion of the American economy. After 1945, the defense factory would function as part of a private production system outside of government control. A set of infrastructures, from legislation that framed surplus disposal and created the national industrial reserve to a host of agencies that oversaw disposal of industrial facilities, established the practices that sought to deliver state property into private hands. Underpinning the regime was the concentration of federal financial and administrative resources in the hands of a small group of government officials. A large bureaucracy led by business-friendly administrators worked within the options set out in the 1944 Surplus Property Act and the financial resources delivered by Congress, the Truman administration, and the military high command to channel industrial space to private hands.

The postwar disposal regime ensured that a few state-financed war plants would remain under the influence of the military. The industrial reserve was created out of the postwar national security state. Even though the focus of the postwar militarized state was upon the creation of an extensive security system to shape and control America's economic and political order, military-industrial officials were concerned about and worked to shape the relationship between industrial mobilization and national security. Military leaders did not want to repeat the mistakes of the past, where industrial unpreparedness had stymied their ability to arm themselves for war. Framing factories within the national security state, military-industrial complex leaders sought some form of control over production. They did this by linking industrial property to national security. As Melvyn Leffler has argued, the national security system was created to defend what many believed to be "the nation's core values, its organizing ideology, and its free political and economic institutions."[62] The industrial site became a calculative productive and symbolic element of that postwar security state.

While the armed forces did not wish to operate industrial plants themselves, they did wish to have immediate and controlled access to such facilities. This forced both the civil state and industrial corporations to make certain calculations about their relationship with industrial property and with the military. Industrialists had to decide whether or not they would purchase or lease government industrial property. Once committed, firms had to work with the military in order to ensure that the national security clause was not violated. The civil state through such agencies as the WAA and the GSA had to provide detailed studies of industrial sites and to maintain defense factories in working order at great cost. Despite the huge financial and time costs allocated to maintaining these plants, the Department of Defense told the 1955 task force on surplus property that "the savings and money made possible by the provision of the national security clause were incalculable."[63] More importantly, in the eyes of many, the value of the military's ability to have control over a large number of specialized, state-owned industrial facilities that could be called upon in a national emergency was even more incalculable.

CHAPTER 7

Disposing of Chicago's War Factories

By the end of the war, metropolitan Chicago was home to more than six hundred government-financed industrial sites. Some were sprawling state-owned complexes that had churned out airplane engines and steel on the city fringe. Others were small additions to central-city factories that had made an assortment of war materials. Regardless of their scale, product, and location, Chicago's defense factories by the spring of 1945 were being closed down, with the loss of tens of thousands of jobs. More than three thousand workers lost their jobs when Studebaker closed its Chicago aircraft engine parts plant in June 1945. Three months later, the last B29 engine rolled off the Dodge-Chicago plant assembly line. Carnegie-Illinois Steel banked three of its four blast furnaces and told workers not to turn up for their shifts. In August, more than seventy thousand workers lost their jobs in the week after the Japanese surrender. Another fifteen thousand jobs disappeared in the following week. On August 18, contracts valued at more than $35 million were terminated by the Chicago Quartermaster Depot.[1] The end of war saw the closing of factories, the loss of industrial jobs, and the termination of munition supply contracts.

The downsizing of the war economy forced national and Chicago leaders to seek answers to questions about the region's industrial property. What were the implications of federal disposal policy for industrial reconversion and the industrial property market? What would be the impact of closing defense factories on the local economy? Chicago's political and business leaders were looking for answers to the same questions as national leaders. In their case, however, the questions of how to frame the industrial site as a marketable commodity and how to dispose of surplus plants were more immediate than for national policymakers as the answers would have long-term effects on local workers, firms, and municipal budgets. Chicago political and business leaders knew that the translation of national policy into the local world would have long-lasting effects on their world.

This was the point made by Ernest Olrich, director of Treasury Procurement, Surplus War Property Division, in June 1944 when he told the city's Retail Merchants Association about the problems of industrial disposal. In his opinion, industrial property and employment were a major concern for those dealing with demobilization and reconversion. It was essential, he averred, that the government create a system that local leaders could use to dispose of defense plants.[2] National disposal policy was important to local leaders because the solution from Washington was going to be played out and resolved (or not) at the local level. Local business executives and politicians did not want to have government-owned industrial facilities such as the Dodge-Chrysler or Studebaker plants become white elephants that would undermine the postwar metropolitan economy or distort the private industrial property market.

Building on surplus property documents, this chapter makes three points about the impact of disposal policy on Chicago's government-owned industrial facilities. First, the success of the disposal program in Chicago hinged on the ability of national and local officials to create new forms of knowledge that framed the defense factory as a commodity to be sold on the private property market. Second, this knowledge was mobilized through a multitiered administrative system running from Washington to Chicago's disposal agencies and private industry. Working with the military and industry, Chicago-based disposal agencies evaluated plancors, answered requests about factories, and negotiated contracts with potential buyers between 1944 and 1950. The area also housed engineering and other private firms that worked on contract for the disposal agencies, as well as the military units that oversaw the disposing of their wartime plants. Third, the importance of the military in the disposal of Chicago's defense factories to private industries is highlighted through its control over industrial space and its determination to ensure that several Chicago defense factories were part of the national industrial reserve. The political, economic, and administrative calculations that came with the federal reframing of industrial sites as objects of disposal had to be mobilized at the local level. The effectiveness of legislation such as the Surplus Property and National Reserve acts was directly tied to what happened at actual industrial sites. Military-industrial complex leaders worked to dispose of wartime government-owned property throughout the early postwar period.

Constructing Knowledge

The intervention of the government and the military in selling off of Chicago's state-owned industrial property required creating information, most notably about the facilities themselves, the economic conditions surrounding the defense plants, and their place in national and local industrial property markets. This material had to be different from what the federal government had previously collected when they were building Chicago's plancors. During the war, government interest centered on creating the conditions that allowed for the rapid construction of industrial space and the building of state-business relations that would increase industrial production. With the end of the war, the government's focus had to shift to other concerns, most notably assessing the location, size, and value of industrial plants; evaluating the relationship of plancors to other factories; ascertaining the internal structure of industries; and determining the character and scale of property markets. The resulting information about state-financed wartime industrial plants took three forms: statistical, textual, and imagistic. This extensive and practical inventory of information was geared to providing decision makers with the information necessary to calculate the place of Chicago's state-owned industrial plants within the broader currents of America's industrial conditions and local property markets.

During the last year of the war the federal government turned its attention to the task of selling off of the defense factories, assessing the nature of the industrial property market, and understanding the relationship between plants and national security. Government agencies started accumulating information for each facility at an early date. A March 1944 survey by the Reconstruction Finance Corporation (RFC) was the first systematic attempt to ascertain the scale and character of the country's defense manufacturing sites. This material became the basis for a published listing of plancors seven months later. In September 1944, the RFC chair, Jesse Jones, sent letters to 370 business leaders, asking what they planned to do with the Defense Plant Corporation (DPC) plants they had operated during the war. Similarly, the DPC undertook comparisons of factory construction and operating costs, subsidized research to find new uses for magnesium manufactured in its factories, analyzed the competitiveness of its plants within each industry, and determined the current reproduction cost of individual facilities. The DPC agency's Plant Utilization Section made studies of the best possible use of its industrial property. Several War Assets Administration (WAA) reports to Congress on various industries including iron and steel, aluminum, and synthetic rubber provided detailed information on the market and production conditions it faced in disposing of wartime industrial sites.[3]

This was not new, of course. The collection of information about industrial property by national, regional, and local groups has a long history. With the exception of the manufacturing census, however, the government's prewar knowledge of Chicago's industrial space was at best sporadic and haphazard. In all cases, knowledge creation was limited and geared to highly specific ends. Credit-rating companies undertook investigations of a range of firm-related issues, including a firm's liquidity and the reputation of potential government suppliers. The military surveyed, somewhat unsuccessfully, Chicago's industrial facilities as part of its interwar mobilization plans. The American government listed the assets of large corporations in their attempt to limit monopolies and to regulate industries. Engineering trade associations posted weekly listings of industrial building contracts. Illinois and Indiana manufacturing associations compiled simple inventories of the location, products, and employees of metropolitan firms. Local industrial associations, most notably the Chicago Association of Commerce, maintained records on the local industrial scene and undertook sporadic surveys of industries. While these materials were sufficient for peacetime purposes, they did not satisfy military and government wartime needs.

Roosevelt's call to arms in 1940 forced his government to rethink both the extent and the type of information that it needed to comprehend the amount and location of factory space needed for industrial mobilization. The calculus about investment in wartime industrial facilities required the federal government and the military to provide descriptive, specialized, and precise information about the country's industrial stock, the types of manufacturing facilities needed to make war materials, and the employment and economic conditions of potential industrial locales. Mobilization of the national economy forced calculating agents to undertake a massive information-gathering exercise after 1940. Material collected during the war, however, was of limited value with the winding down of industrial mobilization. Wartime interest in issues such as construction costs, employment levels, and building contracts was replaced by the search for information that would enable the state to prepare and then sell unwanted industrial property to the private sector. Similarly, the military was intent on assessing the place of wartime industrial facilities in their plans for postwar industrial mobilization. One type of information that federal disposal agencies and the military were looking for was statistical.

An overwhelming amount of statistical material was created by government and military agencies. From simple inventories of state-owned machinery installed in public and private defense plants to detailed data on the monthly output of sulfuric acid, fertilizer, and machine parts, the state stepped up its collection of quantifiable information that would be the basis of its statistical understanding of Chicago's industrial milieu. Government agencies transformed raw data about firm location, industrial output, and consumer demand into material to be analyzed statistically; the regional concentration of specific industries was mapped, and the dynamics of national commodity markets were analyzed by demand curves and sophisticated models. In some cases, the documentation was geared to produce a systematic overview of a particular industrial world. The WAA listings of industrial facilities and its quarterly report to Congress, for example, provided information about Chicago's lessees, the length of the leases, and the use to which defense factories were being put. These inventories consisted of precise information about Chicago's state-owned industrial property.[4]

Calculating agents were able to describe industrial space by gathering statistical material. Descriptions of an industrial plant, from the size of its floor space to the number of parachutes it produced, were made for all of Chicago's war factories. The scrambled plant operated by Cicero's Strom Steel Bearings during the war is a case in point. Government and private officials compiled a huge amount of information about plancor 600, ranging from its size (58,346 square feet) and normal value ($275,000) to detailed financial material about potential purchasers, such as Hess Warming and Ventilating, Sola Electric, and Lion Manufacturing.[5] These data focused on a numerical world characterized by precision and measurement. Statistical enumeration was used to provide comparability to the vast array of manufacturing facilities that were built and made available for private interests. Understanding industrial plants through statistics did not eschew difference. Indeed, the tables and graphs contained in every report established the variability by sector, commodity, investment type, and scale existing among the metropolitan area's defense plants.

By categorizing information, statistics narrowed the government's understanding of the industrial world by insisting on preparing the factory for the marketplace. In this way statistics made that world more comprehensible to the state and other calculating interests, providing them with a single starting point from which decisions could be made. The material placed Chicago industrial property in a comparative light. Information about such issues as a firm's capacity, local competitors, plant values, transportation links, and supplier relationships could be compared to those of the nation and metropolitan Chicago. All of these accumulated materials resulted in the marking up, preparing, and marketing of state-owned industrial property for sale to private firms.

The generation of statistics as the war wound down and during the immediate postwar period facilitated the flow of information between the various calculating agents. This is what happened with the monthly reports that the Chicago Office of the Real Property Disposal Board unit sent to Washington. These reports consisted of several sections with details on the Chicago office's ongoing work on the disposition of wartime surplus plants. The overview section listed the submitted offers and the rejected and accepted bids, and it presented a statistical analysis of the plancors. The Washington section listed firms awaiting action from central headquarters. Other sections provided detailed numerical information about factories withdrawn from the surplus pool, transferred to the General Services Administration, or under negotiation.[6] Routinized, straightforward, and legible, statistical data allowed state, military, and industry officials in Chicago, Washington, and elsewhere to be on the same page.

This statistical material was complemented by an array of textual reports, studies, and correspondence about the defense factories that were to be sold off to private interests or put aside for the national reserve. The material provided a range of information, from details on factory construction to engineering surveys of plants to credit-rating reports of prospective purchasers. The material added flesh to the bare bones of the numerical analyses. In some cases, writers provided interpretations of socioeconomic life. These could be ethnographic, such as a 1949 report on the workings of the WAA's Chicago region office. Written by an insider, the study documented the everyday work life of the office staff. It set out work procedures, practices, and pressures and described the mediating role that Chicago workers played between the Washington bureaucrats, industrial executives, and military officers. What is clear is that the staff resented juggling conflicting aspects of working with the disposal of Chicago's industrial sites. They were caught between the imperatives of implementing national policy, fulfilling military demands, and maintaining workable relations with potential buyers of government property. All of this had to be done while compiling up-to-date information about the factories from government units and outside firms. To add to their difficulties, the building up of this knowledge was hampered by the absence of effective communication between different government agencies and units, the difficulties of reconciling conflicting elements of the Surplus Property Act, and problems of accountability between the owning agencies and the wartime operators.[7]

Even in the face of these difficulties, government agencies compiled an impressive array of textual material about the government industrial property. Most studies generated information that could be used to push forward the agenda of groups such as the Army and Navy Munitions Board (ANMB) and the WAA regarding industrial sites. Officials at the Chicago office of Real Property Disposal Board, for example, sent monthly reports to its head office in Washington. Among other things, these officials had accumulated information about the ongoing work of the Chicago office, individual plancors, local conditions, the problems of working with business, and the state of ongoing negotiations between the regional office and private interests.[8]

In other cases, evidence presented at congressional hearings set out the terms determined by industry or other interests. In April 1948, for example, a subcommittee on surplus property disposal met at the U.S. Courthouse in Chicago. The reason the subcommittee was in Chicago was, according to Ross Rizley, the subcommittee chair, that "over the months, many, many complaints from people in industry and business in connection over the manner in which surplus property is being handled here in the Chicago region." The focus of the hearings was on the inability of local WAA officials to facilitate the sale of surplus steel to industry. Acting upon complaints from industry that surplus steel was not being filtered through to industry quickly enough, Rizley and his colleagues wanted "to look into the situation and see what we can do, if anything, to get this material moving and out into the channels of trade."[9] To this end, the committee interviewed two groups of witnesses: business interests and WAA officials.

This type of textual correspondence to be found in the WAA Chicago office reports and the congressional committee spoke to the ways in which a particular set of relations were struck between federal officials, military leaders, and industrial executives over time. In some cases, as with detailed ANMB and WAA reports or verbatim testimony from congressional committee meetings, the textual material played an important part in the compilation and character of evidence about defense factories. In others, while some of the correspondence was ephemeral, having little value but for the moment, a significant amount had lasting effects on the fate of industrial plants and on government-business cooperation. Whether it was reports by the ANMB on the need for specific types of munitions or a private firm's analysis of a plancor it was seeking to buy, textual knowledge underpinned calculating practices and solidified the budding networks of the military-industrial complex.

The disposal agencies also relied on image-based representations to determine the character of the industrial world and industrial property. The images provided a visual representation of statistical and textual materials. These representations came in various forms, ranging from maps drawn by professional cartographers and plans of industrial facilities drawn by industrial engineers to drawings, photos, and simple maps found in newspaper advertisements and magazines, and to reports by the government and private industry. Maps showing the distribution of war plant investment or the detailed plans of factory space displayed information that could be used by civilian and military disposal officials and potential purchasers of industrial property. A 1944 fertilizer map taken from a chemical trade journal, for example, helped the government work through the demand for the commodity and in the process determined its understanding of the locational pattern of its industrial facilities. The photos published in the *Plant Finder* and other government documents allowed manufacturers to determine the physical character of an industrial facility. Both the fertilizer map and the plancor plans were used in conjunction with statistical and textual analyses to produce new forms of knowledge about industry sites.

Together, the three types of documents created a particular framing of property that could be used to understand the world in which property operated. For the disposal official, this knowledge provided the economic and social parameters of what could be done to surplus property. For military leaders, these types of materials offered information about the suitability of the factory for national security and industrial mobilization. For industrial managers, this documentation provided the means to ascertain whether the facility would fit their production objectives. In other words, the documents were instruments for military-industry complex leaders to evaluate and monitor the role of state-owned industrial property in postwar America.

Kropp Forge illustrates the type of knowledge assembled by the federal government on industrial sites. Before the war, Kropp was a significant Chicago forging firm, making products for the railroad, oil, marine, automotive, and construction industries. During the war it built and operated two additions underwritten by army-sponsored certificates of necessity to manufacture airplane, gun, and machine parts. It also operated plancor 1293, a DPC-financed plant, to make aircraft forgings for the army between April 1943 and August 1945. With the end of the war, the army terminated its contracts with the company, and Kropp dismissed the 225 war workers employed in the government-owned plant.[10] The question of what to do with the facility became an issue for the firm, the DPC, and the military, but the interested parties had little information by which to calculate the factory's economic and strategic value.

The federal government had assembled a smattering of information about plancor 1293 when it was built. This, however, was insufficient for understanding how to place a dollar value on the property, to ascertain the manufacturing site's place in the country's national reserve, or to situate it in relation to other specialized forging facilities, both government and privately owned. In other words, the knowledge necessary to make calculations about the industrial plant was missing. A new set of material about plancor 1293 had to be generated that would frame the industrial site within postwar Chicago's industrial conditions, provide the government with information about how to most effectively dispose of the forging facility, and allow the military to determine whether the industrial plant should be included in the national reserve.

Over the next four years, a wide range of knowledge gathered from a variety of sources was created about the factory by the disposal agencies. Perhaps the largest and most systematic body of information was found in the WAA real property case files, which opened with a prospectus.[11] Following a standardized template, this set out, among other things, an assortment of simple facts about plancor 1293, including the money authorized, committed, and disbursed to make the industrial facility and how it was spent (on land, buildings, etc.); the name of the company operating the plant; and the number of buildings and amount of land and number of machines owned. The remaining file materials are a smorgasbord of statistical, textual, and image-based documents from business, military, and government agents interested in the Kropp Forge–operated plant. Agency officials sent letters and reports to each other about a range of topics. The General Board composed long memoranda that discussed the defense factory's history, legal status, and monetary value; the details of the Kropp bid for purchasing and leasing the plancor; the board's overview of the bid; and recommendations and the reasons for these. Correspondence between Kropp personnel (executives and lawyers) and WAA officials set out the calculations that each side was taking. Documents sent by the company to the WAA, such as the 1947 Annual Report and reports of production rates and military contracts, were used to support the forging company's claim to the property. A press release announced the sale to Kropp.

The creation of material such as found in the plancor 1293 files was critical to the government's ability to dispose of state-owned industrial facilities.

Whether it was records of plancors or other documents, such as studies of individual firms, postwar commodity markets, or the industrial property market, knowledge about industrial sites was more than a repository of information about the assets, location, or number of workers. By framing the industrial site as a calculable object, the statistical, textual, and representational knowledge generated by the state, the military, and industry about industrial space functioned to change the material world of manufacturing and industrial property. This knowledge worked to shift industrial space as a production site owned by the state and geared to the wartime mobilization program to a commodity to be sold to business interests through the industrial property market. The disposal agencies, the military, and business repackaged the defense factory by recalculating what the industrial site was and who had the right to determine its existence.

Chicago's Administrative Structure and Private Enterprise

An effective local administrative system was critical to the disposal of defense plants; successful disposal relied on a multiscalar regime that linked local business and political leaders with national policy makers, officials working in the Washington offices of the disposal agencies and armed forces, and industrial executives. Accordingly, the success of the government's disposal program could only be realized by ensuring that Washington and the business and military groups interested in war plants could work with local disposal officials. The ability to effectively mobilize the new forms of knowledge being created by a range of different agencies was essential to national and local interests. Despite facing several obstacles to the creation of a functioning system, the WAA was able to devise a regional decentralization that coordinated and oversaw the disposal of defense factories. Home to a large collection of state-owned war plants, Chicago was one of the country's most important regional centers. By 1950, local WAA officials had sold a substantial share of the region's surplus war property.

This started slowly. By July 1945, only one large plancor had been made surplus, and only a few minor defense factories had been sold.[12] Acquisitions and sales became more common by 1946. By September 1947, according to Joseph Burke, Chicago's deputy zone administrator, 80 percent of the disposal work had been completed. The list of war plants that had been sold or leased was impressive; it included some of the country's largest manufacturers: Republic Steel, Buick, and the Aluminum Company of America. Several large industrial properties remained on the selling block, however, including those operated by Gary Armor Plate and Wyman-Gordon during the war.[13] According to a 1947 WAA report, the Chicago region as of October 31 had sold ninety-nine

FIGURE 7.1. Selling the Studebaker plancor to National Tea, 1949. Representatives of National Tea Company and the War Assets Administration sign the deal awarding plancor 40 the food-processing firm.
Source: Studebaker Corporation, Accession Number 291–56A-0244, Real Property Case Files, 1952–1957, Federal Property Resources Service records, RG 291, NARA—Chicago.

plants valued at $243 million. Another twenty-six valued at $231 million had been leased. Twenty-nine surplus plancors costing almost $200 million still remained to be disposed of.[14] A trickle of sales continued in the next three years, including large facilities such as those operated during the war by Studebaker in the city's west end (Figure 7.1). Although it is difficult to determine precisely how many plants remained unsold on the eve of the Korean War, a substantial share had found their way into the hands of the private sector.[15]

Despite success, selling Chicago's defense factories was not straightforward. One problem was that the administrative apparatus that had been established in Washington made it very difficult for Chicago officials to dispose of surplus property. Decision making did not flow easily across space. Local officials found that their Washington peers compromised finalizing the deals on which they had worked. The procedure of submitting all documents to the D.C. office for final approval proved slow and cumbersome. Moreover, local attorneys were not authorized to settle litigation cases or to represent the WAA in court. Rather, they had to rely on their Washington counterparts, most of whom did not have knowledge of Chicago conditions.[16] Disposal was also hindered by the slow release of army- and navy-sponsored war plants. W. Reuter, the assistant manager of the RFC's Chicago Loan Agency, complained in a local newspaper that the military's belligerent attitude delayed disposal.[17] These organizational shortcomings made life difficult and caused concern within government circles.

These shortcomings also promoted hostility outside. Growing frustration with the surplus agencies boiled over in the summer of 1946 when public and private opposition to disposal methods "was declared to have reached almost open revolt." In the opinion of professional associations gathered in Washington in June 1946, the disposal system had to be changed.[18] Congressional committees agreed; the flow of information between Washington and the rest of the country had to be streamlined. The state had to more effectively mobilize its knowledge of defense factories; it had to change the basis upon which it made its calculations about the selling of industrial facilities to the private sector.

By the second half of 1946 it was obvious to Washington officials that disposing of surplus war plants could only come about by handing more control to local officials. Facing ongoing criticism and conflicting pressure from military and industrial interests, the WAA implemented changes to its administrative apparatus, most notably the decentralization of authority from Washington to regional offices. The shift of some decision making from D.C. to the regional offices widened the powers of regional officials. The Industrial Advisory Service, the branch that helped business find plants, extended its activities to the regional offices. The operations of the Real Property Disposal Board, which reviewed and gave final approval to sales, were made uniform, and a section was set up in Chicago.[19] By the fall of 1946, a new organizational calculus internal to the Chicago office had been established.[20] The end result was a more effective system rooted in greater local control that facilitated the movement of information and reduced the time it took to make and finalize contracts. Another administrative reorganization took place in 1948 with a "streamlining and girding of the forces to complete the disposal program."[21]

The growing volume of disposal work and administrative decentralization forced the WAA to take over more Chicago office space. The exigencies of disposal, with the incremental disposition of surplus property and control exerted from Washington, ensured that administrative oversight of disposal would proceed in a haphazard manner and with escalating costs. Rather than a thought-out policy of expansion, the Chicago office grew in spurts, adding personnel and office space as resources became available. The chaotic character of plant disposal was exacerbated by the large number of changes to leadership of the Chicago office. There were six regional directors in the first two years of the agency's existence, each of whom brought about personnel changes and emphasized different aspects of factory disposal. The WAA leadership's attempts to rationalize its administrative gaze came to a head in early 1947. Staff reductions took place, adding to workloads, and the zone and regional offices were combined. By the end of 1947 the numbers of workers had been reduced by nearly 50 percent. By early 1947 the agency occupied seven separate spaces scattered around the Loop and the Near North Side. The WAA consolidated these into two spaces: all operations were concentrated on the Navy Pier with the exception of the customer sales office, which was located in the heart of the city's business office district at Wabash Avenue and Van Buren Street.[22]

The difficulty of selling off the remaining wartime industrial plants by 1947 forced the agency to rethink its disposal strategy. Previously, obtaining a fair price as determined by its engineering department and outside private contractors was typically the agency's key concerns. In Chicago, however, even though the WAA continued to search for a fair price, calculations turned to emphasizing the positive effects of the factories on local and regional economies. This was made very clear in September 1947 by Joseph Burke, the Chicago deputy administrator. He told the *Chicago Tribune* that "the price at which we sell is not as important as the permanent gain to the Midwest economy in increased production and higher employment."[23] While still operating within the parameters of the Surplus Property Act, Burke and other agency officials were rethinking how to deploy the knowledge they had generated and how to proceed with the disposal of industrial facilities.

The main issue behind this shift in policy was the ongoing difficulty of selling large, specialized plants that had little utility in postwar industrial America. According to John O'Brien, the disposal program's head, Chicago had too many "white elephants," several of which remained unsold and had very little attraction for private buyers. This was the point made in a valuation report of the plancor operated by Dodge-Chrysler to build bomber engines during the war: the property's conversion to postwar industrial operations was hindered by its size, location, and specialized character.[24] This was the case for several other plancors operated by Gary Armor Plate, American Steel Foundries (castings), the Seneca Shipyards, and Douglas (plane assembly). Many of these plants were unsuitable for peacetime operations. The attempt by WAA officials to turn some of the suburban facilities back into farmland was hindered by the environmental damage caused by chemicals. In other cases, the WAA tried to turn large factories into multiple-tenancy facilities.[25] Increasingly aware that it was next to impossible to obtain a fair price for scrambled and specialized facilities, the agency turned its attention to the impact that the selling of wartime plants would have on the regional economy. As Burke noted, "The industrial economy of the Midwest already profited and is in a position to gain more in the reconversion of government war time production facilities to operation by private industry."[26]

Chicago's federally owned property was subject to detailed examination from disposal agencies and government contractors. Surveys were made of factory sites, machinery, equipment, and location by private engineering firms, the military, and the WAA's engineering division. The value of each plant and the surrounding area's land were appraised by a range of private real estate agents and the WAA's real estate unit. According to William Kirby, the deputy regional director of the WAA's Chicago office, the ability of local disposal officials to sell industrial property was based on "engineering surveys, pictures, plans, and pamphlets" that were "assembled for prospective buyers in a central office."[27] The purpose of these calculations about industrial sites was to help the WAA, the RFC, Congress, the Department of Justice, and other government, military, and private bodies determine the functionality and value of the facilities and the financial status of the firms that sought to buy them. Without these types of calculations it would have been impossible to determine what the appropriate pecuniary and industrial value of the plants were and who had the right to purchase them.

Private industrial engineering companies, of course, were brought in to provide expert advice to WAA officials about industrial sites. The local engineering firm Harry S. Cutmore and Associates made a survey in July 1946 of plancor 1220, the East Chicago site operated by Continental Ordnance during the war. After a detailed discussion of the site, the firm gave a report on the property's best use.[28] A year earlier, Chicago's Burnham and Hammond, Inc., made a two-part appraisal of the war plant run by Ahlberg Bearing. One part of the appraisal consisted of a report on the building, while the other was an assessment of normal reproduction costs.[29] In order to frame the wartime industrial site as a disposal unit, private and government industrial engineers had to determine the scale, cost, quality, and location of defense factories.

A case in point is the 1947 two-volume report by Edwin S. Corman Inc., a Cleveland engineering firm, on a plancor operated by American Steel Foundries. Completed in July 1943 at a cost of $28 million, the foundry's six open-hearth furnaces produced cast armor for tanks. The report's first volume framed the plant as part of a national set of foundries. The technologically advanced steel foundry equipment and a modern layout meant that the plant operated at substantially lower cost per ton than most of its competitors, many of which were housed in "old cramped buildings and yards" and had "few modern facilities for efficient production." Accordingly, Corman recommended that the plancor be sold as a single, integrated unit. The second volume presented a detailed assessment of the plant's reproduction costs and fair value, recommending that fair price was $18.3 million. Corman's report marked the foundry as a viable integrated facility and established its value on the industrial property market.[30]

Another case was Day and Zimmerman's 1945 report on plancor 1235, a $10 million project operated by the Bendix Corporation to make aircraft carburetors. The industrial engineering company was brought in to provide some guidance to government engineers. The January 1945 appraisal report consisted of three main parts. A plan of the property that made up the plancor, complete with property lines, building specifications, and so on, situated the factory in the city's grid system. A financial summary of the plant's main components (land, improvements, buildings, and off-site improvements) provided the DPC with a selling price that could be used on the private property market. This was accompanied by a textual analysis of the manufacturing site that emphasized how the value was calculated.[31]

These outside studies established the calculations that were used to turn the wartime industrial facility from a mobilization site to a commodity to be sold on the private property market. The federal disposal agencies worked with private engineering firms and military real estate branches to describe the character of the factories, to prime the sites for sale on the private industrial property market, and to establish the basis for negotiations between federal agencies, the military, and potential buyers. The WAA and its predecessor agencies operated within the newly created calculative regime that resulted from legislation that directed the agency to dispose of wartime facilities, the flow of financial resources that enabled the creation of knowledge about the plants, and the practices defining how they were to be sold, to whom, at what cost, and under what conditions. This property disposal regime allowed the state to work with private interests and the military to resituate the defense factory as a new object.

The statistical, textual, and image-based representations generated by government and business were used to assess place. The industrial districts in which the factories were located became part of the world that had to be evaluated and ranked. Industrial engineering firms such as Day and Zimmerman offered several services including how to place plants within their wider metropolitan and regional contexts. It was essential that the disposal agency have a better understanding of the economic, labor, housing, and consumer conditions in which a disposed plant was located. The involvement of wartime agencies in industrial production and the ownership of industrial property situated the government projects within the wider region. The state was drawn to accumulate certain forms of knowledge and not others by the fact that it needed information about the manufacturing property it owned. Most notably, the government had to create a greater awareness of the world in which its investments were embedded. The agencies had to know more aspects of the world, including the market of industrial property, the methods of selling industrial facilities, the state of product markets, and the character of locations where industrial plants were to be found. The government's necessary involvement with nongovernmental agents such as property appraisers, auctioneers, and engineering consultants permitted the reframing of the industrial structure of the communities in which the state had invested. An administrative investment went along with a financial one in assessing place.

The impact of these assessments can be understood by the disposal of the manufacturing plant operated by Continental Ordnance during the war. According to Cutmore and Associates, the East Chicago "property is particularly well located for heavy commodity industries, such as foundries, steel fabricating, forging, assembly and other types of metal working." East Chicago, an industrial suburb of Chicago, contained "a good local labor supply," an assortment of commercial and cultural institutions, and a well-developed industrial base. East Chicago was evaluated as an appropriate place for making castings. Measured against other places, it was well located for this type of heavy manufacturing.[32] In other cases, the industrial site was placed within a metropolitan context. In order to situate the possibilities of disposing of the Dodge factory in the city's southwest areas, for example, the WAA looked to the wider world. In 1949 the region's labor and political conditions were considered to be poor and the demand for industrial space to be low. The sale of the Dodge site was hindered by the fact that it was located outside of the region's growth areas, most notably the Clearing and Central Manufacturing industrial districts.[33]

Central to this was the assessment of national and local markets for used industrial property. During the war the government had become a major player in industrial property markets through its purchase of a significant amount of land and buildings. Accordingly, disposal of state-owned industrial land in the postwar period would affect demand for vacant industrial land and for secondhand industrial facilities in metropolitan Chicago. The WAA was well aware of this. Given that one of the principles of the Surplus Property Act was to obtain a high and fair price, the agency was caught between having to fulfill its mandate while permitting the private urban land market to operate under "normal" circumstances. In order to grapple with and better understand this contradiction, the WAA sought to frame their holdings of industrial property within the contexts of the national and local markets. Both the national and regional offices of the WAA undertook frequent and oftentimes detailed and wide-ranging studies of the metropolitan industrial property market.

One such case was a 1947 analysis of the national industrial real estate market by the Washington office. The study's purpose was to give WAA policy makers and valuation officers a better understanding of the problems they were having disposing of surplus property. The agency faced several questions. Would 1947 be as successful as 1946? Would the federal government continue to dominate the national market for industrial property? How should the agency proceed? In their analysis, which was based on "preliminary estimates submitted by American business," the indication was that there would be a general decline in the demand for capital goods nationwide. The estimates suggested that a smaller share of capital goods budgets were going to be spent on used property as companies sought to move their production processes to suburban greenfield sites. For an increasing number of manufacturing firms, secondhand property in the worn-out central-city industrial districts or older noncentral districts such as the Calumet and Pittsburgh's steel-making areas was no longer considered productive. The market for used property, the agency believed, would shift from large corporations to medium- and small-sized firms. The agency needed to tap into this market if it was to dispose of its large supply of surplus sites. In this way, the government's surplus property disposal agency monitored and intervened in the national and local industrial property market.[34]

Disposal calculations also relied on detailed assessments of the financial worthiness of firms seeking to purchase a factory. Many of these assessments were made within the agency by WAA engineers, accountants, and economists, while in others, private firms were contracted to make an evaluation. Regardless of who made the assessment, the intent was to ensure the viability of the property transaction. At the end of 1945, for example, the WAA commissioned a financial report from the Dun and Bradstreet credit-rating company on a potential purchaser of the manufacturing site at 4600 W. Parker. The report on the 20th Century Glove Co., a leather glove manufacturer, was positive, and the facility was awarded to the company. Dun and Bradstreet made a much more extensive report on Allied Control in May 1945. In their report they laid out the firm's financial history, the focus of their post-1941 expansion program, the working history and character of the firm's main executives, the scale and scope of their business making electric relays, solenoids, and switches, and details of their main factory in New York City and the Chicago one they operated for the DPC during World War II.[35] In all cases, the WAA was looking to use financial knowledge to assess the long-term viability of private companies so that the sanctity of the industrial property market was maintained.

The networks created by local WAA offices and related agencies extended to agents other than engineering and credit-rating firms. Local real estate companies were used by the government to buy, sell, and assess property and by industrial firms interested in purchasing a plant. The WAA's Real Estate unit based its prices on information taken from local realtors and looked to maximize returns for its industrial property. To this end, it worked with Chicago real estate companies to find property, to outline the property's history, and to determine the property's fair value. In the case of plancor 1235, the Real Estate division gave other WAA units information about the property's history, analyzed its value in terms of other considerations (employment, conformity to policy, and credit ratings), and made recommendations about its disposal. Manufacturers also employed the property industry. Belmont Radio, for example, used a local realtor, Sturm-Bickel Company, to make an assessment of the cost of plancor 1235 before it put in a bid to buy the west end property.[36] In this and other ways, the government and military generated an extensive body of knowledge about industrial sites that involved a detailed probing of the financial and operational status of manufacturing firms.

The Military and Recalculating Industrial Space

The shadow of the military hovered over the disposal of Chicago's wartime industrial sites. The military's central role mobilizing the nation's industrial firms for wartime production and its responsibility for overseeing the building of billions of dollars of industrial plants during World War II gave the armed forces a stake in what would happen to defense factories at war's end. Further adding to the military's interest in surplus factories was the growing concern with building a large postwar reserve of industrial facilities that could be quickly mobilized in the event of a national emergency.

The military's need to assess and participate in factory disposal began even before defense factories were sold to private companies. As the war wound down, the army and navy had to turn over the plants they had sponsored and financed to civilian agencies for disposal. This was not a straightforward affair. The armed forces were reluctant to release war plants before the end of the war, even though many workers had been laid off and some factories had been closed. It was only at the end of the summer of 1945 that they seriously started to turn their attention to making facilities available for sale. Even when military officials began to prepare industrial sites for disposal, they faced obstacles. In some cases, they had to honor legal contracts that slowed down the surplus process. In others, the termination process, which involved the settlement of outstanding contracts and purchase orders, had to be fulfilled before a factory could be released.[37]

The military was most directly involved in factory disposal through the national industrial plant reserve and the national security clause. As noted earlier, the former consisted of industrial property that were put on standby for use by the military during an emergency. Many Chicago factories became part of this reserve. As of March 1949, at least fifteen reserve plants were located in Chicago. Some had been sold (Howard Foundry, Kropp, Republic Steel, Studebaker, Tantalum, Wyman-Gordon, Youngstown Sheet); others had been leased (Aluminum Co., Chrysler-Dodge, Pullman); and others remained surplus (American Steel Foundry, Continental Foundry, Gary Armor, Pullman, Revere Copper and Brass).[38] These reserve plants were subject to a national security clause imposed by the armed forces, which restricted their sale "in order to insure availability of its basic productive capacity on short notice."[39]

Chicago's defense factories were affected by the national industrial reserve legislation and the national security clause. Two cases show how the importance of maintaining control over strategic materials for defense purposes was central to the military's involvement in industrial matters and how this affected the development of the national reserve in the immediate postwar period. The first, Howard Foundry, operated an army-sponsored aircraft magnesium castings plant during the war. Located at 4900 W. Bloomingdale, plancor 1170 consisted of a modern, one- and two-story building with 148,000 square feet of floor space (Figure 7.2). After the war, magnesium was assessed by the military as "a highly strategic material needed for national defense."[40] Accordingly, a clause was imposed on the facility, which meant that it could only be sold "subject to the provisions and conditions of the national security clause."[41]

The clause brought problems in its wake. Even though a specialized plant such as plancor 1170 was difficult to sell at the best of times, it was even more so when disposal came with a clause. This was made clear by the WAA's appraisal division in May 1948. In a detailed analysis based on three earlier reports by Day and Zimmerman, Nicholson, Porter and List, Inc., and Fugard, Olsen, Urbain and Neiler, the WAA noted that there are "certain costs involved in maintaining a plant of this type under the National Security Clause." To accommodate this, the WAA reduced the plant's fair price from $831,422 to $778,000.[42] The fair price was accepted by Howard, and the company continued to produce magnesium castings under contract with Pratt-Whitney, General Electric (GE), and other corporations. In this case, Howard's place in America's postwar defense program allowed the WAA to work through the restrictions associated with the military's allocation of the factory to the industrial plant reserve while ensuring the continuance of capitalist production relations and the maintenance of private industrial property relations.

Similarly, Chicago's WAA office worked with the ANMB, the Office of War Mobilization and Reconversion, and industry to ensure that America's only producer of tantalum remained a functioning unit under the military's control. During the war the Signal Corps funded a new factory to extract tantalum, tungsten, and molybdenum from ore and to produce metallic powder, sheets, bars, wires, and oxides. The industrial facility was operated by Tantalum Defense Corporation, a subsidiary of North Chicago's Fansteel Metallurgical Corporation. By the end of the war, questions about its postwar status emerged. The military was anxious to keep the plant working even though its capacity was much greater than demand. As S. Powell Warren, a WAA engineer, noted in a 1945 report, the Corps of Engineers "expect to continue the use of the products of this plant at the Manhattan Project in Tennessee."[43] But this could not take place without the key players computing how to get what they wanted while at the same time accommodating other demands. The tension between the military's desire to keep the factory working, Fansteel's need to operate at a profit, and the WAA's mandate to dispose of the plant at a fair price created a set of contested calculations.

Driving the tantalum negotiations was the military's need to create a reserve of industrial plants that would persist past the end of the war and to extend its intervention into industrial matters. Before coming to a permanent solution, Fansteel and the WAA settled on an interim agreement for the month-by-month operation of the factory. This unusual disposal practice was undertaken because

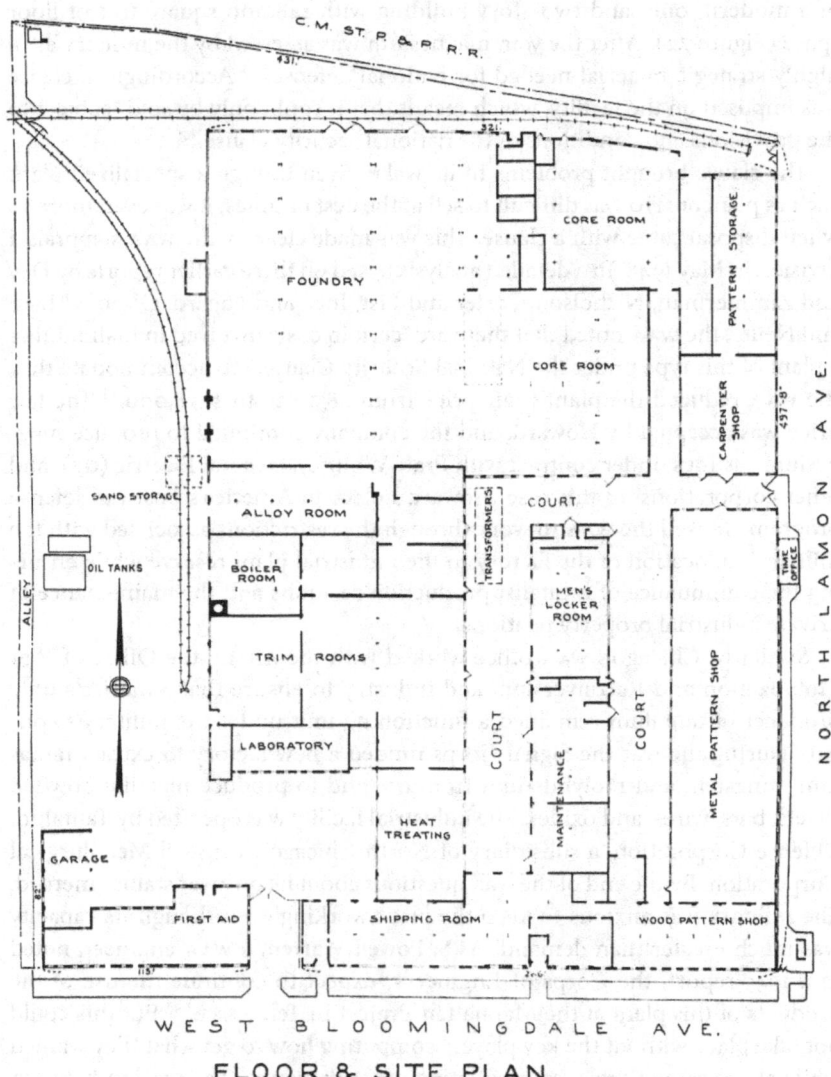

FIGURE 7.2. Floor plan of Howard Foundry. One feature of government ownership of industrial plants was the need to create and assemble precise information about individual facilities.
Source: *Foundry* (Washington, D.C.: Defense Plant Corporation, n.d.).

of the army's need to preserve the facility as a producer of war products and to "insure the future operation and availability for National Security purposes."[44] An October 1946 meeting attended by John Steelman, director of the Office of War Mobilization and Reconversion, and disposal officials finally cemented the military's position. The ANMB made it very clear that they wanted to maintain the plant. Steelman agreed, and told Robert Littlejohn, the WAA administrator, that in his "view it is entirely appropriate for you to give the national security aspect full weight in determining the appropriate rental or sale value of the property and also to give it full weight in choosing between potential purchasers or lessees."[45] As a result, the WAA's Real Property Review Board authorized the sale to Fansteel on January 24, 1947, for $500,000. Even though its wartime construction cost more than $5 million and its fair value was assessed at $2.5 million, the negotiations between the company, the ANMB, and the Atomic Energy Commission around tantalum's place in the world of national security led to disposal at such a low cost.[46]

The disposal of wartime factories such as those operated by Howard and Tantalum involved calculations that ensured that the military would continue to have ongoing relations with the civil state and industry. The development of decentralized administrative capacity in the Chicago office allowed local officials to adjudicate between the competing claims on the region's wartime industrial sites. The WAA and its predecessors in Chicago utilized a variety of local and national public and private experts to determine, among other things, the value of facilities and to whom they should be sold. In some cases, the industrial plant's usefulness to the military and questions about national security were at the forefront of the disposal process. The combination of clauses imposed by the military on sponsored factories and government legislation that allowed for the creation of an industrial plant reserve enabled the military to take a commanding role in determining what happened to many industrial spaces in Chicago and elsewhere.

The military was also involved with factory disposal in less obvious ways. One such way was by working with civil agencies and private industry to assess the state of the nation's industrial stock. From as early as late 1943, the War Production Board (WPB), the Ordnance Department, the DPC, and the WAA commissioned numerous internal and private surveys of defense plants in preparation for the sale of government-owned industrial facilities to private industry. The main concern of these surveys was to assess the ultimate fate of publicly owned industrial sites. While civil officials refocused their calculations from mobilization to disposal, military officers determined the monetary and strategic value of defense property in a postwar setting. Industries also became a focus of military-industry interest. Working with the military's assessment of a factory's national security status, the WAA packaged information about industries in ways appropriate to disposing of industrial sites to private interests.

This was evident with the military-sponsored ordnance plants built during the war. The military's role in the decisions made about the Kankakee Ordnance plant outside of Joliet is a case in point. A sprawling facility that adjoined the Elwood ordnance plant, the Chicago site had been chosen because of its access to large amounts of water, excellent railroad facilities, and a large labor force. Together, the two factories covered 36,000 acres and employed tens of thousands of workers in a thousand buildings with sixteen chemical lines to produce high explosives and sixteen shell-loading assembly lines. The question of what to do with the Kankakee facility at the end of the war had serious repercussions for the army. A major problem was the decline in the army's demand for TNT and other high explosives after August 1945. On top of this, the plant supplied more industrial acid than was needed by Chicago's commercial interests. Moreover, the highly contaminated character of the production system made reconversion back to agricultural pursuits next to impossible. Nevertheless, the army considered it an important facility. An October 1945 report classified the facility as a "nucleus plant" and "the only producer of lead azide" and stated that it should be the "first choice" for retention.[47] Only suitable for the purpose for which it was built, the facility was deactivated in August 1945 and put on standby status two months later.

How did it become a "first choice"? The answer lies in the assessment the military made of industrial surplus plants. The military had little interest in many of the industrial facilities it had financed during the war. Ordnance plants such as Kankakee, however, were different. As producers of high explosives and loaders of ammunition, these plants had a special place in the military's industrial portfolio. An understanding of the place of ordnance plants in this portfolio can be ascertained by an examination of the material created by military and ancillary interests about sulfuric acid and nitric acid, key ingredients in the making of explosives. In order to make the appropriate calculations about the sulfuric and nitric industry, the military had to create a coherent and functional body of information that could guide its decision making.

The calculations started two weeks after the Japanese surrender with a confidential report written by the army's Office of the Chief of Engineers on sulfuric and nitric acid factories. The report laid out the factors that would determine the postwar market for sulfuric acid and the effect this would have on industrial facility disposal. Or, as the Chief of Engineers put it, the report was "to assemble pertinent economic information to assist in the determination of the potentialities of Government-owned" industrial sites.[48] The key word here was *pertinent*. It both suggests that certain material had to be included in the assessment of the state's sites and implies that there is material that should not be included. Pertinent material included information about the extent and character of government and private facilities, the scale of postwar demand for sulfuric acid, and the problems of releasing government-owned facilities onto the private property market. To be considered pertinent meant to be functionally useful for a capitalist reckoning that revolved around issues such as productive capacity, market trends, depreciation costs, transportation facilities, and natural resources. It was through this reckoning that the military established the parameters that determined which industrial sites to sell to private interests.

Informative yet succinct, the report set out the basis for the disposal of state-owned defense factories such as Kankakee to the private sector. It started by laying out the boundaries of the industrial sites under consideration: the name, location, and daily capacity of the thirty defense plants that produced sulfuric acid and nitric acid. This was followed by an outline of the sector's wartime production, showing the tonnage of acids consumed by industries such as fertilizer, iron and steel, and petroleum. It finished with statements about the plants' wartime potential, and how this would affect the postwar market production for sulfuric and nitric acids and the production potential of private firms. In reports such as these, the military worked together with the state and industry to calculate an industry's economic parameters and to frame the roles each member of the military-industrial complex would have in the postwar industry. As a result, through the combined efforts of government agencies and manufacturers, an industrial world was created, one in which government-owned industrial sites were framed and placed in specific ways that defined how they were to be understood as an industrial object.

The August 30 report was linked to other sources of information, which in turn were based on other sources of material. These calculations helped frame the world around which an analysis of the industry was made and the possibilities for the postwar deployment of the industrial site. One such source was an August 27, 1945, confidential report by Alonzo White, chief of the WPB's sulfuric acid unit. In the report, White gave "thumbnail" sketches of every sulfuric acid plant and scrutinized the productive capacity of every industrial site and its potential impact on private production.[49] This involved, among other things, an analysis of the site's capacity, regional resource base, competition with nearby factories, and potential for increasing production. The information, based as it was on material gathered by the various government agencies and industry insiders, created the parameters upon which the industrial sites were understood. White's report, like the one that came from the Chief of Engineers three days later, created the frame through which plant disposal would take place.

After establishing the industrial sites to be analyzed, White then set out the disposal problems faced by the government. A major issue was the regional balance of capacity and demand. While the North was oversupplied, the South had potential for heavy demand from the superphosphate industry. However, he cautioned, the regional conditions could change quickly. Moreover, the close geographic distance between plants and customers would limit the ability of the disposal agencies to sell off the plants. Another pressing issue was what to do with the industrial facilities if they were not disposed of in a timely manner. In White's view, it might be thought that the properties should be held in a standby condition until the private sector had need of them. This, however, would not be wise as the product's corrosive aspects meant that maintenance costs would be prohibitive, and rapid technological change could quickly make the wartime plants redundant. White discussed both issues in greater detail in two papers published in a trade journal in the summer of 1945.[50] His key point was that given the locational restraints on the sale of the product, it was essential to think through the geographic dimensions of the industry, and that this had to be done before new industrial processes and plant design made the government's investment redundant.

This knowledge was used by the military, the main sponsor of sulfuric and nitric acid war plants, to situate Kankakee's position within its broader national program of factory retention and the disposal regime. The army's Advisory Board on Utilization of Surplus Industrial Facilities worked with the disposal agencies and considered in great detail the geographical dimensions of each acid facility and its disposal possibilities. After a detailed examination of the machinery, facilities, labor force, and surrounding districts of plants, the authors turned to how to dispose of these plants. As it so happened, the military refused to place the Kankakee plant for sale on the open market. The regime coalition calculated that this would undermine existing private industrial property that also produced vital defense materials, would adversely affect the industry's structure, and would cause problems for the Chicago area.[51]

Kankakee remained in military hands. By October 1945, the Kankakee plant had merged with the neighboring Elwood plant and was placed in a permanent standby condition with a maintenance workforce of four hundred. Its contracts with the wartime operators—U.S. Rubber and Sanderson and Porter—had already been terminated. It did not stay inactive for very long. Along with other ordnance plants, the Chicago area facility was opened at the end of 1946 to manufacture ammonium nitrate liquor and nitric acid for fertilizer that was to be shipped to American-occupied territory in Europe and Asia to boost agricultural production. The fertilizer program continued for more than three years. The plant was closed in the spring of 1950 when commercial interests in Germany, Korea, and Japan could supply local demand.[52]

Kankakee was reactivated with the advent of conflict in Korea. In November 1950, the plant was selected as headquarters of the Ordnance Ammunition Center, which was to supervise and control the army's expanding ammunition program in the country's fifty-two high-explosive plants. The center's director, Brigadier General Joel Holmes, had clear ideas about the relationship between the military and industry, arguing that "private industry with its vast facilities and resources should be permitted to produce the machines of war with a minimum of interference from government agencies." His staff was largely made up of reserve officers who were "top industrial executives, factory owners, attorneys and engineers."[53] The Ordnance Ammunition Center spent more than $750 million on rehabilitating ordnance plants across America and brought in corporations such as U.S. Rubber at Kankakee, which had operated the factories during the war, to restart nitric and sulfuric acid production. Rehabilitation began in the summer of 1951, and by the following summer, U.S. Rubber had placed most of the chemical production lines in operation. The company employed more than 2,500 by the end of the 1952.[54]

The deliberations involving a range of calculative agents in 1945 and 1946 to determine whether to retain the Kankakee ordnance plant had long-term consequences. Most notably, the army was able to formulate a series of production programs based on knowledge gathered by the WAA, other government agencies, and industry. The factory's function was embedded within a set of multiscalar relations linking the site to regional producers of sulfuric and nitric acids, other ordnance plants, industrial corporations, and fertilizer customers in Europe and Asia. The Kankakee facility was just one of hundreds of factories that became part of the military's calculations about its relationship with business interests. The result was that surplus industrial plants were incorporated into the postwar operations of the armed forces in the name of national security. While the military owned and directly operated few industrial plants after 1945, it did work with civil government agencies and with business to determine the function of many wartime plants in the immediate postwar years.

Conclusion

The disposal of Chicago's state-funded industrial property required the building of new forms of knowledge, the deployment of that knowledge in a local context, and the active engagement of military, government, and industrial officials from across the country with each other. With the end of the war, the federal government's interest in industrial sites shifted from building of war factories to disposal of these state-financed defense factories to private concerns. Accordingly, the federal administration reframed the industrial site as an object to be sold rather than created, and as a result, the state, the military, and industry became embroiled in a set of relations centered on the disposal of industrial sites. These relations by definition were multiscalar and focused on the local.

The reports written by the Chief of Engineers, Alonzo White, and the Chief of Ordnance were produced to allow the officials of the disposal regime to make decisions about how to proceed with disposing of government-owned sulfuric and nitric acid plants. They were not unusual. Report after report for other industries considered the same questions. This was the case with individual factories as well, where material about an industry was paired with information about the site and the locality. In all cases, the WAA, the military, and industry built a body of local and industrial information about war factories and defense industries to help dispose of the manufacturing property that stretched across space. Multiscalar in form, the relations of the military-industrial complex agents were played out in material spaces. The impact of the factories and industries on both national and local markets were examined. The quality and usefulness of the machinery and production units were outlined and compared to private plants. Local conditions, from the character of the labor force to the extent of the transportation system, were analyzed. Through these studies and reports, the civil and military branches of the state reproduced capitalist markets and shaped local economies through the calculations they made about the disposal of government-owned industrial property.

CHAPTER 8

The Site Politics of Defense Factory Disposal

The set of laws, practices, and meanings constituted by national industrial property policy framed the calculative politics of Chicago's industrial sites.[1] As we saw in the previous chapter, those seeking to turn state-owned property into private property built an elaborate structure of regulation to oversee disposal. Disposal of industrial property assets—land, buildings, machinery, roads, and infrastructures—is always place-specific and always contested.[2] An examination of five defense plants operated by Kropp Forge, Republic Steel, Youngstown Sheet and Tube, Bendix Aviation, and Ahlberg Bearing illustrates the site politics of the military-industrial complex in the making of postwar Chicago's industrial property relations. In all five cases, the fate of industrial space lay in the hands of a small number of calculating agents who fought over control of Chicago's wartime industrial sites and attempted to redefine the meaning of property to their own ends. They ranged from disposal officials, who worked within the parameters of the Surplus Property Act to ensure the legal and equitable redistribution of state assets, to industrial and military leaders, who sought to use state rules and regulations for their own benefit. The politics of the disposal of Chicago's war plants, not surprisingly, was not straightforward. A range of conflicting interests sought access to Chicago's manufacturing sites. From the military looking for storage space, charitable institutions seeking office space, and corporations pursuing new manufacturing premises, the transfer of state property to private interests or the military involved a messy politics resulting in a new ordering of the place-based social relations of property.

The National Defense Program and the Calculation of Value

The negotiations between Kropp Forge and the War Assets Administration (WAA) over plancor 1293 provide insights into the way that the politics of the postwar defense program reframed how surplus property was understood by the disposal agencies. Postwar militarization of the industrial economy reworked property relations and, in the case of plancor 1293, repositioned the defense factory in a different way. As noted in chapter 4, Kropp operated a $2.5 million defense factory to make drop forgings for a variety of war producers. The contract between the company and the mobilization agency ended in 1945. Unable to dispose of the factory before the end of the war, the WAA signed a five-year lease in June 1945 with Kropp, which would use the decommissioned plant to manufacture automotive, tractor, and other large forgings. The disposal agency continued to look for a purchaser but was unable to attract bids that matched its fair value of $1,373,300, despite a nationwide advertising campaign and the mailing of promotional letters to more than two thousand concerns (Figure 8.1).[3] Not surprisingly, the WAA did not accept bids of $500,000 and $650,000 from Kropp in 1947 and 1948.[4] As in most other disposal cases, these actions were part of a drawn-out battle among various actors. While the calculations of WAA officials were framed by the Surplus Property Act, the Cicero firm was seeking to purchase industrial property on the cheap. Testing the waters with low bids and unencumbered by competitive bids from other companies, Kropp was looking to find the lowest amount that the WAA could not refuse.

The WAA found itself in a quandary. On the one hand, it had received few serious bids for the scrambled plant, even though it believed that the factory could be sold to companies other than Kropp. On the other, the agency had few viable options given the plant's fair price of $1.3 million and the insertion of a national security clause into the purchase contract. By the summer of 1948, however, the conditions under which Kropp operated had changed. A new calculative element was introduced into the mix as Kropp became part of the nation's program of industrial mobilization. In July 1948 Kropp informed the WAA that it had received contracts to produce "items essential to the maintenance of America's National Defense program now underway" and that the company's sales had increased "primarily due to the defense program."[5] Not only had it obtained contracts to produce forgings for the T180 and T190 jet programs, the T1190 engine program, and the jet landing gear program, but it was also in the process of negotiating more military work.[6] This put pressure on the bearing manufacturer to find space to accommodate these demands. As a result, Kropp looked to the factory to fulfill its expanding production needs and to solidify its place in the postwar defense program. The WAA found itself in a difficult position. While it appeared to be impossible to sell the facility at a fair price to other companies, a legitimate defense contractor was eager to buy it, but at a heavily reduced cost. Weighing up the options, the agency caved and sold the plant to Kropp for $775,000. It was financed by a $95,500 down payment and a $679,500 government-sponsored mortgage, which was to be paid back over five years at 4 percent interest effective August 1, 1948.[7]

FIGURE 8.1. Kropp forging building (plancor 1293). This sales pamphlet provides potential purchasers with an idea of what the plancor looked like. Source: Reconstruction Finance Corporation.

The disposal of plancor 1293 illustrates how defense factories were implicated in the calculative relations of the postwar military-industrial complex. The decisions made during the war about what to build, how to build, where to build, and how industrial plants were connected to other sites were made in the light of decisions about the locational advantages of specific places, existing subcontracting relations, and industrial capacity. Industrial property became an object of calculation during the war that reinforced the changing but increasingly close relationship between the government, the military, and business. This relationship continued after 1945 but took on a new character and meaning. Postwar militarization cohered around the interrelated rise of the national security state and the expansion of the industrial economy. With the heating up of the Cold War, the American government promoted research and development and increased federal funding of defense production while maintaining a relatively light regulatory hand on business.[8]

The growth of a defense economy linked to aerospace, electronics, and other military-related industries fueled the need for specialized producers, which in turn placed ever-greater demands on factory space. Firms seeking to expand their productive capacity had two options; they could purchase property through either the private market or the federal surplus property program. Industrial executives did not make the decision to increase capacity very lightly though. Along with the time to completion and the cost of building, firms were concerned about creating excess capacity. Nevertheless, the expansion of output required the enlargement of industrial production space. One of the issues facing subcontractor firms linked to the defense program such as Kropp was how to accommodate the demand for their products with the industrial facilities they had at their disposal. For most, this required calculating their place in the defense program and the extent and usefulness of their industrial plant.

Kropp's purchase of plancor 1293 in 1948 was such a calculation. The catalyst for the sale was the substantial orders that the forging company had received from several defense contractors and the promise of more to come in the near future. The flow of defense funds to Kropp forced both the company and the WAA to revisit their earlier position regarding the site. The former had previously argued that the state of the factory prohibited them from paying anything close to the disposal agency's "fair value," while the WAA, in memo after memo, and report after report, considered the fair price of $1.3 million to be appropriate. These opposing positions were based on conflicting interpretations about the site, the relative price of industrial land and facilities, and the market for industrial commodities. The arguments about the plant's condition, cost, and functionality were based on the selective use of information gathered by the two parties and the broader politics of postwar industrial mobilization.

Despite the difficulties, the WAA believed before May 1948 that it could find a buyer for the facility other than Kropp. The reason for this was that the state-owned facility was not functionally linked to the existing Kropp property. As C. Roberts, an industrial engineer with the Appraisal Division of the Real Property section, stated in December 1947, the facility is "capable of independent operation . . . and while it is adjacent [to the] lessee's own plant[,] it is not integrated with or dependent upon [the] lessee's plant for operations." This point was made again six months later by another WAA official.[9] This was a consistent message obtained from the information gathered by federal and private reports on the plant over the previous three years. The WAA's attempt to sell the factory to private interests never wavered from its belief that any firm could utilize the industrial property separately from the adjacent Kropp facility.

Things changed very quickly in the last week of May 1948. In a long memo, W. Hauck, chief of the Iron and Steel Branch of the Industrial Division of the WAA's Office of Real Property Disposal, argued that plancor 1293 "must be classified as a scrambled facility."[10] His reasoning was that issues that earlier had not been considered a problem, such as the location of government-owned machinery, were in fact a problem. According to Hauck, the plant could only function independently at a considerable cost and a great delay to the start of productive operations. In his opinion, selling the facility to Kropp would be beneficial to all parties. The government would be able to cross the factory off the list of unsold plants and would receive at least $700,000 for its troubles. The company, meanwhile, would get the additional space it needed to expand production for the defense work. Hauck's calculation appeared to be a winning solution to a problem that was dragging on for far too long.

As this suggests, state-owned industrial facilities such as plancor 1293 became objects of intense scrutiny that were incorporated into postwar America's industrial policy. In some cases, plants were incidental to the country's defense program and industrial-political machinations, while in others, such as plancor 1293, they were directly implicated in the plans of defense producers. As the Kropp case illustrates, the link between the defense program, individual firms, and government industrial property was neither systematic nor well planned. Despite the seemingly coherent postwar policy on state-owned defense factories and the expansion of the defense program, these relationships did not form a "stable 'system' or 'complex,' insofar as such terms imply coherent and centralized intention and direction, only an accretion of interests, forces, and objectives that later looked like a system."[11] Rather, as the Kropp case shows, an ad hoc assembly of competing interests worked to refashion the social relations of industrial property and to resituate government industrial facilities within the industrial and political conditions of postwar America.

This was the position taken by *New York Times* writer Hanson Baldwin, the winner of a Pulitzer Prize for his coverage of World War II. He was very clear about the calculations behind postwar industrial mobilization. In his view, mobilization had to rest on developing an effective national defense program. The success of a program to prepare American industry for a future war rested on military-industry coordination within a national security framework. Industrial mobilization planning, he argued, "means intricate scheduling, stockpiles of the necessary raw materials and a 'master' blueprint that will provide coordinated industrial-military effort." In order to make this possible, the government, the military, and industry had to work more closely. However, Baldwin warned, the industrial mobilization program should not use "World War II as its yardstick; new factors, technological and strategic, have already made all such past calculations obsolete." National security and industrial mobilization were paramount concerns.[12] For Baldwin, the disposal of plants such as plancor 1293 to companies such as Kropp was essential to the success of such a program.

Entangled Steel

Chicago was one of America's leading steel centers in 1939.[13] This position was maintained during the war by injections of state and private investment into steel-making facilities. After the war, the industry's importance for both private and defense expansion ensured that the disposal of state-owned steel mills would undergo intense scrutiny from industrial executives, government officials, and military officers. Surveys, reports, and appraisals of industrial property and the steel industry were done by the WAA and private industrial engineering firms. Federal government, business, and military officials were concerned about a range of steel-related issues, ranging from competition from European producers to the aging structures of the steel industry in the older steel districts and the devaluation of private industrial property. This prompted government-military-industrial leaders to take a special interest in the huge amount of wartime steel facilities that had to be disposed of. The industry's fear that flooding the industry's property market with wartime plants would undermine the postwar industry was in conflict with the government's need to dispose of surplus property, the military's need to have a viable reserve of steel mills available for an emergency, and a community's need to provide employment for workers.[14]

More than $2.58 billion was invested by private firms, the federal government, and the military in new steel-making facilities between 1938 and 1945. The Defense Plant Corporation (DPC) accounted for $1 billion of the state funds, while the army and navy made up the rest. DPC investment was concentrated in a handful of large corporations. Close to $495 million was committed to just seven facilities: U.S. Steel (Geneva, Utah), Braddock, Homestead, and Duquesne (all in Pittsburgh), American Rolling Mills (Houston), and Republic Steel and Inland Steel (both Chicago).[15] Even though the federal government began selling off its steel mills at an early date, disposal was slow, taking several years.

By January 1947, only 44 plants had been sold and 18 leased. By the end of 1950 most of the disposal had been completed: 116 of the 143 large integrated and semi-integrated manufacturing properties listed in the records of the General Services Administration (GSA) had been sold, while another 13 had been transferred to the national industrial reserve, 12 were on long-term lease, and 2 were available for disposal.[16]

Two factories that belonged to the steel facility disposal process are discussed here: Republic Steel in South Chicago (plancor 422) and Youngstown Sheet and Tube in East Chicago (plancor 328). These plancors show how the two properties were subjected to different pressures, most notably executives' sense of the future working of the national steel market, company decisions about how to proceed in the postwar period, and the demands of local interests in maintaining an industrial presence. They illustrate how calculative agents worked within a multiscalar set of industrial and property relations and shaped the on-the-ground story of the two Chicago mills.

Funded by the DPC and operated by Republic Steel, plancor 422 was one of the country's largest government-owned defense facilities (Figure 8.2). Located in South Chicago on a 160-acre site bounded by the company's main plant and the Calumet River, the plant consisted of pig iron and steel-making facilities. Costing almost $91 million, the forty-six buildings were opened in 1943 to manufacture high-quality alloy steel for use in aircraft parts, gun barrels, and other war products. As clearly laid out in the correspondence between the company and the disposal agency, the WAA faced several disposal problems after the termination of its contract with Republic in 1945. Two issues dominated: the difficulty of disposal due to the low demand for the mill's relatively specialized products; and the likely failure of peacetime production resulting from the plant's complicated character.[17] Despite these problems, the mill was sold.

The plant was first advertised for sale in February 1946. Three bids were opened on May 1, all of which were "evaluated and later rejected." As the *New York Times* noted, this was because the bids did "not obtain for the Government the fair value." The disparity between the offered prices and fair value prompted some questions outside of the WAA about the agency's expectations. In May 1946 the Surplus Property Subcommittee of the Committee of Military Affairs made another assessment, but it was not very different.[18] Receiving little help from the report, the WAA re-advertised in the summer, calling for negotiations rather than sealed bids. Once again, the Chicago and Washington offices deemed the submitted proposals inadequate. By November the WAA was at a loss at how to proceed. It had spent considerable time looking for a buyer but "without satisfactory results." In its view, undertaking a third round of advertising would "probably be detrimental for subsequent disposal purposes" and would have deleterious effects on local conditions. The answer, it believed, was to allow previous bidders the chance to resubmit new proposals. This worked.

FIGURE 8.2. "Republic Builds for D.P.C." As indicated in this publication describing a steel plant built as part of the industrial mobilization program, Republic Steel was just one of thousands of plants that received DPC funds to build industrial space for munition production.
Source: Southeast Chicago Historical Society.

On December 20, 1946, the director of the WAA's industrial division recommended that plancor 422 be sold to Republic Steel for $35 million. The recommendation was accepted by the agency's General Board.[19]

What does this tell us about disposal calculations? The recommendation to sell the mill to Republic made it clear that the WAA was not going to receive what they had earlier considered to be the fair price of $45 million. Despite Chicago's attraction as a major steel center, the disposal agency found it extremely difficult to rid itself of the manufacturing facility. On December 20, E. J. Ellinson, the director of the Industrial Division of the Office of Real Property Disposal, wrote a long memorandum that described the plant, outlined the history of negotiations, and assessed Republic Steel's purchase offer for $35 million. In Ellinson's view, the WAA had little choice. If the mill was not quickly disposed of, it would soon become redundant, and any economic or social benefits to the government and to Chicago would disappear. Accordingly, agency officials had to recalibrate their position from one of obtaining a fair price regardless of the offers on the table to one that "better meets" other objectives of the Surplus Property Act.[20] As in the Kropp case, the WAA retreated from its stance that it would only consider "fair" value for the plant. Rather than continuing to insist on $45 million (exclusive of interest), they now recommended accepting Republic's offer of $35 million (inclusive of interest) over twenty years.

The WAA's recalculation was rationalized in several ways. Ellinson explained that the competing bids were unacceptable because the firms were financially and organizationally weak. Republic's proposal, on the other hand, met the objectives of the Surplus Property Act by allowing for effective use of the site and promoting growth of the country's employment and productive facilities. The sale would allow the WAA to receive a high share of the stated fair value, make an immediate end to government expenditures on the plancor, and allow manufacturing operations to continue unimpeded. At the same time, Republic's working capital and administrative and technical organization—"qualified men of long standing and experience in the steel industry"—ensured that it could work with the plant. Finally, an adjoining Republic facility would become the market for the plant's output.[21] By awarding plancor 422 to Republic Steel, the Real Property Review Board was recalculating the place of an industrial plant within the state realm and its place in the larger world of Chicago's industrial and spatial relations.

Although the outcome would be quite different from that of the Republic mill, plancor 328's fate was also situated within the broader circuits of the nation's postwar steel industry. While the WAA and Republic came to a resolution of the seemingly intractable problem of federal fixed-capital investment, this was not the case with plancor 328. The plant was deemed inappropriate to Youngstown's postwar needs, and unable to find another suitable purchaser, the WAA was in a difficult position. The plancor consisted of a more than $2 million investment in land, buildings, and machinery on a two-acre plot in East Chicago. Operated by Youngstown during the war, the electric furnace steel defense plant made alloy ingots for the lessee's own facilities. The mill's problematic nature had been signaled even before the war ended. Open for a year, it was shut in April 1944 due to declining demand for alloy steel. Once closed, it never reopened.[22]

Despite this, however, a unique solution for the disposal of the industrial facilities was found. The solution demonstrates the intersection of the dynamics of national demand for alloy steel, the demand for industrial space in two different cities, and the specific features of two steel firms. There were three obstacles to disposal. First, low demand for electric furnace steel had led to the shutting down of government plants operating in Canton, Ohio, and South Chicago. According to a 1947 study, the situation was dire. Electric furnace production in 1946 was half the 1945 levels, while costs were higher than open-hearth production. It was clear that purchasing the facility would not allow Youngstown or any other firm to make profits. Second, Youngstown was unwilling to make the organizational and manufacturing changes necessitated by the purchase of the war-built mill. The condition of the facilities was not good enough to tempt Youngstown to restructure its corporate division of labor. Finally, the fact that the DPC land was surrounded by lessee-owned land meant that the plancor's tools and machinery could not be reassembled into a self-contained unit that could be operated independently of Youngstown's facilities. The facility was little more than "an adjunct to a highly integrated steel plant consisting among other items of an open hearth and blooming mill plant." Furthermore, the lack of sufficient land ensured that an outside buyer would be unable to build the necessary rolling mill. In light of these obstacles, the WAA gave the mill a fair value of $700,000 even though it had assessed its normal reproduction cost at more than $2 million.[23]

The WAA's advertising campaign elicited only one bid. Feeling that it had no choice, the Chicago office recommended that Youngstown's offer of $510,000 be accepted despite the assessed fair value. The rationale was that if Chicago was to reap the benefit of defense facilities, it had to put the "idle plant into production and provide additional employment."[24] Despite the plant's contribution to local employment and taxes, Washington rejected the offer and authorized the Chicago office to make a counter proposal of $565,587. This was rejected by Youngstown, who informed the WAA in July 1947 that the facility did not fit into their plans. The steel corporation was in the process of implementing a significant expansion plan in East Chicago and elsewhere, and the mill could not be incorporated into the corporation's system. According to Youngstown's executives, the poorly made war facilities would not help the company find new markets or move into new product lines. Accordingly, the steel firm would not purchase or lease the industrial site.

This left the WAA with a problem: How could it dispose of plancor 328? Given the absence of takers for the facilities, what should they do? After several months of assessing national and local conditions, they came to the conclusion that it should be sold as an off-site functional unit.[25] Another round of advertising in the spring of 1948 resulted in four offers. The winning bid was from McLouth Steel of Detroit. The company planned to dismantle the plant and move it to a new site near Detroit.[26] McLouth was desperate to acquire new facilities to meet "an insatiable demand." As the WAA noted, the company's failure "to acquire the Youngstown electric furnace plant would probably result in the suspension of their entire rolling mill facilities because of their inability to secure semi-finished material in the open steel market."[27] With this in mind, the WAA accepted the offer of $1.2 million in June 1948; the plancor was dismantled in August and was reassembled as part of an integrated mill in Trenton just outside of Detroit in the late fall.[28]

The disposal of the Republic and Youngstown plants had quite different outcomes. While one reverted back to the wartime operator, the other was dismantled and moved to another city. In both cases, they were sold far below both their wartime construction cost and what the WAA had assessed as fair price. While their postwar fates were different, multiscalar industrial property relations were common to both outcomes and the determination of what happened to local property. The way in which companies such as Republic, Youngstown, and McLouth framed and worked on local sites was undertaken within broad national and international processes that took account of interbranch competition and capacity, raw material and labor costs, and technological developments.

Site Politics: Plancor 1235

In September 1942 the DPC bought the Sprague, Warner warehouse. The west-end building had been built just a year earlier to accommodate the grocery company's warehousing and packaging facilities. Following the DPC's purchase, the plant became plancor 1235 and was converted to wartime manufacture. The land and buildings cost the DPC $2.4 million, while another $7 million went to machinery and equipment. The facility consisted of two connected buildings with 487,000 square feet of floor space. Modern in design, newly constructed, and close to railroad lines, the plant was a model defense factory. The Bendix Aviation Company operated the DPC facility between 1942 and 1945 to manufacture and undertake research on aircraft aluminum carburetors.[29] A useful manufacturing site during the war, the plant became a site of conflict and negotiation for several interests, including the War Department, several industrial corporations, a handful of national politicians, the Reconstruction Finance Corporation (RFC), the WAA, and the Department of Justice after the war. Unlike the steel mills, the Bendix industrial site was the center of bitter place politics that pitted various companies and their political allies against each other.

The problem started with deliberations about the site by the military. The War Department was looking for a place in Chicago to consolidate its four existing Signal Corps operations into one location. Unable to acquire either the Buick or Studebaker plancors, it turned its attention to plancor 1235. In October, however, the Corps found another site and duly informed the RFC's Office of Defense Plants that the Bendix factory could be sold to private interests. The Corps' alternative site, however, did not work out, and in December, Kenneth Royall, the undersecretary of war, wrote to the RFC stating that the military had "an immediate requirement for the use of the building."[30] But other interests had other plans. Several corporations were also searching for prime Chicago locations. The pressure exerted by one of these firms scuttled the War Department's claim to the property and, in the process, initiated an acrimonious fight for the site.[31] Over the next five months competition for the site led to a battle between three companies: Belmont Radio, Consolidated Grocers, and Helene Curtis.[32] Letters, proposals, memos, surveys, and telephone calls were sent from each firm's executives, lawyers, and political supporters to the WAA's Chicago and Washington offices in an attempt to influence the agency. The competing companies sent out in this barrage of correspondence arguments about employment, finances, mortgages, and other locational options to press their claim to the facility. As a result, the final decision about the fate of plancor 1235 was embedded in a site politics centered on Chicago but stretching out to Springfield, Washington, Baltimore, and elsewhere.

Each company pushed its claim to the site by basing its arguments on the Surplus Property Act. Belmont argued that the war had allowed them to develop new product lines (aircraft, television, communication equipment), resulting in a trebling of employment and the development of economies of scale and cost efficiencies. Acquiring plancor 1235 would allow the company to pass these efficiencies onto the consumer. Walter Murphy, the company's attorney, wrote to Senator Joseph O'Mahoney, chair of the senate subcommittee on surplus property, at the end of January 1946, saying that the plant would "assist a small enterprise like Belmont to grow and develop and keep abreast of the large companies in the field." The purchase would also benefit another electronic company; the Belmont factory on West Dickens would be sold to Zenith Radio for $900,000. This would make "Chicago an important center of the radio industry." Finally, at the end of March, in a desperate bid to stop Helene Curtis from getting the plant, the company mentioned the critical role they had played in convincing the Signal Corps to allow the factory to revert to private industry and not to the military.[33]

Consolidated Grocers pushed an economic angle as well as its unique claim to the manufacturing site. The plant would house the company's Sprague, Warner division, which manufactured and distributed food products to twenty-five thousand food retailers across the country. Nathan Cummings, the firm's president, told the WAA that his company represented "free enterprise." He also claimed that it had a moral right to the property as it was the previous owner and had sold the factory to the DPC in order to aid the war effort. Moving, he complained, had cost the firm a great deal in time and money. The company told the WAA that the shortage of space at the time of the sale forced the firm to move to an old six-story building. The lease, which was coming to an end, could not be renewed. Having to move to another site would increase costs and negatively affect its clients, small businesses across the country. The firm would have to relocate outside of Chicago if it was unable to find a suitable local building.[34] In the company's opinion, plancor 1235 was critical to the success of the firm, Chicago's industrial base, and the nation's grocery industry.

The WAA, however, awarded the factory to the firm that raised the least compelling reasons for why it should receive the plant. In the end, Helene Curtis, a small personal care manufacturer, was awarded the plant at a cost of $2,156,250, taking possession in July 1946.[35] In contrast to Belmont's and Consolidated's substantial arguments, Harold Rosen, Helene Curtis's executive assistant, gave two reasons. First, the industrial plant would allow the firm to start new product lines, most notably heavy-duty restaurant items, which could be manufactured alongside their beauty goods and metal furniture lines. Second, the firm needed more space as it anticipated expanding its workforce from 1,900 to 3,500. The Sacramento Street facility would make this possible.[36] In contrast to Belmont's and Consolidated's detailed reasoning for why they needed the property, Rosen was extremely circumspect. There was no reference to the greater good, no mention of a moral right. It was just a simple economic calculation.

The WAA followed the typical procedure for disposing of plancor 1235. Five sealed bids were received. These were opened by Milnor Hoel, the agency's Chicago director, on February 27. Only three were deemed acceptable: Helene Curtis, Belmont Radio, and Consolidated Grocers. The bids of John Cuneo and National Tea were rejected as not being close to the fair value of $2,125,000 established by a Day and Zimmerman survey. The decision of which of the three bids to accept was based on a four-part calculus: the amount and the terms of the bid, employment, conformity to the Surplus Property Act, and credit ratings. After weighing these, the WAA recommended the Helene Curtis offer. Despite competition from Belmont, the Curtis bid had the highest value ($2,156,250), and this, in the final reckoning, was the most important factor in the WAA's eyes.[37] The WAA officials had made their decision by emphasizing one aspect of the Surplus Property Act.

The arguments laid out in the formal bids from the three companies were not the only instruments that were used to try to influence the WAA's deliberations. While there was a steady stream of correspondence between the firms and the disposal agency, Belmont and Consolidated also applied intense political pressure in the days preceding and following the opening of the sealed bids on February 27, 1946. The two companies mobilized an assortment of place-based political actors in an attempt to sway the WAA's and the RFC's decision about disposing of the industrial property. It was to no avail, but the effort undertaken by the two companies and their supporters provides insights into the site politics of property disposal.

Consolidated turned to their political networks to fight the decision. George Radcliffe, a Democratic senator from Maryland, made a very strong pitch to O. Beasley, the chief of the WAA's General Manufacturing Branch. Radcliffe was an ally of Nathan Cummings, whose wholesaling empire was based in Baltimore. In the senator's view, "The government has an obligation . . . to recognize the fact that the property in question was taken from the Consolidated Grocers' Corporation and that therefore it should be returned to them." He also noted that the firm's "operations are highly important to the activities of many . . . small independent business concerns and that if the Consolidated Grocers' Corporation is not permitted to recover this property, many small independent merchants will be injured." Not content to make his case solely on economic arguments, Radcliffe turned to administrative ones. Any other decision, he suggested, would fly in the "face of the spirit if not the letter of the procedures usually followed for disposition of property."[38] This was followed a few days later by a letter from Scott Lucas, an Illinois Democratic senator. He told General Gregory, the WAA chair, that the property should be returned to the original owners.[39] Consolidated reasoned that national politicians would be able to change the WAA's decision and to influence the politics of the industrial site.

Belmont matched Consolidated's mobilization of powerful allies. In January 30, 1946, the firm's attorney wrote Joseph O'Mahoney, the chair of the senate subcommittee on surplus property, outlining Belmont's case. Four weeks later he sent a letter to Walter Maloney, a D.C. lawyer and a close friend of President Truman, laying out the strengths of Belmont's offer. In his view, neither of the competing companies should have the plancor as Helene Curtis could not pay for it, and Consolidated had been charged as being a monopoly by the Federal Trade Commission. In both cases, this was contrary to the stipulations of the Surplus Property Act. Maloney, in turn, sent Murphy's letter to John Snyder, director of War Mobilization and Reconversion and soon to be secretary of the Treasury. This was followed by letters from other politicians. William Link, the district's congressional representative, told Snyder that Belmont would produce more for the working-class area than the other two firms. C. Wayland Brooks, a Republican senator from Illinois, told Joseph O'Brien, assistant administrator of the WAA's Real Property division, that both he and the head of the Signal Corps supported Belmont's claims. In their opinion, receiving the plant would allow Belmont and Zenith to increase electronic production in Chicago and to "make possible greater efforts in research and experimentation in the field of electronics, radar and television."[40]

What was the WAA to make of the efforts to sway their deliberations? Belmont's and Consolidated's outrage and the correspondence from political heavyweights forced the WAA to reflect on their decision. On March 4, directors of the agency's disposal section met to discuss their earlier decision. Contrary to their earlier judgment, they now believed that all three bids were "deserving of careful consideration" and recommended that no decision be made at the time. The General Board concurred.[41] As John O'Brien, assistant administrator of the WAA's Real Property division, told Senator Radcliffe nine days later, all three bids had their strengths. Concerned about the support for the two bids that were rejected, the board was hesitant to take any action in favor of any one bid and sent the file to the Department of Justice for an opinion. Undaunted by the letters in support of Belmont and Consolidated, Justice agreed with the original decision. On March 18, 1946, the WAA formally accepted the Helene Curtis bid. Three months later, on July 12, the company signed a contract with the WAA on terms of a $539,000 down payment and a $1,617,000 mortgage bearing 4 percent interest per annum, payable quarterly and amortized over a period of ten years.[42]

The signing of the contract, however, was not the end of the matter. Murphy, Belmont's attorney, was right: Helene Curtis was financially unsound. Less than a year after signing the mortgage contract, the beauty products firm wrote the WAA in June 1947 asking to restructure their mortgage. This initiated a new round of deliberations about the site. Rosen explained that the company faced "considerable delay in getting into the building and obtaining the necessary labor and material for conversion of the building." On top of this, changing business conditions had led to low sales and large inventories. In order to boost business they needed to change their financial arrangements with the agency from a ten-year to a fifteen-year mortgage. Helene Curtis had received a commitment from two insurance companies for a new debenture issue of a million dollars, but this was contingent on reducing the mortgage payment. The Real Property Review Board approved the request in mid-August.[43] All seemed set.

But this was not the case. The financial restructuring proved to be a stopgap measure. Less than seven months later, Helene Curtis wanted to sell the factory, and they had a prospective buyer: Kraft Food. The agreed-upon selling price was $2,200,000 plus equipment valued at $347,000, with Kraft paying off the remaining part of the mortgage owing to the RFC. The reason for this drastic action was that the company's fortunes had not improved, and the new mortgage was too large for the firm to carry. The continuing poor business conditions made the property too large for their needs. Employment had dropped from 1,950 in 1946 to 800, while sales fell from $14.3 million in 1946 to $9.3 million in 1947. The sales numbers for the first two months of 1948 were even lower.

The company told the disposal agency that they planned to move to a smaller plant in the Chicago area if allowed to sell the Sacramento Street facility and that they would use the money from the sale to solidify their working capital. Kraft would use the building for offices, cooler space, and cheese manufacture and employ about 1,200.[44]

What did the WAA make of this? As it stood, they had little choice but to submit to the request. The two firms had presented a fait accompli. In April 1948, after an internal investigation into Curtis's claims and the financial stability of the cheese manufacturer, they granted Curtis the right to sell the plant to Kraft.[45] Despite the eventual sale to Kraft, the politics of disposing of the industrial site was contentious, involving numerous actors in various locations who fought over the rights of individual firms to a specific space. In this case, and in contrast to what happened to the steel mills, the fate of an industrial site rested on the calculations made by military officials, government civil agencies, and industrial executives in the face of political and economic pressures and processes.

Building Entanglements: Ahlberg Bearing versus the RFC

On September 12, 1946, the Chicago law firm of Seyfarth and Atwood lodged a complaint in ejectment in the Circuit Court of Cook County. The attorneys, who represented Ahlberg Bearing, informed the court that the company was suing the RFC for $150,000. According to Fred Burkholder, the firm's president, the reason that Ahlberg sought possession of the property named in the complaint was the agency's refusal to remove a government-built encroachment from company property. The land in question was of little material consequence, comprising sixteen inches running the length of the eastern side of the Ahlberg factory.[46] The ensuing court fight, however, involved industrial firms, the federal government, a private land trust, an architect, a building contractor, and attorneys in actions occurring between February 1942 and October 1953. This case would bedevil the WAA's ability to dispose of plancor 653's plant, machinery, and equipment on the property abutting the Ahlberg factory. The site politics behind the court case tells a story about the entanglements that came with the disposal of surplus industrial sites and the conflict associated with the calculative relations of industrial property.

To understand the conflict over the property and the WAA's attempts to dispose of plancor 653, it is best to start at the beginning—the building of the factory. In February 1942, Burkholder wrote to the DPC asking permission to build a two-story factory adjacent to its ball bearing factory on West 47th Street. The construction program would cost $800,000. Ahlberg needed the additional space to fulfill defense contracts to manufacture nonfriction bearings for several firms (Pullman Standard and International Harvester), foreign governments (British, Australian, and South African), and the U.S. Navy and Army. Ahlberg was unable to meet these contracts at its present workspace. The company calculated that the additional capacity would double its 1941 annual output of $1.5 million.[47] The Ahlberg case was a typical mobilization story in which the private sector made various calculations before committing themselves to war production: Ahlberg figured out the firm's capacity, income, and sales resulting from state and private demand, and then it took account of the possibilities of federal funding for building new industrial space. After the DPC's agreement, events moved quickly. By early March, the agency and Burkholder were discussing the purchase of the addition's land for $30,000.[48] Unbeknownst to many of the principal players at the time, this would turn out to be the one of the reasons why the company took the RFC to court in 1946.

Ahlberg had moved several times since it was established in 1908, each time in search of larger quarters. They moved for the last time in 1937, taking a fifteen-year purchase option lease on the West 47th site from the Phipps Industrial Land Trust. As the new wartime factory was to be built on land adjacent to but not owned by Ahlberg, the DPC had to negotiate with the landowner. Accordingly, negotiations between the agency and the Phipps trustees took place in the second week of March 1942. This resulted in a new price for the land: $20,000. The DPC, however, was willing to pay only $17,500; the other $2,500 had to come from Ahlberg. This was duly agreed to, and by March 13 a lease agreement between the bearing maker and the DPC for the new industrial space was ready.[49]

The second issue that bedeviled disposal had to do with the building placed on the DPC-purchased land. At the end of March, Ahlberg, acting for the DPC, signed a contract with Carl Metz, an architect-engineer. The contract stipulated that Metz was to provide architectural and engineering plans for a two-story building costing $150,000 that physically adjoined the east side of the existing factory. Once the plans were completed, Ahlberg contracted with Campbell, Lowrie, and Lautermilch to build the plant for $178,825. The DPC-funded, army-sponsored, two-story addition adjoining the original factory was completed by December 1942.[50] Once the building was constructed, Ahlberg used the factory space to build ball bearings for its various customers until the summer of 1945, when its wartime contracts came to an end.

The resulting court case had to do with the removal of the party wall connecting the original factory and the wartime addition, which was made soon after the completion of the initial defense factory. In Ahlberg's opinion, the wall was an obstacle to the free flow of materials and personnel between the two separately owned properties, and so in December 1942, Phipps approved the removal of the east wall separating the factories. This led to a flurry of letters, telephone calls, and meetings among the different parties. Negotiations were successfully concluded in June 1943, with the proviso that the DPC had to "replace and restore said East wall in substantially the same condition as it was before removal" after the war was over.[51] The issue was put to rest for more than three years. In 1946, however, the demolished wall and the fact that a small portion of the DPC plancor lay in the Ahlberg property—the sixteen-inch encroachment laid out by Burkholder in his complaint—had become a problem. While the 1942 agreement had resulted in the construction of a successful war production unit, the selling of the plant on the open market in 1946 was not so successful. Conflict between Ahlberg and the RFC resulted in delaying the final disposal of the factory until April 1948.

The conflict was triggered by Ahlberg's attempt to purchase the DPC-financed factory. Under the terms of the lease, Ahlberg had the first option to purchase the plant. In August 1945, however, the company informed the WAA that it did not want to purchase the addition, and so the agency put the property up for sale.[52] Several bids were received in the spring of 1946. Surprisingly, Ahlberg was one of the bidders, offering $225,000 in cash. This elicited the scorn of Louis Bean, the special assistant for negotiations of the War Assets Corporation's Plant Disposal Unit. He told Milnor Hoel, the corporation's regional director, that "in cases of this kind where the lessee expects a windfall by reason of the conditions existing that is, it being a so-called scrambled plant, the corporation takes the position that rather than allow a windfall to the lessee it would even go to the extent of removing the property entirely." Its offer to purchase rejected, Ahlberg tried to lease the factory, offering to pay $50,777 for three years.[53] This too was rejected by the disposal agency. The decision, however, backfired. Bean may have had good reason to be angry at the attempts of industrial managers to take advantage of the difficulty faced by the disposal agency in selling scrambled plants. The end result, however, was that the agency realized a much smaller amount of money for plancor 653 than offered by Ahlberg in 1946.

Ahlberg's was not the only bid for the property: Kungsholm Baking Company, which had two Chicago factories, was looking to expand its production facilities and offered $185,000; and a local charity, the Illinois Institute for the Blind (IIB), offered $125,000.[54] By the summer of 1946, Kungsholm had withdrawn its bid, but the IIB bid remained on the table, although negotiations with the WAA progressed slowly. In August, the WAA told Ahlberg that it was terminating the company's right to the facilities.[55] This prompted the bearing manufacturer to demand that the WAA remove the portion of the wartime addition that rested on the east wall of their property. The disposal agency took no action, and so Ahlberg turned to the courts, presenting the complaint in ejectment in September 1946. This litigation not only forced the RFC to deal with the time and costs of a court case, but it also caused a problem in the title of the property and complicated the proposed sale of the property to the IIB.[56]

Despite the pending case, the IIB and the WAA were set to sign the sale contract in January 1947. The signing, however, was delayed at the last hour by the intervention of Ross Rizley, a Republican from Iowa, who chaired the House subcommittee on executive expenditures. On the morning of the signing he informed the WAA that he was sending an investigator to Chicago to look into the deal. The reason, he told Burkholder, was the difference between the IIB's sale price ($125,000) and Ahlberg's bid ($225,000 in cash). Outraged by the discrepancy, Rizley asked the WAA to postpone the sale and to investigate the transaction. As in the case of plancor 1235, the agency agreed to the request, but with different results. The investigation into the charity's dealings found that the IIB's accounting practices were questionable; in early March 1947 the offer to the IIB was withdrawn, and all bids were thrown out. The WAA was back to square one with a court case pending against it. Another solution had to be found.[57]

Given the options, the WAA approved the sale of plancor 653 to Ahlberg for $150,000 cash in April 1947. The decision turned on the agency's desire to rid itself of the court case and Rizley. The sale was conditional upon Ahlberg's withdrawal of the pending suit against the RFC. The transaction was not closed, though, as Ahlberg was short of funds and unable to pay by cash. Despite various proposals, it took more than a year to work out the details.[58] By the end of 1947 the situation was still in flux. As John Loomis, the counsel of the Real Property Disposal division in Washington, told Irving Zemans, his Chicago counterpart, the company was still "not in the position to pay the $150,000.00 cash." Ahlberg wanted a mortgage.[59]

The need for a mortgage set into motion a new calculation, most notably a review of the firm's suitability to receive credit. This necessitated a WAA review of Ahlberg's financial and managerial status. The WAA looked up the company's assets, liabilities, sales, and profits in Standard Corporation Records. A Dun and Bradstreet report had recently downgraded Ahlberg's rating because of its low sales and labor problems. The WAA, however, was looking for a silver lining. It noted that the company's finances appeared to be stronger than they were in the past. In its opinion, the combination of good management and new contracts for the manufacture under license of bearings made by the Bowers and the Jack and Heintz companies suggested that the firm was a going concern. This point was reinforced by another point. The difficulties of disposing of plancor 653 were well known. Given that it was a scrambled plant, there were few favorable options other than selling it to Ahlberg. As one WAA official noted, "The building is not very desirable as a manufacturing plant." He continued by saying that "if the lessee does not exercise their option to purchase this plant site, we might have some difficulty in disposing of it as only a limited type of manufacturing could be utilized in this building." A February 1948 report on the situation recommended that Ahlberg receive the ten-year mortgage.[60]

Accordingly, the WAA agreed to the new financial arrangements. A new payment system was established, consisting of an initial down payment of $10,000 to be paid on December 15, 1947. This was to be followed by $20,000 cash plus interest of 4 percent on April 5, 1948, with the remaining $120,000 plus 4 percent interest to be paid in monthly installments over ten years. In agreeing to the terms, Ahlberg, among other things, had to "release all claims against" the government and to submit "quarterly financial statements."[61] This they did. The mortgage was finally closed in October 1953, and the file was closed. As the fight over plancor 635 by Ahlberg and the WAA shows, property involved a set of organizational procedures that reflect the relationships between different calculative actors. The disposal of plancor 653 and the conflict over the state-owned sixteen-inch abutment running alongside the private factory of Ahlberg Bearing Company demonstrate that this was a highly contentious and place-specific process.

Conclusion

The shift of government-owned property from the public sphere to the private one after 1944 destabilized the settled property relations instituted during the war and reformulated who had the right to take possession of wartime defense factories and under what conditions. As a package of rights held by a single owner, property designates who can use it and who can be excluded from it. In the case of state-owned defense factories, the federal government had the right to determine who had access to the property and to whom it could be sold. An elaborate set of practices and procedures established by the 1944 Surplus Property Act and administered by agencies such as the WAA were implemented by the federal government to oversee the transfer of property rights from one owner (the federal government and military) to another (private companies). While the degree of success by which it achieved its goal of selling off all of its wartime industrial property is debatable, the fact remains that a substantial number of defense factories were shifted from the public to the private sphere between the end of World War II and the beginning of the Korean War. The billions of dollars of state-owned industrial property and thousands of industrial sites created after 1940 across the country were converted to private industrial property between 1945 and 1950.

The process of turning public space into private space after 1944 was not straightforward. The disposal of state property induced a site politics focused on specific spaces (plancors) that stretched from the physical site itself through industrial, military, and federal offices and factories located across the country. The place-based politics of disposal involved a range of calculative actors who tried to shape the disposal process to their own interests. The rights specific to a particular piece of property were fought over in various ways. In some cases, as in the case of plancor 653 and Ahlberg Bearing, the boundaries delineating the extent to which rights could function were subjected to vociferous and legal wrangling. In others, such as the sale of plancor 1293 to Kropp, the ability to mobilize the transfer of property rights to the private sphere hinged on broader national policy such as the postwar defense program that connected industrial mobilization, the Cold War, and industrial space. In yet others, such as the steel mills, the place of a site in a company's future plans set out the parameters of what would happen to the property. In all cases, calculating federal, military, and business actors worked to frame industrial property within a set of public-private relationships centered on a capitalist understanding of property and place. The everyday practices of building and disposing of Chicago's defense factories were embedded in the multiscalar mobilization of various actors, the evaluation of industrial sites, the fixing of industrial capital in space, and placed-based conflicts. Both ideologically and institutionally, the operation of the property disposal regime reflected the broader social relations of property rights in twentieth-century America.

CHAPTER 9

Property, Calculation, and Industrial Space

The recent clash between residents and law enforcement agencies in the St. Louis suburb of Ferguson emphasizes the importance of knowing the origins, operation, and disposal of federally and military-owned property. One key theme that has emerged from the Ferguson conflict is the amount of military equipment deployed by the various police forces involved in the events. While some guns, armored cars, and bazookas were bought through public-private channels, some were not. An August 20, 2014, report in the *Guardian*, for example, pointed to a Department of Defense program that gave surplus military goods to local police departments. While this may have been small in comparison to direct funding from the Department of Homeland Security for population control programs, the country's police forces in places such as Ferguson were using surplus military products to patrol and control America's streets, and to deadly effect.[1] The militarization of Ferguson streets is a reminder that the line between public and private is not clear and that the creation of and market for state property has serious consequences, both inside and outside the public realm. The same is true of the massive amount of industrial property that the federal government created and disposed of between 1940 and 1950. This chapter uses the case of plancor 39 to illustrate this study's key themes: property relations and calculation, industrial mobilization and the military-industrial complex, and the place-based effects of state-owned property.

Plancor 39 and Property Relations

Plancor 39 was a large state-owned aircraft engine plant in the Chicago suburb of Melrose Park.[2] Operated by Buick during the war, the factory was one of the thousands of state-financed defense factories built in all regions of the United States as part of the new calculative property relations of the military-industrial complex. Plancor 39 was not alone. Metropolitan Chicago, home to huge sprawling aircraft engine factories operated by Dodge and Studebaker, was the country's major recipient of federal and military industrial investment. In the five years following Roosevelt's mobilization announcement of May 1940, more than $1.3 billion was funneled to more than six hundred of the region's industrial sites. This huge sum went to purchase substantial amounts of property, to build additions to existing plants, to construct entirely new government-owned factories operated by private companies, and to install new machinery in scrambled private and public industrial spaces. A much smaller amount was indirectly invested in state-authorized certificates of necessity to private industry. The construction and operation of these public and private industrial spaces were fueled by supply contracts valued at almost $10 billion. Metropolitan Chicago was a key node in the militarization of American industrial space and the reformulation of calculative property relations during the war.

The place of Buick-operated plancor 39 in GM's postwar corporate division of labor was being assessed by the fall of 1944. It was clear to all of the key decision makers—in this case, the military, the Reconstruction Finance Corporation (RFC), and the aircraft and automotive industries—that the factory would not be used to make aircraft engines once the war was over. While there was agreement what the property would not be used for, answers about how to actually utilize the plant and who was to own it in the postwar period were more difficult to determine. The Army Air Forces was not keen to hold onto the property as it was looking to downsize its postwar commitments in aircraft manufacture. Meanwhile, the country's aircraft manufacturers were reeling from the massive decline in orders and could not consider adding new capacity to their existing production lines. The RFC was eager to dispose of the facility as quickly as possible. Framed by the strictures of the Surplus Property Act, agency officials sought to obtain a fair price while promoting competition. This, of course, was contradicted by the fact that they wished to sell the factory to GM, one of the country's largest corporations. This would not be easy as Charles Wilson, the company's president, made clear in a letter to Jesse Jones, the secretary of commerce, in September 1944. Wilson outlined which of the sixteen government defense plants they operated during the war were of interest to them in the postwar period. Although Melrose Park had its merits, they found "the purchase price too high for use that can be made of plant" and had more interest in federal plancors in Lima, Fort Wayne, Cleveland, and Indianapolis.[3]

The dilemmas faced by these three central institutions of the military-industrial complex around plancor 39 were played out across the country. The primary operators of defense factories during the war—large, multi-unit corporations with a substantial share of the nation's industrial assets—had to frame the purchase of state-owned property within their postwar expansion plans. The army, navy, and what would become the air force had to decide whether they wanted to continue having direct control over industrial property at the end of the war. The federal government had to face the question of what to do with its billions of dollars of state-owned industrial facilities. The short answer, devised over several years and laid out in the Surplus Property and National Reserve Acts, was that the state would dispose of government factory space by selling it to private interests and by creating a national reserve. As we have seen, this involved calculating how to turn state industrial property into privately held industrial assets. In this way, the push by the military, national security technocrats, and defense-focused industrial executives to create a postwar industrial mobilization program drew wartime defense facilities such as plancor 39 into the scrutiny of industry, the state, and the military.

The building and disposal of state-financed industrial facilities such as the wartime engine plant in Melrose Park illustrate the ways in which property is a bundle of rights that give specific groups of people control over a society's assets and what happens to these assets in space.[4] The federal government's decision in 1940 to finance the construction of defense facilities and then to sell these plants to private interests at the end of the war had repercussions for the relationship between the state, the military, and business in three ways. First, industrial property had to be reframed as a public-private object after 1940 to allow the state and the military to build and mobilize private industrial assets in the service of what was considered the public good. An elaborate, sometimes arcane, and frequently unwieldy body of agencies, legislation, and practices was created to oversee, coordinate, and ultimately, in the final instance, control private property relations. The state as the final arbiter of property rights took control through its investment practices and legislative agenda to determine who had the right to newly created industrial property such as plancor 39. In so doing, the state became the owner of an extensive body of material spaces that were subject to the calculations of a public-private partnership geared to producing munitions for the military, legitimizing federal authority, and increasing corporate profits. Accordingly, the state and the military became directly involved in buying land, building factories, and installing machinery that would be operated by private companies. The refashioning of industrial property after 1940 allowed the federal government to channel an unprecedented amount of resources to the construction of state-owned and privately operated industrial facilities such as plancor 39.

Second, the disposal of billions of dollars of state-owned industrial property destabilized the settled wartime property relations centered on direct federal ownership and indirect subsidies that were put into place after 1940. The recalculation of postwar property relations relied on reframing the defense factory by pulling apart the system that the federal government had created at the beginning of the war. In many ways, the state was able to reestablish the property relations that had existed before Roosevelt's call for expansion in May 1940. The prevailing ideology at the end of the war was that property relations were to be returned, as much as was possible, to their prewar state. The wartime public-private partnership was to be rethought, and industrial property was to be returned to private hands. The discursive and material realities that had made it possible for the state, the army, and GM to create plancor 39 to build defense factories had to be reassembled so that the factory could be sold to private interests and become part of the postwar defense program. To this end, a new set of agencies, legislation, and practices was put in place to enable the transfer of state property to private interests. As with other defense plants across the country, the Surplus Property Act and state-directed disposal agencies were responsible for transferring plancor 39 back into the hands of private companies.

Finally, the changes that took place to industrial property relations during the 1940s forced the institutions of the military-industrial complex to become heavily involved in monitoring and intervening in the property market, both qualitatively and quantitatively. Needing to mobilize industry for defense purposes, the state worked to make industrial property knowable through the creation of statistical, textual, and image-based representations.[5] As we have seen with the building and disposal of plancor 39, a public-private partnership geared to upholding the sanctity of private property had to create a wide-ranging body of information that included documentation on issues as varied as the distribution of factories across the country, the capacity ratios of industries, the cost of vacant land, and the availability of labor. The need to understand the competitive dynamics of the marketplace for industrial plants and land such as the engine factory in Melrose Park required the military and the federal government to become better acquainted with the character of specific industrial sectors and commodities. By monitoring, intervening in, and shaping the private industrial property market between 1940 and 1950, the state plunged headfirst into the calculative "icy waters" described by Karl Marx and Friedrich Engels a hundred years earlier.[6]

The short life of plancor 39 illustrates the four key elements of the calculative relations of property that shaped wartime industrial mobilization and postwar disposal regimes.[7] In the first place, the boundaries that distinguished the real estate and the other elements that went into the building of the engine plant had to be created and made tangible. The material components of property, from the fences that separated one piece of property from another to the concrete, steel, glass, and brick used to build a factory such as the Buick-operated engine factory, had to be clearly identified and defined. Second, a legal apparatus was created that fashioned the content and extent of property relations, defined who had the right to use and transfer property, and determined the ways the property could be used by those who had control over it. In the case of plancor 39, various pieces of legislation, including the National Revenue Act of 1940, the Surplus Property Act of 1944, and the National Security Act of 1947, established the framework for industrial property relations. Third, these relations were shaped by procedures, rules, and practices that typically worked through institutional bodies such as government agencies, military procurement offices, and the corporate purchasing departments. These bodies interpreted the legislation and implemented rules and regulations, usually for their own benefit. Finally, property relations were shaped by issues such as the possibilities opened up by state funding and investment decisions to build a defense factory and the escalating cost of industrial property in times of high demand.

A specific set of calculative relations geared to mobilizing state and private capital, resources, labor, and materials produced plancor 39 and thousands of other industrial spaces during the war. A different set produced the conditions for and the eventual realization of the disposal of property to private interests. The recalculation of state-owned industrial sites by the state once victory appeared inevitable resulted in two main types of property. The first were those manufacturing plants that were directly incorporated into the private sphere. Factories of all sizes—from new, large industrial complexes where corporations such as Dodge and Republic Steel manufactured aircraft engines and steel to the small additions made to existing facilities where companies such as Kropp Forging, Zenith Radio, and Buda made aircraft parts, communication equipment, and diesel engines—were sold to private interests. No longer viewed as spaces of mobilization, industrial facilities such as plancor 39 were now considered as places to be reassessed, revalued, and sold in the private marketplace. They were to pass from public-private spaces of wartime production targeted by intensive federal intervention, monitoring, and evaluation to public spaces functioning in the free marketplace and subject to the prewar regime of relatively light state regulation.

The other type of property consisted of industrial facilities that remained under the control of the federal government and the military. In a handful of cases, plants were put aside and mothballed until they could be mobilized in the advent of war. In other cases, a national security clause was placed upon factories that were sold to private corporations. The clause placed certain restrictions upon the use of and changes to such plants. As of March 1, 1949, 236 state-owned defense factories had been placed on the national industrial plant list. Several of these were located in Chicago, including those operated during the war by Alcoa, American Steel Foundry, Dodge, Howard Foundry, Kropp Forging, Pullman, Republic Steel, Studebaker, and Youngstown Sheet.[8] In this way, plancors were incorporated into the postwar national security state. Negotiations over industrial sites drew the state, the military, and industry into a broader set of interconnections. Being named as part of the national industrial reserve marked an industrial site and required the state and industry to pay closer attention to its material, legal, procedural, and monetary elements. The desire of the military to retain an industrial reserve for national security reasons ensured that the wartime alliance remained in place in the postwar period for the firms involved in the national reserve.

Plancor 39 was subject to the calculations that characterized the making of state-owned and privately owned industrial property between 1940 and 1950. By the summer of 1945, it seemed that GM would purchase the Melrose Park plant. This was certainly the impression given at a meeting held in Washington in August. Eight men from the three different constituencies were present. GM was represented by the corporation's vice-president, the director of the Chevrolet Division, and a company lawyer; the civilian state was represented by Louis Bean and C. Beasley of the RFC; and the military was represented by Major Fabian of the Army Corps of Engineers' Real Estate Division and Colonel Robert Tatlow and Major Bartung from the Production Division of the Army Services Forces. These eight men agreed that General Motors would keep occupancy "as the Army will require" and that the RFC would give the green light for future discussions about the manufacturing property "on receipt of the plan from General Motors."[9]

The discussion about what to do with the facility was compiled from internally generated and contracted knowledge: the 1943 DPC prospectus, the 1944 Lockwood Greene appraisal, and independent GM and army assessments. This information formed the framework for how past calculations about the industrial plant were to be used to determine future uses. Despite the positive signs it gave at the August meeting, GM was not convinced that the engine facility was a necessary part of its expansion strategy. The large corporation was still in the midst of calibrating its postwar plans of where to locate its production facilities. By September 1945, executives at the automotive corporation's head office had decided that the plant's disadvantages outweighed the benefits. Plancor 39 was considered a liability, and GM washed its hands of the wartime factory.[10]

The plant, however, did fit into the postwar property calculations of two other American corporations. In October 1945 Westinghouse and International Harvester submitted bids to purchase the facility. For Pittsburgh-based Westinghouse, the large Melrose Park property would be the company's entry into Chicago. The company told the RFC that after studying a substantial number of factories with respect to "size of plant, geographical location, and ease of adaption to the contemplated operations," it had decided to relocate its motor division from Pittsburgh to the suburbs of Chicago. As one Westinghouse executive stated, "influencing our decision to submit a proposal looking toward the purchase of the Buick, Melrose Park plant, is the desire in the national interest, to utilize if at all possible economically, an existing property."[11] Despite an October bid of more than $7 million, which was increased to $11 million in November, the electrical appliance corporation was not awarded the facility. Instead, the RFC sold it to International Harvester for $13.8 million. The Chicago-based corporation planned on employing five thousand workers to make diesel engines, power lifts, milk coolers, and refrigerators. Based on its calculations of location, condition, size, and profitability, plancor 39 was considered to be a viable industrial space and could be integrated into the corporation's postwar expansion plans.[12] This was played out across the country as the federal disposal agencies negotiated with the military and industry about the future of other wartime defense factories.

Plancor 39, the Military-Industrial Complex, and Corporate Concentration

In the first five years after buying the property, International Harvester expanded the premises and integrated it into the country's postwar industrial mobilization program. With the German surrender, International Harvester announced that it would spend up to $150 million on postwar expansion of existing and new production facilities. The termination of wartime military contracts allowed for the corporation to move back into peacetime production and to expand its product lines. Part of the expansion fund was to be spent on building up its national network of plants. By early 1946, it had extended its empire by building new or acquiring wartime factories in Memphis (farm implements); Waukesha, Wisconsin (foundry); Wood River, Illinois (tractors); and Evansville, Indiana (refrigerators); as well as Melrose Park. A year later it undertook a massive expansion program to build up its farm implement and road vehicle lines. A substantial share of this investment ($37.5 million) went to the corporation's six factories in Chicago. The bulk of this went to expand the Melrose Park facility so that it could concentrate on diesel engines and large tractors. This investment decision was done at the expense of the corporation's other five metropolitan Chicago plants.[13] Federal defense property at Melrose Park, Wood River, and elsewhere was a central feature of International Harvester's corporate postwar expansion plans.

Even though International Harvester turned to the manufacture of civilian products after the war, it remained firmly embedded within the operations of the military-industrial complex. Corporate executives maintained an ongoing relationship with the army. Some writers have pointed to the emergence in the postwar period of a "state manager" (scientist-administrator), who acted as a broker between the three institutions of the military-industrial complex in order to manage conflict and to coordinate technical aspects and problems, and "defense intellectuals," who were civilian professionals employed by the military to oversee the military's involvement in comprehensive planning and personnel communication.[14]

We can also point to a postwar "corporate manager," whose role was to liaise with the military, to manage property and financial issues among the various institutions, and to promote industrial interests within the military. These corporate managers often had experience in the military during the war. Once such person was International Harvester's corporate executive vice-president, General Leven Campbell, who had been the army's chief of ordnance during the war and the director of the country's reconversion program after 1945. After retiring from the army, he went to work for International Harvester. The company's chairman, Fowler McCormick, who was also a member of the National Security Resources Board, played a similar role, mediating between the executive worlds of the private and public sectors. An illustration of this is a speech he gave at the Industrial College of Armed Forces to 223 Chicago industrialists who had received certificates of attendance at the college's two-week information course that provided the ideological rationale for the ongoing relationship between the military and industry. The role of International Harvester's "corporate manager" is shown by the fact that the corporation was chosen by the Industrial College in April 1948 to be visited by seventeen air force, army, and navy officers looking to provide practical knowledge about industrial firms vital to national security.[15] Both Campbell and McCormick acted as corporate managers working directly with the military.

The corporation's place in the defense program was stepped up from the late 1940s as the United States made preparations in anticipation of war in Korea and elsewhere. As with many other corporations, International Harvester was the recipient of postwar research and development funds that were part of a broader industrial planning program initiated by military and industrial leaders. Among other things, the corporation received a government research and development contract at the end of World War II to build an armored vehicle that combined elements of tanks and trucks. The corporation's industrial power division engineering team worked on it for several years, bringing it to fruition in 1950 when International Harvester received a large prime contract to deliver thousands of armored personnel carriers to the army. Plancor 39 was central to this. The armored trucks were to be made at the Melrose Park facility. International Harvester subcontracted out the construction of the vehicle hulls to two of Chicago's railroad equipment corporations (Pullman-Standard and General-American), and it added new buildings and installed new machinery to make the armored vehicles at Melrose Park. By the fall of 1951 the corporation had military contracts valued at $213 million.[16] International Harvester and plancor 39 were firmly integrated in the postwar national defense program.

As the personal contacts and the military contracts illustrate, the military-corporate relationship continued after 1945. In one sense there was nothing new to this as American firms had been working with the military for more than a hundred years. A team of military, political, and business leaders from the early nineteenth century developed a system of interchangeable parts to supply the military. This expanded over the next one hundred years to create a complex centered on military demand, industrial profits, and federal investment.[17] In another sense, though, there was something new to this relationship. This is the point made by Michael Hogan, who notes that after 1945 the military began to "assert an unprecedented degree of political authority and autonomy.... From its center in the Pentagon ... military influence extended throughout the government, and from there to virtually every area of American life."[18] Others such as Melvyn Leffler have pointed to the increasing importance of corporations and their manufacturing facilities in national security.[19] Despite the focus on the military-industrial complex in American life, these writers have paid little attention to the place of industrial property in the continued relevance of the complex in the immediate postwar period. As this study has shown, while factories were not the focus of postwar military interest, they were, nevertheless, as plancor 39 suggests, one part of a broader set of linkages between the military and industry after 1945.

Military interest in industrial property was part of the massive expansion of investment in the national security state and industrial mobilization after World War II. According to Hogan, in the two decades after 1945, the "federal government invested $776 billion in national defense, an amount equal to more than 60 percent of the federal budget, and more if indirect defense and war-related expenditures are included."[20] Part of this funding went to maintain national reserve plants and the expenditures to industrial property that came with prime contracts. While we know very little about this, the expansion of the defense industry and the national security state required a set of material places where defense production could take place. As we saw during the war, once a company such as International Harvester received a prime contract, its executives had to make decisions about what to do with their production space. Several options were open to them; they could refashion existing space, perhaps by rearranging walls and installing new machinery; they could have an addition constructed to accommodate the new work; or they could build entirely new production facilities. It isn't clear how the boundaries of public-private industrial property were determined in these circumstances.

What is clear, though, is that the industrial property relations of the military and industry were mutually constitutive. The former's dependence on corporate America for munitions and corporate reliance on the national security state for large contracts with large profits ensured that industrial property would continue to be an object of concern for military and industrial leaders. Just how this worked after 1945 is unclear, as the structured set of practices centered on state-owned property established during World War II shifted to a more hands-off contractual relationship revolving around private property after the war. The huge number of firms involved in industrial mobilization during the war turned into a smaller, yet powerful, oligopoly of aerospace, electronics, ship, and vehicle industries after the war. The continued functionality of plancors such as the Melrose Park engine factory in the postwar defense industry was clearly linked to the strengthened position of the military-industrial complex in American industrial matters and the creation of a national security state. The research and development and ordnance contracts received by International Harvester after 1945 were linked to industrial mobilization. This, in turn, developed out of New Deal policies and programs. In this context, the long-term legacy of the New Deal was not that of reform, but one of centralization of power within the executive, the state's growing capacity to shape economic activity, and the closer ties between the three institutions of the military-industrial complex.[21] Plancor 39 and other defense factories emerged out of a shifting, negotiated, and corporatist alliance of industrial executives, federal managers, and military leaders that forged distinctive calculative property relations.

The military-industrial complex rested on a corporatist ideology in which military and corporate leaders constructed and sold a vision of the reciprocal relationship of business, the military, and the American population that stressed mutual rights and responsibilities. This involved moving from the collective sensibilities of the New Deal to an emphasis on economic growth and the privatized marketplace. This required rebuilding the public's allegiance to self-help and individualism, reducing state control over industrial matters, ensuring that economic decisions were made in corporate boardrooms, and reliance on the trickle-down effects of increased productivity.[22] Similarly, the military had to convince the population of the growing threat of external forces and the centrality of the military to the defense of America's national security. In this way, industrial assets became part of the calculative effects of the turn to national security.[23] Despite the clear ideological platform and the growing centralization of military-industrial power, the postwar military-industrial complex was not a well-planned or coherent program. As Paul Koistinen notes, it was "a rather amorphous, loosely structured entity" centered on a powerful set of agents who shared a similar ideology and have separate yet linked power bases.[24] These shifting and loosely constructed boundaries "promoted movement among them by individual and initiatives. Indeed, one source of America's success in the production war was the intricate meshing of military and civilian elites."[25] This was clearly the case with corporate managers such as International Harvester's Leven Campbell and Fowler McCormick as they worked together to determine the place of industrial property in American and corporate life.

One of the key trickle-down effects associated with the building and disposal of wartime state industrial property such as plancor 39 was increased corporate concentration. The eight powerful economic coalitions that controlled the lion's share of manufacturing assets in 1939 continued to operate the economic levers of the wartime and postwar industrial economy. The capital assets of the largest 250 corporations grew from $25.9 billion in 1939 to $38.5 billion by the end of the war. Nine billion dollars of this increase came from federal funds for facilities operated by the large firms. The operation of wartime defense factories was overwhelmingly in the hands of a few large corporations. The share of employment of large firms (those with more than five hundred employees) grew from 48 percent in 1939 to 62 percent by 1944. Approximately two-thirds ($117 billion) of war contracts ($175 billion) went to the largest 100 manufacturing firms; more than a half went to only 33 corporations.[26]

The disposal of industrial property did not reduce corporate concentration of the economy. The largest 250 firms acquired 70 percent of all plant disposals. As one writer has noted, the disposal of factories by the War Assets Administration (WAA) "served to perpetuate the high wartime concentration" and "to preserve the war-born industrial concentration of 1940–1945."[27] In some cases, disposal led to the reinforcement of existing industrial concentration, while in others it reconfigured an industry. The operation of plancor 39 by Buick during the war and its purchase by International Harvester in 1945 is an example of the former. General Motors and International Harvester's place in the industrial economy and their position as leaders in the automobile and heavy machinery industries both during and after the war were enhanced by their use of state-financed industrial property.

The disposal of wartime aluminum facilities illustrates another twist on how wartime investment reinforced corporate control of the industrial economy. Before World War II, Alcoa had a monopoly that centered on its vast holdings of bauxite ore, alumina, reduction and smelting mills, rolling mills, and fabricating plants. Building on New Deal precedents, Truman's administration decided to use disposal policy to restructure the industry. As one writer notes, "It was the converging of the anti-trust tradition, the availability of the aluminum facilities for disposal, and uncertainties about post-war production and employment prospects, and the increasing Congressional and public desire for friendly relations between government and business" that established the framework for the creation of a postwar oligopoly.[28] Accordingly, heavy restrictions were placed on Alcoa's purchase of aluminum plants, while two other companies, Reynolds Metals and Kaiser, received preferential treatment acquiring defense factories.

The wartime facility operated by Alcoa in McCook in suburban Chicago is a case in point. The Chicago office of the WAA rejected Alcoa's bid to purchase the 287,000-acre site for $31 million as the attorney general told them that it could not approve disposal of any government property to Alcoa. Instead, the facility was leased to Reynolds.[29] The end result of this and other transactions was that Alcoa came to control 50 percent of total primary capacity, with Reynolds at about 30 percent and Kaiser at 20 percent, and that a new producer (Kaiser) got a start, and an existing one (Reynolds) strengthened. A monopoly became an oligopoly. Unlike the restructuring of the aluminum industry, International Harvester's purchase of plancor 39 did not greatly reorganize the farm implement or truck industries. It did, however, reinforce the concentration of industrial assets in the hands of a few industrial corporations, and it did provide the material facilities for International Harvester's integration into the nation's postwar defense program and the permanent military-industrial complex.

Plancor 39 and Chicago's Postwar Economy

This book has shown how the connection between urban development, militarization, and industrial mobilization between 1940 and 1945 underpinned the development of metropolitan districts, reformulated industrial property relations, and drove the expansion of the region's industrial base.[30] At the center of this relationship were defense factories such as plancor 39. The huge federal and military investment in defense property represented by the Buick-operated wartime industrial facility had implications for the postwar metropolitan economy in Chicago and elsewhere across the country. It could be expected that the impact of wartime investment on postwar metropolitan industrial growth could be quite substantial, especially in the short and medium term, as the fixity of the huge capital investment would provide an anchor for industrial growth.

This impact was uneven as a result of the bipolar distribution of capital investment across metropolitan Chicago. Wartime manufacturing investment created a particular metropolitan industrial geography consisting of a privately financed central district and a state-financed city fringe and suburbs. Many large new defense plants such as the Buick plancor were built on the city's edge during the war. The heavy concentration of large lumps of fixed-capital investment on the very edge of the city and in suburban areas such as Melrose Park, Park Ridge, Joliet, Whiting, and Harvey resulted in large-scale decentralization of industrial space and employment between 1940 and 1945. The outer reaches of the metropolitan district became home to most of the region's new freestanding manufacturing facilities and some of the largest industrial complexes of the day. In contrast, the city center was home to a large number of very small capital investments, typically made to existing factories and by private investors. In this way, Chicago featured an array of industrial spaces, running the gamut from new, multimillion dollar state-financed factories churning out extensive volumes of heavy war munitions, to small, privately financed companies making specialized products under contract to large national corporations. Behind this wartime industrial geography was the calculative actions of a coalition of city politicians, business executives, military leaders, and federal policy makers. Although the aim of the different groups may have been at odds, they were able to work together to forge the basic lineaments of mobilization. National federal, military, and corporate policy makers worked with local interests to build a wartime defense landscape.

Although the question of the impact of state-financed industrial property on the long-term development of Chicago's postwar economy is not the primary concern of this study, we do know something about what happened to metropolitan Chicago's large state-owned plancors after the war. A few, such as the Gary Armor Plate Works, proved difficult to sell because of their size and specialization, and they remained a burden on government coffers and the surrounding area for many years. In contrast, many others were taken up and used for various purposes as illustrated by Chicago's aircraft engine plancors (Buick, Studebaker, and Dodge) and assembly plant (Douglas). The latter was turned into a nonindustrial space; it was sold to the city for the building of O'Hare International Airport. As we have seen, International Harvester has made productive use of the site since its acquisition in 1945. The Buick site is currently operated by Navistar, the successor to International Harvester, and it still makes engines. In other cases, the Studebaker-operated factory during the war was leased by Western Electric in the immediate postwar period and then sold to National Tea in 1950. It is now the Midway Business Center. The Dodge plant has had a more potted history. First, it was leased to Tucker Motor in 1946, and then after that debacle it was taken over by Ford during the Korean War to produce engines. Presently, it is home to several independent functions, including a shopping mall and the Chicago branch of the National Archives.

The postwar history of the large aircraft plancors signals the decline of Chicago's short affair with the aircraft industry and the reversion by companies to older industrial traditions. Despite attempts during the interwar years by the Chicago Association of Commerce to attract aircraft firms, the metropolitan area had never been a prime location for aircraft production. The postwar period was little different. Wartime investment in the huge aircraft engine and assembly factories such as plancor 39 was a specific product of the imperatives of industrial mobilization that could not be sustained in peacetime. Two key reasons underpinned the decline. First, the aircraft industry underwent massive decline between 1944 and the late 1940s. Civil demand shriveled, while reduced military demand kept only a few large prewar companies afloat, none of which were located in Chicago.[31] Second, the automobile corporations reverted back to their core competency, automobiles. While moving into aircraft engine production during the war made economic sense, this was not the case after 1945. The three companies—GM, Chrysler, and Studebaker—were not interested in purchasing expensive, specialized, and complicated factories to build aircraft engines in a metropolis where they had few if any significant ties. As Charles Wilson made clear to the RFC in 1945, the industrial property in Melrose Park did not fit into GM's postwar expansion plans.

While the case of Chicago's aircraft engine plants and the aircraft industry is instructive, there is very little work on the long-term impact of wartime factories on postwar economic development in more general terms. Are Chicago cases such as plancor 39 typical of similar properties in New York City, Philadelphia, Detroit, and Los Angeles? Did industries that developed rapidly in particular places during the war disappear after the war, as did the aircraft industry in Chicago? Most writers have suggested that wartime defense factories added immeasurably to the areas in which they were located. In the South, for example, writers have argued that the importance of defense plants "outran their direct value for peacetime production" and that "more important than physical assets, perhaps, were the intangibles: the demonstration of industrial potential, new habits of mind, a recognition that industrialization demanded community services."[32] But there is little evidence to sustain such a picture for southern districts. With few exceptions, such as the petrochemical complex in southern Texas, defense factories had little effect on industrial development in general and on the emergence of new capital-intensive, high-wage manufacturing in particular after 1945.[33]

The story was different in the West, where wartime expansion reinforced manufacturing facilities established before 1939 and supported the postwar extension of existing industrial clusters centered on aircraft, electronics, and shipbuilding along the Pacific coast.[34] Was this the case in the Manufacturing Belt in the Northeast? Perhaps, but little is known. Ann Markusen and her colleagues have shown that the shift of the defense industry out of the industrial heartland did not take place to any significant degree until after the Korean War.[35] But this tells us nothing about the role of the wartime defense facilities in the anchoring of defense production in the old wartime sites, the movement of the defense industry away from the industrial centers of the Manufacturing Belt, or the effect of wartime plants away from the industrial heartland on places such as Los Angeles or Omaha. According to Alexander Field, the benefits of industrial mobilization "were largely counterbalanced by the negative shock associated with the disruption to the economy resulting from rapid mobilization and demobilization."[36] This disruption was caused by the diversion of talent from the private sector, the excessive demands made to the economy by mobilization, the heavy sectoral imbalance, and the far-too-rapid winding down of the war economy. What this suggests, in other words, is that it is difficult to determine the contribution of wartime state investment on metropolitan Chicago's economy in the postwar period.

Having said that, there is little doubt that plancors such as 39 had a positive effect on the areas in which they were located. The building of government industrial sites does appear to have strengthened the local industrial economy in the postwar years. A significant number of local firms that were rejuvenated by new construction and the installation of new machinery must have used the added capacity to build up their postwar competency. Though as Field has noted, much of the machinery installed during the war was heavily used and greatly deteriorated.[37] Nevertheless, the expansion of the region's productive capacity and new product lines may have helped metropolitan Chicago weather the economic downturn in the immediate postwar period. Wartime industrial space in both the city and the suburbs both during and after 1945 most certainly created multiplier effects through the region in the form of new industrial and service jobs and higher local taxes. Several local manufacturers that acquired defense factories after 1945, such as International Harvester, Pullman-Standard, General-American, and Kropp Forge, received Department of Defense procurement contracts or subcontracts after 1945. How substantial this was is still unknown.

The ability of federal disposal agencies to turn defense factories into functioning industrial facilities after 1945 was heavily influenced by the experience, expertise, and knowledge built up by military-industrial leaders after 1940.[38] During the war a powerful local alliance refashioned existing relations and created new ones, resulting in a new calculus of economic development centered on close military-industry ties. The experience gained by local industrial corporate managers who worked with the military and the state during the war was useful in navigating the increased military spending that accompanied the postwar Cold War hostilities. Military funds allowed manufacturers to gain contracts and profits, workers to gain jobs and incomes, property interests to reap increasing land values, and local politicians to lord over a larger political empire. Cooperation took various forms. In some cases, corporate managers such as Campbell and McCormick worked formal administrative lines to build relationships that were both ephemeral and long-standing. In other cases, individuals embedded in more informal interactions and institutional memberships used conversations over a cigar at a club and long-standing business and familial relationships to build up connections that tied local business and political elites to military bureaucracies. Local and congressional politicians sought to strengthen ties to Washington's policy makers and funding gatekeepers. The body of information about military production needs helped local alliances reach outside to build up their economic base and to refashion the area's industrial landscape to defense production after the war.

The wartime coalition in Chicago consisted of the Chicago Association of Commerce, the Illinois Manufacturers' Association (IMA), the local ordnance department, and various mobilization agencies. Working together, these calculating multiscalar institutions worked to attract capital investment to the metropolis, to build new industrial sites and expand existing ones, and to establish new relations and strengthen existing relations between each other. This continued after the end of the war. The work of a postwar local-military alliance, however, was overshadowed by the emergence of a growth regime composed of downtown business leaders and city officials who sought to revitalize the downtown through control over and restructuring of central city land. This could only be realized by ridding the downtown of obsolete industrial districts and rundown working-class areas, both of which threatened property values and investment activity.[39]

What all of this suggests is that it is difficult to clearly identify the causal relations between postwar industrial expansion and the utilization of defense plants. While this may be the case, what cannot be disputed is that metropolitan Chicago's manufacturing employment went into decline after the war even though it remained America's second largest manufacturing center. Industrial mobilization after 1940 led to a considerable increase in manufacturing employment. The high of a million industrial workers during the war was not to be repeated in the postwar years. The total number of production, scientific, and administrative workers in the manufacturing sector remained stable at about 950,000 between 1947 and 1963. The most dramatic change, however, was on the metropolitan area's industrial geography. The city of Chicago lost a considerable number of factories and jobs after World War II. Manufacturing employment fell from 667,000 in 1947 to 508,000 in 1963. Over the same period, the city saw its share of metropolitan manufacturing drop from 71 percent to just over half. The city experienced both absolute and relative decline. After the war, manufacturers closed factories and laid off workers in increasing numbers. In an increasing number of cases, they shut their doors forever. In others, they moved to the Chicago suburbs or to the southern United States or overseas. This was a common phenomenon across the Manufacturing Belt.[40]

The story was different in the suburbs, where manufacturing employment grew from 278,000 in 1947 to 450,000 in 1963. The deindustrialization of Chicago and the expansion of the suburban industrial economy were driven by some combination of local factors: lower land costs, an increasing labor pool, the building of an expressway system, lower unionization rates, and a shifting consumer market. The process was also structural, as industrial executives chose to disinvest in the city center by closing down local branches and shifting production to other parts of the country and the world.[41] The old industrial districts of the city center were fatally squeezed by capital's locational calculus. Did wartime investment influence this double movement of central-city disinvestment and suburban investment? As we have seen, most wartime construction occurred on the city fringe and in the suburbs such as Melrose Park. For some writers, this was critically important for the development of the metropolitan industrial geography in the postwar period. Perry Duis argues that factory construction on the urban fringe was "perhaps the most important war legacy for Chicago," as it spurred economic development around defense factories and "helped trigger an outlying housing boom that preceded the 1949 Federal Housing Act." As he notes, the "massive wave of defense plant construction" during the war "helped hasten . . . industrial dispersal" in the postwar years.[42]

How much of the city-suburban differential can be accounted for by wartime factories is unclear. The massive fixed-capital investments in Chicago's city fringe and suburban districts during the war generated multiplier effects that spilled over into the postwar period. Most notably, they would have contributed to the development of new technologies, product lines, interfirm relations, employment, and tax revenue, as we have seen with plancor 39 and some of the other defense factories. What we don't know is the extent to which these war factories contributed to either central-city decline or suburban growth. Very few firms would have been able to purchase large industrial complexes such as plancor 39, while the postwar impact of small additions made to existing factories are difficult to assess. Related to this is the high rate of private investment in industrial plants after the war. There are some indications that firms invested heavily in new manufacturing facilities beginning in 1947, especially in the suburbs.[43] Whether wartime investment anchored postwar investment is unknown. Despite the evidence from plancor 39 and the emphatic claims of Duis or those writing about the southern industry, we know little about the long-term effects of defense factories on the metropolitan economy.

Conclusion

What is known about the long-term effects of defense plants is that the calculative relations of industrial property were twice reformulated between 1940 and 1950. With the advent of war in 1940, industrial assets were subjected to new forms of calculation in which the federal government and the military worked with corporations to determine how factories were to be built, where they were to be built, and who was to build them. Factories were no longer considered the sole prerogative of private capitalist interests. The state became involved in factory space in an entirely new way through its ownership of industrial land, investment in industrial facilities, and control of industrial output. After the war, property was changed once again, this time by the disposal of industrial assets to private interests. The calculative relations generated by these two movements created a more intense form of political and economic intimacy between the state, the military, and industry—one that continued after the end of the war. A range of powerful military and industrial leaders reworked their long-term relationships through their involvement in mobilizing and disposing of new manufacturing space. The ability of these leaders to implement and reproduce these relations rested on actualizing the relations in place. Mobilization of a defense economy rested on gaining control over industrial property and building new industrial space and additions to existing factories in specific sites. The multiscalar actions of calculations by military-industrial leaders were central to the historical geographies of industrial property, economic development, and the militarization of America's metropolitan space.

APPENDIX

Wartime Factory Expansion

The fixed-capital investment data for wartime industrial plants were taken from two sources. *War Manufacturing Facilities* is a consolidated directory listing all war facilities receiving federal and military funds for expansion and machinery during the war. While the directory may not have been complete, it does account for a vast share of the total expenditure.[1] Missing from the list are the 5,000 plancors that were valued at less than $50,000 each. The aggregate expenditure of $180.5 million represents a minuscule share of all public expenditures and private authorizations. The data in the directory are arranged by company and factory location (with operating division and subsidiaries grouped under the parent company). The report presents the estimated cost of distributed funds by source of public and private funds and description of the product. There are a total of 605 investments in manufacturing facilities valued at $1,378,989,000 in metropolitan Chicago.[2] Of this, it was possible to allocate 508 investments to one of two actions—an addition to an existing facility or the building of a new factory.

The second source—the *War Industrial Facilities Authorized*—also provides the name of the plant operator, the product, the cost of the facility, and the source of public funds.[3] There are differences though. The data only go through December 31, 1944. While this is not as extensive as the 1946 publication, the amount of new construction awards in 1945 was comparatively small, so for all intents and purposes it covers the vast majority of fixed-capital investment.[4] It sorts the material by state, county, and municipality rather than company. Finally, it breaks the cost down to that spent on structures and expenditures for both publicly and privately financed facilities. The two publications complement each other very nicely.

The municipality but not the street address was listed in both directories, so it was necessary to cross-list the additions and new factories with the 1924, 1940, and 1950 *Industrial Directories*, Moody's, and the *Chicago Commerce*. Of the 605 wartime projects in metropolitan Chicago (1940–1945), I have been able to find an address for 562 of them, accounting for 93 percent of the number of wartime projects and 99 percent of the total cost. In other words, I am able to identify the geographic coordinates of the vast majority of the projects established during the war. I made the street address listing for metropolitan Chicago, which I defined as consisting of the Illinois counties of Lake, Cook, DuPage, Kane, McHenry, and Will and the Indiana counties of Lake and Porter.

The 605 metropolitan Chicago firms received funds totaling $1.3 billion to build new factories and install new machinery, and 1,430 firms received military supply contracts valued at $9.8 billion. While these facts are undeniable, the character of Chicago's investment in war facilities, however, is open to question. While contemporary observers and more recent scholars agree that approximately $1.3 billion was invested in industrial plants and equipment by private firms and the government in Chicago during the war, there is disagreement about what that funding was invested in. In her monumental description of the Illinois war effort, Mary Watters states that 400 new factories were built and about 1,450 expanded between 1940 and 1945.[5] The *Commerce*, the mouthpiece of the Chicago Association of Commerce (CAC), estimated in its March 1945 edition that "more than 300 new plants" had been built and that another 1,200 had "been expanded" during the war.[6] Finally, Perry Duis and Scott La France, using a March 1946 *Commerce* article, state that more than a third of factory construction investment went to more than 300 new factories and more than 1,400 additions.[7]

These numbers are completely out of line with those I compiled from the two official sources noted above. As previously noted, the former has listings of every private and public industrial investment up to the end of 1944, while the former recorded every wartime investment. Between them, they provide a complete picture of American industrial investment in buildings, machinery, and equipment during the war. What they show is that the total number of wartime time projects funded by private and public sources in metropolitan Chicago between 1940 and 1945 is a long way off from the totals of Duis and La France, Watters, and the CAC.

There are two serious discrepancies. The first is the number of projects. My total of 605 expanded and new factories is much lower than the 1,500 stated by the CAC and the 1,800 stated by Watters and by Duis and La France. Of course, the government could not account for every expansion; it would have been unable to count every plant that built new industrial space. However, given its control over investment and construction materials, it is difficult to believe that the government could have missed a significant number of construction projects. Moreover, it would have been unthinkable for many firms, a large number of which had a great amount of unused capacity by the end of the 1930s, to take the time, trouble, and expense of expanding their production space. On the other hand, it is not unthinkable that the city's boosters would have inflated the numbers in order to entice more firms to the city and to lift industrial morale among local business people. Given this, there can be little doubt that previous writers have seriously overstated the number of projects that received fixed-capital wartime investment from private and public sources. The probable reason for this is that the CAC was doing its utmost to promote Chicago's strengths, image, and confidence. The association was not immune to exaggerating the scale of Chicago's industrial mobilization and growth. It appears that Watters and Duis and La France have too easily accepted the CAC's version of Chicago's wartime investment.

The second discrepancy is the number of new factories. According to my data, writers have vastly overestimated the number of "new" plants. Again, the reliance on the CAC's numbers has led others writers astray. In this the case, the issue may have to do with how a new factory and an addition are defined. It would seem that many of the factories counted as "new" actually were additions to existing factories. This is definitely the case if one defines a new industrial property as a new building in a location that is not adjacent to the property of an existing industrial firm. That is, a new plant is one situated at a site where no existing industrial building was present. Following this logic, an addition is a new building that is part of or adjacent to an existing industrial building or property. Following these definitions, there were only 42 new factories constructed in metropolitan Chicago during the war, not the 300 or 400 mentioned by other writers. The remaining capital investment projects consisted of 456 additions to existing factories and 105 equipment-only projects. Together these totaled 605 projects with a total value of $1,378,989,000.

The distinction between a new factory and additions to a factory is important because capital investment in an existing location had different meanings than investment in a new plant elsewhere. The former implies that the firm has made a decision that the existing location is a valuable one. It could be valuable in several senses: 1) the cost of building elsewhere is too expensive; 2) the firm is unwilling, for many reasons, to locate elsewhere; 3) production would be too disjointed if the firm maintained the former plant and built a new one; and 4) the existing site continues to have real advantages. In other words, the production of new factory space, either as additions or as new plants, was related to the mobilization of industrial and government officials and to how these agents mobilized a set of other agents, such as real estate brokers, architects, engineers, and city officials.

NOTES

Introduction

1. Franklin Delano Roosevelt, "Fireside Chat Radio Address, May 26, 1940," *American Presidency Project*, by Gerhard Peters and John T. Woolley, http://www.presidency.ucsb.edu/ws/index.php?pid=15959, accessed June 3, 2014.

2. Roosevelt, "Fireside Chat."

3. Gregory Hooks, *Forging the Military-Industrial Complex: World War II's Battle of the Potomac* (Urbana: University of Illinois Press, 1991); Paul Koistinen, *Arsenal of World War II: The Political Economy of America Warfare, 1940–1945* (Lawrence: University Press of Kansas, 2004); V. R. Cardozier, *The Mobilization of the United States in World War II* (Jefferson, N.C.: McFarland, 1995); Keith Eiler, *Mobilizing America: Robert Patterson and the War Effort, 1940–1945* (Ithaca: Cornell University Press, 1997); Harold Vatter, *The U.S. Economy in World War II* (New York: Columbia University Press, 1985).

4. For a discussion of property as a social relation see Nicholas Blomley, "Law, Property, and the Geography of Violence," *Annals of the Association of American Geographers* 93 (2003): 86–107; C. B. Macpherson, *Property: Mainstream and Critical Positions* (Toronto: University of Toronto Press, 1978), 1–13; Joseph Singer, *Entitlement: The Paradoxes of Property* (New Haven: Yale University Press, 2000); Lynn Staeheli and Don Mitchell, *The People's Property? Power, Politics, and the Public* (New York: Routledge, 2008).

5. My interest is on industrial property as an object worked on by military-complex leaders, that is, as a calculative object. I do not cover issues internal to production (such as mechanization, labor relations, and gender and racial divisions of labor) or everyday life (such as living costs and housing shortages). Other studies have focused on these questions in great detail. For work that looks at calculation see Michel Callon, "The Embeddedness of Economic Markets in Economics," in *The Laws of the Markets*, ed. Michel Callon (Oxford: Blackwell, 1998), 4–6; Timothy Mitchell, *Rule of Experts: Egypt, Techno-Politics, Modernity* (Berkeley: University of California Press, 2002), 19–53; Reuben Rose-Redwood, "'A Regular State of Beautiful Confusion': Governing by Numbers and the Contradictions of Calculable Space in New York City," *Urban History* 39 (2012): 624–38.

6. Sarah Jo Peterson, *Planning the Home Front: Building Bombers and Communities at Willow Run* (Chicago: University of Chicago Press, 2013); Perry Duis and Scott La

France, *We've Got a Job to Do: Chicagoans and World War II* (Chicago: Chicago Historical Society, 1992); Roger Lotchin, *Fortress California, 1910–1961: From Warfare to Welfare* (New York: Oxford University Press, 1992); Robert Spinney, *World War II in Nashville: Transformation of the Homefront* (Knoxville: University of Tennessee Press, 1998).

7. Doreen Massey, "Power-Geometry and the Progressive Sense of Place," in *Mapping the Futures: Local Culture, Global Change*, ed. Jon Bird, Barry Curtis, Tim Putnam, George Robertson, and Lisa Tickner (London: Routledge, 1993), 59–69; Neil Brenner, *New State Spaces: Urban Governance and the Rescaling of Statehood* (New York: Oxford University Press, 2004); Andrew Herod, "Scale: The Local and the Global," in *Key Concepts in Geography*, ed. Nicholas J. Clifford, Sarah L. Holloway, Stephen P. Rice, and Gill Valentine, 2nd ed. (London: SAGE, 2009), 217–35.

8. Michael J. Hogan, *A Cross of Iron: Harry S. Truman and the Origins of the National Security State, 1945–1954* (New York: Cambridge University Press, 1998); Hooks, *Forging the Military-Industrial Complex*; Koistinen, *Arsenal of World War II*; Gary Weir, *Forged in War: The Naval-Industrial Complex and American Submarine Construction, 1940–1961* (Washington, D.C.: Department of the Navy, 1993).

9. Ben Baack and Edward Ray, "The Political Economy of the Origins of the Military-Industrial Complex in the United States," *Journal of Economic History* 45 (1985): 369–75; Benjamin Cooling, *Gray Steel and Blue Water Navy: The Formative Years of America's Military-Industrial Complex, 1881–1917* (Hamden, Conn.: Archon Books, 1979); Robert Cuff, *The War Industries Board: Business-Government Relations during World War I* (Baltimore: Johns Hopkins University Press, 1973); Kurt Hackemer, "The U.S. Navy and the Late Nineteenth-Century Steel Industry," *Historian* 57 (1995): 703–12; Paul A. C. Koistinen, *Mobilizing for Modern War: The Political Economy of American Warfare, 1865–1919* (Lawrence: University Press of Kansas, 1997); Paul A. C. Koistinen, *State of War: The Political Economy of American Warfare, 1945–2011* (Lawrence: University Press of Kansas, 2012).

10. For example, see Lotchin, *Fortress California*, 15–22.

11. Private investment during the war had to be authorized by the military or the federal government. Most investment received state subsidies through accelerated depreciation.

12. Richard Walker and Robert Lewis, "Beyond the Crabgrass Frontier: Industry and the Spread of North American Cities, 1850–1950," in *Manufacturing Suburbs: Building Work and Home on the Metropolitan Fringe*, ed. Robert Lewis (Philadelphia: Temple University Press, 2004), 16–31; Philip Scranton, *Proprietary Capitalism: The Textile Manufacture at Philadelphia, 1800–1885* (New York: Cambridge University Press, 1983); Robert Lewis, *Chicago Made: Factory Networks in the Industrial Metropolis* (Chicago: University of Chicago Press, 2008). The earliest study of industrial suburbanization is probably Graham Taylor, *Satellite Cities: A Study of Industrial Suburbs* (New York: Appleton, 1915).

13. Studies that emphasize the national at the expense of the local are Elberton Smith, *The Army and Economic Mobilization* (Washington, D.C.: GPO, 1959); Vatter, *U.S. Economy in World War II*; Jack Ballard, *The Shock of Peace: Military and Economic Demobilization after World War II* (Washington, D.C.: University Press of America, 1983); James Cook, *The Marketing of Surplus War Property* (Washington, D.C.: Public Affairs Press,

1948); Gerald White, *Billions for Defense: Government Financing by the Defense Plant Corporation during World War II* (University: University of Alabama Press, 1980).

14. For exceptions see Walter Adams and Horace Gray, *Monopoly in America: The Government as Promoter* (New York: Macmillan, 1955), 117–41, and Harold Stein, "The Disposal of the Aluminum Plants," in *Public Administration and Policy Development: A Case Book*, ed. Harold Stein (New York: Harcourt, Brace, 1952). For a discussion of how studies of the military-industrial complex have neglected local practices see Lotchin, *Fortress California*, 15–22. See the papers in *Enterprise and Society* 12 (2011): 1–199, for a recent overview and several studies of the complex.

15. White, *Billions for Defense*; Stein, "Disposal of the Aluminum Plants," 313–61.

16. Andrew Herod, *Scale* (New York: Routledge, 2011).

17. Much of the work on local wartime mobilization has been done by Roger Lotchin. See his *Fortress California*; "World War II and the Growth of Southern City Planning: A Gigantic Force?," *Planning Perspectives* 18 (2003): 355–76; and *The Bad City in the Good War* (Bloomington: Indiana University Press, 2003). Also see Geoffrey Rossano, "Suburbia Armed: Nassau County Development and the Rise of the Aerospace Industry, 1909–1960," in *The Martial Metropolis: U.S. Cites in War and Peace*, ed. Roger Lotchin (New York: Praeger, 1984), 61–87; Martin Schiesl, "Airplanes to Aerospace: Defense Spending and Economic Growth in the Los Angeles Region, 1945–1960," in Lotchin, *Martial Metropolis*, 135–49.

18. Michael Bernstein and Mark Wilson, "New Perspectives on the History of the Military-Industrial Complex," *Enterprise and Society* 12 (2011): 6. Mark Wilson argues that the relationship between a firm and the state is "often absent in studies" of the military-industrial complex. Most case studies are limited to the corporation's influence over the state and the development of new production methods. See his "Making 'Goop' out of Lemons: The Permanente Metals Corporation, Magnesium Incendiary Bombs, and the Struggle for Profits during World War II," *Enterprise and Society* 12 (2011): 12. Peterson's study of Willow Run in *Planning the Home Front* illustrates the strength of the case study approach for examining militarized space.

19. Federally funded industrial investment also flowed to rural areas. For studies of rural defense factories see Thomas Scott, "Winning World War II in an Atlanta Suburb: Local Boosters and the Recruitment of Bell Bomber," and Richard Combes, "Aircraft Manufacturing in Georgia: A Case Study of Federal Industrial Investment," both in *The Second Wave: Southern Industrialization from the 1940s to the 1970s*, ed. Philip Scranton (Athens: University of Georgia Press, 2001), 1–42. Also see Lotchin, "World War II."

20. The real property case materials consist of War Asset Administration files held at College Park, Maryland, and the regional office where the plancor was located. While there is some overlap in the material covered, the two sets of files contain different material. Information about the plancor can also be found in other War Asset Administration records, such as those of the Real Property Review Board, and in other record groups, such as Federal Property Resources.

21. Every government-owned industrial factory was given a unique code that consisted of two parts: letters identifying the funding agency and a number. In some cases, the agency identifier started with plancor (U.S. Army); in other, it started with Nobs

(U.S. Navy) or Ord (ordnance). I use "plancor" throughout the study to refer generally to industrial plants and machinery financed by the federal government and the military.

Chapter 1. Calculation and Industrial Property

1. Karl Marx and Friedrich Engels, *The Communist Manifesto* (Harmondsworth, UK: Penguin, 1967), 82.

2. Karl Marx, *Capital* (New York: Vintage, 1977); Michel Foucault, *The History of Sexuality*, vol. 1: *An Introduction* (London: Penguin, 1998); David Harvey, *The Urban Experience* (Baltimore: Johns Hopkins University Press, 1989); James Scott, *Seeing Like a State: How Certain Schemes to Improve the Human Condition Have Failed* (New Haven: Yale University Press, 1998).

3. The simultaneity of quantitative and qualitative has been given a neologism: "qualculation." I will stick with "calculation." See Michel Callon and John Law, "On Qualculation, Agency and Otherness," *Environment and Planning D: Society and Space* 23 (2005): 717–33.

4. Karl Polanyi, *The Great Transformation: The Political and Economic Origins of Our Time* (Boston: Beacon Press, 1957 [1944]); Max Weber, *Economy and Society* (Berkeley: University of California Press, 1978 [1922]); Sidney Pollard, *Peaceful Conquest: The Industrialization of Europe, 1760–1970* (Oxford: Oxford University Press, 1982).

5. David Harvey, *Limits to Capital* (Chicago University of Chicago Press, 1982), 371. Also see Fred Block, "Polanyi's Double Movement and the Reconstruction of Critical Theory," *Papers in Political Economy* 28 (2008): 2–14; Ann Davis, "Endogenous Institutions and the Politics of Property: Comparing and Contrasting Douglass North and Karl Polanyi in the Case of Finance," *Journal of Economic Issues* 42 (2008): 1101–22.

6. Reuben Rose-Redwood, "With Numbers in Place: Security, Territory and the Production of Calculable Space," *Annals of the Association of American Geographers* 102 (2012): 295–319.

7. Jeremy Crampton and Stuart Elden, "Space, Politics, Calculation: An Introduction," *Social and Cultural Geography* 7 (2006): 681–85; Chris Carter and Alan McKinlay, "Cultures of Strategy: Remaking the BBC, 1968–2003," *Business History* 55 (2013): 1228–46; D. Asher Ghertner, "Calculating without Numbers: Aesthetic Governmentality in Delhi's Slums," *Economy and Society* 39 (2010): 185–217; Emma Norman, "Who's Counting? Spatial Politics, Ecocolonisation and the Politics of Calculation in Boundary Bay," *Area* 45 (2013): 179–87; Timothy Mitchell, *Rule of Experts: Egypt, Techno-Politics, Modernity* (Berkeley: University of California Press, 2002).

8. Andrew Barry, "The Anti-Political Economy," *Economy and Society* 31 (2002): 269–70.

9. Michel Callon and Fabian Muniesa, "Economic Markets as Calculative Collective Devices," *Organization Studies* 26 (2005): 1229–50; Anne Cronin, "Calculative Spaces: Cities, Market Relations, and the Commercial Vitalism of the Outdoor Advertising Industry," *Environment and Planning A* 40 (2008): 2734–50; Don Slater, "From Calculation to Alienation: Disentangling Economic Abstractions," *Economy and Society* 31 (2002): 234–49.

10. Callon and Muniesa, "Economic Markets," 1231.

11. Lynn Staeheli and Don Mitchell, *The People's Property? Power, Politics and the*

Public (New York: Routledge, 2008), 53; Nicholas Blomley, "Law, Property, and the Geography of Violence," *Annals of the Association of American Geographers* 93 (2003): 86–107.

12. Both the federal government and the military financed different types of industrial space, from entire newly constructed factories to extensions to existing privately owned industrial facilities. I use the term "defense factory" here as shorthand for all types of industrial space financed by the federal government and military.

13. Slater, "From Calculation to Alienation," 238.

14. Michel Callon, "The Embeddedness of Economic Markets in Economics," in *The Laws of the Markets*, ed. Michel Callon (Oxford: Blackwell, 1998), 19–23.

15. On the different types of property see C. B. Macpherson, *Property* (Toronto: University of Toronto Press, 1978), 1–13. On property relations in urban areas see Nicholas Blomley, "Landscapes of Property," *Law and Society Review* 32 (1998): 567–612; Staeheli and Mitchell, *People's Property?*

16. For path dependency see Ron Martin and Peter Sunley, "Path Dependence and Regional Economic Evolution," *Journal of Economic Geography* 6 (2006): 395–437; Paul Pierson, "Increasing Returns, Path Dependence, and the Study of Politics," *American Political Science Review* 94 (2000): 251–67.

17. Some key studies are Benjamin Cooling, *Gray Steel and Blue Water Navy: The Formative Years of America's Military-Industrial Complex, 1881–1917* (Hamden Conn.: Archon, 1979); David Hounshell, *From the American System to Mass Production, 1800–1932: The Development of Manufacturing Technology in the United States* (Baltimore: Johns Hopkins University Press, 1984); Paul Koistinen, *The Military-Industrial Complex. A Historical Perspective* (New York: Praeger, 1980); Gregory Hooks, *Forging the Military-Industrial Complex: World War II's Battle of the Potomac* (Urbana: University of Illinois Press, 1991); Jacob Vander Meulen, *The Politics of Aircraft: Building an American Military Industry* (Lawrence: University Press of Kansas, 1991); Paul Koistinen, *State of War: The Political Economy of American Warfare, 1945–2011* (Lawrence: University Press of Kansas, 2012). Also see Michael Bernstein and Mark Wilson, "New Perspectives on the History of the Military-Industrial Complex," *Enterprise and Society* 12 (2011): 1–9.

18. For an overview see Rachel Woodward, "From Military Geography to Militarism's Geographies: Disciplinary Engagement with the Geographies of Militarism and Military Activities," *Progress in Human Geography* 29 (2005): 718–40, and "Military Landscapes: Agendas and Approaches for Future Research," *Progress in Human Geography* 38 (2014): 4–61.

19. Woodward, "Military Landscapes," 42.

20. For work that explores militarization in America during World War II and the Cold War see John Cloud, "American Cartographic Transformations during the Cold War," *Cartography and Geographic Information Science* 29 (2002): 261–82; Trevor Barnes, "Geographical Intelligence: American Geographers and Research and Analysis in the Office of Strategic Services, 1941–1945," *Journal of Historical Geography* 32 (2005): 149–68; Matt Farish, "Archiving Areas: The Ethnogeographic Board and the Second World War," *Annals of the Association of American Geographers* 95 (2005): 663–79; Patrick Vitale, "Wages of War: Manufacturing Nationalism during World War II," *Antipode* 43 (2011): 783–819.

21. Calculation is inherently cartographic. This is touched on in chapter 7. For a

broader examination of this see Susan Schulten, *Mapping the Nation: History and Cartography in Nineteenth-Century America* (Chicago: University of Chicago Press, 2012).

22. Blomley, "Law, Property, and the Geography of Violence"; Staeheli and Mitchell, *People's Property?*

23. Koistinen, *Military-Industrial Complex*; Koistinen, *State of War*; Ben Baack and Edward Ray, "The Political Economy of the Origins of the Military-Industrial Complex in the United States," *Journal of Economic History* 45 (1985): 369–75.

24. Koistinen, *Military-Industrial Complex*, 8. Also see Cooling, *Gray Steel and Blue Water Navy*; Kurt Hackemer, "The U.S. Navy and the Late Nineteenth-Century Steel Industry," *Historian* 57 (1995): 703–12; Merritt Roe Smith, *Harpers Ferry Armory and the New Technology: The Challenge of Change* (Ithaca: Cornell University Press, 1977).

25. Koistinen, *Military-Industrial Complex*, 11–12.

26. Gerald White, *Billions for Defense: Government Financing by the Defense Plant Corporation during World War II* (University: University of Alabama Press, 1980), 1.

27. On the state see Ray Hudson, *Producing Places* (New York: Guilford Press, 2001), 48–95; Theda Skocpol, "Political Response to Capitalist Crisis: Neo-Marxist Theories of the State and the Case of the New Deal," *Politics and Society* 10 (1980): 155–201. For studies of the American state see Stephen Skowronek, *Building a New American State: The Expansion of National Administrative Capacities, 1877–1920* (New York: Cambridge University Press, 1982); Bartholomew Sparrow, *From the Outside In: World War II and the American State* (Princeton: Princeton University Press, 1996); Alan Brinkley, *The End of Reform: New Deal Liberalism in Recession and War* (New York: Alfred Knopf, 1995).

28. Hooks, *Forging the Military-Industrial Complex*, 5.

29. Skocpol, "Political Response to Capitalist Crisis," 156; Ira Katznelson and Bruce Pietrykowski, "Rebuilding the American State: Evidence from the 1940s," *Studies in American Political Development* 5 (1991): 306; John Jeffries, "The 'New' New Deal: FDR and American Liberalism, 1937–1945," *Political Science Quarterly* 105 (1990): 397–418; Robert Leighninger, *Long-Range Public Investment: The Forgotten Legacy of the New Deal* (Columbia: University of South Carolina Press, 2007).

30. David Hart, *Forged Consensus: Science, Technology, and Economic Policy in the United States, 1921–1953* (Princeton: Princeton University Press, 1998).

31. Hart, *Forged Consensus*, 117–44; Barton Bernstein, "The Debate on Industrial Reconversion: The Protection of Oligopoly and Military Control of the Economy," *American Journal of Economics and Sociology* 26 (1967): 159–72; Brinkley, *End of Reform*.

32. Robert Cuff, *The War Industries Board: Business-Government Relations during World War 1* (Baltimore: Johns Hopkins University Press, 1973); Koistinen, *Military-Industrial Complex*.

33. James Cook, *The Marketing of Surplus War Property* (Washington, D.C.: Public Affairs Press, 1948), 15–31; Jack Ballard, *The Shock of Peace: Military and Economic Demobilization after World War II* (Washington, D.C.: University Press of America, 1983); Louis Cain and George Neumann, "Planning for Peace: The Surplus Property Act of 1944," *Journal of Economic History* 41 (1981): 129–35; Harold Stein, "The Disposal of the Aluminum Plants," in *Public Administration and Policy Development: A Case Book*, ed. Harold Stein (New York: Harcourt, Brace, 1952), 313–61; White, *Billions for Defense*.

34. Industrial sites could be sold off to any potential buyer, such as local governments, wholesalers, or transportation companies, although most were purchased by manufacturing firms.

35. It is difficult to know the precise number and value of the factories that remained unsold. The annual reports of the WAA to Congress are unclear about the number remaining on the books. The agency's final report stated that 82 percent of the real property acquired by the agency had been sold to private companies, transferred to federal agencies, or sold at a discount for public benefit purposes by June 30, 1949. WAA, *Quarterly Progress Report: Second Quarter, 1949* (Washington, D.C.: WAA, 1949), 3–4.

36. Michael J. Hogan, *A Cross of Iron: Harry S. Truman and the Origins of the National Security State, 1945–1954* (New York: Cambridge University Press, 1998); Daniel Yergin, *Shattered Peace: The Origins of the Cold War and the National Security State* (Boston: Houghton Mifflin, 1977); Jeffery Dorwart, *Eberstadt and Forrestal: A National Security Partnership, 1909–1949* (College State: Texas A&M University Press, 1991); Melyvn Leffler, *A Preponderance of Power: National Security, the Truman Administration, and the Cold War* (Stanford: Stanford University Press, 1992); Douglas Stuart, *Creating the National Security State: A History of the Law That Transformed America* (Princeton: Princeton University Press, 2008); Elizabeth Fones-Wolf, *Selling Free Enterprise: The Business Assault on Labor and Liberalism, 1945–1960* (Urbana: University of Illinois Press, 1994).

37. Jennifer Light, *From Warfare to Welfare: Defense Intellectuals and Urban Problems in Cold War America* (Baltimore: Johns Hopkins University Press, 2003); Hart, *Forged Consensus*, 175–205; Robert Cuff, "Ferdinand Eberstadt, the National Security Resources Board, and the Search for Integrated Mobilization Planning, 1947–1948," *Public Historian* 7 (1985): 37–52; Alfred D. Sander, "Truman and the National Security Council: 1945–1947," *Journal of American History* 59 (1972): 369–88.

38. Leffler, *Preponderance of Power*; Cuff, "Ferdinand Eberstadt"; Hogan, *Cross of Iron*; Yergin, *Shattered Peace*.

39. Harry Thompson and Lida Mayo, *The Ordnance Department: Procurement and Supply* (Washington, D.C.: Government Printing Office, 1991), 12.

40. Michael Storper and Richard Walker, *The Capitalist Imperative: Territory, Technology and Industrial Growth* (Cambridge, Mass.: Blackwell, 1989), 138.

41. Harvey, *Urban Experience*; Hudson, *Producing Places*; Robert Lewis, *Chicago Made: Factory Networks in the Industrial Metropolis* (Chicago: University of Chicago Press, 2008); Edward Muller, "The Pittsburgh Survey and 'Greater Pittsburgh': A Muddled Metropolitan Geography," in *Pittsburgh Surveyed: Social Science and Social Reform in the Early Twentieth Century*, ed. Maurine Greenwald and Margo Anderson (Pittsburgh: University of Pittsburgh Press, 1996); Allen Scott, *Metropolis: From the Division of Labor to Urban Form* (Berkeley: University of California Press, 1988); Storper and Walker, *Capitalist Imperative*.

42. Hudson, *Producing Places*, 257. Also see Andrew Herod, *Scale* (New York: Routledge, 2011) and the essays in Kevin Cox, ed., *Spaces of Globalization: Reasserting the Power of the Local* (New York: Guilford, 1997).

43. Lewis, *Chicago Made*.

44. The state and the military used war conditions to survey the city as well as indus-

trial property. This, however, is not the subject of the present study. The framework of calculation laid out here could provide a framework for getting at the broader question of surveying the metropolis.

45. Hudson, *Producing Places*, 255–85; Doreen Massey, "The Conceptualization of Place," in *A Place in the World? Place, Culture and Globalization*, ed. Doreen Massey and Pat Jess (London: Macmillan, 1995), 59–69.

46. They have examined wartime governance, the gendered character of work, and the building of civil defense. See Roger Lotchin, ed., *The Martial Metropolis: U.S. Cites in War and Peace* (New York: Praeger, 1984); Roger Lotchin, *The Bad City in the Good War* (Bloomington: Indiana University Press, 2003); Catherine Lutz, *Homefront: A Military City and the American Twentieth Century* (Boston: Beacon Press, 2001); Robert Spinney, *World War II in Nashville: Transformation of the Homefront* (Knoxville: University of Tennessee Press, 1998); Marilynn Johnson, *The Second Gold Rush: Oakland and the East Bay in World War II* (Berkeley: University of California Press, 1993).

47. Perry Duis, "Symbolic Unity and the Neighborhood: Chicago during World War II," *Journal of Urban History* 21 (1995): 184–217; Perry Duis and Scott La France, *We've Got a Job to Do: Chicagoans and World War II* (Chicago: Chicago Historical Society, 1992).

48. Sarah Jo Peterson, *Planning the Home Front: Building Bombers and Communities at Willow Run* (Chicago: University of Chicago Press, 2013).

49. Gary Weir, *Forged in War: The Naval-Industrial Complex and American Submarine Construction, 1940–1961* (Washington, D.C.: Department of the Navy, 1993), 58.

50. Roger Lotchin, *Fortress California, 1910–1961: From Warfare to Welfare* (New York: Oxford University Press, 1992), 5.

51. Harvey, *Limits to Capital*.

52. For the quote see Hudson, *Producing Places*, 257. See also Doreen Massey, "Power-Geometry and the Progressive Sense of Place," in *Mapping the Futures: Local Culture, Global Change*, ed. Jon Bird, Barry Curtis, Tim Putnam, George Robertson, and Lisa Tickner (London: Routledge, 1993), 59–69; Allan Pred, *City-Systems in Advanced Economies* (London: Hutchinson, 1977).

53. John Logan and Harvey Molotch, *Urban Fortunes: The Political Economy of Place* (Berkeley: University of California Press, 1987); Harvey, *Urban Experience*; Kevin Cox and Andrew Mair, "Locality and Community in the Politics of Local Economic Development," *Annals of the Association of American Geographers* 78 (1988): 307–25; Greg Hise, *Magnetic Los Angeles: Planning the Twentieth-Century Metropolis* (Baltimore: Johns Hopkins University Press, 1997); Clarence Stone, *Regime Politics: Governing Atlanta, 1946–1988* (Lawrence: University Press of Kansas, 1999).

Chapter 2. Industrial Sites and Wartime Mobilization

1. Civilian Production Administration, *Industrial Mobilization for War: History of the War Production Board and Predecessor Agencies, 1941–1945* (Washington, D.C.: Government Printing Office, 1947), xiii.

2. Alan Brinkley, *The End of Reform: New Deal Liberalism in Recession and War* (New York: Alfred Knopf, 1995); Byron Fairchild and Jonathan Grossman, *The Army and Industrial Manpower* (Washington, D.C.: Department of the Army, 1959); Mark Foster,

Henry J. Kaiser: Builder in the Modern American West (Austin: University of Texas Press, 1989); David Hart, *Forged Consensus: Science, Technology, and Economic Policy in the United States, 1921–1953* (Princeton: Princeton University Press, 1998); Gregory Hooks, *Forging the Military-Industrial Complex: World War II's Battle of the Potomac* (Urbana: University of Illinois Press, 1991); Paul Koistinen, *Arsenal of World War II: The Political Economy of America Warfare, 1940–1945* (Lawrence: University Press of Kansas, 2004); Elberton Smith, *The Army and Economic Mobilization* (Washington, D.C.: Government Printing Office, 1959); Gary Weir, *Forged in War: The Naval-Industrial Complex and American Submarine Construction, 1940–1961* (Washington, D.C.: Department of the Navy, 1993); Gerald White, *Billions for Defense: Government Financing by the Defense Plant Corporation during World War II* (University: University of Alabama Press, 1980).

3. Philip Funigiello, *The Challenge to Urban Liberalism: Federal-City Relations during World War II* (Knoxville: University of Tennessee Press, 1978); Mark Gelfand, *A Nation of Cities: The Federal Government and Urban America, 1933–1965* (New York: Oxford University Press, 1975); Roger Lotchin, *Fortress California, 1910–1961: From Warfare to Welfare* (New York: Oxford University Press, 1992); Robert Spinney, *World Two II in Nashville: Transformation of the Homefront* (Knoxville University of Tennessee Press, 1998).

4. Hooks, *Forging the Military-Industrial Complex*, 98–107; Koistinen, *Arsenal of World War II*, 53–64; Keith Eiler, *Mobilizing America: Robert P. Patterson and the War Effort, 1940–1945* (Ithaca: Cornell University Press, 1997), 44–45, 60–63; White, *Billions for Defense*, 1–3.

5. Jack Ballard, *The Shock of Peace: Military and Economic Demobilization after World War II* (Washington, D.C.: University Press of America, 1983), 159.

6. Hal Foust, "Green Jubilant over Promise of More Arms Jobs," *Chicago Tribune*, November 26, 1941, 3.

7. Civilian Production Administration, *War-Created Manufacturing Plant: Federally Financed, 1940–1944* (Washington, D.C.: Government Printing Office, November 15, 1945). It is unclear from the reports what constituted an "existing" factory. For my purposes here, a new factory had to be physically separate from an existing one. Civilian Production Administration, *War-Time Manufacturing Plant Expansion: Privately Financed 1940–1945* (Washington, D.C.: Government Printing Office, 1946), 5 and Appendix Table 1-A.

8. Civilian Production Administration, *War-Time Manufacturing Plant Expansion*, 39–40. Also see Civilian Production Administration, *War-Created Manufacturing Plant*, 3.

9. Civilian Production Administration, *War-Created Manufacturing Plant*, 21–22; Civilian Production Administration, *War-Time Manufacturing Plant Expansion*, 32.

10. Marilynn Johnson, *The Second Gold Rush: Oakland and the East Bay in World War II* (Berkeley: University of California Press, 1993), 60. Nelson Lichtenstein, *Labor's War at Home: The CIO in World War II* (New York: Cambridge University Press, 1982); Ruth Milkman, *Gender at Work: The Dynamics of Job Segregation by Sex during World War II* (Urbana: University of Illinois Press, 1987).

11. Civilian Production Administration, *War-Time Manufacturing Plant Expansion*, 3–4; Robert Higgs, "Private Profit, Public Risk: Institutional Antecedents of the Mod-

ern Military Procurement System in the Rearmament Program of 1940–1941," in *The Sinews of War: Essays on the Economic History of World War II*, ed. Geofrey Mills and Hugh Rockoff (Ames: Iowa State University Press, 1993), 166–98; Hooks, *Forging the Military-Industrial Complex*, 125–62.

12. United States, Congress, Senate, *Hearing before the Surplus Property Subcommittee of the Committee on Military Affairs and Industrial Reorganization and the Subcommittee on Industrial Reorganization of the Special Committee on Economic Policy and Planning*, 79th Congress, 1st Sess. (Washington, D.C.: Government Printing Office, October 29, 1945), 4.

13. After the war, Lovett had a role in the creation of the CIA, was secretary of defense under Truman between 1951 and 1953, and was responsible for Korean War mobilization and long-term preparedness measures. Lovett is an outstanding example of the continuity of personnel over the war and postwar periods and as such links the concerns of wartime mobilization with those of postwar security.

14. David Lynch, *The Concentration of Economic Power* (New York: Columbia University Press, 1946), 111–42; Smaller War Plants Corporation, *Economic Concentration*, 15–20; Hooks, *Forging the Military-Industrial Complex*, 99–102.

15. For quotes see Smaller War Plants Corporation, *Economic Concentration*, 25.

16. Brinkley, *End of Reform*, 106–36.

17. Smaller War Plants Corporation, *Economic Concentration*, 25; Jim Heath, "American War Mobilization and the Use of Small Manufacturers, 1939–1943," *Business History Review* 46 (1972): 295–319; Brinkley, *End of Reform*, 192–94.

18. For quotes see Gregory Hooks, "The Weakness of Strong Theories: The U.S. State's Dominance of the World War II Investment Process," *American Sociological Review* 58 (1993): 43; and Smaller War Plants Corporation, *Economic Concentration*, 32.

19. Jesse H. Jones with Edward Angly, *Fifty Billion Dollars and My Thirteen Years with the RFC (1932–1945)* (New York: Macmillan, 1951), 338.

20. Koistinen, *Arsenal of World War II*, 54–55; White, *Billions for Defense*, 3–4.

21. Alan Brinkley, "World War II and American Liberalism," in *The War in American Culture: Society and Consciousness during World War II*, ed. Lewis Erenberg and Susan Hirsch (Chicago: University of Chicago Press, 1996), 313–30.

22. Hans Klagsbrunn, "Some Aspects of War Plant Financing," *American Economic Review* 33 (1943): 119.

23. Klagsbrunn, "Some Aspects of War Plant Financing," 119–22; Eiler, *Mobilizing America*, 63–65; Hooks, "Weakness of Strong Theories"; John Salmond, *The Conscience of a Lawyer: Clifford J. Durr and the American Civil Liberties, 1899–1975* (Tuscaloosa: University of Alabama Press, 1990), 62–63; White, *Billions for Defense*, 15–16.

24. White, *Billions for Defense*, 10.

25. Brinkley, *End of Reform*; Philip Funigiello, "Kilowatts for Defense: The New Deal and the Coming of the Second World War," *Journal of American History* 56 (1969): 604–20; Robert Leighninger, *Long-Range Public Investment: The Forgotten Legacy of the New Deal* (Columbia: University of South Carolina Press, 2007).

26. Brinkley, *End of Reform*, 137–74; Funigiello, "Kilowatts for Defense."

27. Address delivered by President Roosevelt to the Congress, May 16, 1940. Also see

U.S. Department of State, *Peace and War: United States Foreign Policy, 1931–1941* (Washington, D.C.: Government Printing Office, 1983 [1943]), 525–31.

28. Franklin Roosevelt, "Fireside Chat, May 26, 1940," http://www.presidency.ucsb.edu/ws/index.php?pid=15959, accessed September 27, 2012.

29. White, *Billions for Defense*, 3; Hooks, *Forging the Military-Industrial Complex*, 98–107.

30. Ira Katznelson and Bruce Pietrykowski, "Rebuilding the American State; Evidence from the 1940s," *Studies in American Political Development* 5 (Fall 1991): 306. Also see John Jeffries, "The 'New' New Deal: FDR and American Liberalism, 1937–1945," *Political Science Quarterly* 105 (Fall 1990): 397–418; Jyette Klausen, "Did World War II End the New Deal? A Comparative Perspective on Postwar Planning Initiatives," in *The New Deal and the Triumph of Liberalism*, ed. Sidney Milkis and Jerome Mileur (Amherst: University of Massachusetts Press, 2002), 193–230.

31. Jason Scott Smith, *Building New Deal Liberalism: The Political Economy of Public Works, 1933–1956* (Cambridge: Cambridge University Press, 2006), 258. Also see Leighninger, *Long-Range Public Investment*.

32. Hooks, *Forging the Military-Industrial Complex*, 128; William Barber, *Designs within Disorder: Franklin D. Roosevelt, the Economists, and the Shaping of American Economic Policy, 1933–1945* (New York: Cambridge University Press, 1996); Brinkley, *End of Reform*; Vatter, *U.S. Economy in World War II*.

33. Fairchild and Grossman, *Army and Industrial Manpower*, 20.

34. Hooks, *Forging the Military-Industrial Complex*, 43.

35. Koistinen, *Arsenal of World War II*; U.S. Civilian Production Administration, *Industrial Mobilization for War*; White, *Billions for Defense*; Hooks, *Forging the Military-Industrial Complex*.

36. Koistinen, *Arsenal of World War II*, 13–71; Barton Bernstein, "The Removal of War Production Board Controls on Business, 1944–1946," *Business History Review* 39 (1965): 243–60; Vatter, *U.S. Economy in World War II*, 32–50.

37. Hooks, "Weakness of Strong Theories," 44.

38. Barton Bernstein, "The Debate on Industrial Reconversion: The Protection of Oligopoly and Military Control of the Economy," *American Journal of Economics and Sociology* 26 (1967): 160.

39. Higgs, "Private Profit, Public Risk"; Hooks, *Forging the Military-Industrial Complex*, 125–62. There were three key elements of the wartime procurement system: negotiated contracts (which replaced competitive bidding); cost of production plus a fixed fee (which was guaranteed by the federal government); and advance payments by the army and navy of up to 30 percent of the contract price during the performance of the work.

40. Hooks, "Weakness of Strong Theories," 48–50.

41. White, *Billions for Defense*, 6. There were two early financing strategies: the creation of government corporations to build and lease government-owned factories and the contract between private interests that built war plants with government loans to be paid back over five years. Klagsbrunn, "Some Aspects of War Plant Financing," 120–22.

42. Smith, *Army and Economic Mobilization*, 474.

43. White, *Billions for Defense*, 7–9.

44. Klagsbrunn, "Some Aspects of War Plant Financing," 120–23.

45. White, *Billions for Defense*, 6, 11–18; Jones, *Fifty Billion Dollars*, 340–42. The total amount invested in defense factories by the other government agencies was $8.9 billion, with the War Department contributing $5.4 billion, the Navy Department close to $2.9 billion, and the Maritime Commission $600 million.

46. White, *Billions for Defense*, 1–6.

47. Sanborn is the best-known insurance map publisher. Its large collection of urban maps is available through university and public libraries. The Library of Congress has extensive holdings.

48. Lewis Atherton, "The Problem of Credit Rating in the Ante-Bellum South," *Journal of Southern History* 12 (1946): 534–56; R. Hidy, "Credit Rating before Dun and Bradstreet," *Bulletin of the Business Historical Society* 13 (1939): 81–88; James Madison, "The Evolution of Commercial Credit Reporting Agencies in Nineteenth-Century America," *Business History Review* 48 (1974): 164–86; James Norris, *R.G. Dun and Co., 1841–1900: The Development of Credit-Reporting in the Nineteenth Century* (Westport, Conn.: Greenwood Press, 1978); Rowena Olegario, *A Culture of Credit: Embedding Trust and Transparency in American Business* (Cambridge, Mass.: Harvard University Press, 2006).

49. Koistinen, *Military-Industrial Complex*, 10.

50. For the quote see Smith, *Army and Economic Mobilization*, 35. Also see Robert Cuff, *The War Industries Board: Business-Government Relations during World War I* (Baltimore: Johns Hopkins University Press, 1973); Paul Koistinen, *The Military-Industrial Complex: A Historical Perspective* (New York: Praeger, 1980), 10.

51. For quote see Brian Waddell, *The War against the New Deal: World War I and American Democracy* (De Kalb: Northern Illinois University Press, 2001), 48. Also see Smith, *Army and Economic Mobilization*, 39–47; Koistinen, *Military-Industrial Complex*, 11–12.

52. Waddell, *War against the New Deal*, 46–48.

53. Calvin Hoover, "The Requirements of a War Economy," *Annals of the American Academy of the Politics and Social Science* 218 (1941): 78–86.

54. Morris Copeland, "Production Planning for a War Economy," *Annals of the American Academy of Political and Social Science* 220 (1942): 94–105.

55. The question of interagency rivalry is a key theme of Hooks, *Forging of the Military-Industrial Complex*; Koistinen, *Arsenal of World War II*. In "Production Planning," Copeland talks about the slowness of the country's institutions.

56. Koistinen, *Arsenal of World War II*, 289–91.

57. Bernstein, "Removal of War Production Board Controls"; Vatter, *U.S. Economy in World War II*, 32–50.

58. For quote see Koistinen, *Arsenal of World War II*, 21, cf. 82–86, 120–21.

59. War Production Board, *Concentration of Civilian Production by the War Production Board* (Washington, D.C.: Government Printing Office, 1944).

60. Koistinen, *Arsenal of World War II*, 82–86, 115–25, 291–92; Robert Connery, *The Navy and the Industrial Mobilization in World War II* (Princeton: Princeton University Press, 1951), 352–56. White, *Billions for Defense*, 50–66.

61. Quoted in Eiler, *Mobilizing America*, 63.

62. McCloy was legal counsel to large industrial conglomerates including I.G. Farben before 1941. After the war he became president of the World Bank.

Chapter 3. Mobilizing Chicago's Wartime Industrial Property

1. "Arms Output Now Soaring," *Commerce*, December 1941, 31; Roger Biles, *Big City Boss in Depression and War: Mayor Edward Kelly of Chicago* (DeKalb: Northern Illinois University Press, 1984), 144–18; Perry Duis and Scott La France, *We've Got a Job to Do: Chicagoans and World War II* (Chicago: Chicago Historical Society, 1992), 67–96.

2. "Arms Output Now Soaring," 30.

3. "War Plant Building Near Billion Dollars," *Commerce*, March 1944, 40–42; United States, *Sixteenth Census of the United States: 1940: Manufactures, 1939*, vol. 3; Mary Watters, *Illinois in the Second World War: Operation Home Front*, vol. 2 (Springfield: State of Illinois, 1952), 1–136, 246.

4. United States, *Census: Manufacturers*, vol. 3; Robert Lewis, *Chicago Made: Factory Networks in the Industrial Metropolis* (Chicago: University of Chicago Press, 2008).

5. "Invest Millions as Chicago Area Factories Grow," *Chicago Tribune*, January 2, 1940, 23; "New Plants Top 232 Millions; U.S. Rents Vast Space in City," *Chicago Tribune*, April 25, 1942, 23.

6. "Business-Civic Team Urged for Greater Chicago," *Chicago Tribune*, October 7, 1939, 8; Arthur Evans, "Tackle Program to Give Chicago New Industries," *Chicago Tribune*, October 28, 1939, 9; "Chicago Group Begins Drive for New Industries," *Chicago Tribune*, January 30, 1940, 20; Biles, *Big City Boss*, 116–18; Duis and LaFrance, *We've Got a Job to Do*, 67–96. For Lyon see N. H. Engle, "Leverett Samuel Lyon," *Journal of Marketing* 24 (1959): 67–69.

7. "Chicago Warned It Must Fight to Get New Industries," *Chicago Tribune*, June 20, 1939, 23.

8. "Chicago Warned," 23.

9. "Business-Civic Team"; Evans, "Tackle Program"; "Chicago Group Begins Drive"; Chicago Association of Commerce, *The Chicago Association of Commerce Report for 1940* (Chicago: Chicago Association of Commerce, 1941): 33–34.

10. Duis and La France, *We've Got a Job to Do*, 67–96. For a regional context see Harold Vatter, *The U.S. Economy in World War II* (New York: Columbia University Press, 1985), 14, 35–36.

11. "Shell Plants in Midwest Is Defense Plan," *Chicago Tribune*, July 17, 1940, 25.

12. "Plane Industry Clings to Open Coastal Areas," *Chicago Tribune*, August 24, 1940, 19; "Strategic Sites for Industry," *Chicago Tribune*, September 8, 1940, 16.

13. "Form Clearing House for U.S. Bid Request," *Chicago Tribune*, September 13, 1940, 35.

14. "Form Clearing House"; Hal Foust, "Another Chicago Advantage—Its Vast Labor Reservoir," *Chicago Tribune*, November 11, 1941, 1; "Green, Kelly Win Pledge of Arms Aid for State," *Chicago Tribune*, November 25, 1941, 1; "Hartz Resigns Chicago OPM Contract Post," *Chicago Tribune*, December 4, 1941, 37; Byron Fairchild and Jonathan Grossman, *The Army and Industrial Manpower* (Washington, D.C.: Department of the Army, 1959), 104–5; William Strand, "Reveal Growth of Arms Plants in Coast Areas," *Chicago Tri-*

bune, January 11, 1942, B6, and "Study Removal of Arm Plants to Inland Areas," *Chicago Tribune*, January 3, 1942, 7.

15. Vatter, *U.S. Economy*, 36; Gregory Hooks, *Forging the Military-Industrial Complex: World War II's Battle of the Potomac* (Urbana: University of Illinois Press, 1991); Paul Koistinen, *Arsenal of World War II: The Political Economy of America Warfare, 1940–1945* (Lawrence: University Press of Kansas, 2004).

16. Glenn McLaughlin, "Wartime Expansion Industrial Capacities," *American Economic Review* 33 (1943): 110–11; Fairchild and Grossman, *Army and Industrial Manpower*, 101–9.

17. "Large Centers to Be Avoided in Arms Building," *Chicago Tribune*, November 26, 1940, 23.

18. John Salmond, *The Conscience of a Lawyer: Clifford J. Durr and American Civil Liberties, 1899–1975* (Tuscaloosa: University of Alabama Press, 1990); Roger Lotchin, "'Mars Has a Hand in Your Pocket': Urban California in the Second Great War," in *Fortress California, 1910–1961: From Warfare to Welfare* (New York: Oxford University Press, 1992), 131–69; Gerald White, *Billions for Defense: Government Financing by the Defense Plant Corporation during World War II* (University: University of Alabama Press, 1980).

19. U.S. Congress, Senate, *Hearings before a Special Committee Investigating the National Defense Program, part 1* (Washington, D.C.: Government Printing Office, 1941), 65.

20. Biles, *Big City Boss*.

21. "Committee of 3 to Press City's War Aid Claims," *Chicago Tribune*, May 20, 1940, 11.

22. "Green, Kelly Win Pledge," 1; Hal Foust, "Green Jubilant over Promise of More Arms Jobs," *Chicago Tribune*, November 26, 1941, 3; Hal Foust, "Green Will Urge in Capital: Help Non-war Plants," *Chicago Tribune*, November 24, 1941, 4; Duis and La France, *We've Got a Job to Do*, 70–71; Watters, *Illinois*, vol. 1: 6–7.

23. "Green, Kelly Win Pledge," 1; Foust, "Green Jubilant over Promise," 3.

24. *An Analysis of the Chicago Industrial Area with Respect to National Defense Production and New Plant Establishment* (Chicago: Chicago Association of Commerce, 1940); *The Chicago Industrial Area for National Defense Production and New Plant Establishment* (Chicago: Chicago Association of Commerce, 1940); *The Chicago Industrial Area: A Review of 1944* (Chicago: Chicago Association of Commerce, 1946). The Chicago Plan Commission was responsible for *Residential Chicago*, vol. 1 of *The Report of the Chicago Land Use Survey* (Chicago: Chicago Plan Commission, 1942); *Land Use in Chicago*, vol. 2 of *The Report of the Chicago Land Use Survey* (Chicago: Chicago Plan Commission, 1943); *Industrial and Commercial Background for Planning Chicago* (Chicago: Chicago Plan Commission, 1942); *Forty-Four Cities in the City of Chicago* (Chicago: Chicago Plan Commission, 1942); Charles Blessing and Harold Mayer, *The Calumet Industrial District: A Preface to a Comprehensive Development Plan* (Chicago: Chicago Plan Commission, 1942).

25. Chicago Association of Commerce, *Analysis*, 2.

26. Blessing and Mayer, *Calumet Industrial District*, 3.

27. Chicago Association of Commerce, *Analysis*, 2, 12.

28. Chicago Association of Commerce, *Chicago Industrial Area*, n.p.

29. Chicago Association of Commerce, *Analysis*, 2 (emphasis in the original).

30. "War Plant Building Near Billion Dollars," *Commerce*, March 1944, 40–42. The policy of locating industry inland was partially successful. Although the fourteen interior states categorized as inland by the mobilization agencies received $21.6 billion of wartime supply contracts and $4.5 billion of new construction and equipment contracts, their share of the national totals at 11 percent and 21 percent trailed the East Coast (38 and 35 percent), and Great Lakes (36 and 31 percent). The totals were similar to those found in the West Coast states (14 and 12 percent).

31. "War Plant Building," 40.

32. "National Defense Committee Formed by Manufacturers," *Chicago Tribune*, September, 1939, 31.

33. "Free Factories from Shackles! General Warns," *Chicago Tribune*, May 19, 1940, 9.

34. "Chicago's National Defense Role," *Commerce*, March 1941, 44; Watters, *Illinois*, 2:15–17.

35. Chicago Association of Commerce, *Report for 1940*, 3. Jeffrey Charles, "Chambers of Commerce," in *The Encyclopedia of Chicago*, ed. James Grossman, Ann Durkin Keating, and Janice Reiff (Chicago: University of Chicago Press, 2004), 126.

36. Chicago Association of Commerce, *Report for 1940*, 31, 32.

37. Ibid., 31–34.

38. For Chicago see "Chicago Defense Group Planned to Get War Work," *Chicago Tribune*, December 12, 1940, 3; and "Name Chicago Commission on Military Work," *Chicago Tribune*, March 6, 1941, 31. For Illinois see "State Defense Council Calls First Meeting," *Chicago Tribune*, January 2, 1941, 12; "Green Signs Bill Creating State Defense Council," *Chicago Tribune*, April 18, 1941, 10.

39. "Council of Defense Is Credited with Aiding Arms Boom in State," *Chicago Tribune*, February 8, 1942, 11.

40. Chicago Association of Commerce, *The Chicago Association of Commerce Report for 1942* (Chicago: Chicago Association of Commerce, 1943), 17. Also see Wayne Thomis, "Chicago Is Vast Factory to Aid in U.S. Defense," *Chicago Tribune*, May 18, 1940, 3; Chicago Association of Commerce, *Report for 1940*, 30–34; Chicago Association of Commerce, *The Chicago Association of Commerce Report for 1941* (Chicago: Chicago Association of Commerce, 1943), 6–18; Chicago Association of Commerce *The Chicago Association of Commerce Report for 1943* (Chicago: Chicago Association of Commerce, 1944), 6–18; Chicago Association of Commerce, *The Chicago Association of Commerce Report for 1944* (Chicago: Chicago Association of Commerce, 1945), 7–21.

41. For the RFC see Neil Jacoby and Raymond Saulnier, *Business Finance and Banking* (New York: National Bureau of Economic Research, 1947), 121–23. For the Defense Problem Service see "Chicago's National Defense Role," *Commerce*, March 1941, 42–44; "Arm's Output Now Soaring," *Commerce*, December 1941, 59–76; Chicago Association of Commerce, *Report for 1941*, 11, 9.

42. Chicago Association of Commerce, *Report for 1944*, 14–16; "Chicago's National Defense Role"; "Arm's Output Now Soaring."

43. "Plan for Arms Clinic Attracts Wide Response," *Chicago Tribune*, October 15, 1941, 32.

44. Lloyd Norman, "Huge Arms Clinic Opens Today; Select Seven Cities for Work," *Chicago Tribune*, October 22, 1941, 31.

45. Lloyd Norman, "Firms Besiege Arms Clinic in Hunt for Work," *Chicago Tribune*, October 23, 1941, 31.

46. Vincent Carosso, *Investment Banking in America: A History* (Cambridge, Mass.: Harvard University Press, 1970).

47. Thomas Furlong, "Seeks Greater Reserve Board Credit Powers," *Chicago Tribune*, November 15, 1940, 29; "First Big Bank Loan on Plane Contract Near, "*Chicago Tribune*, November 19, 1940, 25; "Banks to Lend 200 Million to Bendix Aviation," *Chicago Tribune*, September 27, 1942, B7; John Fisher, "Banks' Billions Await Call to Pay for Plants," *Chicago Tribune*, September 26, 1940, 27; Civilian Production Administration, *War-Time Manufacturing Plant Expansion: Privately Financed 1940–1945* (Washington, D.C.: Government Printing Office, 1946), 20–22.

48. U.S. Civilian Production Administration, *War Industrial Facilities Authorized, July 1940–August 1945: Listed Alphabetically by Company and Plant Location* (Washington, D.C.: Government Printing Office, 1946), various pages. "First Big bank Loan on Plant Contract Near," *Chicago Tribune*, November 19, 1940, 25.

49. "RFC to Share in Bank Loan to Davidson Manufacturing," *Chicago Tribune*, December 6, 1941, 28; "Banks to Lend 200 Million to Bendix Aviation," *Chicago Tribune*, September 27, 1942, B7. Established in 1888, the Harris investment banking firm specialized in municipal bonds but also provided industrial loans. See Mark Wilson, "Harris Trust and Savings Bank," in Grossman et al., *Encyclopedia of Chicago*, 927; Carosso, *Investment Banking*.

50. U.S. Congress, House, "Certificates of Necessity and Government Plant Expansion Loans," 82nd Congress, 1st Sess. (Washington: Government Printing Office, May 1951), 17, 22.

51. Hans Klagsbrunn, "Some Aspects of War Plant Financing," *American Economic Review* 33 (1943): 119–20; R. Elberton Smith, *The Army and Economic Mobilization* (Washington, D.C.: Government Printing Office, 1959), 456–75; White, *Billions for Defense*, 1–10.

52. Jacoby and Saulnier, *Business Finance*, 121–28, 187–95; Anna Youngman, *The Federal Reserve System in Wartime* (New York: National Bureau of Economic Research, 1945), 1–14; Watters, *Illinois*, 2:6–7.

53. The V, VT, and T loans were, respectively, for war production, wartime contract termination, and termination contracts.

54. John Fisher, "Banking Future Held Dependent on Arms Finance," *Chicago Tribune*, November 13, 1940, 31.

55. "Chicago National Defense Role," *Commerce*, March 1941, 44; Watters, *Illinois*, 2:34–36, 123; "Name Officials to Aid in Arms Subcontracting," *Chicago Tribune*, March 26, 1941, 25.

56. Fisher, "Banking Future," 31.

57. *United States Government Manual: October 1939* (Washington, D.C.: Government Printing Office, 1939); *United States Government Manual: Summer 1944 (Revisions through August 1)* (Washington, D.C.: Government Printing Office, 1944).

58. "Chicago Realty Men in Capital for Office Shift," *Chicago Tribune*, December 27, 1941, 3.

59. "Reserve Bank Takes Over More Space as Its Activities Expand," *Chicago Tribune*, April 4, 1942.

60. Al Chase, "Chicago Offices of RFC Moved to 208 S. La Salle," *Chicago Tribune*, September 3, 1942, 27; "Chicago Offices of ODS Moved to 366 West Adams," *Chicago Tribune*, January 10, 1943, 19.

61. "Chicago's National Defense Role," *Commerce*, March 1941, 44.

62. William Carey, "Central-Field Relationships in the War Production Board," *Public Administration Review* 4 (1944): 31–42.

63. M. George Goodrick, "WPB Decentralization within the Chicago Region," *Public Administration Review* 4 (1944): 210.

64. "Begin Chicago Plant Survey for Air Corps," *Chicago Tribune*, March 22, 1942, 19.

65. Fred Preston, "Address," *The Commercial Club of Chicago, 64th Year Book, 1941–1942* (Chicago: Executive Committee, 1942), 558–59.

66. "Arms Output Now Soaring," 32–46; Watters, *Illinois*, 2:14–15.

67. Otto Maha, "Historical Progress of Hannifin Manufacturing Company Ordnance Division" (Chicago, typescript, December 7, 1945): 3–4; IHLR; "Firm Produces Mechanism for High Caliber Gun," *Chicago Tribune*, July 12, 1941, 12.

68. Letter from W. T. Crane to M. L. Flaningam, September 6, 1946, 1–2; Burgess-North Mfg. Co. Records, IHLR.

69. "Schools Aid Defense," *Commerce*, December 1941, 53–58; Richard Thompson, *Crystal Clear: The Struggle for Reliable Communications Technology in World War II* (Hoboken, N.J.: IEEE Press, 2007); Watters, *Illinois*, 1:8, 92, 424.

Chapter 4. Chicago's Wartime Industrial Sites

1. War Production Board, *War Manufacturing Facilities Authorized through December 1944 by State and County* (Washington, D.C.: Government Printing Office, 1945). Civilian Production Administration, *War Industrial Facilities Authorized, July 1940–August 1945: Listed Alphabetically by Companies and Plant Location* (Washington, D.C.: Government Printing Office, 1946). See the Appendix for a discussion of my totals and those of other writers.

2. "Two Aviation Engine Plants for Chicago," *Commerce*, February 1941, 40.

3. Wayne Thomis, "Chicago Is Vast Factory to Aid U.S. Defense," *Chicago Tribune*, May 18, 1940, 3.

4. Perry Duis, "Symbolic Unity and the Neighborhood: Chicago during World War II," *Journal of Urban History* 21 (1995): 196–200.

5. "U.S. Naval Activities, World War II, by State" (Washington, D.C.: Department of the Navy, 1945), http://www.ibiblio.org/hyperwar/USN/ref/USN-Act/index.html, accessed July 10, 2012.

6. Jacob Vander Meulen, *Building the B-29* (Washington, D.C.: Smithsonian Institution Press, 1995), 13–20; Wesley Stout, *Great Engines and Great Planes* (Detroit: Chrysler Corporation, 1947), 1–2, 48–54; William Cunningham, *The Aircraft Industry: A Study in Industrial Location* (Los Angeles: Morrison, 1951), 87, 130.

7. Vander Meulen, *Building the B-29*, 86–88; Stout, *Great Engines*, 2; Irving Brinton

Holley, *Buying Aircraft: Matériel Procurement for the Army Air Forces* (Washington, D.C.: Government Printing Office, 1964), 319–20.

8. Thomas Scott, "Winning World War II in an Atlanta Suburb: Local Boosters and the Recruitment of Bell Bomber," in *The Second Wave: Southern Industrialization from the 1940s to the 1970s*, ed. Philip Scranton (Athens: University of Georgia Press, 2001), 1–23; Cunningham, *Aircraft Industry*, 94, 133.

9. Cunningham, *Aircraft Industry*, 131; Holley, *Buying Aircraft*, 309–10; "Kelly Proposes Four Sites for Erection of Plane Factories," *Chicago Tribune*, February 14, 1942, 11.

10. "Postwar Possibilities," 2; Cunningham, *Aircraft Industry*, 91–93, 121, 136n; Vander Meulen, *Building the B-29s*, 88–89; "Chrysler Erecting Huge War Plant," *New York Times*, December 14, 1942, 37.

11. Stout, *Great Engines*, 47.

12. "Chrysler Plans Expansion of Plant in Chicago," *Chicago Tribune*, June 4, 1942, 29; "Pass Ordinance Closing Off Streets for Plant Site," *Chicago Tribune*, February 20, 1942, 28.

13. "City Extending Water Service to War Plants," *Chicago Tribune*, September 20, 1942, 11. Also see "Chrysler Corp. Chicago Plant Largest Maker of B-29 Engines," *Wall Street Journal*, June 13, 1944, 6; "Chrysler Erecting Huge War Plant." For Kahn and the development of industrial architecture see Lindy Biggs, *The Rational Factory: Architecture, Technology, and Work in America's Age of Mass Production* (Baltimore: Johns Hopkins University Press, 1996).

14. Stout, *Great Engines*, 54. Also see "Chrysler Corp. War Output Hits Peaks in December," *Wall Street Journal*, January 2, 1943, 5; Vander Meulen, *Building the B-29s*, 89, 95–98; Sarah Jo Peterson, *Planning the Home Front: Building Bombers and Communities at Willow Run* (Chicago: University of Chicago Press, 2103), 179–205; Duis and LaFrance, *We've Got a Job to Do*, 69–71; "Fuller (George A.) Co.," in *The Encyclopedia of Chicago*, ed. James Grossman, Ann Durkin Keating, and Janice Reiff (Chicago: University of Chicago Press, 2004), 925.

15. Amortization was the most important method for investing in manufacturing facilities before Pearl Harbor. Paul Koistinen, *Arsenal of World War II: The Political Economy of America Warfare, 1940–1945* (Lawrence: University Press of Kansas, 2004), 57–58.

16. Watters, *Illinois*, 2:35.

17. For quote see Chicago Association of Commerce, *The Chicago Association of Commerce Report for 1942* (Chicago: Chicago Association of Commerce, 1943), 17. Also see Chicago Association of Commerce, *The Chicago Association of Commerce Report for 1941* (Chicago: Chicago Association of Commerce, 1942), 11.

18. "Prospectus Plancor 1836," October 1, 1943, Box 31, Real Property Disposal Case Files, RG 270, National Archives and Records Administration (NARA)—Chicago; "Borg and Beck Division of Borg-Warner Corporation," September 30, 1946, Wartime Company Histories, Illinois War Council (IWC), RG 518, Illinois State Archives (ISA), Springfield.

19. "Memorandum to the Real Property Review Board," December 18, 1947, Folder: Kropp Forge Aviation Company, Cicero, Illinois, Appraisals, vols. 1 and 2, PL. 1293, Box 160, Real Property Disposal Case Files, RG 270, NARA—Chicago.

20. "Letter from Roy Kropp to the WAA," July 26, 1948, Accession Number: 291-56A-0244, Ahlberg Bearing Company, Records of the Chicago Regional Office, Real Prop-

erty Case Files, 1952–1957, Federal Property Resources Service records, RG 291, NARA—Chicago; "Letter from Kropp Forge to the WAA," December 22, 1947, Folder: Kropp Forge Company, Plancor 1293, Chicago, Illinois (R-111-53), Box 8, Records of the Real Property Review Board, 1946–1949, RG 270, NARA—College Park, Md.

21. "Minutes," WAA Advisory Council meeting, November 26, 1947, 1, Folder: Scrambled Facilities, Subject File, 1946–1948, Box 13, General Board Advisory Council, RG 270, NARA at Chicago.

22. "Minutes," WAA Advisory Council meeting, November 26, 1947, 1.

23. "Prospectus," October 1, 1943, Folder: Gaertner Scientific Corporation, Chicago, Plancor 1397, Box 120, Real Property Disposal Case Files, RG 270, NARA—Chicago.

24. "Appraisal by Fugard, Olsen, Urbain and Neiler," March 20, 1946, "Memo to Henry Radoux," April 4, 1946, and "Memo to the Board," July 30, 1946, Folder: Stauffer Chemical Co., Hammond, Ind. Plancor 2331, Box 231; Real Property Disposal Case Files, RG 270, NARA—Chicago.

25. Coleman Woodbury and Frank Cliffe, "Industrial Location and Urban Redevelopment," in *The Future of Cities and Urban Redevelopment*, ed. Coleman Woodbury (Chicago: University of Chicago Press, 1953), 269, 271.

26. Philip Funigiello, *The Challenge to Urban Liberalism: Federal-City Relations during World War II* (Knoxville: University of Tennessee Press, 1978), 10; Arnold Silverman, "Defense and Deconcentration: Defense Industrialization during World War II and the Development of Contemporary American Suburbs," in *Suburbs Re-Examined*, ed. Barbara Kelly (New York: Greenwood Press, 1989), 157–63; Duis, "Symbolic Unity and the Neighborhood," 184–217.

27. The eighteen metropolitan districts covered a range of sizes and regions: large centers with a mixed manufacturing base (New York and Philadelphia) and more specialized places that ran the gamut from large (Detroit and San Francisco) to small (Rochester and Toledo). Together, they provide an extremely good cross-section of the country's industrial base.

28. The ideal measure for 1939 would have been new capital investments. As this was not included in the 1939 census, wage earners was the next best measure.

29. John Kain, "The Distribution and Movement of Jobs and Industry," in John Kain, *Essays on Urban Spatial Structure* (Cambridge, Mass.: Ballinger, 1975), 84.

30. Equipment accounted for only $41.5 million of the more than $1.3 billion. Firms that had enough existing capacity typically invested in machinery to meet production demands but did not build new factory space.

31. "Invest in the Middle West," *Commerce*, May 1944, 45–47; Watters, *Illinois*, 2:67; Chester Placek and Donald Taylor, "Tantalum," *Industrial and Engineering Chemistry* 48 (1956): 686–95; various issues of *Commerce*.

32. See essays in Robert Lewis, ed., *Manufacturing Suburbs: Building Work and Home on the Metropolitan Fringe* (Philadelphia: Temple University Press, 2004); Philip Scranton, *Proprietary Capitalism: The Textile Manufacture at Philadelphia, 1800–1885* (New York: Cambridge University Press, 1983); Robert Lewis, *Chicago Made: Factory Networks in the Industrial Metropolis* (Chicago: University of Chicago Press, 2008).

33. Chicago Plan Commission, *Industrial and Commercial Background for Planning Chicago* (Chicago: Chicago Plan Commission, 1942), 49.

34. Lewis, *Chicago Made*, 141–66, and Robert Lewis, "Networks and the Industrial Metropolis: Chicago's Calumet District, 1870–1940," in *Industrial Cities, History and Future*, ed. Clemens Zimmerman (Chicago: University of Chicago Press, 2013), 89–114.

35. Charles Blessing and Harold Meyer, *The Calumet Industrial District: A Preface to a Comprehensive Development Plan* (Chicago: Chicago Plan Commission, 1942).

36. "Charles Blessing," *New York Times*, December 19, 1992; "Harold Mayer," *Chicago Tribune*, July 29, 1994. After cutting their teeth with the Chicago Plan Commission, both went on to have illustrious planning and academic careers.

37. Blessing and Mayer, *The Calumet Industrial District*, 37.

38. Ibid., 3–26.

39. "Chicago Held Eligible for Defense Plants," *Chicago Tribune*, August 14, 1940, 27; Byron Fairchild and Jonathan Grossman, *The Army and Industrial Manpower* (Washington, D.C.: Department of the Army, 1959), 101–9.

40. "Chicago Held Eligible," 27.

41. Curtis E. Lemay and Bill Yenne, *Superfortress: The Story of the B-29 and American Air Power* (New York: McGraw-Hill, 1988), 23–59; Meulen, *Building the B-29*, 13–20.

42. Hal Foust, "Site in Country Proposed for Bomber Plant," *Chicago Tribune*, December 5, 1941, 2.

43. "Memo to General Board," May 9, 1946, Folder: Continental Ordnance Corp., East Chicago, Ind. PL. 1220 Ind. 57. Appraisal Data, Box 74, Real Property Disposal Case Files, RG 270, NARA—College Park, Md.; "WPB Orders Halt on Ordnance Unit," *New York Times*, November 29, 1942, 50.

44. "U.S. Naval Activities."

45. "Daniel Seifer to M. L. Flaningam," 2–3, August 27, 1946, Diamond Wire and Case Co., Wartime Company Histories, IWC, RG 518, ISA. For a discussion of technological innovation in Chicago see Duis and La France, *We've Got a Job*, 78–81.

46. War Production Board, *War Manufacturing Facilities Authorized through December 1944 by State and County*; War Production Board, *Listing of Major War Supply Contacts by State and County* (Washington, D.C.: WPB, 1944).

47. "Builds Ship Sectionally," *New York Times*, December 15, 1942, 37.

48. "Declaration," March 22, 1946, Folders: Pressed Steel Car Co., Chicago (Disposal Data,) WD 592 ILL 70, Box 201, Real Property Disposal Case Files, RG 270, NARA—Chicago; *Steelcar Line* (Chicago: Pressed Steel Car Co., 1945), 4; Letter from the Pressed Steel Car Company to the Illinois State Historical Society, December 27, 1946, Wartime Company Histories, IWC, RG 518, ISA.

49. Lloyd Norman, "'Ghost Plant' Makes Tanks: Corn to Shells in 16 Months," *Chicago Tribune*, February 27, 1942, 7.

50. Ibid.

51. "Chicago Area to Make New Light Tanks," *Chicago Tribune*, February 11, 1942, 29.

52. "Memo. to General Board," September 27, 1946, Folder: Buda Company, Harvey, Illinois, Box 36, Real Property Disposal Case Files, RG 270, NARA—Chicago; "Letter from H. Conenour to M. Flaningham," September 6, 1945, Wartime Company Histories, IWC, RG 518, ISA; "Expand Harvey Plant of Tank Engine Maker," *Chicago Tribune*, August 2, 1940, 27.

53. C. Roberts, "Engineer's Report," p. 2, February 20, 1947, Folder: Wyman-Gordon

Company, Harvey, Illinois (Final Disposition), Plancor 89, RR-ILL87, Box 258, Real Property Disposal Case Files, NARA—Chicago. Also see "Memorandum to the Advisory Council, Exhibit A," p. 8, November 19, 1947, Projects 46K-46P, Box 13, General Board Advisory Council, RG 270, NARA—College Park, Md.

54. "H. Stoddard to H. Klagsbrunn," September 9, 1944, Folder: Wyman-Gordon, Harvey, ILL.(Disposal Data), PL. 89, ILL 87, Box 258, Real Property Disposal Case Files, RG 270, NARA—Chicago.

Chapter 5. War Factories and Industrial Engineering

1. There are few histories of the industry, but see Samuel Lincoln, *Lockwood Greene: The History of an Engineering Business, 1832–1958* (Brattleboro, Vt.: Stephen Green Press, 1960).

2. Lenore Fine and Jesse Remington, *The Corps of Engineers: Construction in the United States* (Washington, D.C.: Office of the Chief of Military History, 1972), 109–10.

3. David Noble, *America by Design: Science, Technology and the Rise of Corporate Capitalism* (New York: Knopf, 1977), 33–49; David Hounshell, *From the American System to Mass Production, 1800–1932: The Development of Manufacturing Technology in the United States* (Baltimore: Johns Hopkins University Press, 1984); Alfred Chandler, *The Visible Hand: The Managerial Revolution in American Business* (Cambridge, Mass.: Belknap, 1977), 282, 439.

4. Lincoln, *Lockwood Greene*, 1–49; Howard Emerson and Douglas Naehring, *Origins of Industrial Engineering: The Early Years of a Profession* (Norcross, Ga.: Industrial Engineering and Management Press, 1988); Noble, *America by Design*; Hounshell, *From the American System*; Chandler, *Visible Hand*.

5. James Munce, *Industrial Architecture: An Analysis of International Building Practice* (New York: F. W. Dodge, 1960), 9–11; Lindy Biggs, *The Rational Factory: Architecture, Technology and Work in America's Age of Mass Production* (Baltimore: Johns Hopkins University Press, 1996).

6. Fine and Remington, *Corps of Engineers*, 309–41.

7. William Enright, "Vast Construction of Plants Is Ahead," *New York Times*, September 22, 1940, F7.

8. Lincoln, *Lockwood Greene*, 705–20; Emerson and Naehring, *Origins of Industrial Engineering*; "Got Fee of $1,128,030 on Ordnance Works," *New York Times*, March 1, 1941, 6.

9. "H.K. Ferguson Co.," *Wall Street Journal*, August 28, 1941, 9; "Ferguson Firm Saves Month in Building Rubber Plant," *Wall Street Journal*, March 29, 1943, 12; "H.K. Ferguson Co. to Get 'E' Award for Work on Arsenal," *Wall Street Journal*, April 14, 1943, 11; "U.S. Detinning Capacity to Be Increased 67% by Expansion Program," *Wall Street Journal*, October 12, 1942, 5.

10. "All-Timber Warehouses Urged to End Shortage," *Wall Street Journal*, April 3, 1942, 14; "Research Must Solve Post-War Problems States H.K. Ferguson," *Wall Street Journal*, February 25, 1942, 9; "May Cut Costs 50%," *Wall Street Journal*, September 17, 1942, 5; "U.S. Warship Losses Replaced by New Buildings, Report Says," *Wall Street Journal*, April 2, 1943, 10; "U.S. to Increase Aluminum Output," *New York Times*, March 6, 1942, 29.

11. U.S. Congress, Senate, *Hearings before a Special Committee Investigating the Na-*

tional Defense Program, Part 6, 77th Congress, 1st Sess. (Washington, D.C.: Government Printing Office, 1941), 1914.

12. Fine and Remington, *Corps of Engineers*, 184–92.

13. U.S. Senate, *National Defense Program*, 1752; "S&P Celebrate 50 Years," *New York Times*, March 4, 1946, 32; Chemical Corps Association, *The Chemical Warfare Service in World War II* (New York: Rinehold, 1948), 20. For another case study see Rita Walsh and Duane Peter, *The World War II Ordnance Department's Government-Owned Contractor-Operated (GOCO) Industrial Facilities: Ravenna Ordnance Plant Historic Investigation* (Plano, Tex.: Geo-Marine, 1995).

14. U.S. Senate, *National Defense Program*, 1914–18.

15. Fine and Remington, *Corps of Engineers*, 135; also see 72, 130–43.

16. Responsibility for building of army production facilities shifted from the Quartermaster Department to the Corps of Engineers in December 1941.

17. U.S. Senate, *National Defense Program*, 1756–62.

18. U.S. Taking Arms Plant Site Now, Objectors Told," *Chicago Tribune*, September 25, 1940, 8; Fine and Remington, *Corps of Engineers*, 177–78.

19. "U.S. Taking Arms Plant Site Now."

20. Ibid.; Clayton Kirkpatrick, "Munitions Plant Towns to Avoid Hangover," *Chicago Tribune*, November 11, 1941, 8. For the army's wartime land acquisition programs see Fine and Remington, *Corps of Engineers*, 174–84; Smith, *Army and Economic Mobilization*, 441–44.

21. Fine and Remington, *Corps of Engineers*, 174–84; Smith, *Army and Economic Mobilization*, 441–44.

22. Mary Watter, *Illinois in the Second World War*, vol. 1, *The Production Front* (Springfield, Ill.: State of Illinois, 1952), 23–24, 248, 304. Also see Sarah Jo Peterson, *Planning the Home Front: Building Bombers and Communities at Willow Run* (Chicago: University of Chicago Press, 2013), 42–76; Kate Brown, *Plutopia: Nuclear Families, Atomic Cities, and the Great Soviet and American Plutonium Disasters* (New York: Oxford University Press, 2103), 16–18.

23. Kirkpatrick, "Munitions Plants Towns to Avoid Boom Hangover; "20,000 Builders to Get Jobs on Defense Works," *Chicago Tribune*, November 30, 1940, 23; Ward Walker, "Arms Plant Trade Booms 3 Towns," *Chicago Tribune*, February 16, 1941, S1; Watter, *Illinois*, 2:23–24, 248, 304; "Big Plant at Elwood Goes into Production," *Chicago Tribune*, July 13, 1941, 11; "Big Shell Plant Starts," *New York Times*, July 13, 1941, 23.

24. A firm partner, Francis Blossom, worked with the War Department evaluating potential defense contractors. The Truman Committee was charged with looking into allegations that Blossom participated in the determination of the Elwood contract. He was found not guilty. For the company's testimony see U.S. Senate, *National Defense Program*, 1756–62, 1913–37.

25. The list consisted of three types of business: purchased material and equipment, leased equipment, and subcontractors. The latter list had the subcontractor's name, address, and type of work performed. The other lists consisted of vendor, street address, product purchased or leased, and the cost or rental of the product.

26. For a similar story in an earlier period see Robert Lewis, *Chicago Made: Fac-*

tory Networks in the Industrial Metropolis (Chicago: University of Chicago Press, 2008), 117–40, 189–214.

27. "Chicago Firms to Help Build Defense Plant," *Chicago Tribune*, January 21, 1941, 21.

28. "Prospectus," October 1, 1943, Folder: General Motors Corp.—PL. 39—Melrose Park, ILL, vol. 1, October 1, 1943, thru December 31, 1945 (ILL 16), Box 127, Real Property Disposal Case files, RG 270, NARA—Chicago (hereafter Buick WAA files).

29. The Albert Kahn Associated Architects and Engineers Company was the leading industrial architectural firm in the country by the end of the 1930s. See Robert Lewis, "Redesigning the Workplace: The North American Factory in the Interwar Period," *Technology and Culture* 42 (2001): 670; "Buick to Start Its Big Aircraft Motor Plant Here Monday," *Chicago Tribune*, March 15, 1941, 1; "Let Steel Contract on Buick's Melrose Park Engine Plant," *Chicago Tribune*, February 14, 1941, 29.

30. "Two Aviation Engine Plants for Chicago," *Commerce*, February 1941, 40.

31. William Cunningham, *The Aircraft Industry: A Study in Industrial Location* (Los Angeles: Morrison, 1951), 91; Watters, *Illinois*, 2:24–25.

32. "Prospectus," Buick WAA files.

33. "Prospectus," and "Semi-monthly Status Report," September 30, 1943, Buick WAA files.

34. Lockwood Greene Engineers, "Plancor 39: Aviation Engine Plant, Defense Plant Corporation, Melrose Park, Illinois. Appraisal," August 26, 1944; and "Lockwood Green Engineers Inc. to DFC," September 9, 1944, Buick WAA files.

35. "$34,451,384 Order for Shell Loading Plant Let by Army," *Wall Street Journal*, November 9, 1940, 3; "Cuts Fee of Agent on War Plant Site," *New York Times*, February 21, 1941, 8.

36. Gail Farr and Brett Bostwick, *Shipbuilding at Cramp and Sons* (Philadelphia: Philadelphia Maritime Museum, 1991); Joel Davidson, *The Unsinkable Fleet: the Politics of U.S. Navy Expansion in World War II* (Annapolis: Naval Institute Press, 1996), 57; William Chaikin and Charles Coleman, *Shipbuilding Policies of the War Production Board, January 1942–November 1945* (Washington, D.C.: Civilian Production Administration, 1947); "Definite Program Formulated to Reopen Cramp's Shipyard," *Wall Street Journal*, July 16, 1940, 4; "Cramp's Shipyard," *Wall Street Journal*, July 26 1940, 2; "Cramp Shipyard," *Wall Street Journal*, August 31, 1940, 4; "Naval Contracts Offered to Cramp's," *New York Times*, August 7, 1940, 3.

37. Orville Dwyer, "A Pasture into Shipyard in Just 8 Months," *Chicago Tribune*, January 24, 1943, 11; James Reston, "Ships That Grow on the Prairie," *New York Times*, June 20, 1943, SM10; "Summary of Chicago Bridge and Iron Co—Nobs 462 Plant Facilities for N.I.R.A. Program," March 1949, Folder: Chicago Bridge and Iron Plant, Seneca, Illinois—Nobs-462, Box, 45, Real Property Disposal Case files, RG 270, NARA—Chicago.

38. Civilian Production Association, *War Industrial Facilities*; "G. T. Horton Headed Bridge Concern, 71," *New York Times*, March 20, 1945, 19; Dwyer, "Pasture Turns into a Shipyard"; "Boat-a-Week Keeps Seneca Yard Hustling," *Chicago Tribune*, June 6, 1943, B7; Reston, "Ships That Grow"; "End of War Job Shrinks Illinois 'City,'" *Washington Post*, June 3, 1945, M14; "Chicago Bridge and Iron Company, Seneca, Illinois," August 11, 1948,

Folder: Chicago Bridge and Iron Plant, Seneca, Illinois, Nobs-462, Mr. Buck-Work File, Box 45, Real Property Disposal Case files, RG 270, NARA—Chicago.

39. "Chicago Bridge and Iron Company, Seneca, Illinois" August 11, 1948. For the advertisement see "Display Ad 6," *Washington Post*, June 25, 1946, 6.

40. Fair value refers to the price obtained for the industrial property given market conditions and the particularities of the facilities themselves, while reproduction cost refers to the cost of building the facilities given typical market conditions.

41. Day and Zimmerman, "Report No. 4605, vol. 1; Valuation Report on Property Identified as Nobs 462, Chicago Bridge and Iron Company (Shipbuilding Division) Plant, Located as Seneca, Illinois," November 13, 1946, 2, 3, Folder: Chicago Bridge and Iron Plant, Seneca, Illinois—Nobs-462, Work File, Box 44, Real Property Disposal Case files, RG 270, NARA—Chicago.

42. Day and Zimmerman, "Report No. 4605," 10, 18. Also see Watter, *Illinois*, 2:89–91.

43. Office of Community War Services, "Seneca, Illinois: 'The Prairie Shipyard,'" February 1944, 2, 5, War Records and Research Federal Papers; Illinois War Council papers, RG 518, ISA; emphasis is mine.

44. Office of Community War Services, "Seneca, Illinois," 2, 5; Day and Zimmerman, "Report No. 4605," 15. Also see Watter, *Illinois*, 2:307–9.

45. Fine and Remington, *Corps of Engineers*, 155.

Chapter 6. The Disposal Regime

1. Gregory Hooks, "The Weakness of Strong Theories: The U.S. State's Dominance of the World War II Investment Process," *American Sociological Review* 58 (1993): 45.

2. Gerald White, *Billions for Defense: Government Financing by the Defense Plant Corporation during World War II* (Tuscaloosa: University of Alabama Press, 1980), 90–93.

3. Louis Cain and George Neumann, "Planning for Peace: The Surplus Property Act of 1944," *Journal of Economic History* 41 (1981): 129–30. The report was turned into a publication: A. Kaplan, *The Liquidation of War Production* (New York: McGraw-Hill, 1944).

4. "Orderly Disposal of Federal War Plants to Industry Urged," *Chicago Tribune*, December 6, 1943, 26.

5. Clifton Mack and James Knox, "Disposition of Government Property," *Harvard Business Review* 22 (1943): 54–63; John Sumner, "The Disposition of Surplus War Property," *American Economic Review* 34 (1944): 458–71. Also see Harry Tosdal, "Disposal of War Surpluses," *Harvard Business Review* 22 (1944): 346–57; Edwin Martin, "The Disposition of Government Financed Industrial Facilities in the Postwar Period," *American Economic Review* 33 (1943): 128–36.

6. "Studies Disposal of War Surpluses," *New York Times*, April 16, 1944, RE1.

7. "Sale of U.S. Holdings Held Vast Problem," *Chicago Tribune*, April 22, 1944, 19.

8. White, *Billions for Defense*, 90–93.

9. Sumner, "Disposition of Surplus War Property," 360–65.

10. For the politics of the disposal agencies see Harold Stein, "The Disposal of the Aluminum Plants," in *Public Administration and Policy Development: A Case Book*, ed. Harold Stein (New York: Harcourt, Brace, 1952), 313–61; White, *Billions for Defense*, 88–112.

11. The SWPA became the Surplus Property Board in October 1944, which became the Surplus Property Administration in September 1945. This was replaced by the WAA in March 1946. The WAA was abolished in June 1949. Cain and Neumann, "Planning for Peace."

12. Surplus Property Act of 1944, October 3, 1944, Ch. 479, 58, Stat. 765; Cain and Neumann, "Planning for Peace," 129–35.

13. White, *Billions for Defense*, 94–98.

14. Colonel R. Tatlow, "Memorandum for the Director, Readjustment Division, Headquarters, Army Services Forces," p. 1, Folder: 600.9 (facilities list and data), September 1945–, Subject File of the Central Office of Real Property, 1946–1949, 600.3 to 600.9 (Facility list and data), Box 67, RG 270, NARA—College Park, Md. Unsurprisingly, after the war, Tatlow took a job in the industry as president of Abbott, Merkt and Co., a New York City industrial engineering firm.

15. Martin, "Disposition of Government Financed," 136.

16. Tatlow, "Memorandum for the Director."

17. Surplus Property Administration, *The Liquidation of War Surpluses: Quarterly Progress Report, Fourth Quarter 1945* (Washington: Government Printing Office, 1945), 18–23.

18. WAA, *The Integration of Surplus Proposal: Quarterly Progress Report, First Quarter, 1946* (Washington, D.C.: WAA, 1946), 42; WAA, *The Acceleration of Surplus Proposal: Quarterly Progress Report, Second Quarter, 1946* (Washington, D.C.: WAA, 1946), 37. A small number of state-owned industrial properties made their way to public agencies, groups, and organizations. The majority, however, were sold to private interests. This chapter focuses on the disposal of industrial property to private interests, unless otherwise noted.

19. "Monthly Report, October 1947," November 26, 1947, Box 84, Subject File, 1946–1949, Office of Information, RG 270, NARA—College Park, Md.; "Army, Navy to Free 386 Surplus Plants," *New York Times*, August 24, 1945; WAA, *Quarterly Progress Report: Second Quarter, 1949* (Washington: WAA, 1949), 3–4.

20. "Government-Owned Industrial Plants for Sale or Lease," *Wall Street Journal*, September 17, 1945, 8.

21. "Government-Owned Steel Plant for Sale or Lease," *New York Times*, June 22, 1946, 10.

22. White, *Billions for Defense*, 100.

23. Reconstruction Finance Corporation, *Second Advanced Listing of Government-Owned Industrial Plants to Be Disposed of by Reconstruction Finance Corporation* (Washington, D.C.: Government Printing Office, 1945), n.p.

24. WAA, *Plant Finder: A Buyer's Guide to Government-Owned Industrial Plants* (Washington, D.C.: Office of Real Property Disposal, WAA, April 1949), n.p.

25. WAA, *Planning for Liquidation: Quarterly Progress Report, Fourth Quarter, 1947* (Washington, D.C.: WAA, 1948), 13, 14.

26. WAA, *Quarterly Progress Report: First Quarter, 1948* (Washington, D.C.: WAA, 1948), 7–8. For the Garland plant see "WAA Will Auction Two Dozen Plants," *New York Times*, October 4, 1948, 30; "To Auction War Plant," *New York Times*, July 20, 1948, 35. For other cases see "To Auction War Plant," *New York Times*, October 31, 1948, R1.

27. WAA, *Quarterly Progress Report, Fourth Quarter, 1948* (Washington, D.C.: WAA, 1949), 9.

28. WAA, *How to Buy or Lease Surplus Real Estate* (Washington, D.C.: WAA, 1946).

29. Orin Burley, *Industrial Expansion and Government Plant Disposal: Fourth Federal Reserve District* (Cleveland: Federal Reserve Bank of Cleveland, 1945), 5–6; Robert Cuff, *The War Industries Board: Business-Government Relations during World War 1* (Baltimore: Johns Hopkins University Press, 1973).

30. Michael Hogan, *A Cross of Iron: Harry S. Truman and the Origins of the National Security State, 1945–1954* (New York: Cambridge University Press, 1998). Also see Robert Cuff, "Ferdinand Eberstadt, the National Security Resources Board, and the Search for Integrated Mobilization Planning, 1947–1948," *Public Historian* 7 (1985): 37–52; Alfred Sander, "Truman and the National Security Council: 1945–1947," *Journal of American History* 59 (1972): 369–88; Daniel Yergin, *Shattered Peace: The Origins of the Cold War and the National Security State* (Boston: Houghton Mifflin, 1977).

31. White, *Billions for Defense*, 110.

32. Surplus War Property Administration, *Surplus War Property*, vol. 1, *The Basic Facts*, and vol. 2, *The Basic Procedures* (Washington, D.C.: Public Affairs Press, 1944). The report noted that although the military designated their property as standby, this did not have congressional approval.

33. Office of the Chief of Engineers, "Report in War-Department-Owned Nitric Acid Facilities," p. 7, August 30, 1945, Folder: Postwar Possibilities for Utilization of War Department-Owned Industrial Facilities, Box I213, RG 156, NARA—College Park, Md.

34. Philip Dodd, "U.S. Proposes 'Reserve' War Plants in City," *Chicago Tribune*, October 30, 1945, 12; White, *Billions for Defense*, 110.

35. Munitions Board, *Report to the Congress on the National Industrial Reserve under Public Law 833, 80th Congress* (Washington, D.C.: Government Printing Office, 1949).

36. Army Service Forces, "Industrial Installations," 3.

37. "Truman Aids Plan for Preparedness," *New York Times*, June 20, 1946, 24.

38. "Sixty War Plants Will Be Retained," *New York Times*, December 23, 1946, 11.

39. Bess Furman, "Universal Training a Must, Patterson Warns Women," *New York Times*, January 27, 1947, 1.

40. "Army Seeks Caves, Mines for Underground Plants," *New York Times*, August 4, 1947, 1.

41. Munitions Board, *Report to the Congress*, 1.

42. "18 Industrialists Aid Mobilization," *New York Times*, March 31, 1947, 27.

43. Munitions Board, *Report to the Congress*, 1.

44. Sections 2 and 5, "An Act to Authorize Leases of Real or Personal Property by the War and Navy Department, and for Other Purposes," Public Law 364, 80th Congress, August 5, 1947.

45. Section 5, Public Law 364, 80th Congress. These facilities fell into three types: those operated by private corporations, those run by the military, and those that were no longer operating.

46. WAA, *Planning for Liquidation: Quarterly Progress Report, Fourth Quarter, 1947* (Washington, D.C.: WAA, 1948), 18–19; Munitions Board, *Report to the Congress*, 1.

47. U.S. Congress, Senate, *Hearings before the Committee on Armed Services, Eightieth*

Congress, Second Session on S. 2554, A Bill to Promote the Common Defense by Providing for the Retention and Maintenance of a National Reserve of Industrial Productive Capacity, and for Other Purposes (Washington, D.C.: Government Printing Office, 1948), 5.

48. Robert Young, "Halt Sale of War Plants: Plan Survey for Possible Conversion," *Chicago Tribune*, April 9, 1948, 1.

49. "200 U.S. Plants Being Studied for Use in War," *Chicago Tribune*, April 25, 1948, 12.

50. Samuel Tower, "Surplus Sales Ban Urged for Defense in an 'Emergency,'" *New York Times*, April 25, 1948, 1.

51. "Board Stops the Sale of 100 War Plants for Possible Use in the Emergency 'Reserve,'" *New York Times*, May 6, 1948, 19.

52. John Norris, "Committee Votes Plant Reserve Bill," *Washington Post*, May 26, 1948, 3.

53. "An Act to Promote the Common Defense by Providing for the Retention and Maintenance of a National Reserve of Productive Capacity, and for Other Purposes," Section 2, Public Law 883, 80th Congress (hereafter National Industrial Reserve Act).

54. Munitions Board, *Report to the Congress*, 2; White, *Billions for Defense*, 112.

55. National Industrial Reserve Act, Section 10.

56. WAA, *Quarterly Progress Report: Fourth Quarter, 1948*, 9–10.

57. "National Industrial Plant Reserve status as of March 1, 1949," 600.3 to 600.9 (Facility list and data), Box 67, Subject File of the Central Office of Real Property, 1946–1949, RG 270, NARA—College Park, Md.; Munitions Board, *Report to the Congress*, 5–7.

58. "Industry Readied for Mobilization," *New York Times*, July 7, 1950, 29.

59. General Services Administration, *Annual Report of the Administrator of General Services for the Year Ending June 30, 1950* (Washington, D.C.: General Services Administration, 1950), 20–21.

60. Task Force on Use and Disposal of Federal Surplus Property, *Report on Use and Disposal of Federal Surplus Property* (Washington, D.C.: Government Printing Office, 1955), 182.

61. SWPA, *Surplus War Property*, 1.

62. Melyvn Leffler, *A Preponderance of Power: National Security, the Truman Administration, and the Cold War* (Stanford: Stanford University Press, 1992), 13.

63. Task Force on Use and Disposal of Federal Surplus Property, *Report*, 187–88.

Chapter 7. Disposing of Chicago's War Factories

1. "Last B-29 Motor Turned Out by Dodge-Chicago," *Chicago Tribune*, September 1, 1945, 19; "3 Studebaker Aircraft Units to Shut in June," *Chicago Tribune*, May 12, 1945, 19; Perry Duis and Scott La France, *We've Got a Job to Do: Chicagoans and World War II* (Chicago: Chicago Historical Society, 1992), 115–16; "War Jobs to End This Week for 15,000 Workers," *Chicago Tribune*, August 19, 1945, 9.

2. Ernest Olrich, "Disposing of Surplus War Goods and Properties," *Commerce*, July 1944, 23–24, 26.

3. Steven Fenberg, *Unprecedented Power: Jesse Jones, Capitalism, and the Common Good* (College Station: Texas A&M University Press, 2011), 488, 491; Gerald White, *Billions for Defense: Government Financing by the Defense Plant Corporation during World War II* (University: University of Alabama Press, 1980), 100–101.

4. WAA, "Industrial Facilities under Lease (in Whole or in Part), June 1, 1949," General Services Administration, Records Relating to Industrial Facilities under Lease, 1942–1956, Box 4, Records of the Reconstruction Finance Corporation, RG 234, NARA—College Park, Md. Hundreds of statistical reports and inventories on state-owned industrial sites are filed in the RFC and WAA records at NARA. The first and last quarterly reports are Surplus Property Board, *Surplus Property: Quarterly Progress Report* (Washington, D.C.: Government Printing Office, 1945), n.p.; and WAA, *Quarterly Progress Report: Second Quarter, 1949* (Washington, D.C.: WAA, 1949).

5. See the folders in boxes 231 and 232 in the Real Property Disposal Case Files, RG 270, NARA—Chicago.

6. WAA, "Real Property Report No. 14," October 25 1948, Folder: 319.1 Activity Reports, October '48–December '49, Box 44, Subject File of the Central Office of Real Property, 1946–1949, Activity Reports (319.1), RG 270, NARA—College Park, Md.

7. War Assets Administration, "Historical Report, Chicago Region," ca. April 1949, Folder: Historical Report—Chicago Region, Box 21; Chicago-Cincinnati, Office of Administration Services, Historical Unit, Historical Records 1943–1949, RG 270; NARA—College Park, Md.

8. WAA, "Real Property Report No. 14."

9. U.S. Congress, House, Committee on Expenditures in the Executive Departments, Investigations, Disposition of Surplus Property, *Hearings before the Surplus Property Subcommittee of the Committee on Expenditures in the Executive Departments*, 80th Congress, 2nd Sess. Pursuant to H. Res. 90 and H. Res. 100, Part 8 (Washington D.C.: Government Printing Office, 1948), 2185.

10. "War Jobs to End," 9.

11. The files for plancor 1293 can be found in Box 160: Real Property Disposal Case Files, WAA records, RG 270, NARA—Chicago; and Box 8: Records of the Real Property Review Board, 1946–1949, NARA-College Park, Md.

12. "Interest Rises in Chicago Area War Factories," *Chicago Tribune*, July 29, 1945, B14.

13. "10 Major War Plants Remain for WAA Sale," *Chicago Tribune*, September 14, 1947, 9.

14. WAA, "Special Report No. 2: Industrial Real Property—WAA Acquisitions, Disposal and Available for Disposal Activity and Returns for Sales by Zones and Regions and Agencies from Which Acquired as of October 31, 1947," p. 1, November 26, 1947, Box 84, Office of Information, Subject File, 1946–1949, RG 270, NARA—College Park, Md.

15. "Memo," April 13, 1949, Folder: Plancor 40—Studebaker Corporation, Chicago, Illinois, Box 232, Real Property Disposal Case Files, RG 270, NARA—Chicago.

16. WAA, "Historical Report, Chicago Region" [ca. April 1949], pp. 1–2, Box 21, Folder, Historical Report—Chicago Region; Office of Administration Services, Historical Unit, Historical Records 1943–1949, RG 270, NARA—College Park.

17. "Interest Rises in Chicago Area."

18. "Surplus Disposal Stirs Wide Protest," *New York Times*, June 8, 1946, 34.

19. WAA, *The Acceleration of Surplus Proposal: Quarterly Progress Report, Second Quarter, 1946* (Washington, D.C.: WAA, 1946), 37.

20. WAA, "Historical Report, Chicago Region," 3–8.

21. WAA, *Analysis of Progress for the Calendar Year 1948* (Washington, D.C.: WAA—Region 5, 1949), n.p., Folder: Analysis of Program, 1948, WAA Region #5, Real Property Analysis, Regional Histories, Chicago–Cincinnati, Box 21, Office of Administration Services, Historical Unit, Historical Records 1943–1949, RG 270, NARA—College Park, Md.

22. WAA, "Historical Report, Chicago Region," 3–8; WAA Executive Order Better Sales Methods," *Chicago Tribune*, April 14, 1947, 7; "Chicago WAA Begins Move to Navy Pier," *Chicago Tribune*, December 4, 1947, 46; "WAA Rents Navy Pier Space for Offices Here," *Chicago Tribune*, February 2, 1947, 4.

23. "10 Major War Plants Remain," 7.

24. "Valuation Report," November 29, 1949, Box 51, Folder: Postwar Possibilities for Utilization of Government-Owned Industrial Facilities, Plancor 792, Chrysler Corporation (Dodge Plant), Chicago, Cook County, Illinois, RG 270, NARA—Chicago.

25. "Half of Surplus Industry Units Held of No Use," *Chicago Tribune*, November 26, 1946, 29.

26. "10 Major War Plants Remain," 7.

27. "WAA Starts Drive to Sell 48 Plants," *New York Times*, October 31, 1946, 48.

28. "Harry Cutmore & Associates Inc. Report," July 19, 1946, 1–2, 6, Box 74, Folder: Continental Ordnance Corp., East Chicago, Ind. PL. 1220 Ind. 57, Appraisal Data, Real Property Disposal Case Files, RG 270, NARA—College Park, Md.

29. Burnham and Hammond, Inc., "Appraisal: Replacement Cost as of Today: Land, Buildings, Equipment Exclusive of Overtime, Bonuses, Etc.," March 1945, Box 3, Real Property Disposal Case Files, RG 270, NARA—Chicago (hereafter Ahlberg WAA case).

30. Edwin S. Corman Inc., Engineers [Cleveland], "WAA, American Steel Foundries Cast Armor Plant, Appraisal, Volume 1: Valuation Report," p. 8, March 26, 1947, and "WAA American Steel Foundries Cast Armor Plant, Appraisal, Volume 2: Reproduction Cost of Property," March 26, 1947, Box 14, Real Property Disposal Case Files, RG 270, NARA—Chicago.

31. Day and Zimmerman, "Report No. 4218 Covering an Appraisal of the Defense Plant Corporation Property Identified as Plancor No. 1235, Chicago, Illinois," January 9, 1945, Box 28, Folder: Bendix Aviation Corp., Chicago, ILL-1235 (3 of 10), Real Property Disposal Case Files, RG 270, NARA—Chicago.

32. "Harry Cutmore & Associates Inc. Report."

33. "Valuation Report," November 29, 1949, Folder: Chrysler-Dodge Corp., Chicago, ILL. PL 792 and Folder: Summary of Report No. 4401–B Covering an Appraisal of the Reconstruction Finance Corporation Property Identified as Plancor No. 792—Part 2, Chrysler Corporation—Dodge Chicago Plant, Chicago, Box 51, Real Property Disposal Case Files, RG 270, NARA—Chicago.

34. WAA, *The Economic Outlook and the Market for Surplus Property* (Washington, D.C.: WAA, March 1947), 7.

35. "Dun and Bradstreet Report on 20th Century Glove Co.," June 11, 1945, Box 2, Real Property Disposal Case Files, RG 270, NARA—Chicago; "Dun and Bradstreet Report on Allied Control Co. Inc.," May 18, 1945, Box 5, Real Property Disposal Case Files, RG 270, NARA—Chicago.

36. "Memo to Plant Disposal Section from Real Estate Unit," March 1, 1946, Folder:

Bendix Aviation Corp., Chicago, ILL-1235 (5 of 10), Box 28, Real Property Disposal Case Files, RG 270, NARA—Chicago (hereafter Box 28, Bendix WAA); "Belmont Radio to the RFC, December 11, 1945, Box 28, Bendix WAA.

37. White, *Billions for Defense*, 101–2.

38. WAA, "National Industrial Plant Reserve Status as of March 1, 1949," Subject File of the Central Office of Real Property, 1946–1949, 600.3 to 600.9 (facility list and data), Box 67, RG 270, NARA—College Park, Md.

39. "Memo to the Real Property Review Board," January 25, 1947, Folder: Tantalum Defense Corporation, North Chicago, Ill. (R-ILL-96) Plancor 495, Box 236, Real Property Disposal Case Files, RG 270, NARA—Chicago (hereafter Tantalum WAA).

40. "Zone Administrator to the Chairman, Real Property Review Board," June 5, 1947, Folder: Howard Foundry Company, Inc. Plancor 1170, Chicago, Illinois, Box 7, Records of the Real Property Review Board, 1946–1949, RG 270, NARA—College Park, Md. (hereafter Howard WAA).

41. "Memo to the General Board," p. 3, July 15, 1948, Howard WAA.

42. "Memo to the General Board," May 28, 1948, Howard WAA files. Also see "Minutes of the Meeting of July 25, 1948," p. 1, Folder: WAA Board Actions July–Aug–Sept 1948, WAA Board Actions, 1947–1948, Box 15, Records of the Real Property Review Board, 1946–1949, RG 270, NARA—College Park, Md.

43. S. Powell Warren, "Engineer's Summary Report," p. 2, October 15, 1945, Tantalum WAA.

44. "Memo to the Real Property Review Board," January 24, 1947, Tantalum WAA.

45. "John Steelman to Robert Littlejohn," October 23, 1946, Tantalum WAA.

46. "Minutes of Meeting of January 24, 1947," Folder: Board January 24, 1947, Box 14, General Board Action Files, 1946–1949, January 21–28, 1947, RG 270, NARA—College Park, Md.

47. H. Whitaker, J. Willard, and H. Pond, "Postwar Possibilities for Utilization of War Department-Owned Industrial Facilities: Kankakee Ordnance Works, Joliet Arsenal," February 15, 1946, Box I214, RG 156, NARA—College Park, Md.; Alonzo White, "Potentials of War Department-Owned Sulphuric Acid Facilities," August 27, 1945, Folder: Postwar Possibilities for Utilization of War Department-Owned Industrial Facilities, Box I213, RG 156, NARA—College Park, Md.; Army Service Forces, "Industrial Installations," 29.

48. Office of the Chief of Engineers, "Memorandum: Study of Sulphuric and Nitric Acid Production and Utilization," August 30, 1945, Folder: Postwar Possibilities for Utilization of War Department-Owned Industrial Facilities, Box I213, RG 156, NARA—College Park, Md.

49. White, "Potentials of War Department."

50. Alonzo White, "Sulphuric Acid: Current Position and Outlook," *Chemical Engineering News* 23 (1945): 1154–59; Alonzo White, "Production, Consumption, and Stocks by Market Areas in the U.S., 1943–1944," *Chemical Engineering News* 23 (1945): 1334–35.

51. Army Service Forces, "Industrial Installations Recommended for Retention in Postwar Military Establishment [sic]," p. 18, no date, Box 172, Post WWI Divisions, Services and Other Units, RG 156, NARA—College Park, Md.

52. "U.S. Will Make Fertilizer in 17 War Plants," *Chicago Tribune*, August 27, 1946, 25. See "Army to Close 8 Fertilizer Making Units," *Chicago Tribune*, January 6, 1950, B11.

53. Harold Arbeen, "Joliet Group Is Munitions Boss of Army," *Chicago Tribune*, May 31, 1951, C8.

54. Arbeen, "Joliet Group"; Harold Arbeen, "Huge Arsenal at Joliet Does Big Job Again," *Chicago Tribune*, June 3, 1951, A9; "Outlay Planned to Rehabilitate Army TNT Unit," *Chicago Tribune*, July 7, 1952, C6.

Chapter 8. The Site Politics of Defense Factory Disposal

1. Nicholas Blomley, "Law, Property, and the Geography of Violence," *Annals of the Association of American Geographers* 93 (2003): 86–107; Lynn Staeheli and Don Mitchell, *The People's Property? Power, Politics, and the Public* (New York: Routledge, 2008); Franz von Benda-Beckmann, Keebet von Benda-Beckmann, and Melanie Wiber, "The Properties of Property," in *Changing Properties of Property*, ed. Franz von Benda-Beckmann, Keebet von Benda-Beckmann, and Melanie Wiber (New York: Berghahn Books, 2006), 1–39.

2. Ray Hudson, *Producing Places* (New York: Guildford, 2001), 255–85; Doreen Massey, "The Conceptualization of Place," in *A Place in the World? Place, Culture and Globalization*, ed. Doreen Massey and Pat Jess, 2nd ed. (London: Macmillan, 1995), 59–69.

3. "Memorandum to General Board," ca. June 1948, Accession Number: 291–56A-0244, Kropp Forge Company, Records of the Chicago Regional office, Real Property Case Files, 1952–1957, RG 291, NARA—Chicago.

4. "Memorandum to the General Board," February 24, 1948, Folder: Kropp Forge Aviation Company, Cicero, Illinois, Appraisals, vols. 1 & 2, PL. 1293, Box 160: Real Property Disposal Case Files, RG 270, NARA—Chicago (hereafter Kropp file).

5. "Kropp Forge Company," *Wall Street Journal*, September 15, 1948, 11.

6. "Letter from Roy Kropp to the WAA," July 26, 1948, Accession Number: 291–56A-0244, Kropp Forge Company, Records of the Chicago Regional office, Real Property Case Files, 1952–1957, RG 291, NARA—Chicago (hereafter Kropp FPRS file); "Memorandum to the General Board," August 10, 1948, Kropp file.

7. "Chattel Mortgage," December 10, 1948, Kropp FPRS file.

8. David Hart, *Forged Consensus: Science, Technology, and Economic Policy in the United States, 1921–1953* (Princeton: Princeton University Press, 1998); Daniel Yergin, *Shattered Peace: The Origins of the Cold War and the National Security State* (Boston: Houghton Mifflin, 1977); Jeffery Dorwart, *Eberstadt and Forrestal: A National Security Partnership, 1909–1949* (College Station: Texas A&M University Press, 1991); Douglas Stuart, *Creating the National Security State: A History of the Law That Transformed America* (Princeton: Princeton University Press, 2008); Elizabeth Fones-Wolf, *Selling Free Enterprise: The Business Assault on Labor and Liberalism, 1945–1960* (Urbana: University of Illinois Press, 1994).

9. "Memorandum to the Real Property Review Board," December 18, 1947, Kropp file; "Memorandum to the Real Property Review Board," May 21, 1948, Kropp file.

10. "Memorandum to the Real Property Review Board," May 28, 1948, Kropp file.

11. Michael Sherry, *In the Shadow of War: The United States since the 1930s* (New Haven: Yale University Press, 1995), 142.

12. Hanson Baldwin, "Mobilizing Industry," *New York Times*, April 21, 1946, 29.

13. Kenneth Warren, *The American Steel Industry, 1850–1970: A Geographical Interpretation* (Pittsburgh: University of Pittsburgh Press, 1973).

14. Ralph Fogg, "Survey of Facilities of the Iron and Steel Industry," December 7, 1944, Folder: Reports—Real Property Acquisitions, Box 84, Reports, Monthly Progress (319.1), Reports, Real Property (319.1), Subject File 1946–1949, RG 270, NARA—College Park, Md.; Surplus Property Administration, *War Plants Disposal: Joint Hearings before the Subcommittee on Surplus Property of the Committee on Military Affairs and the Industrial Reorganization Subcommittee of the Special Committee on Postwar Economic Policy and Planning* (Washington, D.C.: Government Printing Office, 1946); Arthur Manley, "Disposal Plan for Iron and Steel Plants and Facilities," March 4, 1948, 602 Disposal Schedules to 602 Ordnance Plants, Box 77, Subject File of the Central Office of Real Property, 1946–1949, RG 270, NARA—College Park, Md.; "Iron and Steel Plants Disposal Status as of 12/31/50," Folder: War Assets Administration Board Actions 1946, Board Actions Jan.–Feb.–March 1947, Box 14, Youngstown Sheet and Tube Co., East Chicago, Indiana, to War Assets Administration—Board Actions, 1946–1947, Records of the Real Property Review Board, 1946–1949, RG 270, NARA—College Park, Md.

15. Fogg, "Survey of Facilities"; United States, Surplus Property Administration, *Report to Congress in Disposal of Government Iron and Steel Plants and Facilities* (Washington, D.C.: Government Printing Office, 1945), 5–10.

16. Gerald White, *Billions for Defense: Government Financing by the Defense Plant Corporation during World War II* (University: University of Alabama Press, 1980), 107–8; James Cook, *The Marketing of Surplus War Property* (Washington, D.C.: Public Affairs Press, 1948), 19–21; "Iron and Steel Plants."

17. "Memo to the Chicago Regional Real Property Disposal Board," October 28, 1946, Folder: Republic Steel Corp (Plancor 422), South Chicago, Illinois, Box 8, Real Property Review Board, 1946–1949 records, RG 270, NARA—College Park, Md. (hereafter Republic file); "Republic Steel to the WAA," April 30, 1946, "Republic Steel to the WAA," Sept 30, 1946, and "Memo to Real Property Review Board," Nov. 1, 1946, Republic file.

18. U.S. Congress, Senate, Committee on Military Affairs, *War-Plant Disposal: Bids for Geneva and South Chicago Steel Plants: Report of the Surplus Property Subcommittee of the Committee on Military Affairs* (Washington, D.C.: Government Printing Office, 1946); "Bids on Steel Plant at Chicago Rejected," *New York Times*, June 1, 1946, 25.

19. "Memo to Real Property Review Board," November 1, 1946, Republic file. See *New York Times*, February 15, 1946, 40, and June 22, 1946, 10; *Wall Street Journal*, September 6, 1946.

20. "Memo to Real Property Review Board," p. 16, December 20, 1946, Republic file.

21. Ibid.

22. "Prospectus," October 1, 1943; Folder: Youngstown Sheet and Tube Company, East Chicago, Indiana, (Disposal Data) vol. 1, October 1943 thru December 31, 1947, IND. 42, PL. 328, Box 259, Real Property Disposal Case Files, RG 270, NARA—Chicago (hereafter Youngstown file); "Engineer's Report," (ca. spring 1947), Youngstown file; "Memo to the Real Property Review Board," June 12, 1947, Youngstown file.

23. "Engineer's Report"; "Memo to the Real Property Review Board," June 12, 1947, Youngstown file; "Prospectus", Youngstown file.

24. "Memo to the Real Property Review Board," June 12, 1947, 3, Youngstown file.

25. "E. G. Rhett to J. Mauthe," June 20, 1947, Youngstown file; "Memo to the Real Property Review Board," September 3, 1947, Youngstown file; "Inter-WAA Letter," November 18, 1947, Youngstown file.

26. "Memo to Files," May 25, 1948, Youngstown file; Folder: Youngstown Sheet and Tube Company, East Chicago, Indiana, (Disposal Data), vol. 2, January 1948, IND. 42, PL. 328, Youngstown file.

27. "Memo to General Board," June 10, 1948, pp. 1, 2, Youngstown file; Folder: Youngstown Sheet and Tube Company, East Chicago, Indiana, (Final Disposition), IND. 42, PL. 328, Youngstown file.

28. "WAA Memo," August 30, 1948, Youngstown file; Folder: Youngstown Sheet and Tube Company, East Chicago, Indiana (Final Disposition), IND. 42, PL. 328, Youngstown file; "McLouth Steel Corp. Will Build Integrated Mill in Detroit Suburb," *Wall Street Journal*, October 23, 1948, 3.

29. "Declaration of Surplus Real Property," 8 January 1948, Box 28, Folder: Bendix Aviation Corp., Chicago, ILL-1235 (12 of 13), Real Property Disposal Case Files, RG 270, NARA—Chicago (hereafter Bendix file); "Day and Zimmerman Report," January 9, 1945."

30. "Kenneth Royall to the RFC," December 1, 1945, Box 28, Bendix file.

31. Belmont Radio convinced the RFC and the War Department that plancor 1235 should be used for industrial purposes rather than military ones. There is nothing in the archives to contradict this point. "Proposal of Belmont Radio Corporation," February 27, 1946, Box 28, Bendix file.

32. Consolidated Grocers was created in 1945 by merging several companies, one of which was Sprague, Warner, the original occupant at 505 Sacramento. Before the war, National Industries was called National Mineral. It changed its name to Helene Curtis in October 1946.

33. "Nathan Summer to the RFC," December 11, 1945; "Walter Murphy to Senator Joseph O'Mahoney," January 30, 1946; "Proposal of Belmont Radio Corporation," February 27, 1946; "Walter Murphy to the Department of Justice," March 29, 1946; all in Box 28 of the Bendix file.

34. "S. Kennedy to the WAA," February 27, 1946, and "Nathan Cummings to the WAA," March 13, 1946, both in Box 28, Bendix file.

35. "Memo to the General Board," ca. March 1948, Box 28, Bendix file.

36. "Harold Rosen to the RFC," December 11, 1945, Box 28, Bendix file.

37. "Claude Wells to Plant Disposal Section," March 1, 1946, Box 28, Bendix file.

38. "Senator George Radcliffe to O. Beasley," March 2, 1946, Box 28, Bendix file.

39. "Scott Lucas to E. B. Gregory," March 11, 1946, Box 28, Bendix file.

40. "Walter Murphy to Joseph O'Mahoney," January 30, 1946; "Walter Murphy to Walter Maloney," February 24, 1946; "Walter Maloney to John Snyder," February 26, 1946; "William Link to George Snyder," February 28, 1946; "C. Wayland Brooks to Joseph O'Brien," March 6, 1946; all in Box 28, Bendix file.

41. "F. Berquist to the Board," March 4, 1946, Box 28, Bendix file.

42. "John O'Brien to Senator George Radcliffe," March 13, 1946, Box 28, Bendix file; "Harold Rosen to Robert Littlejohn," June 6, 1947, Box 29, Bendix file.

43. "Rosen to Littlejohn," Box 28, Bendix file; "Memo to the Real Property Review

Board," August 12, 1947, Box 28, Bendix file; "Minutes of Meeting of August 12, 1947," Box 34, Bendix file.

44. "Harold Rosen to Joseph Burke," March 18, 1948; "Fact sheet," March 25, 1948; "Kraft Foods to the WAA," March 25, 1948; all in Box 28, Bendix file.

45. "Transcript of Proceedings of Special Meeting of the General Board," April 9, 1948, and "Director of the Industrial Division to Regional Director, Chicago," May 6, 1948, both in Box 28, Bendix file.

46. "Complaint in Ejectment," September 12, 1946, Civil Case File 46 C 1784, Ahlberg Bearing Company vs. Reconstruction Finance Corporation, Civil Case Files, 1938–1980, U.S. District Court records, Northern District of Illinois at Chicago, RG 21, National Archives—Chicago (hereafter Ahlberg vs. RFC). The case was moved from the state to the U.S. District Court for the Northern District of Illinois, Eastern Division, in early November.

47. "F. O. Burkholder to the DPC," February 12, 1942, Ahlberg vs. RFC. This is the first document in the file. It is unknown whether Ahlberg approached the army or the navy before talking with the DPC. We also do not know if the company had spoken to the DFC before the February 12 letter. Regardless, it was in the winter of 1942 that the seeds of the court conflict were sown.

48. "F. O. Burkholder to the DPC," March 5, 1942, Ahlberg vs. RFC.

49. "Complaint in Ejectment," p. 5, Ahlberg vs. RFC; "Lump Sum Form of Construction Contract for Defense Plant Corporation—Plancor 653," May 4, 1942, Ahlberg vs. RFC. Phipps owned and operated one of Chicago's industrial districts, the Kenwood Industrial District. See Robert Lewis, "Planned Districts in Chicago: Firms, Networks and Boundaries, 1900–1940," *Journal of Planning History* 3 (2004): 29–49.

50. "Lump Sum Form."

51. "Modification of Lease and Supplemental Agreement," December 30, 1942; "Lump Sum Form"; "Agreement," June 7, 1943, p. 2; and "Modification of Lease and Supplemental Agreement," December 30 1942; all in Ahlberg vs. RFC.

52. "Memo from A Burnside," August 28, 1945, Ahlberg vs. RFC; "Letter from A Hobson," January 10, 1946, Ahlberg vs. RFC.

53. "Letter from F. O. Burkholder," February 8, 1946; "Letter from Louis Bean," n.d.; and "Letter from Alberg," March 15, 1946; all in Ahlberg vs. RFC.

54. "Letter from Kungsholm Bakery," March 9, 1946, and "Letter from F Berquist," March 19, 1946, both in Ahlberg vs. RFC.

55. "Letter from F. O. Burkholder," August 8, 1946, Ahlberg vs. RFC.

56. "Answering Brief of Reconstruction Finance Corporation with Regard to Plaintiff's Motion to Dismiss Counterclaim," November 20, 1946, Ahlberg vs. RFC.

57. "Block $40,000 WWA Sale: Bare $137,000 Offer," *Chicago Tribune*, January 29, 1947, 1; "WAA Withdraws Building Sale to Group for Blind," *Chicago Tribune*, March 13, 1947, 14. Interestingly, there is no material in the WAA archives that documents this issue.

58. Joseph Hearst, "Permits Firm to Buy 'Part' of Own Plant," *Chicago Tribune*, April 12, 1947; W. Day, "Advisory Report," February 9, 1948, Ahlberg vs. RFC.

59. "Memo from John Loomis," December 8, 1947, Accession Number: 291-56A-0244, Ahlberg Bearing Company, Real Property Case Files, 1952–1957, RG 291, National Archives—Chicago (hereafter Ahlberg Real Property case file).

60. "Schedule," n.d., and "Advisory Report," February 1948, both in Ahlberg Real Property case file.

61. "Approval of the Mortgage," p. 2, February 19, 1948; "Contract of Sale," April 12, 1948; and "Ending of the Mortgage," October 15, 1953; all in Ahlberg Real Property case file.

Chapter 9. Property, Calculation, and Industrial Space

1. Amanda Holpuch, "Michael Brown Shooting," *Guardian*, August 20, 2014, http://www.theguardian.com/world/live/2014/aug/20/michael-brown-attorney-general-ferguson-protests, accessed August 20, 2014.

2. As noted in chapter 5, the ground for the aircraft engine suburban factory was broken in March 1941, and the $125 million factory with one million square feet of floor space opened in January 1942. Over three years of operations some 16,000 workers made more than 74,000 radial aircraft engines for B-24 bombers under license to Pratt and Whitney.

3. "CE Wilson to Jesse Jones," September 22, 1944, Folder: General Motors Corp.—PL. 39—Melrose Park, ILL. vol. 1, Oct. 1 1943 thru Dec. 31, 1945 (ILL 16), Box 127, Real Property Disposal Case Files, WAA Records, RG 270, NARA—Chicago (hereafter Buick WAA files).

4. Nicholas Blomley, "Law, Property, and the Geography of Violence," *Annals of the Association of American Geographers* 93 (2003): 86–107; Lynn Staeheli and Don Mitchell, *The People's Property? Power, Politics, and the Public* (New York: Routledge, 2008); Franz von Benda-Beckmann, Keebet von Benda-Beckmann, and Melanie Wiber, "The Properties of Property," in *Changing Properties of Property*, ed. Franz von Benda-Beckmann, Keebet von Benda-Beckmann, and Melanie Wiber (New York: Berghahn Books, 2006), 1–39.

5. On the state and the making of markets see Michel Callon, ed., *The Laws of the Markets* (Oxford: Blackwell, 1998); Timothy Mitchell, *Rule of Experts: Egypt, Techno-Politics, Modernity* (Berkeley: University of California Press, 2002); Karl Polanyi, *The Great Transformation: The Political and Economic Origins of Our Time* (Boston: Beacon, 2001 [1944]).

6. Karl Marx and Friedrich Engels, *The Communist Manifesto* (Harmondsworth, UK: Penguin, 1967), 82.

7. Michel Callon, "The Embeddedness of Economic Markets in Economics," in *The Laws of the Markets*, ed. Michel Callon (Oxford: Blackwell, 1998), 1–57.

8. WAA, "National Industrial Plant Reserve Status as of March 1, 1949," Box 67, Subject File of the Central Office of Real Property, 1946–1949; 600.3 to 600.9 (Facility list and data), WAA Records, RG 270, Washington—College Park, Md.

9. "Memorandum Re: General Motors," August 8, 1945, Buick WAA files.

10. "Letter from P. Bukowski to D. Rhett, December 1, 1944, and Louis Bean, "Memorandum for the Files," July 27, 1945, both in Buick WAA files.

11. "Westinghouse, I.H.C.," *Chicago Tribune*, October 14, 1945, A6. Letter from Westinghouse to RFC, October 10, 1945, Buick WAA files.

12. "Press Release," November 23, 1945, Buick WAA files; "Harvester Co. Buys Surplus RFC Plant," *Chicago Tribune*, November 24, 1945, 24.

13. "Harvester Plans Expansion Moves," *New York Times*, May 11, 1945, 25; "Int. Harvester Profit, Sales Down in Year," *Chicago Tribune*, March 7, 1946, 33; "37.5 Millions Spent in Area by Harvester," *Chicago Tribune*, July 24, 1947, A7. For a discussion of corporate labor policy see Robert Ozanne, *A Century of Labor-Management Relations at McCormick and International Harvester* (Madison: University of Wisconsin Press, 1967).

14. Gregory McLauchlan, "The Advent of the Nuclear Weapons and the Formation of the Scientific-Military-Industrial Complex in World War II," in *The Military-Industrial Complex: Eisenhower's Warning Three Decades Later*, ed. Gregg Walker, David Bella, and Steven Sprecher (New York: Peter Lang, 1992), 101–27; Jennifer Light, *From Warfare to Welfare: Defense Intellectuals and Urban Problems in Cold War America* (Baltimore: Johns Hopkins University Press, 2003).

15. "Army, Navy, Air Men Will Visit Chicago Plants," *Chicago Tribune*, April 6, 1948, B7; "Industrial College of the Armed Forces Awards Certificates," *Chicago Tribune*, June 19, 1948, 11.

16. "Int. Harvester Unit to Build War Vehicle," *Chicago Tribune*, August 26, 1950, B5; "Pullman-Standard and Gen-American to Construct Armored Vehicle Hulls," *Chicago Tribune*, December 3, 1950, B5; "Truck Makers Shift into High on Army Output," *Chicago Tribune*, October 22, 1951, B12.

17. David Hounshell, *From the American System to Mass Production, 1800–1932: The Development of Manufacturing Technology in the United States* (Baltimore: Johns Hopkins University Press, 1984); Ben Baack and Edward Ray, "The Political Economy of the Origins of the Military-Industrial Complex in the United States," *Journal of Economic History* 45 (1985): 369–75.

18. Michael Hogan, *A Cross of Iron: Harry S. Truman and the Origins of the National Security State, 1945–1954* (New York: Cambridge University Press, 1998), 469. Also see Gregory Hooks, "The Danger of an Autarkic Pentagon: Updating Eisenhower's Warning of the Military-Industrial Complex" in Walker, Bella, and Sprecher, *Military-Industrial Complex*, 129–80; Paul Koistinen, *State of War: The Political Economy of American Warfare, 1945–2011* (Lawrence: University Press of Kansas, 2012), 88–112, 218–20.

19. Melyvn Leffler, *A Preponderance of Power: National Security, the Truman Administration, and the Cold War* (Stanford: Stanford University Press, 1992), 13.

20. Hogan, *Cross of Iron*, 474.

21. John Mollenkopf, *The Contested City* (Princeton: Princeton University Press, 1983), 47–96; Hooks, "Danger of an Autarkic Pentagon," 138–51.

22. Elizabeth Fones-Wolf, *Selling Free Enterprise: The Business Assault on Labor and Liberalism, 1945–1960* (Urbana: University of Illinois Press, 1994); Harold Vatter, *The U.S. Economy in World War II* (New York: Columbia University Press, 1985); Louis Galambos and Joseph Pratt, *The Rise of the Corporate Commonwealth: U.S. Business and Public Policy in the Twentieth Century* (New York: Basic Books, 1988), 129–54.

23. Leffler, *Preponderance of Power*.

24. Paul Koistinen, *The Military-Industrial Complex: A Historical Perspective* (New York: Praeger, 1980), 14.

25. Michael Sherry, *In the Shadow of War: The United States since the 1930s* (New Haven: Yale University Press, 1995), 71.

26. James Cook, *The Marketing of Surplus War Property* (Washington, D.C.: Public Affairs Press, 1948), 32–34.

27. Ibid., 34–35. Also see Louis Cain and George Neumann, "Planning for Peace: The Surplus Property Act of 1944," *Journal of Economic History* 41 (1981): 131–34; Gerald White, *Billions for Defense: Government Financing by the Defense Plant Corporation during World War II* (University: University of Alabama Press, 1980), 123.

28. Harold Stein, "The Disposal of the Aluminum Plants," in *Public Administration and Policy Development: A Case Book*, ed. Harold Stein (New York: Harcourt, Brace, 1952), 315.

29. "Memo to the Board," February 28, 1946, and "Memo to the General Board," May 1946, Box 8, Real Property Disposal Case Files, RG 270, NARA—Chicago.

30. Roger Lotchin, *Fortress California, 1910–1961: From Warfare to Welfare* (New York: Oxford University Press, 1992).

31. G. Simonson, "The Demand of the Aircraft Industry, 1907–1958," *Journal of Economic History* 20 (1960): 377–79; William Cunningham, *The Aircraft Industry: A Study in Industrial Location* (Los Angeles: L. L. Morrison, 1951); Louis Eltscher and Edward Young, *Curtiss-Wright: Greatness and Decline* (New York: Twayne, 1998), 130.

32. White, *Billions for Defense*, 125–61; George Brown Tindall, *The Emergence of the New South, 1931–1945* (Baton Rouge: Louisiana State University Press, 1967), 701.

33. Robert Lewis, "World War II Manufacturing and the Postwar Southern Economy," *Journal of Southern History* 73 (2007): 837–66.

34. Martin Schiesl, "Airplanes to Aerospace: Defense Spending and Economic Growth in the Los Angeles Region, 1945–1960," in *The Martial Metropolis: U.S. Cites in War and Peace*, ed. Roger Lotchin (New York: Praeger, 1984), 135–49; Allen Scott and Doreen Mattingly, "The Aircraft and Parts Industry in Southern California: Continuity and Change from the Inter-War Years to the 1990s," *Economic Geography* 65 (1989): 48–71; Anne Markusen, Peter Hall, Scott Campbell, and Sabrina Dietrick, *The Rise of the Gunbelt: The Military Remapping of Industrial America* (New York: Oxford University Press, 1999).

35. Markusen et al., *Rise of the Gunbelt*, 82–117.

36. Alexander Field, *A Great Leap Forward: 1930s Depression and U.S. Economic Growth* (New Haven: Yale University Press, 2011), 80.

37. Ibid., 79–105.

38. Lotchin, *Fortress California*, 15–22.

39. Joel Rast, *Remaking Chicago: The Political Origins of Urban Industrial Change* (De Kalb: Northern Illinois University Press, 1999); Joel Rast, "Regime Building, Institution Building: Urban Renewal Policy in Chicago, 1946–1962," *Journal of Urban Affairs* 31 (2009): 173–94.

40. Barry Bluestone and Bennett Harrison, *The Deindustrialization of America: Plant Closings, Community Abandonment, and the Dismantling of Basic Industry* (New York: Basic Books, 1982); Guian McKee, *The Problem of Jobs: Liberalism, Race, and Deindustrialization in Philadelphia* (Chicago: University of Chicago Press, 2008); Steven High, *Industrial Sunset: The Making of North America's Rust Belt, 1969–1984* (Toronto: University of Toronto Press, 2003).

41. Dominic A. Pacyga, *Slaughterhouse: Chicago's Union Stock Yard and the World It*

Made (Chicago: University of Chicago Press, 2015), 137–76; Dominic A. Pacyga, *Chicago: A Biography* (Chicago: University of Chicago Press, 2009), 308–21; Gregory Squires, Larry Bennett, Kathleen McCourt, and Philip Nyden, *Chicago: Race, Class, and the Response to Urban Decline* (Philadelphia: Temple University Press, 1987); David Bensman and Roberta Lynch, *Rusted Dreams: Hard Times in a Steel Community* (New York: McGraw-Hill, 1987).

42. Perry Duis, "Symbolic Unity and the Neighborhood: Chicago during World War II," *Journal of Urban History* 21 (1995): 210, 211.

43. William Clark, "Big Industrial Construction Expected Soon," *Chicago Tribune*, July 14, 1946, A7; "June Expansion by Industry in Chicago Large," *Chicago Tribune*, June 29, 1947, A9; "Building Booms in Suburbs as City Moves Out," *Chicago Tribune*, May 6, 1951, S2; "Billions in New Plants," *Chicago Tribune*, October 21, 1951, B9.

Appendix. Wartime Factory Expansion

1. Civilian Production Administration, *War Industrial Facilities Authorized, July 1940–August 1945: Listed Alphabetically by Companies and Plant Location* (Washington, D.C.: Government Printing Office, 1946).

2. The directory also listed infrastructural and transportation expenditures. These were not included in the study.

3. War Production Board, *War Manufacturing Facilities Authorized through December 1944 by State and County* (Washington, D.C.: Government Printing Office, 1945).

4. More than 80 percent of investment in wartime defense factories had taken place before the end of 1943. Smaller War Plants Corporation, *Economic Concentration and World War II* (Washington, D.C.: Government Printing Office, 1948), 37.

5. Mary Watters, *Illinois in the Second World War*, vol. 2 (Springfield: State of Illinois, 1952), 22.

6. "War Plant Building over $80,000,000," *Commerce*, March 1945, 45–46.

7. Perry Duis and Scott La France, *We've Got a Job to Do: Chicagoans and World War II* (Chicago: Chicago Historical Society, 1992), 68.

MANUSCRIPT SOURCES

Chicago History Museum
    Chicago Association of Commerce and Industry (CAC)
    Illinois Manufacturers' Association Records (IMA)
Chicago Public Library
    Special Collections (CPL, SC)
    Municipal Reference (CPL, MR)
Illinois State Archives
    Illinois War Council (World War II) records (IWC)
NARA—College Park
    Office of the Chief of Ordnance, RG 156 (OCO)
        Post WWI Divisions, Services and other Units; Industrial Service; Production Service Division.
        Post WWI Divisions, Services and other Units; Industrial Division; Ammunition Branch, Facilities and Resources Section
    Reconstruction Finance Corporation, RG 234 (RFC)
        Office of the Secretary;
        Office of the Controller;
        Final Accountability Reports.
    War Assets Administration, RG 270 (WAA)
        Advisory Council
        Central Office of Real Property
        General Board, Advisory Council
        Office Files of the WAA Administrator, Jess Larson
        Office of Administrative Services, Historical Unit
        Office of Administration
        Real Property Review Board
NARA—Chicago
    U.S. District Court, Northern District of Illinois at Chicago, RG 21 (USDC)
        Civil Case Files, 1938–1939
    War Assets Administration, RG 270 (WAA)
        Real Property Disposal Case Files (RPDC)

Manuscript Sources

    Federal Property Resources Service, RG 291
        Real Property Case Files
    University of Chicago, Special Collections
        Merriam Charles E. Merriam papers
    University of Illinois, Manuscripts and Rare Books
        Metropolitan Housing Council (MHC)
            Postwar Economic Advisory Council of Chicago

INDEX

Acme Steel plant, 63
advertising: for Chicago's locational assets, 58, 62, 69; for surplus industrial facilities, 24, 135–36, 140
agglomeration economies, 26
Ahlberg Bearing Company, 164; RFC court case, 10, 192–96
aircraft engine plants, 103, 143; Buick, 119–23, 198–204; Dodge-Chrysler, 78, 81, 83–85, 152, 202; Douglas Aircraft, 70, 79, 81, 92, 210; in postwar Chicago, 209–10; Studebaker, 152–53, 161
aircraft industry: landing craft, 86, 88; production, 36, 65, 88; state and private financing, 35; supply contracts, 38
Alcoa (Aluminum Company of America), 92, 160, 208
aluminum, 208
American Steel Foundries, 163, 164, 168, 202
armored personnel carriers, 205
Army and Navy Munitions Board (ANMB), 50, 53, 79, 86, 98; industrial reserve program, 144–46; plant negotiations, 169, 171; reports, 157–58
Army Industrial College, 50
auctions, 141
aviation industry, 64–65, 75. *See also* aircraft industry; Bendix Aviation Company

Baker, Murray, 62
Baldwin, Hanson, 181–82
Baltimore, Md., 188, 190
banks. *See* financial institutions
Baruch, Bernard, 132
Baruch-Hancock report (1944), 130, 132
Bean, Louis, 194, 203

Belmont Radio Corporation, 167, 188, 189–90, 251n31
Bendix Aviation Company, 70, 177, 187–88
Bendix Corporation, 164
Bernstein, Michael, 7, 221n18
Berquist, Fred, 131
Blessing, Charles, 97
Blossom, Francis, 240n24
Boeing Aircraft Company, 29, 81, 88
bomber plants: construction of, 28, 81, 83–84, 113; disposal of, 163; locations of, 98–99
Borg-Warner Corporation, 71, 88
British Purchasing Commission, 102
B-29 bomber (Superfortress), 81, 83–84
Buda Company, 100, 103, 202
Buick aircraft engine plant: Chicago's postwar economy and, 209; engineer assessment of, 119–23; property relations of, 198–204
Burgess-Norton Pool, 74
Burke, Joseph, 160, 163
Burkholder, Fred, 192–95
business attitudes, 38–39, 46, 48; national reserve program and, 144–45; on state intervention in industry, 43, 61

calculation: by airplane corporations, 29; Buick engine plant and, 119–23, 203–4; concepts, 11–12, 13–14; factory construction and, 81, 84–86; factory disposal and, 125–26, 140, 142, 150, 167, 172–73; industrial reserve and, 143, 146; knowledge and, 48–49, 51; metropolitan areas and, 26, 30; postwar industrial mobilization and, 181–82; spaces of, 15–17; of value of plants, 164–65
calculative agents: Chicago industrial sites and, 177; corporate executives as, 78;

259

calculative agents (*continued*)
    federal government as, 121; financial institutions as, 70–72; industrial engineers as, 107–9, 116, 118, 127; industrial reserve and, 149; information gathering by, 155–56; networks, 76–77; role of, 5, 15–18, 51, 75
Callon, Michel, 13
Calumet district, 27, 63, 93; industrial history, 96–99; wartime investment and construction, 77, 99–103, 104
Campbell, Leven, 205, 207, 212
Canton, Ohio, 186
capital: circulation of, 28–29; federal government, 42; for industrial property, 48, 70, 106, 197; manufacturing, 35; private, 8, 34, 96, 100, 202; wartime, 57. *See also* fixed-capital investment
capitalism, 13–14, 18, 42
Central Intelligence Agency, 24, 142
certificates of necessity, 47, 71, 77, 94, 100, 199; for additions to properties, 85–86, 96
Chemical Warfare Service, 113
Chicago: administrative system, 160–63; city boosters, 59, 62–65; employment, 213; firms, 117–18, 215–16; industrial investment, 57–59, 65, 77–80, 104, 198–99; manufacturing zones, 6, 93–96, 104, 209; new factory construction, 80–85, 89; postwar economy, 209–211; supply contracts, 59–60, 63, 216; wartime agencies, 72, 212; wartime economy, 1, 56, 65, 66–68, 104. *See also* Calumet district; Joliet, Ill.; Melrose Park, Ill.
Chicago Association of Commerce (CAC), 56, 73, 80, 86, 217; booster program, 58, 59, 64; growth coalition, 62; industrial records, 155; role of, 67–69, 120, 212
Chicago Bridge and Iron Company, 107, 125
Chicago Commerce, 56, 68, 215–16
Chicago Commission on National Defense, 67, 69
Chicago Ordnance District, 73–74, 80, 102–3, 113
Chicago Plan Commission, 63
Chicago Quartermaster Depot, 152
Chicago Tribune, 8, 59, 73, 114, 163
Chrysler Motor Company, 81, 84, 210. *See also* Dodge-Chrysler
Cicero, Ill., 57, 104
Cincinnati, Ohio, 92, 118
Civilian Production Administration (CPA), 32, 35
class, 15,18; capitalist, 67, 132; calculative politics, 13, 76; labor markets and, 29; military-industrial alliance, 76, 142
Clayton, Will, 134
Clement, Col. J., 112–13
Committee on Economic Policy, 131
Committee on the National Defense Program, 67
commodities, 108, 152–53, 160, 165, 166
Congress. *See* U.S. Congress
Consolidated Grocers' Corporation, 188–90, 251n32
Continental Motors plant (Garland, Tex.), 141
Continental Ordnance Corporation, 99, 164, 165
Copeland, Morris, 51
corporate concentration, 38–39, 208–9
corporate leaders or managers, 1, 3, 6, 40, 212; at International Harvester, 205, 207; role of, 78–79, 105, 204; use of industrial knowledge, 52–53
corporations: automobile, 210; economic control, 37–38, 55, 104; factory investment, 77–80; industrial reserve program and, 143, 150; military relations, 204–7; scale and scope of, 110
Corps of Engineers, 107–8, 114, 115, 124, 169
Cramer, Stuart, 147
Cramp Shipyards, 124
credit-rating companies, 49, 154, 167
Cummings, Nathan, 189, 190

Davidson Manufacturing Corporation, 70
Day and Zimmerman, 46; appraisal for Bendix Corporation, 164–65; appraisal of Seneca shipyards, 107, 124–27; wartime tasks, 123–24
decentralization: Chicago administrative, 160, 162, 171; industrial, 6, 63, 64, 72–73, 96, 209
Defense, Department of, 142, 151, 198, 212
defense factory construction: additions and renovations, 85–89, 93, 96, 217; calculations about, 81, 84–86; in Calumet district, 99–103; in Chicago, 80–85, 93–94; complexities of, 106; corporate/private investment in, 35–36, 77–80, 85–86, 230n45; federal mobilization plan for, 44–47; local processes of, 6; network relationships and, 14; role of engineers in, 110–11; state investment in, 16, 33–36, 77–78, 94; in suburban areas, 90–92

defense factory disposal: auctions, 141; calculations about, 125–26, 140, 142, 150, 167, 172–73; concerns and difficulties with, 131–32, 133–34; corporate control of, 208; engineer assessments, 122–27; GSA plan for, 148–49, 151; information gathering on, 153–60; legislation on, 24, 130–31, 133; military's role in, 168–69, 171–75; politics of, 177, 187–92, 196–97; postwar regime on, 129–30, 132–33, 150; promotional campaign, 24, 135–36, 140; selling of Chicago plants, 156–57, 160–67, 210; selling of factories, 23–24, 130–31, 135, 140–41. *See also* disposal agencies

Defense Plant Corporation (DPC): Ahlberg Bearing contract, 192–94; Buick plant and, 119–23; Chrysler contract, 84; engineering firms and, 108, 111; financing of war factories, 41, 47–48, 77, 89, 120, 182; knowledge acquisition, 53, 124, 136, 154; role of, 43; Sprague, Warner warehouse purchase, 187

Defense Problem Service, 68–69
Defense Production Clinic, 69
Detroit, Mich., 29, 65, 122, 187, 210
Diamond Wire and Cable Company, 101
disposal agencies, 15, 109, 122; formation of, 130, 133; knowledge assemblage by, 153, 159; obstacles, 133–34, 162; plant assessments, 163–65. *See also* War Assets Administration

Dodge-Chrysler, 79, 119, 153, 163, 166; airplane engine factory, 78, 81, 83–85, 152, 202, 210
"dollar-a-year" men, 38, 45
Douglas Aircraft, 70, 79, 81, 92, 210
Duis, Perry, 28, 90, 213–14, 216–17
Dun and Bradstreet, 49, 167, 195

East Chicago, Ind., 97, 164, 166; steel production, 99–100, 183, 186
economy. *See* war economy
educational institutions, 74–75
Edwin S. Corman Inc., 164
electric furnace steel, 186–87
electronics sector, 65, 94, 180, 211. *See also* radio industry
elites, 45, 58, 97, 98, 207; political, 67, 75, 212
Ellinson, E. J., 185
Elwood Ordnance plant, 74, 107, 112–18, 172, 174; construction award, 112; locational considerations for, 113–15
employment. *See* job growth
Engels, Friedrich, 11, 12

engineers / engineering firms. *See* industrial engineering firms
Enright, William, 110
Eugene Dietzgen Company, 117
explosives, 35, 118, 172, 174

Fansteel Metallurgical Corporation, 94, 169, 171
federal government: engineering firms and, 107–9; financial institutions and, 71–72; industrial disposal regime, 129–33, 154, 175, 200; industrial mobilization plan, 3, 5, 44–48; information gathering, 155–57; intervention in industrial production, 33–34, 40–44; investment in wartime factories, 6, 21–22, 30, 32–33, 198–99; military-industrial relations, 5, 19; national security and, 24–26; property ownership, 88–89, 202; supply contracts, 3, 36, 56
Federal Reserve Bank of Chicago, 71, 72
Federal Works Agency (FWA), 43, 126, 148
Ferguson, Mo., 198
fertilizer industry, 158, 174–75
Field, Alexander, 211
financial institutions, 37, 70–72, 119
fixed-capital investment, 9, 27, 185; in Chicago firms, 77–78; city/suburban share of, 90–94, 104, 209; data analysis on, 215, 217; in new wartime factories, 35, 98
Folsom, Marion, 131
Ford-Lansing airport, 99
Ford Motor Company, 28, 74, 210
Forrestal, James, 147
Foucault, Michel, 11, 12–13
Funigiello, Philip, 90

Gaertner Scientific Corporation, 89
Gary, Ind., 57, 93, 97, 100
Gary Armor Plate Works, 160, 163, 168, 210
General Electric Company, 117, 169
General Motors Corporation, 145; Melrose Park plant, 120, 122–23, 199, 203, 208, 210
General Services Administration (GSA), 124, 148–49, 151, 156, 183
George A. Fuller Company, 84
George S. Armstrong and Company, 111
Great Depression, 40, 41, 58
Greater Chicago Plan, 58
Green, Dwight, 34–35, 59, 62, 67; promotion of Chicago, 98–99
greenfield sites, 30, 81, 93, 100, 166
Guardian, 198

Hancock, John, 132
Hannifin Manufacturing Company, 74
Harry S. Cutmore and Associates, 164, 166
Hartz, W. Homer, 60, 69
Harvey, David, 11, 12
Harvey, Ill., 100, 103, 209
Hauck, W., 181
Helene Curtis Industries, 188–92, 251n32
H. K. Ferguson Company, 111
Hoel, Milnor, 189, 194
Hogan, Michael, 206
Hooks, Gregory, 22, 38
Hoover, Calvin, 50–51
housing, 51, 97
Housing Act (1949), 213
Howard Foundry Company, 168–69, 171, 202
Hudson, Ray, 26, 29

Illinois Council of Defense (ICD), 62, 67, 98–99
Illinois Institute for the Blind (IIB), 194–95
Illinois Manufacturers' Association (IMA), 73, 80, 212; Committee on National Defense, 66
Industrial College of Armed Forces, 50, 205
industrial directories, 135, 215–16
industrial dispersal, 59, 213
industrial engineering firms, 46, 84, 122, 127–28; appraisals of industrial plants, 109–10, 119, 124, 164; calculative expertise of, 107–9, 111, 112, 118; supply contracts, 110–11. *See also* Day and Zimmerman; Lockwood Greene Engineers Inc.; Sanderson and Porter
Industrial Mobilization Plan (1930), 20, 50
industrial property: calculations and, 13–15, 21, 26, 151, 180; corporate control over, 55; engineering firms and, 107–9, 111; key elements of, 2; local and national markets and, 166–67; metropolitan geography of, 6; military interest in, 4, 19–21, 206; national security and, 24–25; place and, 28–29; public and private investment in, 34–36; state-owned, 141–42, 150, 155–56, 200
industrial property relations: changes to, 5, 201–2; legislation, 201–2; local and nonlocal, 56–57; of military-industrial complex, 2, 177, 180–81, 198–204, 206; ownership and, 33; in postwar Chicago, 177, 178, 183; private, 169
industrial reserve. *See* national industrial reserve
industrial sites: agents and, 1–2, 16–17; as calculative spaces, 14–16; complications of, 106; creation and conversion of, 4–5, 7, 30, 63–65; economic boundaries of, 33; financing/investments, 22–23, 46–48, 57–58; militarized state and, 19–21; military control of, 146–48, 151; recalculation of, 202; scale of, 27; state intervention in, 40–44, 89–90. *See also* defense factory construction; defense factory disposal
Inland Steel Company, 97, 182
interior policy, 59, 114, 233n30
International Harvester Company, 74, 100, 210, 212; military-corporate relations, 204–9; postwar expansion, 204; purchase of plancor 239, 120, 203–4
inventory: of defense factories, 123, 154; industrial, 49–50, 51–52, 66; war manufacturers, 73
isolationism, 20, 43, 66

jet programs, 178
job growth, 56, 175, 208; in defense industries, 35–36, 38
Johnson, Louis, 108
Johnson, Marilynn, 36
Joliet, Ill., 86, 104, 112, 115, 117
Jones, Jesse H., 39, 61, 62, 154, 199
Justice, Department of, 109, 131, 164, 187, 191

Kahn, Albert, 84, 110, 120
Kain, John, 93
Kaiser Aluminum, 208
Kankakee Ordnance plant, 111, 172–75
Kelly, Edward, 62, 67, 81, 83
Klagsbrunn, Hans, 40–41, 103
knowledge, industrial: calculative, 50–52; of Chicago industrial sites, 154–55, 175; engineering firms and, 107, 109, 121–22; on factory disposal, 153–54, 167, 176; image-based, 158; industrial reserve, 143; "pertinent" information on, 172–73; production and assemblage of, 48–49, 52–54, 65–66, 120; statistical, 155–57; textual, 157–58
Knudsen, William, 53, 61, 98
Koistinen, Paul, 207
Koppers United, 92
Kraft Foods Company, 141, 191–92
Kropp Forge Company, 88, 158–59, 202, 212; purchase of plancor 1293, 177–78, 180–82, 197
Kungsholm Bakery, 194

labor supply, 29, 60, 63, 108, 166
La France, Scott, 28, 216–17
Landing Ships, Tanks (LSTs), 124–25
Larson, Jess, 140–41, 147
Leffler, Melvyn, 24, 150, 206
legislation: antimonopoly, 25, 49; industrial disposal, 24, 130–31, 133; industrial property, 2, 16, 48; industrial reserve, 146–48, 153; property relations and, 201–2; on state intervention in industry, 43. *See also* New Deal; Surplus Property Act
liberals, 42–44
local alliances, 29, 30, 212
Lockwood Greene Engineers Inc.: appraisal of Buick plant, 107, 119–23, 203; work volume, 110–11
Loomis, John, 195
Los Angeles, Calif., 3, 8, 29, 92, 210–11
Lotchin, Roger, 7, 28
Lovett, Robert A., 36–38, 54, 81, 83, 228n13
Lucas, Scott, 60, 190
Lyon, Leverett, 58, 59, 62

Mack, Clifton, 131
magnesium, 154, 168–69
maps, 158
Marx, Karl, 11, 12
May, Stacy, 53
Mayer, Harold, 97
McCloy, John, 54, 231n62
McCormick, Fowler, 205, 207, 212
McKeough, Raymond, 60
McLouth Steel Corporation, 187
Melrose Park, Ill., 6, 104, 203, 209, 213. *See also* plancor 39
metropolitan geographies: calculation and, 26; Chicago manufacturing districts, 93–94, 96, 166, 213; industrial investment in, 6, 90–92, 209, 237n27
Metz, Carl, 193
military: engineering firms and, 107–9, 111, 127–28; factory disposal and, 168–69, 171–75; funding for factory expansion, 101–2; industrial mobilization and, 79–80, 96, 98; industrial reserve, 143–48, 150, 168; interwar preparedness, 44; land acquisition, 115–16; leaders, 21–22, 46, 52, 75, 150, 158; power, 25; procurement, 46, 69, 77, 81, 202; supply contracts, 56, 70, 100–101, 143, 216
military-industrial complex, 21, 43–44, 75; agents, 14, 33; calculative relations of, 28, 30, 180, 214; corporate relations, 38–39, 204–7; emergence and concept, 5, 18–19, 40, 48, 54–55; industrial engineers and, 111–12, 120, 128; local processes of, 6; national security and, 129–30, 150; site politics of, 177; state-controlled plants and, 148
Milwaukee, Wis., 118
mobilization agencies: Chicago, 72, 76; civil and military, 48, 68, 104, 107; difficulties and failures of, 34, 60, 61; efforts to secure funds, 77; emergence of, 21–22, 43, 44–45; industrial capacity and, 88; information gathering, 51–54, 108; leaders and bureaucrats and, 3, 8, 38; relations with engineers, 108–10; scale and, 29; utilization of knowledge, 51–52
Murphy, Walter, 188, 190–91

National Association of Manufacturers (NAM), 36, 37
National Association of Real Estate Boards, 132
National Defense Act (1920), 20, 50, 73
National Defense Advisory Committee (NDAC), 45, 46–47, 52–53, 111
national industrial reserve: Chicago sites, 153, 202; creation of, 25, 130, 142–46, 150; GSA reserve, 148–49, 151
National Industrial Reserve Acts (1947 and 1948), 16, 25, 130, 147–48, 153
national security, 42, 149, 171, 206–7; calculations on, 144; coalition, 145; emergence of, 142, 150, 180; ethos, 144; postwar industrial regime and, 23–24, 129–30, 133. *See also* national security clause
National Security Act (1947), 24
national security clause, 147–48, 151, 168–69, 202
National Security Council, 24, 142
National Security Resources Board, 147, 205
Navistar, 210
navy. *See* U.S. Navy
Navy Industrial Association, 145
Nelson, Donald M., 61, 83, 145
networks: business, 116–17, 212; of calculative agents, 76–77; defense factory, 14; engineering, 112, 116, 118; of individuals, 13; industrial, 33, 75, 81; property relations and, 21; social, 29; WAA, 167; wartime industrial mobilization, 18, 30

Index

New Deal, 20, 66; agencies, 43, 45, 48, 60, 72; industrial mobilization program and, 41–42, 44; policies, 22, 207
New York City, N.Y., 8, 118, 119, 210
New York Times, 136, 181, 183
nitric acid, 143, 172–75
North Chicago, Ill., 6, 93–94, 104
Nye Committee (Special Senate Committee to Investigate the Munitions Industry, 1936), 20

objects: calculative relations of, 13–15, 18; defense factory as, 112, 130, 133, 165; industrial sites as, 33, 34, 43, 97, 108, 173; state, 71
O'Brien, Joseph, 163, 190–91
Odlum Floyd, 62
Office of Community War Services (OCWS), 126–27
Office of Price Administration (OPA), 131, 133
Office of Production Management (OPM), 45, 52–53, 60, 62; regional offices, 72–73
Office of War Administration, 133
O'Hare International Airport, 210
Olrich, Ernest, 152–53
O'Mahoney, Joseph, 188
Ordnance, Chief of, 144, 175, 205
Ordnance Department, 91, 102, 112, 113. *See also* Chicago Ordnance District

Patterson, Robert P., 54, 61, 143, 145
Philadelphia, Pa., 63, 112, 123–24, 210
Phipps Industrial Land Trust, 193
Pine Bluff Arsenal, 113
Pittsburgh, Pa., 92, 167, 203
place: industrial property and, 28–29; social relations of, 27, 76
plancors: advertisements for, 136; definition, 221n21; difficulties selling, 163; disposal of, 124, 125, 154, 161; engineer appraisals, 164–65; information gathering on, 159–60; plans, 158; private sector and, 132
plancor 39, 210, 214; construction, 119, 253n2; engineer assessment of, 121–23; military-corporate relations of, 204–9; property relations of, 198–204, 209
plancor 328, 183, 185–87
plancor 422, 183–85
plancor 600, 156
plancor 653, 192–96
plancor 1170, 168–69
plancor 1235, 187–89, 195, 251n31; assessment of, 164–65, 167

plancor 1293, 159, 177–78, 180–82, 197
Plant Finder, 136, 140, 158
police, 198
political sociology, 12–13
postwar America: defense program, 178, 180–82, 201, 205; economic direction of, 23, 129, 142, 208; industrial conversion, 131, 144, 196; industrial disposal regime, 129–30, 204; manufacturing decline, 172, 186, 199, 210, 213; property relations, 199–200; safety of, 132
Pratt and Whitney Aircraft Company, 119, 120, 169, 253n2
Pressed Steel Car Company, 102
private industry: Chicago boosters and, 64–65; factory disposal and, 129–30, 141, 153, 171–75; federal mobilization program and, 2–3, 41–43; financing of factory additions, 85–86; operation of defense plants, 47–48, 132; selling of wartime plants to, 23–24; state-owned facilities and, 88–89
procurement system, 36–37, 229n39; agencies, 69, 73, 102; corporate control of, 104; military, 46, 69, 77, 81, 202
property markets: capitalist, 12; local and national, 166–67, 176; military-industrial complex and, 201; private, 108, 134, 150, 153, 165, 173; state intervention in, 132, 142, 153–54
property relations: calculative agents and, 22, 76; networks and, 21; prewar conditions, 132; pricing and, 14; public-private imperatives, 115, 196; restructuring of, 2, 19, 54, 76, 177
property rights, 12, 16, 54, 89; individual, 115; of private sector, 129; transfer of, 196–97, 200–201
public-private partnerships: formation of, 3–4, 67, 128; industrial plant disposal and, 129, 150, 196–97, 200; industrial reserve program and, 143, 146; networks, 117; property relations and, 200–202, 206
Pullman-Standard Car Manufacturing, 100–102, 205, 212

Quartermaster Department, 107–8, 113, 123
Querl, E. P., 58, 62, 97

radio industry, 65, 74, 101, 188. *See also* Belmont Radio Corporation
Ratcliffe, George, 190
real estate industry, 115–16, 132, 134; property assessments, 167; resources, 141

Real Property Disposal Board, 135, 185; Chicago division, 156–57, 162; Washington division, 195
Reconstruction Finance Corporation (RFC), 41, 48, 72, 154; Ahlberg Bearing court case, 192–96; business loans, 68, 70; factory disposal practices, 134–36, 199
Republic Steel Corporation, 97, 136, 160, 202; disposal of plancor 422, 183–85
research and development, 144, 180, 205, 207
Revenue Act (1940), 70, 86
Reynolds Metals, 208
Rizley, Ross, 157, 195
Roberts, C., 181
Rock Island Ordnance plant, 116
Roosevelt, Franklin D.: call for industrial expansion, 34; industrial disposal regime, 6, 131, 133; industrial mobilization program, 1, 2–4, 40–44; interior wartime policy, 59, 114, 233n30
Rosen, Harold, 189, 191
Royall, Kenneth, 145, 188
rubber. *See* synthetic rubber industry
Rutherford, Col. H., 98

Sanderson and Porter, 46, 107; factory design and construction, 114–16; subcontractors and business networks, 116–18, 174; wartime contracts, 112–13
scale: economies of, 105, 188; metropolitan, 26–27; national and regional, 8, 18, 75
scrambled plants, 156, 194–95; in Calumet district, 103; definition of, 88–89
Senate Special Committee to Investigate the National Defense Program. *See* Truman Committee
Seneca shipyards, 107, 124–27
Seyfarth and Atwood, 192
shipbuilding, 102, 112
shipyards, 28, 107, 124–27
Signal Corps, 169, 188, 190
Silverman, Arnold, 90
Skokie, Ill., 104
Slater, Dan, 14
Smaller War Plants Corporation (SWPC), 38, 39
Smith, Harrison, 112–14
Snyder, John, 190
South Chicago, Ill., 100, 183, 186
Soviet Union, 26, 144
Sperry Gyroscope Company, 84–85
Sprague, Warner and Company, 187, 188–89, 251n32

Springfield, Ill., 75, 188
Standard Oil Company (Ind.), 100
Standard Railway Equipment Company, 86, 88
standby plants, 132, 142; in Chicago, 168, 174; military-controlled, 143, 146; total number of, 148
state manager, 71, 204
Stauffer Chemical, 89
steel industry, 92, 118, 167; Acme Steel plant, 63; in Calumet district, 97, 99–102, 104; Carnegie Steel, 86; plant disposal, 182–87; public-private investment in, 182; sale of surplus steel, 157; shipyard building and, 125; suburban expansion, 8, 57. *See also* American Steel Foundries; Republic Steel Corporation; U.S. Steel Corporation; Youngstown Sheet and Tube Company
Steelman, John, 147, 171
Stone and Webster Engineering Company, 110–11
Strom Steel Bearings, 156
Studebaker Corporation, 79, 93, 199; engine plant closure, 152–53, 161, 210
subcontracting, 36, 77, 85, 104, 180, 240n25; by Sanderson and Porter, 116–17
suburbs/suburbanization: Chicago manufacturing districts, 6, 93–96, 104, 209; employment in, 213; industrial investment, 6, 90–92, 214. *See also* Calumet district; Joliet, Ill.; Melrose Park, Ill.
sulfuric acid, 89, 172–75
Sumner, John, 131, 133
supply chains, 36
supply contracts, 28–29, 30, 48; for Chicago firms, 59–60, 62, 65, 77, 199, 216; corporate dominance, 1, 38; engineering, 110–11, 112–13, 124; federal investment in, 3, 36, 56; geographic distribution of, 61; locally awarded, 72; military, 56, 70, 100–101, 143, 216
Surplus Property Act (1944), 134, 150, 153, 177, 178; objectives, 24, 133, 166, 185; public-private property transfer, 200, 201
Surplus Property Board (SPB), 134
Surplus War Property Administration (SWPA), 133, 134, 143, 243n11
surveys: of Calumet district, 97; of Chicago industries, 63, 68, 80, 155, 163–64; of defense plants, 171; engineering, 113, 121; of government-owned factories, 136, 154; technical, 149
synthetic rubber industry, 27, 32, 110–11, 154

tank manufacturing, 36, 74, 102, 124–25
tantalum, 93–94, 169, 171
Tatlow, Col. Richard, 134–35, 203, 243n14
tax amortization, 47, 70–71, 236n15
Truman Committee, 116–18, 132, 143, 240n24

unemployment, 152, 213
University of Chicago, 74; Committee on Human Development, 126
U.S. Air Force, 84, 98, 101, 103, 199, 205
U.S. Army, 67, 71, 73, 100; Construction Division, 108, 112; investment in defense factories, 44; national security and, 146; Office of the Chief of Engineers, 143, 172–73, 175; supply contracts, 56, 101–2, 159. See also military
U.S. Congress, 42, 48, 131, 133–34; committee meetings, 157–58; industrial reserve program and, 144–47; reorganization of, 142
U.S. Navy, 67, 71, 80, 146; request for shipyards, 124–25; supply contracts, 56, 101, 124. See also military
U.S. Rubber, 174–75
U.S. Steel Corporation, 97, 100, 182

Valliant, Col. Rigby, 115
value: fair, 185–86, 189, 242n40; of industrial sites, 108–9, 124, 126, 154; land or property, 115–16, 122–23; of surplus property, 133, 164, 171, 180
visible minorities, 15

Wall Street Journal, 136
War Assets Administration (WAA), 88, 119, 208, 225n35; administrative changes, 133, 162–63; assessment of Seneca shipyards, 125–27; Chicago office reports, 157–58; factory disposal negotiations, 182–83, 185–87, 188–92, 192–96; industrial facilities listings, 155; industrial reserve and, 147, 151, 169; Kropp Forge negotiations, 177–78, 180–82; plant disposal strategies, 24, 122, 134–36, 140–41, 160, 163–65; Price Review Board, 135; property market study, 166–67; Real Estate unit, 164, 167; real property case files, 159, 221n20; Real Property Review Board, 171, 185, 190–91

War Department, 50, 103, 111, 134, 145; industrial site politics and, 187–88
war economy: in Chicago, 1, 56, 65, 66–68, 104; corporate/private control over, 3, 55; creation and planning of, 3–4, 48, 50–51; downsizing of, 152; industry demand and, 211; place and, 5, 29; shift from/to peace economy, 6, 57, 61, 133, 150
War Industries Board, 49
War Problem School, 69, 86
War Production Board (WPB), 22, 45, 53, 171; Construction Bureau, 52
War Resources Board, 45
Washington, D.C., 72, 75; defense disposal and, 156–57, 160–62
Watters, Mary, 216
W. C. Ritchie, 86
Weir, Gary, 28
Western Electric Company, Inc., 79, 101, 145, 210
Westinghouse Electric and Manufacturing Company, 203
White, Alonzo, 173–74, 175
Whiting, Ind., 100, 209
Willow Run, Mich., 28
Wilson, Charles, 199, 210
Wilson, Mark, 7, 221n18
wire, electrical, 101
Wisconsin Structural Steel, 118
women, 15
World War I mobilization: administrative structure of, 25; calculations about, 16–17, 30; corporate control of, 38–39, 55; federal program, 1, 2–3, 5, 44–46; industrial reserve and, 149; military-industrial complex and, 19, 27–28; networks, 18, 32–33; planning, 49–51; scale and, 27–28; state intervention, 33–35, 48. See also mobilization agencies
Wright aircraft engines, 81, 84
Wyman-Gordon Company, 103, 160, 168

Youngstown Sheet and Tube Company, 97, 183, 185–87, 202

Zenith Radio Corporation, 188, 190, 202

GEOGRAPHIES OF JUSTICE AND SOCIAL TRANSFORMATION

1. *Social Justice and the City*, rev. ed.
   BY DAVID HARVEY

2. *Begging as a Path to Progress: Indigenous Women and Children and the Struggle for Ecuador's Urban Spaces*
   BY KATE SWANSON

3. *Making the San Fernando Valley: Rural Landscapes, Urban Development, and White Privilege*
   BY LAURA R. BARRACLOUGH

4. *Company Towns in the Americas: Landscape, Power, and Working-Class Communities*
   EDITED BY OLIVER J. DINIUS AND ANGELA VERGARA

5. *Tremé: Race and Place in a New Orleans Neighborhood*
   BY MICHAEL E. CRUTCHER JR.

6. *Bloomberg's New York: Class and Governance in the Luxury City*
   BY JULIAN BRASH

7. *Roppongi Crossing: The Demise of a Tokyo Nightclub District and the Reshaping of a Global City*
   BY ROMAN ADRIAN CYBRIWSKY

8. *Fitzgerald: Geography of a Revolution*
   BY WILLIAM BUNGE

9. *Accumulating Insecurity: Violence and Dispossession in the Making of Everyday Life*
   EDITED BY SHELLEY FELDMAN, CHARLES GEISLER, AND GAYATRI A. MENON

10. *They Saved the Crops: Labor, Landscape, and the Struggle over Industrial Farming in Bracero-Era California*
    BY DON MITCHELL

11. *Faith Based: Religious Neoliberalism and the Politics of Welfare in the United States*
    BY JASON HACKWORTH

12. *Fields and Streams: Stream Restoration, Neoliberalism, and the Future of Environmental Science*
    BY REBECCA LAVE

13. *Black, White, and Green: Farmers Markets, Race, and the Green Economy*
    BY ALISON HOPE ALKON

14. *Beyond Walls and Cages: Prisons, Borders, and Global Crisis*
    EDITED BY JENNA M. LOYD, MATT MITCHELSON, AND ANDREW BURRIDGE

15. *Silent Violence: Food, Famine, and Peasantry in Northern Nigeria*
    BY MICHAEL J. WATTS

16. *Development, Security, and Aid: Geopolitics and Geoeconomics at the U.S. Agency for International Development*
    BY JAMEY ESSEX

17. *Properties of Violence: Law and Land-Grant Struggle in Northern New Mexico*
    BY DAVID CORREIA

18. *Geographical Diversions: Tibetan Trade, Global Transactions*
    BY TINA HARRIS

19. *The Politics of the Encounter: Urban Theory and Protest under Planetary Urbanization*
    BY ANDY MERRIFIELD

20. *Rethinking the South African Crisis: Nationalism, Populism, Hegemony*
    BY GILLIAN HART

21. *The Empires' Edge: Militarization, Resistance, and Transcending Hegemony in the Pacific*
    BY SASHA DAVIS

22. *Pain, Pride, and Politics: Social Movement Activism and the Sri Lankan Tamil Diaspora in Canada*
    BY AMARNATH AMARASINGAM

23. *Selling the Serengeti: The Cultural Politics of Safari Tourism*
    BY BENJAMIN GARDNER

24. *Territories of Poverty: Rethinking North and South*
    EDITED BY ANANYA ROY AND EMMA SHAW CRANE

25. *Precarious Worlds: Contested Geographies of Social Reproduction*
    EDITED BY KATIE MEEHAN AND KENDRA STRAUSS

26. *Spaces of Danger: Culture and Power in the Everyday*
    EDITED BY HEATHER MERRILL AND LISA M. HOFFMAN

27. *Shadows of a Sunbelt City: The Environment, Racism, and the Knowledge Economy in Austin*
    BY ELIOT M. TRETTER

28. *Beyond the Kale: Urban Agriculture and Social Justice Activism in New York City*
    BY KRISTIN REYNOLDS AND NEVIN COHEN

29. *Calculating Property Relations: Chicago's Wartime Industrial Mobilization, 1940–1950*
    BY ROBERT LEWIS

30. *In the Public's Interest: Evictions, Citizenship, and Inequality in Contemporary Delhi*
    BY GAUTAM BHAN

31. *The Carpetbaggers of Kabul and Other American-Afghan Entanglements: Intimate Development, Geopolitics, and the Currency of Gender and Grief*
    BY JENNIFER L. FLURI AND RACHEL LEHR

32. *Masculinities and Markets: Raced and Gendered Urban Politics in Milwaukee*
    BY BRENDA PARKER

www.ingramcontent.com/pod-product-compliance
Lightning Source LLC
Chambersburg PA
CBHW011753220426
43672CB00017B/2945